# Contributions to Economics

The series *Contributions to Economics* provides an outlet for innovative research in all areas of economics. Books published in the series are primarily monographs and multiple author works that present new research results on a clearly defined topic, but contributed volumes and conference proceedings are also considered. All books are published in print and ebook and disseminated and promoted globally. The series and the volumes published in it are indexed by Scopus and ISI (selected volumes).

Valentina Vasile • Elena Bunduchi
Editors

# The Economic and Social Impact of the COVID-19 Pandemic

## Romania in a European Context

Springer

*Editors*
Valentina Vasile
Institute of National Economy - Romanian Academy
Bucharest, Romania

Elena Bunduchi
Institute of National Economy - Romanian Academy
Bucharest, Romania

Faculty of Economics and Law
George Emil Palade University of Medicine, Pharmacy, Science, and Technology of Targu Mures
Targu Mures, Romania

ISSN 1431-1933 ISSN 2197-7178 (electronic)
Contributions to Economics
ISBN 978-3-031-47779-9 ISBN 978-3-031-47780-5 (eBook)
https://doi.org/10.1007/978-3-031-47780-5



This Springer imprint is published by the registered company Springer Nature Switzerland AG
The registered company address is: Gewerbestrasse 11, 6330 Cham, Switzerland

# Contents

# Chapter 1
# Preliminary Comments. A Scientometric Dimension of the Economic and Social Impact of COVID-19

**Valentina Vasile and Razvan Vasile**

**Abstract** As a conjunctural phenomenon, the pandemic crisis, through its implications and effects, affected the work and life model, and emphasized the low resilience of society, as a whole, to flexibly and effectively manage the effects, to adapt. The externalities were both positive and negative, and many of the effects are still present, with public policies aiming to build a "new normal". The costs of the pandemic have been analysed by experts, and we refer not only to the economic ones but also to the social, cultural, psychological and other effects. The introductory chapter of the volume presents, on the one hand, a synthesis of the specialized literature, highlighting the interest of experts to understand, measure and analyse the complexity of the impact of the pandemic, and, on the other hand, motivates the thematic selection of the volume's chapters. A scientometric analysis was developed, based on the publications in the WoS database, for the period 2020–2022 and the dependencies of the keywords were defined. The arguments for the research subjects selected to be analysed in volume were inventoried, and the aspects of interest addressed in detail in each of the chapters were briefly presented. So, the main message of the present volume could be summarized as follow "after each crisis we redefine ourselves, a "new normal" is built from the economic, social and cultural perspective, we move to a new phase of human progress, in which the balances of development are reconfigures. Main drivers should be: solidarity, inclusion, innovation, complex approach of problem-solving, and accountability."

---

V. Vasile (✉)
Institute of National Economy-Romanian Academy, Bucharest, Romania

R. Vasile
National Institute of Economic Research "Costin C. Kiritescu" - Romanian Academy, Bucharest, Romania



V. Vasile, E. Bunduchi (eds.), *The Economic and Social Impact of the COVID-19 Pandemic*, Contributions to Economics,
https://doi.org/10.1007/978-3-031-47780-5_1

## Economic and Social Impact of COVID-19: A Brief View Based on Literature Review

As a conjunctural phenomenon, the COVID-19 pandemic generated multiple effects on the economic and social environment, demonstrating once again that society as a whole was unprepared for the management of both the actual medical problem and especially its effects. Although, at the local (national or regional) level, cases of risks generated by medical problems have also been recorded in the past, and history has also recorded and documented other pandemic situations, in the current case, the weaknesses of the system of health, especially the lack of prevention (respectively of preparation with material and human resources, a deficient logistical structure to set up special treatment areas, poor flexibility of the integrated management system, lack of spaces and protocols for managing associated problems, etc.), led to extreme protection measures (isolation of people in households, prohibition of free movement of the population, prohibition of some activities considered non-essential, application of experimental treatments, without prior testing according to existing procedures, etc.) with important effects on the functioning of the healthcare system as such, beyond the pandemic, and not only. The general measure was a lockdown (slowing down the movement of people, closing some current activities, including postponing the provision of medical services for the chronically ill) with brutal effects on economic, social and cultural activities.

The costs of the pandemic have been analysed by experts, and we refer not only to the economic ones but also to the social, cultural, psychological and other effects. The specialized literature demonstrates the interest of experts to understand, analyse and show the complexity of the impact, in the short term but especially in the medium and long term. If at the beginning of the pandemic (end of 2019) only 34 scientific papers were published on the theme of management and impact, in 2020–2022 we witnessed an explosion of papers on this theme (approx. 400,000), and in the first part of the year 2023, 50,000 have already been published, only if we consider the papers indexed in the WoS database. This proves not only the interest but also the multitude of facets of the impact – from medical research to identify treatments and vaccines to the identification of costs, risks and impact on the environment or certain economic, social or cultural activities, on the ICT sector and the need for digital skills, on the need to continue the education of the young generation even in conditions of isolation, etc.

The externalities were both positive and negative, and the effects are still felt in the present. From an economic point of view, the pandemic was considered by experts as "the worst economic contraction since the Great Depression". The IMF deems that it was "far worse than the Global Financial Crisis" (IMF, 2020a, 2020b). The immediate economic effect was a sudden contraction of the global economy by 2.8% in 2020 compared to 2019, with differences by country groups and economies (IMF, 2023a).

The effects of the pandemic were felt on multiple levels, both by the population (from the cost of living to job security) and by the business environment (limitation of some activities, additional costs and changes in work organization). The effect on costs was caused by additional expenses for specific health protection products, medicines, vaccines, etc., with inflation constantly increasing (following the pandemic, it was also amplified by the energy crisis and the conflict in Ukraine, which affected food prices, especially for cereals and food products, in general). The closure or restriction of activity for some fields of activity generated economic contraction, inflation and unemployment (Fig. 1.1), the most affected being the countries most vulnerable to the international markets, with great openness to foreign commercial relations and reduced competitiveness. The economic recovery from 2021 managed to absorb the unemployment from the pandemic period only partially, countries like Romania still recording unemployment rates above the pre-pandemic level. Moreover, the mobility for work during the pandemic experienced divergent developments: (a) on the one hand, the temporary return of some categories of multiyear immigrants, employed in the host countries in non-essential activities, was observed, and, (b) on the other hand, a migration of those in essential jobs or of graduates from less developed countries to those with a higher level of economic development was stimulated, which offered additional incentives and facilities for employment in deficit sectors, in essential activities for the functioning of the economy in pandemic conditions (health, transport services, local services, of general interest, agriculture, food industry, medical research, etc.). Therefore, for many less developed countries, the mobility for work continued, with the destructuring of employment in essential sectors, which amplified the economic and social effects of the pandemic crisis and prolonged them, generating adverse effects, namely, the future reduction of the stock of native human capital necessary for economic recovery. We are currently facing "the scarring impact of the pandemic; a slower pace of structural reforms" (IMF, 2023b).

Remote work during the pandemic led to an increase in the demand for internet connections and the level of its use in 2020, in the case of social distancing restrictions and lockdowns. On the other hand, the risk of data security has increased, so, for some countries that entered the pandemic with a high degree of digitization (such as Estonia, the Netherlands, Denmark and Norway, to mention only the EU area as an example), there were no increases in internet use during 2020, but even a slow decrease, due to the vulnerability of digitalized industries, enterprises and jobs (Natalia, 2022). In other countries, such as Italy, Spain and France, digital acceleration has seen increases of 60–80% in the internet traffic (OECD, 2020; Su et al., 2020) but with the accentuation of digital inequality (Van Deursen, 2020; Grishchenko, 2020; Nguyen et al., 2021; Lamberti et al., 2021) and other digital marginal effects (Maneejuk & Yamaka, 2020; Emara & Zhang, 2021; Appiah-Otoo & Song, 2021; Perez-Castro et al., 2021).

Many studies have carried out bibliometric analyses on the impact of COVID-19, with emphasis on certain aspects such as factors (restrictions of physical interaction; limitation of economic, social and cultural activities; production of medicines and vaccines; medical services; etc.) or economic effects (reduction of activity and working hours, changing working conditions, forms of employment, job security, the need for digital skills, communication and managerial activities, reduction of

GDP = Gross domestic product, constant prices, percent change

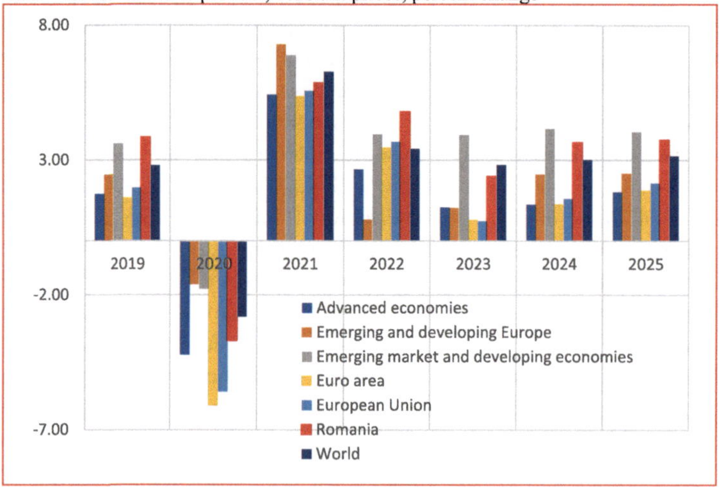


Inflation = Inflation, average consumer price, percent change

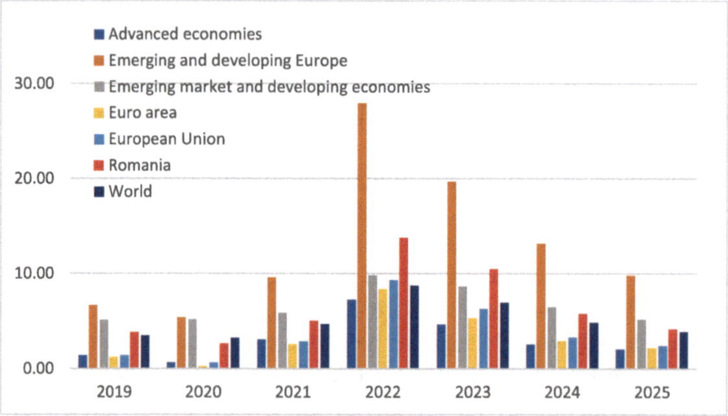


Unemployment rate = Percent of total labor force

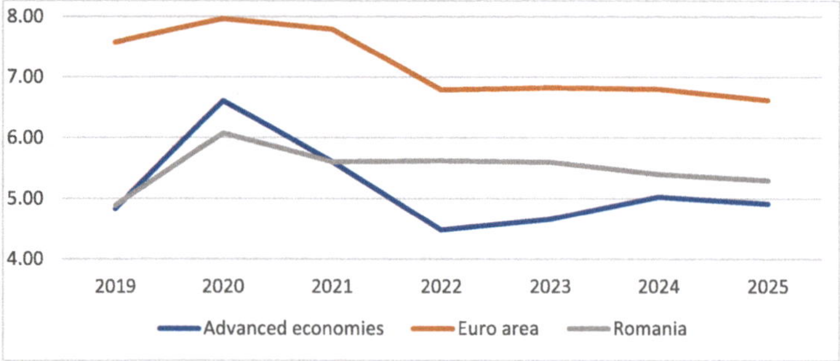


**Fig. 1.1** Dynamics of main economic indicators (2019–2022) and forecasts (Source: IMF database, online https://www.imf.org/en/Publications/WEO/weo-database/2023/April, accessed on 20 July 2023)

commercial relations, forced digitization of business, a slower pace of structural reforms, etc.), social effects (loss of jobs and sources of income, unemployment, a slow post-pandemic recovery in labour supply, social alienation, household debt distress, increased social discrimination, decreased level of well-being), medical effects (access to medical services for chronic diseases, treatments for COVID-19 and access to the vaccine), behavioural effects (burnout at work, isolation and loneliness, disruptions to routines, amplified family stressors, increased risks for adolescent psychiatric issues), cultural effects, etc.

So, according to previous bibliometric analysis performed by the experts, the common output was that the pandemic crisis hit harder the supply chain performance; put pressure on the health sector, transport, tourism and cultural activities; and increased stress in performing the activities related to food processing, commerce, personal services, education and public services but also on the financial innovation instruments, the sharing economy performance or public policies efficiency (Cantó et al., 2022; Rizvi et al., 2022; Fauzi, 2022; Santeramo, 2022; Alshater et al., 2022; Ciucan-Rusu et al., 2022; Surugiu et al., 2023; Vavoura & Vavouras, 2022; Goel et al., 2021; Wei et al., 2021; Guan et al., 2020; Nagy et al., 2021; Mody et al., 2021; Li & Xu, 2021). Our bibliometric research is focused on thematic research interest related to and effects on economic activities. If in 2020–2021 the papers were focused on the impacts, such as costs, economic distress, discrimination, inequalities and governance weaknesses, the structural impact of the epidemic on the industry and psychological impact of financial market response, in 2022–2023, the scientific discourse shifted to medium- and long-term effects and postcrisis recovery issues—robust recovery, employment disruption, digital intensity of companies, circular economy, innovation in supply chain management, safety economy and the "new normal" (economic and social), to mention the most important topics.

The data in Fig. 1.2 shows the distribution by year of publication of the scientific papers that analysed individual problems regarding the economic and social impact of the pandemic, published in the WoS database.

Starting from the papers published in the WoS database and the topics of interest for this volume, in order to define and include topics of interest (less studied or with controversial analyses, or with results still inconclusive in terms of importance or effects), we analysed in detail, going up to when analysing the entire content of the published works, two thematic levels: (a) economic impact of COVID-19, economic growth, economic resilience, economic recovery and economic effects, and (b) social impact of COVID-19—social inclusion, social discrimination and social effects. The analysis highlighted that the two categories intertwine and are of interest not only to economists or sociologists but also to experts in the various fields of activity, the separation being difficult to analyse.

The graphs below, grouped in Fig. 1.3, illustrate the chain of links and the intensity of concerns regarding the detailed thematic aspects. Considerring the economic impact, the subareas of interest were centred on several thematic groups, namely, crisis management- development—health policy (red colour); the effects of the pandemic and the areas affected—economic effects—Income, inequality—life-mobility, effects on health—anxiety, mental health (green); resources-funding and

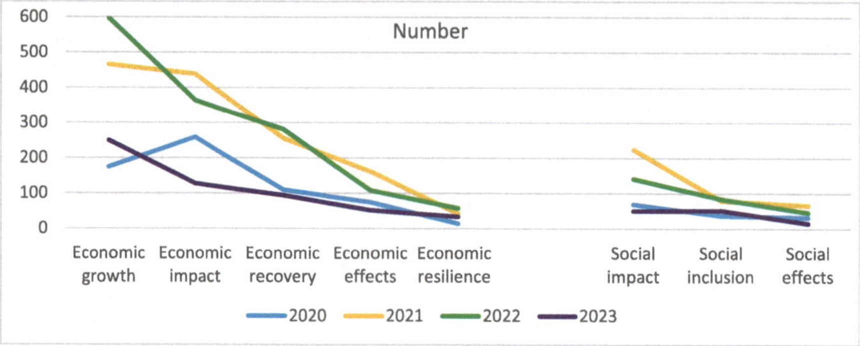


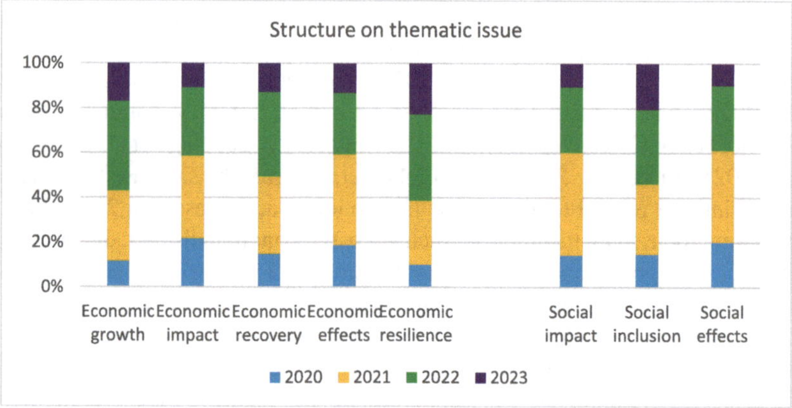


**Fig. 1.2** Selection of thematic papers published regarding the impact of the pandemic crisis on the economic and social environment, in the period 2020–2023 (July) (Source: WoS database, accessed on 30 July 2023)

economic growth (blue); adaptation- economic resilience- governance (yellow); digital transformation—entrepreneurship—growth—innovation—performance (purple); recovery—inflation—financial crisis—fiscal policy (blue); environment-pollution (orange). This thematic diversity indicates the complex effects of the pandemic highlighted only partially in the current analysis. For the articles that focused on the social impact, it should be mentioned that we identified fewer thematic clusters than in the case of the economic impact, respectively, five compared to eight, and the most important thematic links were as follows: economic-social interference—from management, performance communication and innovation, sustainability at social impact risk resilience, challenges (red); health and pandemic effects on persons—anxiety, mental health, stress (green); community, policy, participation and public services—education, health (blue); behaviour, discrimination (yellow).

It is thus obvious that the pandemic crisis, through its implications and effects, has affected the work and life model. The effect of the pandemic crisis on economic

A. COVID-19 and economic impact, economic growth, economic effects, economic, recovery, economic resilience (3718/15)

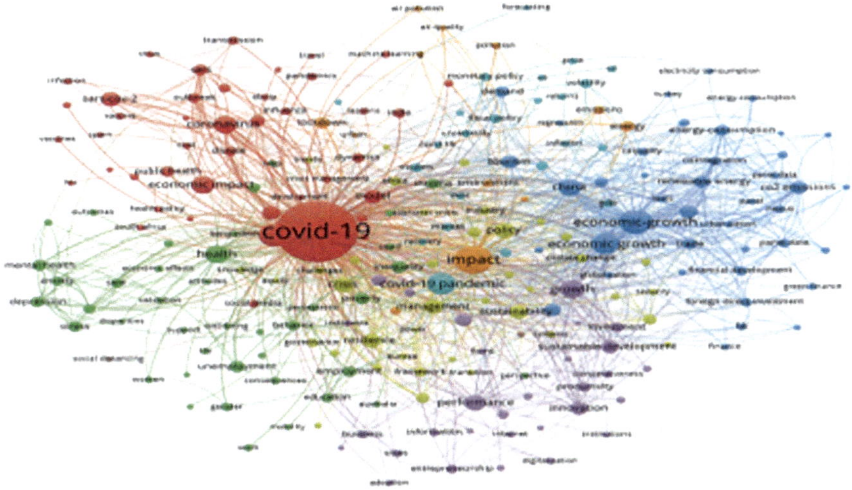


B. COVID-19 and social impact, social effects, social inclusion (926/10)

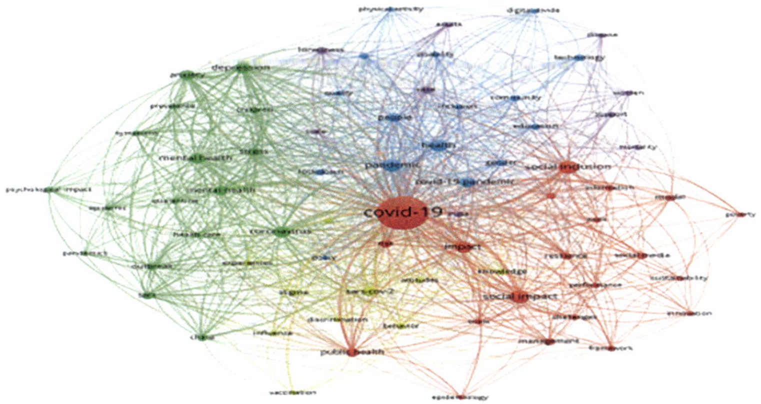


**Fig. 1.3** The distribution of thematic areas and the chain of links in the analysis of the economic and social impact of COVID-19 (Source: WoS database, accessed on 30th of July, 2023, WOSviewer soft). (**a**) COVID-19 and economic impact, economic growth, economic effects, economic, recovery, economic resilience (3718/15). (**b**) COVID-19 and social impact, social effects, social inclusion (926/10)

activities and employment was uneven, and the measures to counteract the economic and social effects only partially mitigated the negative externalities generated by the crisis. Moreover, some economic activities registered increases including during the pandemic, but they put pressure on inflation through increased costs (construction, courier services, transport services, the pharmaceutical industry and trade in sanitary products, the industry of protective materials and associated trade, trade in products and services specific to the ICT field, etc., to list only a few of them). From the perspective of employment and the protection of employees' incomes, employment flexibility schemes (work from home, flexible work schedule, financial aid schemes for working capital, partial subsidization of wages for the period of inactivity due to pandemic restrictions, etc.) were difficult to access by small companies and vulnerable categories of personnel. The felt effects were on working time and working conditions, job security (some activities were outsourced through digitization) and earnings from work.

If the employment in the non-essential sectors was significantly reduced, in unequal proportions, the staff employed in essential activities (frontline workers) continued to work, in difficult conditions, with multiple risks (of infection, unequal working time and often overtime hours, isolation from family, etc.). Employment for these categories has increased, as have the material incentives offered to them. The labour market in essential activities is strongly segmented: on the one hand, the staff employed in such activities is mainly in lower-quality and higher insecurity jobs and low-paid, and, on the other hand, there are specialized, highly qualified staff from the health sector and ICT (but not limited), with high salaries, who received additional financial incentives precisely to remain employed, in their countries of origin and not to migrate where the advantages were greater for similar activities (the more developed countries could afford to promote such a policy to cover the employment deficit). Regardless the field of activity, young people, migrant workers, low-educated people, women and other vulnerable categories were over-represented among those affected during the pandemic by the employment crisis, being either those with a higher risk of dismissal (occupying jobs that could not be done in the remote system), those who are low-paid or those who have jobs with partial employment and/or for limited periods (OECD, 2021, 2022; Ker et al., 2021; Ciuhu et al., 2022).

From the employment and its structure by activities perspective, the pandemic period highlighted the importance of activities that ensure essential products and services in society, respectively the role of the workforce and the need for appropriate policies on the labour market for them, for job security and avoiding the employment deficit (Eurofound, 2020; Vasile et al., 2020, 2023).

However, we must not omit the adverse effects generated by the pandemic on young people and the need for policies to retain them on the labour market in their countries of origin, through integrated policies (working conditions, pay for work, social recognition, career progress, continuous training) for "meaningful jobs regardless of their age". Employment recovery after COVID-19 crisis and also the experience of employment/education during the pandemic have redefined the position of young people in relation to the labour market (OECD, 2023; Ghita et al., 2023a, 2023b).

## The Main Aspects Analysed in This Volume

Starting from the analysis of the problems generated by the management of the pandemic, in economic and social terms, as well as based on the specialized literature, in our approach to analysis, we focused on some aspects that influenced national economies, relations on international markets and the model of work and life, in general. In addition, as the impact studies published so far have already shown, the effects of the pandemic were different across countries and regions (in diversity, duration and intensity); the factors aggravating the unfavourable aspects, including the major structural changes in the economic and social environment, have redefined the model of work and life, creating the coordinates of "the new normal", in which they took shape as basic requirements: robust economic recovery, taking into account innovation and digital transformation as transversal factors of economic growth and competitiveness, and smart management of environmental factors, building economic and social resilience.

Less developed countries face multiple vulnerabilities such as a) a greater dependence on foreign capital (the important share of foreign direct investments), b) a greater risk on foreign markets (the degree of openness to exports) and c) a increased mobility of the labor force for financial reasons (external migration for work, for remittance). From this perspective, the volume presented, as a case study, the situation of Romania, which faces all the mentioned vulnerabilities, to which others are added.

Romania, as a member state of the European Union since 2007, although with an important potential of natural and human resources, records slippages in governance, failing to create its internal self-development mechanisms. It is an emerging economy (IMF, 2022), and, although in 2020 and 2022 it was classified by the World Bank as a high-income economy (WB, 2020, 2022), it is based on a volatile economic growth, centred on growing consumption and imports, in terms of economic performance indicators being ranked last among EU member countries.

Although it ranks seventh in the EU in terms of human potential (NIS, 2022a, 2022b, 2023), the loss of human capital through migration for work, especially of higher education graduates, erodes, in the medium and long term, the potential for growth and economic performance and deepens income and social gaps. Moreover, during the pandemic, labour migration from the category of essential workers, with the exception of health sector personnel, could not be stopped by the public policy measures implemented by the government to manage internal crises (in health, education, agriculture, etc.). Performance in the absorption of structural funds and, more recently, funds through the Recovery and Resilience Plan is reduced and does not develop the necessary development infrastructure to achieve SDGs and social inclusion; on the contrary, the gaps (in real terms) and discrimination, in its various forms, are increasing (UNDP, 2023). The overlapping crises, specific to the last decade, are managed by the galloping increase of the external debt and the rescheduling of payments, and the budget deficit becomes chronic. The underground economy still represents over 1/5 of GDP (Schneider et al., 2010; Schneider &

Asllani, 2022; Zaman & Goschin, 2015), which makes it difficult to reset and recover economically and socially. In such a context, the pandemic effects were more intense, and the period of robust macroeconomic rebalancing is being prolonged, the economy is fragile, and the inflation generated by the price of energy and the prices of basic consumer products (food, utilities) will substantially erode the results expected in terms of social development and the well-being of the Romanian population (EC, 2023; SPI, 2023).

The volume was structured in three parts, each addressing in detail economic problems associated with the characteristics of the COVID-19 crisis, respectively: (a) the effects generated by the period of restrictions on the business environment; (b) the paradigm changes of employment and industrial relations determined by digitization, as an alternative to the closure of some companies and the facilitation of communication for carrying out daily activities, work and life in the household and in the community; and (c) the resilience of the health sector and the risks associated with the management of the pandemic crisis in the conditions of a deep crisis of the sector, already installed before the pandemic – labour shortage, problems of securing material resources, management of medical waste, etc.

The analyses carried out in this volume aim at both the pre-, during and post-pandemic evolution, as well as the impact, in the short, medium and long term.

After a brief presentation of the literature review from the scientometric perspective, in this chapter, in which we highlighted the experts' interest in analysing the impact of the COVID-19 crisis on economic and social development, with the identification of positive and negative externalities that determined adjustments of macroeconomic balances and of the dynamics of the business environment, by fields of activity and industries, in Chapter "Another Crisis, Different Responses?—Determinants of Crisis and Mixed Impact on Economic Development: A Comparative Approach of the EU Countries", the asymmetry of the effects of exogenous crises (pandemic type) compared to endogenous ones (financial crisis of 2008–2009) on economic growth (performance in the use of production factors) and some indicators of social progress (dynamics of NEETs and the poverty rate) was highlighted. It was aimed to analyse the complex effect of crises, the fact that, regardless of the type of crisis, the post-recovery period does not mean a return to the previous situation, but rather a resetting of the balances, in which the dynamics of recovery after the crisis is different on fields of activity and categories of indicators (such as employment rate, gross fixed capital formation and trade openness), in some cases, the precrisis parameters are not reached, and in other situations, they are easily exceeded. The recent development of society is marked by overlapping crises with numerous irreversible consequences. Whether it's a financial crisis or a pandemic, these events set off chain reactions, influencing both the economic and social landscape. Their effects significantly impacted the labour market, introducing new challenges and reshaping the existing norms. This chapter conducts a comparative analysis of the pandemic and 2008–2009 financial crises, concentrating on their impact on economic development and the restructuring of the labour market. The recovery after each crisis varied, with some EU countries experiencing only partial recovery and diverse outcomes across countries. Policy measures adopted during the crises also displayed varying levels of effectiveness. The 2008–2009 and COVID-19 crises significantly influenced employment levels, resulting in substantial changes in job structure and content. The recovery efforts differed by country, and the chapter investigates the effects on the labour market. It could be argued that the coexistence of overlapping crises represents the new development standard. Therefore, it becomes essential to focus on the notion of resilience-building, and any analysis of this scenario should involve comparing quick recovery with a strong emphasis on economic and social development. Prioritizing resilience in crisis management strategies is critical to achieving fair and inclusive growth.

Part I "The Challenges of the Pandemic and the Business Environment: Towards a New Normal?" consists of four chapters, in which we aimed to highlight the main effects of the COVID-19 crisis on the business environment, respectively, to what extent the characteristics and limitations of the crisis disrupted the development of the business environment (change of priorities in the digital transition of companies, reconfiguration of the model of business as a result of the restrictions regarding social distancing and the protection measures specific to the pandemic crisis, how commercial relations were affected and what were the state's challenges to ensure the budget revenues necessary to manage the crisis).

So, in Chapter "Digital Transformation: Challenges and Limits for the New Normal?", an analysis was made of the digital intensity of companies and the extent to which the pandemic period interrupted or, on the contrary, accelerated the digital transition. The analyses carried out took into account the specific technical endowment for the large-scale use of the facilities offered by ICT products/services, as well as the acquisition by employees of digital skills, which have become a transversal requirement for all workplaces. This chapter also highlighted the extent to which, in the post-pandemic period, companies gave up (totally or to what extent) the facilities generated by digitization for current activities – communication at company level, operational management, redefining the content of jobs, remote employment, hybrid employment, e-commerce, etc., thus building/redefining "a new normal" for business development model.

Chapter "Thinking Beyond COVID-19: What's Next for Romanian's SMEs?" aims to underline the multiple aspects determined by the restrictions imposed by the pandemic for most of the business activities, with a special focus on the SME sector in Romania, trying to bring solutions and proposals for adapting to the restrictions without closing the business and postcrisis recovery. The most frequent problems faced by companies, and in particular SMEs, were interruptions in the production value chain, with syncope in supply, which led to a shortage of resources and financial blockages generated by delayed payments or temporary suspension of some. In many cases, especially for micro-enterprises, the lack of an online payment alternative, the difficulty of accessing funds to support the financing of working capital and supporting the transition of some activities online have represented serious barriers in the adaptation/survival of companies.

In Chapter "Distortions and Gains in Foreign Trade Activity During the Post-pandemic Era", a detailed analysis of international trade was made, especially because it supported the health system with sanitary materials, specific intervention equipment, medicines and vaccines. Trade was reduced during the pandemic for most products not directly related to the management of activities in the health sector and goods strictly necessary for current consumption that could not be provided locally. The relaunch of general international commercial relations was achieved with the removal of restrictions for the business environment and with the transition of companies to the extensive use of ICT facilities for the completion of transactions. The global trade recovered starting with 2021 and for many countries, in 2022, the export and import flows were above the levels before the pandemic year. However, the impact on different products and/or services was different, and the supply chains were put under serious pressure; several factors should be considered for the future – inflation, energy crisis, increasing shipping costs and geopolitical instability.

"Tax Burden During the Pandemic: Lessons Learned and Challenges" is the chapter that concludes the first part of the work. Countries' budgets have seen a reduction in tax revenues during this pandemic. Governments have taken various tax measures to help taxpayers fight the pandemic's adverse effects, mainly aimed at relaxing taxation and/or rescheduling some payment obligations. In other cases, the policymaker has adopted (temporary) tax exemptions which have increased the budget deficit and restructured public expenditures, especially those that supported the management of the pandemic and the relaunch of the business environment.

The major effect of the pandemic limitations/restrictions refers to the labour force, which was affected in multiple ways – the duration of work, working conditions, forms of employment, earnings from work and mobility. It is also the reason why the second part of the volume addresses the analysis of the way of work.

Part II "Constraints on Labor Market Participation: Changing the Employment Paradigm" includes, similarly, four other chapters, but the theme focuses on the workforce, changes in industrial relations and the functioning of the labour market. It started from the limitations imposed by the pandemic restrictions on employment models and work as such, and the general and specific effects were analysed. The general ones concerned the expansion of the use of ICT products/services and the reorganization of workplaces, the relocation of many to the employees' homes and/or their adaptation to the requirements of social distancing and the implementation of requirements/limitations related to the physical interaction of employees or of them with business partners, including with clients. In fact, the paradigm of work and forms of employment have changed; the importance of certain activities, professions and jobs has been redefined. The specific effects take into account aspects related to mobility for work and its limitations during the pandemic period, namely, the reconsideration of the importance of essential workers, the utility and benefits of remote work and hybrid work and the segmentation of employment in the new economic and social context created by the pandemic. We also included the analysis of changes in the structure of occupations and in the demand/supply ratio on the labour market, of the flexibility of the labour market, but also the impact of the COVID-19 pandemic on the main vulnerable categories in the labour market – women, young people and the elderly.

The analyses were aimed at highlighting the irreversible mutations that underpin the reconstruction of post-pandemic employment models and industrial relations, in general, which will fundamentally change initial and continuing training programmes and redefine the foundations of strategies and policies regarding education for the labour market.

In Chapter "The (Post)Pandemic Employment Model", the vulnerabilities of the labour market and the change of the employment model are analysed, with an emphasis on the dynamics of the transformation of jobs and the characteristics of emerging forms of employment. It explores the key factors influencing these changes, their implications for workers and organizations and potential long-term effects on the labour market. By examining the adoption of remote work, gig economy platforms and flexible arrangements, this research sheds light on the evolving landscape of employment and offers insights into the future of work. Nevertheless, the changing employment paradigm driven by the pandemic presents opportunities for digital transformation of the labour market in order to cope with adapted/flexible/renewed models of business.

A special chapter was addressed to "The impact of the pandemic on the participation in the labour market of vulnerable groups: women, young people, the elderly, self-employed workers". The evolution of the main indicators of the labour market was analysed, under two main aspects: The first one aims to identify the initial changes in the situation of vulnerable groups on the labour market, as an immediate effect of the outbreak of the pandemic (and that covers the period 2019–2020, as well as an estimate of the evolution of labour indicators for the next 2 years). The second aspect aims to compare the estimates made with the real evolution of the same indicators for the years 2021 and 2022, in order to highlight the final impact of the pandemic crisis on the labour market situation of the selected vulnerable groups. In order to capture the changes in the labour market, absolute and relative indicators of employment and unemployment were used, structured by some sociodemographic characteristics (age, education, gender and others) but also by a series of variables related to the type of employment and work regime (work schedule, type of ownership, activity sector, work type, major occupational groups, employment status, etc.).

Another important aspect for highlighting the effects of the pandemic on the workforce was the external mobility of workers in general and, in particular, of healthcare personnel. In Chapter "Propensity for Migration of Healthcare Professionals: Push-Pull Factors Analysis", the factors of migration identified by healthcare students from Romania are analysed. As a result of the shortage of doctors that Romania is facing, the authors found that the propensity towards migration is identified even among students. Future medical specialists tend to migrate both for studies and for work. The reasons behind this decision are similar, but not limited to lack of career perspective, poor working condition and wage differential. The tendency to return is not obvious, so half of the respondents never want to return to Romania.

Furthermore, the insights gained from qualitative analysis can provide a foundation for crafting informed policies in both the medical and educational domains. Policymakers can tailor strategies that aim to retain talented healthcare professionals by addressing the identified push and pull factors. These strategies might include improving the quality of medical education, offering competitive compensation and benefits packages, enhancing working conditions and creating opportunities for career advancement.

Chapter "Features of the Policies Adopted for the Mitigation of the Pandemic Recession Impact on the Labour Market Operation" concludes the analysis from the second part of the volume and presents the features and the effects of the measures designed and implemented by the different states in the pandemic context. Generally, the pandemic restrictions had an extended negative impact on the labour market operation by sharply blocking the labour demand and creating damages on the labour supply. The chapter analyses the evolution of the rate of unemployment and the main features of the labour market policies implemented in the framework of European Union in order to mitigate the negative impact of COVID-19 pandemic, the common elements and the differences of the labour market policies promoted in the old member states and in new member states as Romania.

Finally, in the last part of the volume Part III "Health Sector: New Identity, Old Challenges", we addressed the problems of the health sector, the key activity that facilitated the management of the crisis, both from the perspective of the health status of the population and of health risk management—the quality of services, the allocation of resources, the management of the necessary changes in the labour market of the health sector activity and, respectively, the reduction of risks generated by medical waste.

Chapter "Impact of COVID-19 on Healthcare Labor Market in European Countries and Romania in particular" highlights the vulnerabilities of the health sector to mitigate the pandemic, with a special analysis of the health labour market. The weaknesses start from the reduced flexibility of the sector to articulate itself to the specific requirements of the type of pandemic, to which are also added the shortages of specialty personnel, as well as the vulnerabilities of the health labour market and the lack of attractiveness for young people, in less developed countries where the sector is also faced with equipment not updated according to the advance of science, with a deficient management in incentive remuneration and professional career development.

The final thematic chapter, "Issues Regarding the Management of Hazardous Medical Waste During the Covid-19 Crisis in Romania", presents some aspects related to the risks for environmental protection from the generation of medical waste, on the availability of medical waste disposal capacities.

At the end of the volume, "Conclusions: Looking Forward. Main Challenges and Limits", the main aspects resulting from the analysis were synthesized and useful results for decision-makers were presented—from lessons learned to examples of good practices and from the analysis of policy effectiveness to recommendations for changes necessary for an integrated/articulated vision of post-pandemic economic and social development strategies. Possible directions for continuation/deepening of the analyses in the volume were also highlighted.

The effects of the pandemic are still being felt and will continue to affect the business environment and the quality of life of citizens, from multiple perspectives. Therefore, the present volume is a first approach to the complex analysis of the effects of the pandemic crisis (on the three defining coordinates of the impact—turbulence on the business environment, the reconstruction of the typology and work models and the deep reform of the health sector, through the management in emergency regime of essential deficiencies and weaknesses) and thus completes the specialized literature. We did not propose to have a comprehensive character, on the analysis components addressed, but to emphasize the main aspects that clearly support that the return to the pre-pandemic situation is not possible, and the viable solution is to adjust the work and life model, of supporting the development of the economic and social resilience of national economies, in the context of the integrated approach to old and new problems. This implies, on the one hand, connecting the requirements of robust economic growth, for the benefit of the national economy and the population, of sustainable development with a smart management of environmental issues and of social inclusion and poverty reduction and, on the other hand, of adequacy to the demands of digital transformation and development for all.

We hope that the reader will be challenged by the approaches and analyses carried out and to develop other thematic research directions, some already suggested during the work, to generate technological transfer by taking recommendations, using research tools and/or capitalizing on the results, by customizing/adapting in other areas of economic and social activities.

## References

Alshater, M. M., Atayah, O. F., & Khan, A. (2022). What do we know about business and economics research during COVID-19: A bibliometric review. *Economic Research-Ekonomska Istraživanja, 35*(1), 1884–1912.

Appiah-Otoo, I., & Song, N. (2021). The impact of ICT on economic growth-comparing rich and poor countries. *Telecommunications Policy, 45*(1), 102082. https://doi.org/10.1016/j.telpol.2020.102082

Cantó, O., Figari, F., Fiorio, C. V., Kuypers, S., Marchal, S., Verbist, G., Romaguera-de-la-Cruz, M., & Tasseva, I. V. (2022). Welfare resilience at the onset of the COVID-19 pandemic in a selection of European countries: Impact on public finance and household incomes. *Review of Income and Wealth, 68*(2), 293–322.

Ciucan-Rusu, L., Vasile, V., Stefan, D., Comes, C.-A., Stefan, A.-B., Timus, M., Oltean, A., Bunduchi, E., & Popa, M.-A. (2022). Consumers behavior determinants on online local market platforms in COVID-19 pandemic—A Probit qualitative analysis. *Mathematics, 10*, 4281. https://doi.org/10.3390/math10224281

Ciuhu, A.-M., Ghita, S.-I., Vasile, V., & Boboc, C. (2022). Occupational gender disparities–before and after Covid-19. *Romanian Statistical Review nr., 2*(2022), 31–50. https://www.revistadestatistica.ro/2022/06/romanian-statistical-review-2-2022/

European Commission. (2023). *European social progress index 2020*. Accessed July 30, 2023, from https://ec.europa.eu/regional_policy/information-sources/maps/social-progress/2020_en

Eurofound. (2020). *Living, working and COVID-19, COVID-19 series*. Publications Office of the European Union. https://doi.org/10.2806/467608

Emara, N., & Zhang, Y. (2021). The non-linear impact of digitization on remittances inflow: Evidence from the BRICS. *Telecommunications Policy, 45*(4), 102112. https://doi.org/10.1016/j.telpol.2021.102112

Fauzi, M. A. (2022). E-learning in higher education institutions during COVID-19 pandemic: Current and future trends through bibliometric analysis. *Heliyon, 8*(5), article e09433.

Ghiță, S. I., Boboc, C. R., Saseanu, A. S., & Vasile, V. (2023a). How does the supply of tertiary graduates correlate with the labour market? Evidence from European countries. In R. Pamfilie, V. Dinu, C. Vasiliu, D. Pleșea, & L. Tăchiciu (Eds.), *9th BASIQ International Conference on New Trends in Sustainable Business and Consumption*. Constanța, Romania (pp. 96–103). ASE. https://doi.org/10.24818/BASIQ/2023/09/062

Ghiță, S., Boboc, C., Vasile, V., & Ciuhu, A. M. (2023b). Female labor precariousness during the pandemic lessons for a future better normal. In A. M. Dima & E. R. Danescu (Eds.), *Fostering recovery through metaverse business modelling. ICESS 2022*. Springer Proceedings in Business and Economics. Springer. https://doi.org/10.1007/978-3-031-28255-3_10

Goel, R. K., Saunoris, J. W., & Goel, S. S. (2021). Supply chain performance and economic growth: The impact of COVID-19 disruptions. *Journal of Policy Modeling., 43*(2), 298–316.

Grishchenko, N. (2020). The gap not only closes: Resistance and reverse shifts in the digital divide in Russia. *Telecommunications Policy, 44*(8), 102004. https://doi.org/10.1016/j.telpol.2020.102004

Guan, D. B., Wang, D. P., Hallegatte, S., Davis, S. J., Huo, J. W., Li, S. P., Bai, Y. C., Lei, T. Y., Xue, Q. Y., Coffman, D., Cheng, D. Y., Chen, P. P., Liang, X., Xu, B., Lu, X. S., Wang, S. Y., Hubacek, K., & Gong, P. (2020). Global supply-chain effects of COVID-19 control measures. *Nature Human Behaviour, 4*(6), 577–587.

IMF. (2020a). *World economic outlook*, April 2020: The Great Lockdown. https://www.imf.org/en/Publications/WEO/Issues/2020/04/14/weo-april-2020

IMF. (2020b). *World economic outlook update, June 2020: A crisis like no other, an uncertain recovery*. https://www.imf.org/en/Publications/WEO/Issues/2020/06/24/WEOUpdateJune2020

IMF. (2022). *world economic outlook database, April 2022–emerging market and developing economies/emerging and developing europe (16 countries)*. Accessed July 20, 2023, from https://www.imf.org/en/Publications/WEO/weo-database/2023/April

IMF. (2023a). *World economic outlook, April 2023: A rocky recovery*. https://www.imf.org/en/Publications/WEO/Issues/2023/04/11/world-economic-outlook-april-2023

IMF. (2023b). *World economic outlook update, July 2023: Near-term resilience, persistent challenges*. https://www.imf.org/en/Publications/WEO/Issues/2023/07/10/world-economic-outlook-update-july-2023

Ker, D., Montagnier, P., & Spiezia, V. (2021). Measuring telework in the COVID-19 pandemic. In *OECD digital economy papers, no. 314*. OECD Publishing. https://doi.org/10.1787/0a76109f-en

Lamberti, G., Lopez-Sintas, J., & Sukphan, J. (2021). The social process of internet appropriation: Living in a digitally advanced country benefits less well-educated Europeans. *Telecommunications Policy, 45*(1), 102055. https://doi.org/10.1016/j.telpol.2020.102055

Li, B., & Xu, Z. (2021). A comprehensive bibliometric analysis of financial innovation. *Economic Research-Ekonomska Istraživanja, 35*(1), 367–390.

Maneejuk, P., & Yamaka, W. (2020). An analysis of the impacts of telecommunications technology and innovation on economic growth. *Telecommunications Policy, 44*(10), 102038. https://doi.org/10.1016/j.telpol.2020.102038

Mody, M. A., Hanks, L., & Cheng, M. (2021). Sharing economy research in hospitality and tourism: A critical review using bibliometric analysis, content analysis and a quantitative systematic literature review. *International Journal of Contemporary Hospitality Management, 33*(5), 1711–1745.

Nagy, A. M., Konka, B., & Török, Á. (2021). The COVID problem reflected by economics–a bibliometric analysis. *Acta Oecon., 71*(S1), 205–221.

Natalia, G. (2022). An inverted digital divide during Covid-19 pandemic? Evidence from a panel of EU countries. *Telemat Inform, 72*, 101856. https://doi.org/10.1016/j.tele.2022.101856

Nguyen, M. H., Hargittai, E., & Marler, W. (2021). Digital inequality in communication during a time of physical distancing: The case of COVID-19. *Computers in Human Behavior, 120*, 06717. https://doi.org/10.1016/j.chb.2021.106717

NIS. (2022a). *Resident population on January 1, 2022 and international migration in 2021 (Romanian).* https://insse.ro/cms/sites/default/files/com_presa/com_pdf/poprez_ian2022r_0.pdf

NIS. (2022b). *Population and housing census, 2021–provisional results (Romanian).* https://insse.ro/cms/sites/default/files/com_presa/com_pdf/cp-date-provizorii-rpl2021_0.pdf

NIS. (2023). *The workforce in Romania: Employment and unemployment in 2022 (Romanian).* https://insse.ro/cms/ro/content/for%C5%A3a-de-munc%C4%83-%C3%AEn-rom%C3%A2nia-ocupare-%C5%9Fi-%C5%9Fomaj-%C3%AEn-anul-2022-romana

OECD. (2020). *Policy responses to coronavirus (Covid-19).* Keeping the Internet up and running in times of crisis. https://www.oecd.org/coronavirus/policy-responses/keeping-the-internet-up-and-running-in-times-of-crisis-4017c4c9/.

OECD. (2021). *OECD employment outlook 2021: Navigating the COVID-19 crisis and recovery.* OECD Publishing. https://doi.org/10.1787/5a700c4b-en

OECD. (2022). *The unequal impact of COVID-19: A spotlight on frontline workers, migrants and racial/ethnic minorities.* https://read.oecd-ilibrary.org/view/?ref=1133_1133188-lq9ii66g9w&title=The-unequal-impact-of-COVID-19-A-spotlight-on-frontline-workers-migrants-and-racial-ethnic-minorities

OECD. (2023). *Retaining talent at all ages.* OECD Publishing. https://doi.org/10.1787/00dbdd06-en

Perez-Castro, M. A., Mohamed-Maslouhi, M., & Montero-Alonso, M. A. (2021). The digital divide and its impact on the development of Mediterranean countries. *Technology in Society, 64*, 101452. https://doi.org/10.1016/j.techsoc.2020.101452

Rizvi, S. K. A., Yarovaya, L., Mirza, N., & Naqvi, B. (2022). The impact of COVID-19 on the valuations of non-financial European firms. *Heliyon, 8*(6), e09486.

Santeramo, F. G. (2022). Circular and green economy: The state-of-the-art. *Heliyon, 8*(4), e09297.

Schneider, F., Buehn, A., & Montenegro, C. E. (2010). Shadow economies all over the world. New estimates for 162 countries from 1999 to 2007. *Policy Research Working Paper, 5356.* https://documents1.worldbank.org/curated/en/311991468037132740/pdf/WPS5356.pdf

Schneider, F., & Asllani, A. (2022). *Taxation of the Informal Economy in the EU.* https://www.europarl.europa.eu/RegData/etudes/STUD/2022/734007/IPOL_STU(2022)734007_EN.pdf

SPI. (2023). *Global index 2022: Overview, social progress imperative.* Accessed July 30, 2023, from https://www.socialprogress.org/global-index-2022overview/

Su, C. C., Liu, J., & Zhou, B. (2020). Two levels of digitalization and internet use across Europe, China, and the U.S. *International Journal of Communication, 14*, 5838–5859.

Surugiu, M. R., Vasile, V., Mazilescu, R., Surugiu, C., & Vasile, R. (2023). Determinants of the resilience building in tourism. A case study on Romania in the context of the pandemic crises. *Journal of Tourism Management Research, 10*(1), 15–31. https://doi.org/10.18488/31.v10i1.3237

UNDP. (2023). *Human development reports: Romania. IHDI–inequality-adjusted HDI, table 3: Inequality-adjusted human development index (2021).* https://hdr.undp.org/inequality-adjusted-human-development-index#/indicies/IHDI. Accessed on July 30, 2023.

Van Deursen, A. J. A. M. (2020). Digital inequality during a pandemic: Quantitative study of differences in COVID-19–related internet uses and outcomes among the general population. *Journal of Medical Internet Research, 22*(8), e20073. https://doi.org/10.2196/20073

Vasile, V., Bunduchi, E., Stefan, D., & Comes, C-A. (2023). Migrant critical workers during and after COVID-19 pandemic, pp. 197–214, in International labour mobility: How remittances shape the labour migration model, Palgrave Macmillan, . doi:https://doi.org/10.1007/978-3-031-18683-10.

Vasile V., Boboc, C., Ghiță, S., Apostu, S., Pavelescu, F-M., & Mazilescu, C.R. (2020). *The effects of the Sars Cov 2 pandemic on employment. The role of public policies and the resilience of the labor market in the context of the adaptation of the business environment*/Efectele pandemiei

Sars Cov 2 asupra ocupării. Rolul politicilor publice şi rezilienţa pieţei muncii în contextul adaptării mediului de afaceri, (in Romanian). https://doi.org/10.13140/RG.2.2.33243.18723, Projects: COVID-19 Impact–Economic and social evidences. https://acad.ro/SARS-CoV-2/doc/d19-Efectele_pandemiei_asupra_ocuparii.pdf

Vavoura, C., & Vavouras, I. (2022). Sustainable economic development in the European Union and COVID-19. *Evolutionary and Institutional Economics Review, 19*, 449–467. https://doi.org/10.1007/s40844-021-00217-1

WB. (2020). *The World Bank.* "World Bank list of economies (June 2020)". Accessed July 20, 2023, from hupo.org.

WB. (2022). *The World Bank.* "New World Bank country classifications by income level: 2022–2023". Accessed July 20, 2023, from blogs.worldbank.org

Wei, X., Li, L., & Zhang, F. (2021). The impact of the COVID-19 pandemic on socio-economic and sustainability. *Environmental Science and Pollution Control Service, 28*(48), 68251–68260.

Zaman, G., & Goschin, Z. (2015). Shadow economy and economic growth in Romania. Cons and pros. *Procedia Economics and Finance, 22*, 80–87. https://doi.org/10.1016/S2212-5671(15)00229-4

# Chapter 2
# Another Crisis, Different Responses? Determinants of Crisis and Mixed Impact on Economic Development: A Comparative Approach of the EU Countries

**Valentina Vasile, Raluca Mazilescu, and Marius-Razvan Surugiu**

**Abstract** The pandemic and the financial crisis of 2008–2009 are comparatively analysed in this chapter from the perspective of their impact on economic development and the restructuring of the labour market. These two crises affected employment levels and led to significant changes in job structures and the content of jobs. The postcrisis recovery varies among the EU member states and candidate countries, and in some cases, only partial recovery has occurred due to the specific conditions of each country and differences in the efficiency of policy measures.

## Introduction

Society's recent development is characterised by overlapping crises with multiple irreversible effects. Whether the cause is a financial crisis or a pandemic, these events trigger chain effects, impacting the economic and social environment. Their impact affected the labour market, bringing new challenges and redesigning the status quo.

This chapter provides a comparative analysis of the pandemic and 2008–2009 financial crisis, focusing on their impact on economic development and restructuring the labour market. The recovery following each crisis differed, with some EU countries experiencing only partial recovery and varying outcomes across countries. Policy measures employed during the crises also exhibited different levels of effectiveness. Both the 2008–2009 and Covid-19 crises significantly affected employment levels and brought about substantial changes in job structure and content of jobs. Recovery efforts varied by country, and the chapter examines the effects on the labour market using indicators such as employment rate, NEET rate, and job vacancy rate.

V. Vasile (✉) · R. Mazilescu · M.-R. Surugiu
Institute of National Economy - Romanian Academy, Bucharest, Romania



V. Vasile, E. Bunduchi (eds.), *The Economic and Social Impact of the COVID-19 Pandemic*, Contributions to Economics,
https://doi.org/10.1007/978-3-031-47780-5_2

One may point out that the overlapping crises could be viewed as the new normal of development. Consequently, it becomes crucial to address the concept of building resilience, and any examination of this situation should involve comparing rapid recovery with robust economic and social development. Also, fostering resilience is imperative to ensure equitable and inclusive growth when devising a crisis management approach.

The foundation of this investigation lies in the observation that the financial crisis of 2008–2009 and the Covid-19 pandemic had far-reaching consequences on diverse economic sectors. These effects were characterised by delayed, amplified, and prolonged impacts. An important research question in this context is whether the recovery from these crises varied among countries.

The main objectives of this research are the following: to check if the crises influenced the selected indicators; to identify the recovery period, meaning the period in which the value of the indicators (after the crisis) reached the pre-crisis levels; and to check the relationship between the selected indicators.

The authors selected this topic because they recognise that all crises, regardless of their nature, causes, or intensity, have a detrimental impact on the economy and create broader and multiple effects on various levels, including social, cultural, and institutional aspects. Furthermore, the financial crisis of 2008–2009 and the Covid-19 pandemic were stark reminders of our lack of preparedness in building resilience to withstand and recover from such challenging situations effectively.

Resilience can be defined in various ways and encompasses many components. However, the common objective in disaster recovery and preparedness efforts is building resilience. A crucial element of resilience involves effectively utilising available resources at a particular moment to achieve maximum productivity. In this context, resilience pertains to the overall ability of an economy to manage, recover, and reconstruct itself after a shock, thereby minimising aggregate consumption losses. Emphasising this aspect highlights the community's capacity to anticipate, adapt, and capitalise on environmental changes.

The OECD's definition of economic resilience underscores a significant aspect. According to their definition, economic resilience can be enhanced by implementing policies that aim to mitigate the risks and consequences of severe crises. Identifying the most effective measures that balance promoting growth and managing crisis risk is essential when there is a trade-off between the two. This involves considering a range of macroeconomic and structural policies to enhance economic resilience effectively (OECD, 2023).

Indeed, macroeconomic resilience can be broken down into two main components (Hallegatte, 2014): instantaneous resilience, focused on the ability of an economy to restrict the magnitude of immediate production losses when faced with a certain level of asset losses, and dynamic resilience, revolving around the capacity of an economy to rebuild and recover over time following a crisis.

Resilience in economics refers to the capacity to restore balance in the business environment, rebuilding and adapting after a disruptive event while absorbing and mitigating the impact of the shock. This concept encompasses understanding how a shock affects different segments of society and their vulnerability to such events. A sustainable recovery, however, involves navigating and overcoming similar crises, even if they have other underlying causes.

Developing resilience is a collective ethical obligation. Several critical elements are deemed significant, including evaluating risks and embracing adaptability, fostering strategic foresight and readiness for change, adjusting to market demands in a globalised context, and assuming social responsibilities at both national and local levels.

Economic disturbances can emerge due to a combination of factors, encompassing industry downturns, financial constraints, limited innovation, erosion of comparative or competitive strengths, bureaucratic obstacles, and the influence of national or global events on consumer demand and expenditure. Natural disasters, human-made calamities, and social unrest can also contribute to disruptions. The economic resilience of a community or nation hinges on the capacity of its leaders to anticipate and evaluate these risks, make informed decisions based on diverse inputs, and proactively undertake measures to mitigate potential risks.

The chapter's main contribution lies in its comparative examination of the impacts of the two most recent crises on the labour market. It assesses both the extent of their influence and the duration of the recovery period, aiming to determine the degree to which economic recovery relies on the labour market's resilience.

The chapter reviews relevant literature, highlighting specific aspects that align with the research topic. It outlines the research methodology and presents the findings from analysing labour market indicators. The last section offers remarks, conclusions, and recommendations emphasising labour market resilience as crucial for sustainable development.

## Literature Review

Examining the literature reveals a focus on analysing crises and sustainable economic and social recovery. The discussions show that there is a changing growth paradigm, taking into consideration the monetary vs social profit. Also, the disruption can be associated with the objective of reaching pre-crisis performance indicators.

When the topic is focused on economic resilience, an exciting idea emerges to absorb the shocks and transform the status quo, showing the importance of preparedness for the (next) crisis. Other topics discussed in the literature are the main lessons learned after the financial crisis, managing the main factors determining the crises and measures to diminish the adverse effects and the recovery vulnerability. Other authors discuss the importance of the nature of the crises, the recovery versus "the new normal".

The occurrence of crises like the 2007–2008 global financial crisis (endogenous) and the 2019 coronavirus pandemic (exogenous) serves as a stark reminder of the consequences when risks materialise, putting the resilience of interconnected economies and societies to the ultimate challenge (OECD, 2021a).

Global openness and integration bring about both advantageous and disadvantageous consequences. On the positive side, they lead to significant benefits such as

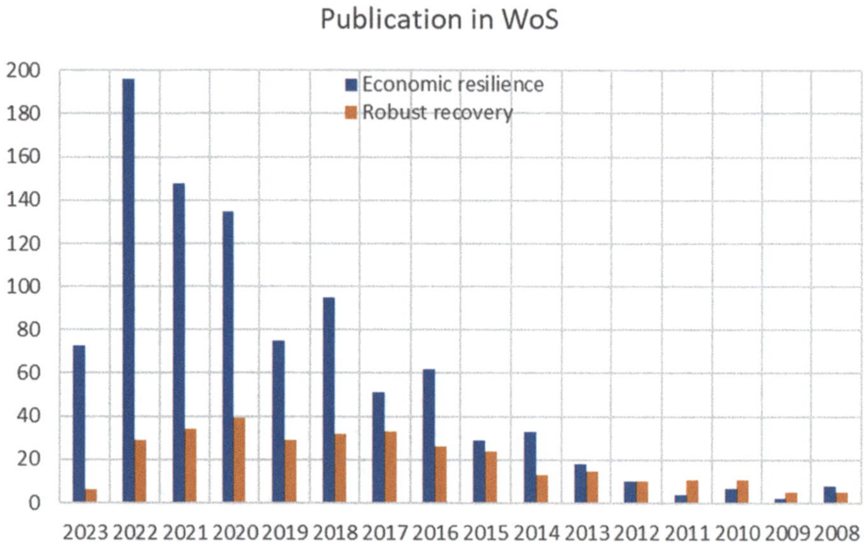


**Fig. 2.1** Publication in WoS (works on economic resilience and robust recovery), 2008–2023 (Source: WoS database)

increased productivity gains, easier diffusion of technology, and decreased poverty. However, on the negative side, these open and integrated systems are susceptible to crisis contagion, where external crises can quickly spread and result in severe global economic downturns. This is due to the interconnectedness of various systems and sectors, causing impacts to cascade and amplify the effects of such crises.

The results from the analysis of the literature show that (Figs. 2.1, 2.2, and 2.3):

- In the realm of capacity and resources, it is crucial to identify what needs to be accomplished and determine the appropriate institutions that will carry out these tasks. This demonstrates a sense of responsibility in implementing measures effectively.
- Additionally, fostering collaboration and trust is essential because achieving solid economic growth relies on a harmonious partnership between the private and public sectors and healthy and respectful collaborative relationships.
- Furthermore, it is essential to align approaches to change, employing effective leadership and intelligent decision-making to adapt to new conditions. This includes the challenge of renewing and redesigning strategies and reconfiguring priorities.
- Investing in innovation plays a central role in successfully overcoming crises.
- A balanced recovery could be achieved by focusing on community-based development for all, emphasising the development of capabilities and interest in addressing social, institutional, and systemic challenges.
- To ensure risk assessment and investment in prevention are practical, supportive measures and adapted policy tools are necessary, requiring the collaboration and contribution of all stakeholders involved.

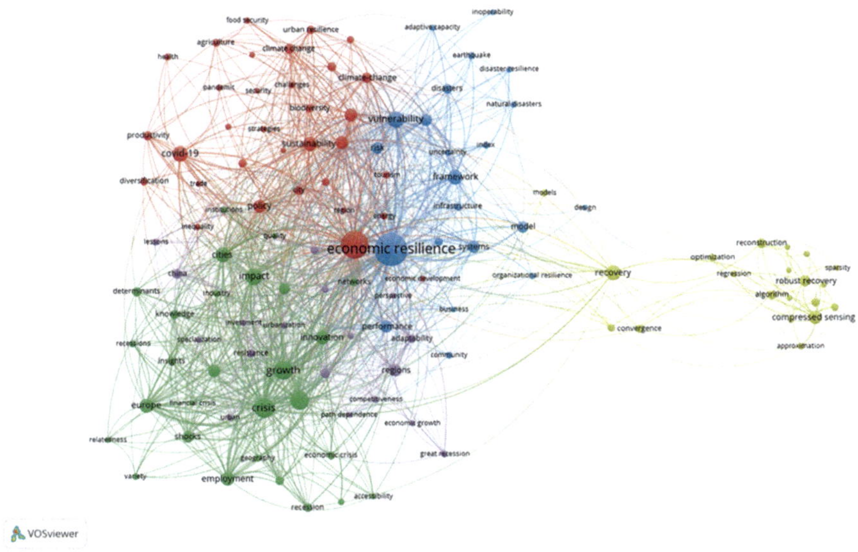


**Fig. 2.2** Economic resilience vs robust recovery after the crisis: economic resilience and robust recovery (10) (Source: WoS database, processed with VOSviewer)

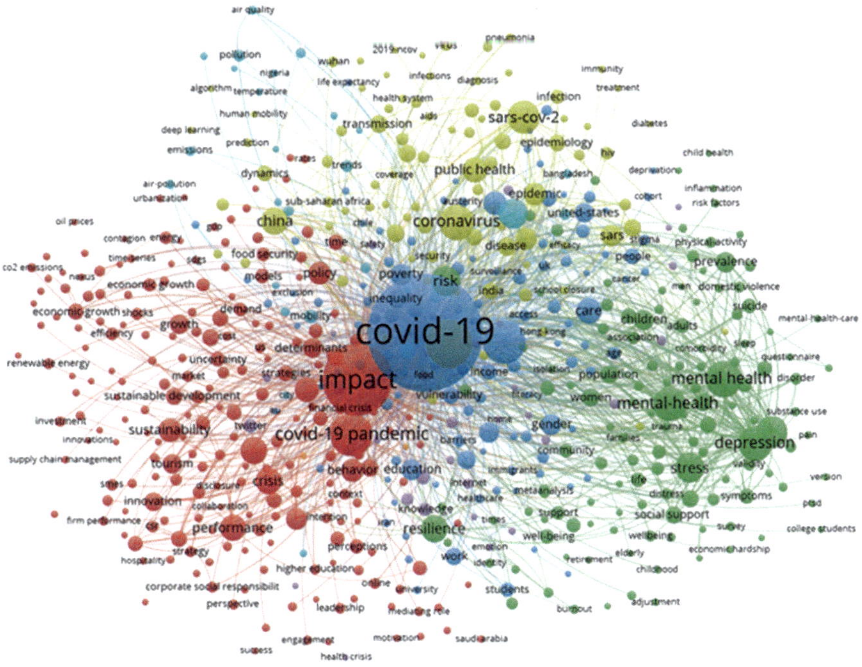


**Fig. 2.3** Economic resilience vs robust recovery after the crisis: Covid-19 and economic and social impact (10) (Source: WoS database, processed with VOSviewer)

Crises, irrespective of their type, have significantly influenced the labour market from various standpoints. The financial crisis of 2008–2009 had a profound and enduring impact on the labour market, taking over a decade for the global unemployment rate to return to pre-crisis levels. However, youth unemployment has not reached pre-crisis levels (Lee et al., 2020). Likewise, the Covid-19 pandemic-induced crisis had a detrimental effect on the labour market, resulting in approximately four times higher losses in working hours in 2020 compared to the global financial crisis. The surge in the unemployment rate during pandemic was also significantly higher than during the 2008–2009 crisis (ILO Monitor, 2021).

The repercussions were particularly harsh on young individuals (Verick, 2009) and women (Fleming, 2021; Ciuhu et al., 2022) and led to a restructuring of employment across various industries, transforming the employment model and giving rise to asymmetric effects (OECD, 2022).

Macroeconomic stimulus measures and labour market policies only partially mitigated the crisis. Still, their implementation was crucial in preventing severe economic contraction and safeguarding the labour market from deterioration (Verick & Islam, 2010). Cho and Newhouse (2011) analysed the Great Recession's impact (2007–2009) on various types of workers in different middle-income countries. The study revealed that young people bore the brunt of the adverse effects on employment.

Junankar (2011) analysed the influence of the last international financial crisis on unemployment across different countries. The findings highlighted variations in its impact on other nations, with employment declines observed in the construction and manufacturing sectors. In contrast, the financial and business industries experienced a surge in unemployment. Several countries resorted to measures such as increased expenditure on active labour market policies and policies encouraging firms to reduce working hours instead of laying off workers to stabilise their economies. Countries have pursued various strategies to limit redundancies, including measures focused on unemployment benefits, employment guarantee schemes, and minimum wages (Verick & Islam, 2010).

The pandemic crisis adversely affected the labour market, leading to heightened vulnerability and a rapid surge in long-term unemployment (OECD, 2021b). Su et al. (2021) analysed various European countries, revealing that the pandemic substantially increased unemployment.

According to the IMF (2022), the crisis pronounced impacted specific groups, including low-skilled workers, young individuals, those with temporary employment arrangements, and workers in contact-intensive services. Job retention schemes were crucial in mitigating the pandemic's impact on the labour market.

Different countries adopted a range of policy measures to counteract the effects of the pandemic crisis on the labour market, as reported by the ILO-OECD (2020). These measures included implementing protocols to reduce workers' exposure to Covid-19 in the workplace, promoting remote working, securing jobs, saving companies, and ensuring essential services. Additionally, income security and employment support were provided to affected workers. Job retention schemes were widely used to prevent layoffs and maintain income stability, while some countries implemented restrictions on dismissals during the crisis to curtail layoffs. Measures to support firms' liquidity, such as subsidies, loan guarantees, and tax-related measures, were also implemented (ILO-OECD, 2020).

The two crises had similar effects: increased unemployment, wage cuts, rising restructuring demands, and a surge in job applications. However, their causes were different. The coronavirus pandemic impacted various industries due to a health emergency, while the 2007–2008 crisis began in the financial sector and spread systematically. The worst-hit sectors in the financial crisis were banking, real estate, and construction, whereas, during the pandemic, tourism, hospitality, food services, and the automotive industry faced the brunt. During the 2007–2008 financial crisis, high-salary employees were the first to be laid off, but companies retained these valuable employees during the pandemic. Advanced digitalisation benefits companies and workers with the widespread adoption of remote work during the pandemic (Cristea, 2020).

In the case of Germany, the Covid-19 crisis has had a more profound impact on economy and labour market than the last financial crisis. During the pandemic, a more comprehensive range of sectors were affected than in the past. However, the number of people who lost their jobs has been limited, as many workers have entered into part-time schemes. Part-time schemes were utilised much more extensively during the pandemic than during the financial crisis. For instance, in the hotel industry (accommodation and gastronomy), approximately 93% of employees were registered for part-time schemes. Unemployment was primarily concentrated in hospitality industry (Gehrke & Weber, 2020).

The outbreak of the pandemic and the implementation of essential public health measures in Ireland led to the highest increase in unemployment in March 2020. While job losses have been observed across all sectors, the tourism, food industry, and retail trade sectors experienced the most significant impact (Coates et al., 2020).

The crisis asymmetrically impacts the labour market across industries and worker groups in Austria. The tourism sector saw the most significant job losses, with employment in the industry declining by nearly 40%, accounting for approximately 75,000 jobs. Other sectors severely affected by the crisis were arts and culture, entertainment and recreation, and temporary employment agencies, with employment dropping by 12% to 15% (Böheim & Leoni, 2020).

During the global financial crisis, young and low-educated workers in the USA experienced a more significant impact, whereas women and Hispanics were more severely affected by the Covid-19 pandemic. Interestingly, jobs that can be done remotely through teleworking, those involving social interactions, and the essential ones have historically exhibited fewer cyclical fluctuations. The historical lack of cyclical changes in occupations suitable for teleworking can be attributed to a higher proportion of skilled workers. In contrast to the global financial crisis, sectors involving social interactions experienced more significant declines in employment during the Covid-19 pandemic. At the same time, jobs conducive to teleworking and essential jobs saw lesser declines. Both crises affected low-income workers the hardest, underscoring the significant distributional impact of the global financial crisis and the pandemic (Shibata, 2020).

The pandemic crisis has had a profound impact on various countries and industries. For instance, in the USA, nearly 1.6 million workers in the hotel sector faced layoffs or contract suspensions, while an additional 3.9 million jobs in the tourism industry (hotel-supported jobs) were lost (American Hotel and Lodging Association, 2020).

In the USA, Cortes and Forsythe (2022) examined how the Covid-19 pandemic affected employment, and they demonstrated that the pandemic exacerbated pre-existing inequalities. Thus, although employment declines affected many, they were notably more severe and enduring in lower-paying occupations and industries.

In India, the pandemic had a more substantial impact than the global financial crisis, with the migrant population particularly affected. Low-income households, without alternative sources of income and lacking social security benefits, bore the brunt of the crisis (Khanna, 2020).

Globally, the tourism industry suffered severe losses due to measures taken to curb the spread of the SARS-CoV-2. Slow recovery was anticipated even after easing isolation measures, posing business challenges (ILO, 2020). For instance, Brazil's tourism industry faced significant losses of approximately 80% in accommodation services, with parks and attractions closed. The sector faced potential losses of around $6.2 billion (Euromonitor, 2020).

Various countries experienced substantial disruptions in their hospitality and food industries. In France, over 75,000 restaurants, 3000 clubs, and 40,000 cafes were forced to close, impacting around 1 million employees on technical unemployment (La Chaîne Info, 2020). The UK's tourism-dependent regions saw about 80% of hotel and food industry workers on furlough schemes, with 1/3 of total jobs facing the risk of long-term disappearance (The Guardian, 2020).

Across the world, airlines and tourism businesses have adjusted their staffing levels, while some companies halted hiring and implemented temporary unemployment measures in collaboration with unions to avoid layoffs. Many organisations were exploring coping strategies for the crisis, including reduced working hours (CNN Business, 2020).

Malik et al. (2021) developed an analysis for the USA, UK, Japan, and Indonesia. They showed that the economic slowdown resulting from the pandemic has a detrimental effect on the unemployment rate. According to the authors, the government should focus on maintaining aggregate demand and supply while ensuring the smooth functioning of supply chains amid various restrictions. Additionally, the paper suggests maximising alternative budget resources. Moreover, it emphasises the need to strengthen the labour system and prioritise the development of health and food security industries as key post-pandemic policies.

Fiaschi and Tealdi (2022) examined the changes in employment patterns among persons aged 20–29 in Italy. The findings reveal that the pandemic exacerbated the situation of higher inactivity rates compared to other EU countries, and a temporary but not persistent trend of young individuals aged 20–24 returning to education was identified.

According to Dvořák et al. (2020), despite all the adverse effects of the pandemic, there were also some positive economic outcomes. One notable positive impact is increased financial inclusion and broader access to the financial system. Additionally, the adoption of digitalisation and information technology has significantly advanced in large and small enterprises and higher education institutions during the pandemic. Moreover, the Covid-19 crisis has heightened awareness about climate change, showcasing the potential for reducing CO2 emissions through decreased economic activity. Furthermore, the pandemic has prompted optimising workloads and the elimination of unnecessary tasks in many businesses and public institutions.

The Covid-19 pandemic introduced new working models less widespread before the crisis. Many employees transitioned to remote work, and companies swiftly adapted to support and protect their workforce, leading to structural changes in the employer-employee relationship. To address labour market challenges, digitisation emerged as a practical solution, facilitating access to resources for the population and continuing professional development activities during this difficult period (Mindrican & Matei, 2023).

Despite the negative impact on various economic sectors, the Covid-19 pandemic has accelerated digitisation. Many industries have found essential support in transferring activities to the online environment or intensifying their digital operations.

## Methodology

The investigation regarding the recovery period for selected indicators covers 2008–2022, and a comparative analysis of EU and candidate countries is developed with data from Eurostat. The indicators used were the NEET rate, employment rate, at-risk-of-poverty rate, job vacancy rate, trade openness, and gross fixed capital formation.

Statistical analysis focused on the recovery period after the crisis, with a comparative approach for the EU and candidate countries.

Also, an econometric analysis was developed in this study. Following various computations, one might emphasise the importance of the cointegration relationships between the variables (long-term). In the empirical analysis, an annual dataset for the 2012–2021 period is used for EU countries (old and new ones) and also for candidate countries (only for Montenegro, North Macedonia, Serbia, and Türkiye, due to the lack of data). The variables used are presented in Table 2.1.

The econometric analysis was followed by a graphical representation (with data for 2012 and 2021 and EU countries) of the relationships between the variables. We developed this analysis to see if there is a convergence at the level of EU countries. The relationships considered are:

- EMPL vs TO, considering that TO can lead to increased exports of goods and services, which can positively impact employment in labour-intensive industries. TO can expose domestic industries to competition from imports, and if domestic industries are unable to compete with lower-priced imports, they may experience

**Table 2.1** The variables used in the analysis

| Acronym | Explanation | Unit of measure | Source |
|---|---|---|---|
| GDP_CAPITA | Gross domestic product per capita | Percentage of EU-27 total (based on million purchasing power standards), current prices, market prices | Eurostat |
| EMPL | Employment rates by sex, age, and citizenship (%), total; from 15 to 74 years | Percentage | |
| GFCF | Gross fixed capital formation (investments) | Current prices, million euro | |
| NEET | Young people neither in employment nor in education and training by sex, age, and labour status (NEET rates), total | Percentage | |
| P | At-risk-of-poverty rate (cut-off point: 60% of median equivalised income after social transfers), total | Percentage | |
| TO | Trade openness ((exports +imports)/GDP x 100)) | Percentage | |
| JVR | Job vacancy rate (number of job vacancies/(number of occupied posts + number of job vacancies) x 100), annual average | Percentage | |

Note: All variables were transformed in the index by authors (present year/past year x 100)
Source: developed by authors

a decline in sales and profitability, leading to potential job losses. Countries with a high level of TO tend to have more export-oriented industries, which may experience growth due to increased demand for their products in international markets, potentially leading to higher employment opportunities.

- GFCF vs TO, considering that TO can attract investments, stimulating job creation in the host country. Thus, foreign companies may invest in domestic industries, leading to increased employment opportunities. GFCF indicates investments in infrastructure and production capacities, and improved infrastructure can enhance a country's export potential by reducing transportation costs, improving logistics, and making it more attractive for investors. Investments in fixed capital can lead to the expansion and modernisation of industries, increasing their export capacity. Upgraded facilities and technologies can help industries produce more efficiently and competitively, enabling them to participate more actively in international markets.
- GFCF vs P, considering that GFCF can stimulate economic growth, which, in turn, can lead to more job opportunities. As the economy expands, it may generate additional employment opportunities, potentially reducing P as more people find jobs and increase their incomes. Investments in capital and

technology through GFCF can improve productivity in various industries. Higher productivity can lead to increased wages for workers, which may help lift individuals or households out of poverty and reduce the overall P.

- GFCF vs NEET, considering that GFCF can contribute to economic growth, which may increase job opportunities in various sectors. A growing economy with expanding industries is more likely to offer employment prospects, potentially reducing the NEET rate.
- GDP_CAPITA vs P, considering that a higher GDP_CAPITA generally indicates a more prosperous economy with more employment opportunities. As the economy grows and generates more jobs, it can potentially reduce the number of people at risk of poverty by providing income-earning opportunities for a broader population segment.

The analysis emphasises certain aspects of labour market resilience and the capacity for a robust recovery postcrisis period. Moreover, the chapter investigates the duration required for specific labour market indicators to return to their pre-crisis levels. It recognises that resilience can also be measured by an indicator linked to the time taken to recover to pre-crisis values.

During our analysis, we encountered limitations concerning data availability for the job vacancy rate. Numerous EU member states lacked data for the entire period, leading to data gaps.

## Dynamics of the Selected Indicators (2008–2022)

Our statistical analysis focuses on observing the shock's characteristics, including its magnitude and duration of reduction or decline. Additionally, we closely examined the recovery period by analysing the years it took to return to the pre-crisis level.

The findings revealed the presence of propagated crises, referring to imported crises that had significant and long-lasting impacts. During the recovery period, there were noticeable variations between countries, which can be categorised as follows:

(a) Some countries experienced a reduced but rapid recovery, and this rebound was not sustainable. For instance, Romania's export increased, but it was coupled with rising deficits in the trade balance.
(b) Other countries faced prolonged recovery periods with associated complementary effects, such as asymmetric employment recovery characterised by chronic structural deficits. This was linked to increased external work mobility, inflexible job markets, and a low rate of job vacancies. There was also a deficit of employment opportunities in industries capable of supporting infrastructure investments like construction and construction materials, leading to a migration of workers for employment abroad. Additionally, there was an increased employment deficit in the agricultural sector due to the migration of low-skilled workers from rural areas.
(c) In certain countries and across various indicators, the pre-crisis levels were not restored, indicating a shift towards a "new normal" model.

## *NEET Rate*

Examining the NEET rate reveals varying impacts of both crises on different countries. The newer member states were more affected during the financial crisis than the older ones. In 2009 compared to 2008, three new member states, namely, Estonia (+5.8 p.p.), Latvia (+5.7 p.p.), and Lithuania (+3.3 p.p.), recorded the highest increases in the share of NEET. On the other hand, out of eight countries with a rise of 1 p.p. or less in the share of NEET, six were older member states, including Belgium, Greece, Italy, Portugal, Austria, and Germany. Luxembourg experienced a decline in the share of NEET during the same period (−0.4 p.p.). Among the EU candidate states, data were available only for Türkiye and North Macedonia, which had a similar pattern to Luxembourg. Despite the financial crisis, evolution was favourable, i.e. the share of NEET decreased by −2.1 p.p. in Türkiye and −3 p.p. in North Macedonia.

During the Covid-19 pandemic, the NEET rate was more severely impacted than during the financial crisis. Countries like Montenegro, Türkiye, Lithuania, Ireland, Spain, Germany, North Macedonia, and Estonia witnessed an increase in the share of NEET between 3.8 p.p. and 1.3 p.p. However, the outbreak of the coronavirus pandemic led to improved employment prospects among young people in only one of the new member states, Latvia (−0.8 p.p.), and in two of the old member states: Denmark (−0.3 p.p.) and Belgium (−0.1 p.p.). Overall, at the EU-27 level, the impact of the financial crisis on the share of NEET was more significant (+1.6 p.p. in 2009/2008) compared to the pandemic crisis (+1 p.p. in 2020 vs 2019).

Regarding the NEET indicator, the recovery following the financial crisis exhibited the following trends. The two candidate countries with data until 2020, North Macedonia and Türkiye, showed an exciting evolution of the NEET share after the financial crisis. While the worst situation was recorded in 2008, a decrease started in 2009, indicating a faster recovery.

Among the EU member states (MSs), several countries demonstrated a swift recovery of the NEET share to pre-financial crisis levels, which we'll refer to as the "recovery period". These countries are three old MSs, namely, Germany, Austria, and Sweden, that achieved complete NEET recovery after the financial crisis in 2010 (2 years) and even reached lower levels than in 2008. Luxembourg and Latvia experienced recovery in 2015, taking 7 years to get pre-crisis NEET levels.

13 EU MSs fully recovered within 10 years or less, including eight old MSs and five new member states (NMSs). Other five old MSs passed through a lengthy recovery period, meaning more than 10 years

Other countries, namely, Greece, Netherlands, and Finland, took more than 10 years to return to pre-financial crisis NEET levels, achieving recovery in 2021 (13 years). France and Italy had a recovery period of 14 years, reaching pre-crisis NEET levels in 2022.

However, no recovery was registered until 2022 in one old MS (Denmark) and three NMSs (Croatia, Cyprus, and Romania). The NEET share in these countries did not return to pre-financial crisis levels until the end of the analysed period (2022), which may be attributed to overlapping crises.

## *Employment Rate*

Old member states seemed more affected than the new ones. The top eight countries that recorded the highest decreases in employment rate in 2009 vs 2008 include five old member states (Ireland (−5.7 p.p.), Spain (−4 p.p.), Denmark (−2.6 p.p.), Finland (−2.3 p.p.), and Sweden (−2.1 p.p.)) and three new member states (Latvia (−7.7 p.p.), Estonia (−5.6 p.p.), and Lithuania (−4.1 p.p.)). Out of the five countries with minor decreases in the employment rate, two were old MSs (Greece (−0.4 p.p.) and Netherlands (−0.3 p.p.)), two were NMSs (Croatia (−0.3 p.p.) and Malta (−0.2 p.p.)), and one was a candidate (Türkiye (−0.4 p.p.)). In other European countries, the financial crisis's adverse effects on the employment rate were delayed: in Poland, a slight decrease was recorded in 2010. Afterwards, it maintained an upward trend; in Luxembourg, the employment rate dropped in 2011, while in North Macedonia, the same happened only in 2013. Germany was the only EU MS where the employment rate increased in 2009–2019.

The employment rate of old member states also seemed more affected by the pandemic crisis. Out of the nine states that recorded the most significant decreases in the rate of employment, only two were new member states, Estonia (−1.8 p.p.) and Bulgaria (−1.6 p.p.), and the other two were candidate countries: Montenegro (−5.2 p.p.) and Türkiye (−2.9 p.p.). The most affected old member states were Spain (−2.1 p.p. in 2020 vs 2019), Germany (−1.7 p.p.), Ireland (−1.6 p.p.), Portugal (−1.3 p.p.), and Austria (−1.2 p.p.).

The prospects of employment improved after the outbreak of the coronavirus pandemic in only one NMS, namely, Malta (+0.7 p.p.), and in one candidate country: Serbia (+0.2 p.p.).

At the aggregated level of EU-27, the impact of the financial crisis on the employment rate was slightly larger than the one of the pandemic crisis (−1.1 p.p. in 2009 vs 2008, compared to −1 p.p. in 2020 vs 2019).

The new member states seemed to have had the fastest recovery of the employment rate to the pre-financial crisis level (we will use the term "recovery period"). Four of the top six countries with the best performances were NMSs (Malta, Poland, Hungary, and Romania). In Malta and Türkiye, the employment rate wholly recovered after the financial crisis after 2 years (in 2010) (reached higher levels than in 2008), followed by Austria and Poland (3 years), with recovery in 2011, and Hungary and Romania (4 years)—with recovery in 2012.

The employment rate at the EU-27 level recovered to the pre-financial crisis level after 8 years in 2016.

Out of the ten EU countries where the recovery period of employment rate exceeded 10 years, the majority were old MS (seven), the other three being NMSs.

The member states with the most extended recovery period of the employment rate were Ireland, France, Finland, and Cyprus, where the values of this indicator returned to the pre-financial crisis level after 14 years, in 2022, following another crisis (the Covid-19 pandemic).

Nevertheless, in two old MSs (Denmark and Spain) and one new MS (Greece), the employment rate did not return to the pre-financial crisis level until the end of the analysed period (2022), all the more so since the adverse effects of the pandemic were also manifested.

An interesting trend was observed in Germany and Luxembourg, where the employment rate grew upwards despite the financial crisis. A similar situation was recorded in North Macedonia (EU candidate country). The data were incomplete for the other EU candidate countries (Montenegro and Serbia) or missing.

After the outbreak of the pandemic crisis, the employment rate recovered to the pre-pandemic levels, after 2 years (in 2021), in 11 EU member states, 6 of them being OMSs (Denmark, Ireland, Greece, France, Luxembourg, and Netherlands) and 5 NMSs (Croatia, Cyprus, Hungary, Poland, and Slovakia). In the other 13 EU member states, the recovery period was longer: the employment rate returned to the level of 2019 or above in 3 years (in 2022).

Among the candidate countries, data for 2019–2022 were available only for Serbia, where the employment rate returned to the pre-pandemic level in 2022 after 3 years.

However, there were some member states where the adverse effects on the employment rate were more challenging to overcome. In Germany, Latvia, and Romania, the employment rate has not returned to the pre-pandemic levels (by the end of 2022). At the same time, Malta's employment rate continued to rise after 2019, seemingly unaffected by the pandemic.

## *At-Risk-of-Poverty Rate*

Due to data constraints (available from 2011 onwards), an analysis of the effects of the financial crisis on the at-risk-of-poverty rate could not be carried out.

The old MSs seemed to record the sharpest increases in poverty after the pandemic crisis. Out of the 11 states where the at-risk-of-poverty rate grew by more than 0.2 p.p. in 2020 compared to 2019, the majority (seven) were old MSs: Netherlands (+0.2 p.p.), Spain (+0.3 p.p.), France, Austria and Finland (+0.6 p.p.), Ireland (+0.7 p.p.), and Germany (+1.3 p.p., from 14.8% to 16.1%), while only three were NMSs: Lithuania (+0.3 p.p.), Slovenia (+0.4 p.p.), and Bulgaria (+1.2 p.p., from 22.6% to 23.8%).

Despite the pandemic crisis, an opposite situation was observed in three candidate countries (Albania, Serbia, and Montenegro), where the at-risk-of-poverty rate recorded the most significant decreases (ranging between −1.2 p.p. and − 1.9 p.p.). Latvia and Estonia were the NMSs that saw the most significant improvement in this indicator, while the same happened for Portugal and Sweden (old MSs).

An interesting case is represented by Malta, Poland, and Romania, where the pandemic crisis did not negatively affect the at-risk-of-poverty rate, which constantly decreased during 2019 and 2022. In Belgium, Sweden, and Cyprus, the at-risk-of-poverty rate declined between 2019 and 2021 but increased in 2022, reaching a level below the pre-pandemic rate. The same happened in Czechia and Estonia, except the at-risk-of-poverty rate achieved in 2022 was higher than that of 2019. Besides a delayed effect of the pandemic crisis, this situation could also be generated by other factors, which are not related to the pandemic, such as the increase in energy prices. In France, Netherlands, and Austria, the at-risk-of-poverty rate constantly increased during 2019–2022.

At the aggregated level of EU-27, the pandemic crisis determined an increase of +0.2 p.p. in the at-risk-of-poverty rate from 16.5% in 2019 to 16.7% in 2020.

The NMSs seemed to have had the fastest recovery of the at-risk-of-poverty rate, which returned to the pre-pandemic crisis level after 2 years. Out of the top six countries with the best performances, three were NMSs (Bulgaria, Lithuania, and Slovenia), while only two were old MSs (Ireland and Finland) and one was a candidate (Türkiye). In another seven EU countries, the at-risk-of-poverty rate reached the levels before the pandemic after 3 years in Germany, Spain, Luxembourg, and Portugal (old MSs) and Croatia, Latvia, and Hungary (NMSs). In Greece and Slovakia, the values of this indicator did not return to the pre-pandemic level until the end of the analysed period (2022).

## *Job Vacancy Rate*

Data for job vacancy rates during 2008–2022 were available only for nine EU member states (seven NMSs and two old MSs). Another nine EU states (including one candidate country) don't have the complete series. Still, the available data can be used to analyse the trend in the context generated by the pandemic.

First, the financial crisis triggered a decrease in the job vacancy rate in EU member states, whose intensity varied across countries. The top four countries that recorded the highest declines in job vacancy rate in 2009 vs 2008 included three NMSs and one old MS: Czechia (−2 p.p.), Estonia (−1.6 p.p.), and Lithuania and Netherlands (−1.2 p.p.). On the other hand, the most minor decrease was recorded in Luxembourg (−0.2 p.p.), followed by Slovakia and Slovenia (−0.3 p.p.).

The recovery to the pre-financial crisis levels (2008) took only 2 years in Luxembourg, 6 years in Hungary and Slovenia, 8 years in Latvia, and 9 years in Czechia, while in Netherlands and Lithuania, the job vacancy rate needed the most extended period to return to the pre-crisis level, respectively, 10 and 13 years. At the same time, in Estonia and Slovakia, the job vacancy rate did not recover to the pre-financial crisis levels by the end of 2022.

The outbreak of the pandemic crisis and the containment measures adopted by the governments had a substantial impact on the business environment, which was also manifested by a drop in the job vacancy rate that saw the most significant losses in

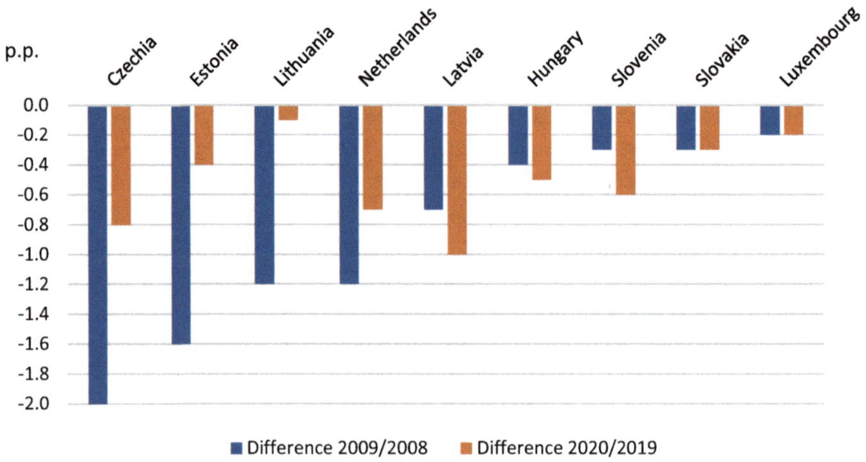


**Fig. 2.4** The evolution of the job vacancy rate in some EU member states in the first year after the financial crisis (2009) and the first year after the pandemic (2020), compared to the pre-crisis levels (percentage points) (Source: authors' calculations based on Eurostat (2023). Job vacancy rate, annual data, NACE Rev. 2, https://ec.europa.eu/eurostat/databrowser/view/JVS_A_RATE_R2/default/table?lang=en&category=labour.jvs)

Latvia (−1 p.p. in 2020 compared to 2019), followed by Czechia, Germany (−0.8 p.p.), and Netherlands (−0.7 p.p.). The disruptions generated by the pandemic barely impacted the job vacancy rate in Luxembourg (−0.2 p.p. in 2020 compared to 2019), Bulgaria, and Lithuania (−0.1 p.p.).

From a comparative perspective, the drop in the job vacancy rate in the first year after the financial crisis was more significant compared to the first year after the pandemic in Czechia, Estonia, Lithuania, and Netherlands. However, in Latvia, Hungary, and Slovakia, the adverse impact of the pandemic on the job vacancy rate overpassed those of the financial crisis (Fig. 2.4).

In the majority of EU countries (Lithuania, Luxembourg, Netherlands, Slovenia, Portugal, Croatia, Poland, Sweden, and Finland), the job vacancy rate recovered to the pre-pandemic levels after 2 years in 2021, while the recovery period was 3 years for Estonia, Hungary, Germany, and Bulgaria. It is essential to mention that there are four NMSs (Latvia, Slovakia, Romania, and Czechia) where the job vacancy rate did not recover after the pandemic. In North Macedonia, the only candidate country with available data, the job vacancy rate in 2020 remained at the level of 2019, despite the pandemic outbreak.

## *Trade Openness*

Trade openness highlights the vulnerabilities of one country to external shocks. An investigation of the effects of the financial crisis on trade openness in the EU countries was impossible as data were available starting with 2011. However, during 2011–2019, trade openness at the EU-27 level rose from 84.7% to 95.2%. Beginning in 2013, trade openness recorded the highest values in Luxembourg, followed by Malta and Ireland.

The Covid-19 pandemic caused the blocking, temporary interruption, and even breaking of the existing supply chains worldwide, phenomena that the trade openness index can illustrate. The analysis of this indicator before and after the outbreak of the pandemic highlights that the most substantial adverse effects were recorded in two candidate countries (Montenegro, where the trade openness lost 21.8 p.p. in 2020 compared to 2019, and Albania—with −16.5 p.p.), followed by two NMSs, namely, Slovakia (−15 p.p.) and Bulgaria (−14.4 p.p.), and one old member state, Luxembourg (−12.6 p.p.). On the other hand, among the countries where the trade openness diminished to the most minor extent (with less than 5 p.p.), there are four NMSs (Latvia (−1.3 p.p.), Poland (−2.4 p.p.), and Estonia and Hungary (−5.3 p. p.)), two old MSs (Italy (−4.6 p.p.) and Ireland (−4.5 p.p.)), and one candidate country (Türkiye, where the trade openness decreased by 1.7 p.p.). Cyprus was the only EU member state where trade openness continued to grow despite the pandemic, from 152% in 2019 to 183.4% in 2022. In Malta, the adverse effects of the pandemic on trade openness were felt only in 2021 and not in 2020, as happened in the rest of the EU member states and candidates. Still, in 2021, the value of Malta's trade openness was more significant than the one in 2019, before the pandemic (323% compared to 316%).

Against the background of the pandemic crisis, trade openness at the aggregated level of EU-27 declined by 6 p.p., from 95.2% in 2019 to 89.2% in 2020.

The analysis of the recovery period for trade openness revealed that the new MSs and the candidate countries had the resources to overcome faster the challenges triggered by the pandemic shock. Returning to the levels in 2019 was accomplished after 2 years in the majority of the two categories of countries mentioned above (9 out of 11 NMSs and 5 out of 7 candidate countries). On the other hand, a shorter recovery period (2 years) was recorded only in 9 out of 14 old MSs (Austria, Belgium, Denmark, Germany, Greece, Italy, Luxembourg, Netherlands, Spain). In comparison, recovery required more time for the other four countries (3 years—France, Finland, Portugal, and Sweden). By contrast, only two NMSs (Bulgaria and Hungary) and two candidate countries (Montenegro and Albania) faced a similar situation. Moreover, Ireland's trade openness did not return to the pre-pandemic level by the end of 2022.

## *Gross Fixed Capital Formation*

Gross fixed capital formation (GFCF) represents the investments made in a country from new value-added and illustrates the vulnerabilities to internal shocks.

The analysis of the impact of the financial crisis on the gross fixed capital formation of EU member states could not be developed due to data limitations.

Between 2011 and 2022, GFCF for EU-27 was marked by an expansion of over 52%, from 2357.2 billion euro in 2011 to 3592.8 billion euro in 2022.

The outbreak of the SARS-CoV-2 pandemic contributed to increasing uncertainty in the business environment, diminishing, stopping, or postponing the realisation of some investments. An analysis of GFCF before and after the pandemic revealed that declined in almost two-thirds of the EU countries and all candidate countries in 2020. The most significant decreases were recorded in Ireland, where gross fixed capital formation decreased by 18% in 2020 compared to 2019, followed by Montenegro (−13.7%), Slovakia (−10.3%), and Spain (−8.8%). The countries where the gross fixed capital formation diminished to a minor extent (with less than 2%) include three old MSs (Luxembourg (−1.5%) and Germany and Portugal (−0.8%)), one NMS (Latvia: −1.4%), and two candidate countries (Albania (−1.5%) and North Macedonia (−1.1%)). However, the pandemic did not cause disturbances at GFCF level in the other ten EU countries, maintaining its growth trend. This group of countries include five old MSs, namely, Netherlands, Finland, Greece, Sweden, and Denmark, and five NMSs: Romania, Lithuania, Bulgaria, Cyprus, and Estonia. The growth rate varied widely, depending on each country's economic and pandemic conditions. In Netherlands, Finland, Romania, and Greece, the gross fixed capital formation increased by less than 1% in 2020 compared to 2019. In Denmark and Cyprus, it expanded by 5–6%, while Estonia recorded the highest growth, namely, +21.4%, during the same period.

Against the background of the pandemic crisis, the EU-27 gross fixed capital formation fell by 4.6%, from 3115.4 billion euro in 2019 to 2971.5 billion euro in 2020.

Among the countries that recorded a decline in gross fixed capital formation during the pandemic, the majority (19 out of 24) had the resources and the conditions to reverse the adverse effects of the pandemic quickly. They returned to the pre-pandemic gross fixed capital formation levels after 2 years in 2021. Seven of them were old MSs (Austria, Belgium, Germany, France, Italy, Luxembourg, and Portugal), six were NMSs (Czechia, Croatia, Hungary, Latvia, Malta, and Slovenia), and the other six were candidate countries (Albania, Bosnia and Herzegovina, Kosovo, North Macedonia, Serbia, and Türkiye). In Spain, Poland, and Slovakia, the recovery of this indicator needed 3 years.

A distinct category includes Ireland and Montenegro, where the gross fixed capital formation declined in 2020 and reached the minimum level in 2021. Even if the trend reversed in 2022, the increase was insufficient to reach the pre-pandemic levels.

## Empirical Analysis

In the analysis, an annual dataset for the 2012–2021 period is used for EU countries (old and new member states) and also for candidate countries (only for Montenegro, North Macedonia, Serbia, and Türkiye, due to the lack of data). The variables used in

**Table 2.2** The descriptive statistics for the series

| | GDP_CAPITA | EMPL | GFCF | NEET | P | TO |
|---|---|---|---|---|---|---|
| Mean | 100.7480 | 1.009031 | 1.047616 | 0.986244 | 99.87773 | 101.3148 |
| Median | 100.4854 | 1.010545 | 1.037572 | 0.980392 | 99.51691 | 101.2102 |
| Maximum | 131.0145 | 1.093079 | 2.088695 | 1.318182 | 117.2043 | 124.8219 |
| Minimum | 89.22156 | 0.899614 | 0.627564 | 0.577778 | 86.70520 | 79.93502 |
| Std. Dev. | 3.179128 | 0.021240 | 0.120897 | 0.102482 | 4.716078 | 5.364290 |
| Skewness | 2.603257 | -0.918086 | 3.012097 | 0.265903 | 0.394847 | 0.212164 |
| Kurtosis | 29.59490 | 7.657510 | 24.39048 | 4.591637 | 4.044025 | 4.943891 |
| Jarque-Bera | 9271.758 | 316.4322 | 6234.777 | 35.55358 | 21.63426 | 49.97941 |
| Probability | 0.000000 | 0.000000 | 0.000000 | 0.000000 | 0.000020 | 0.000000 |
| Sum | 30526.65 | 305.7363 | 317.4276 | 298.8318 | 30262.95 | 30698.38 |
| Sum Sq. Dev. | 3052.270 | 0.136242 | 4.414041 | 3.171800 | 6716.900 | 8690.234 |
| Observations | 303 | 303 | 303 | 303 | 303 | 303 |

Source: developed by authors

the analysis are GDP per capita, employment rates, gross fixed capital formation, NEET rate, at-risk-of-poverty rate, and trade openness. Job vacancy rate is not used in the empirical analysis due to the lack of data. The descriptive statistics for the series are presented in Table 2.2.

The first step of the analysis is related to developing the panel unit root test and requires all variables to have the same properties. The variables should have the same order of integration. The results are presented in Table 2.3.

For this test, the null hypothesis is "panel data have unit root", and the alternative hypothesis is "there is no unit root in panel data". In our case, we obtained the probability values of >5% for data in level for all groups of countries. This means that we cannot reject the null hypothesis. In level, the variables are nonstationary.

We obtained the probability values of <5% for data in first difference. This means that we can reject the null hypothesis. In first difference, the variables do not have unit root, so they become stationary. In this case, we decided to run the panel cointegration test and analyse two relationships: (a) the nexus between GDP_CAPITA, EMPL, GFCF, and TO (nexus no. 1, or N1) and (b) the nexus between GDP_CAPITA, NEET, and P (nexus no. 2, or N2).

Thus, we checked the relationships for:

- All groups of countries (panel with data for new member states, old member states, and candidate countries; see Tables 2.4 and 2.5)
- New member states (panel with data for new member states; see Tables 2.6 and 2.7)
- Old member states (panel with data for old member states; see Tables 2.8 and 2.9)
- Candidate countries (panel with data for candidate countries; see Tables 2.10 and 2.11)

For the panel of all groups of countries (panel with data for new member states, old member states, and candidate countries), the probability value is less than 5% in

**Table 2.3** Panel unit root test

| | GDP_CAPITA | D(GDP_CAPITA) | EMPL | D(EMPL) | GFCF | D(GFCF) |
|---|---|---|---|---|---|---|
| Method | Statistic | | | | | |
| Panel unit root test: summary<br>Null: unit root (assumes common unit root process) | | | | | | |
| Levin, Lin & Chu t* | 0.93781 | −21.0407*** | −0.32905 | −17.8593*** | 1.09035 | −22.3620*** |
| Null: unit root (assumes individual unit root process) | | | | | | |
| ADF-Fisher chi-square | 33.7493 | 404.922*** | 39.6641 | 328.691 | 25.2695 | 412.906*** |
| PP-Fisher chi-square | 31.5186 | 485.270*** | 34.2301 | 336.650 | 17.9403 | 464.198*** |
| | NEET | D(NEET) | P | D(P) | TO | D(TO) |
| Method | Statistic | | | | | |
| Panel unit root test: summary<br>Null: unit root (assumes common unit root process) | | | | | | |
| Levin, Lin & Chu t* | 3.37953 | −22.0612*** | −0.80216 | −27.9811*** | 0.04532 | −20.7756*** |
| Null: unit root (assumes individual unit root process) | | | | | | |
| ADF-Fisher chi-square | 36.1006 | 396.403*** | 35.7095 | 429.224*** | 28.9298 | 358.530*** |
| PP-Fisher chi-square | 47.4111 | 403.130*** | 31.5882 | 456.659*** | 14.9251 | 398.766*** |

Note: * *p*-value ≤0.1, ** *p*-value ≤0.01, *** *p*-value ≤0.001
Source: developed by authors

**Table 2.4** Panel cointegration test, all groups of countries, N1

Pedroni Residual Cointegration Test
Series: GDP_CAPITA EMPL GFCF TO
Date: 05/24/23 Time: 12:37
Sample: 2012 2021
Included observations: 310
Cross-sections included: 31
Null Hypothesis: No cointegration
Trend assumption: No deterministic trend
Automatic lag length selection based on SIC with a max lag of 0
Newey-West automatic bandwidth selection and Bartlett kernel

| Alternative hypothesis: common AR coefs. (within-dimension) | | | | |
|---|---|---|---|---|
| | Statistic | Prob. | Weighted Statistic | Prob. |
| Panel v-Statistic | -3.527662 | 0.9998 | -2.598758 | 0.9953 |
| Panel rho-Statistic | 2.915695 | 0.9982 | 2.451300 | 0.9929 |
| Panel PP-Statistic | -7.950639 | 0.0000 | -3.832923 | 0.0001 |
| Panel ADF-Statistic | -5.643216 | 0.0000 | -3.724229 | 0.0001 |
| Alternative hypothesis: individual AR coefs. (between-dimension) | | | | |
| | Statistic | Prob. | | |
| Group rho-Statistic | 5.049180 | 1.0000 | | |
| Group PP-Statistic | -5.162553 | 0.0000 | | |
| Group ADF-Statistic | -4.005755 | 0.0000 | | |

Source: developed by authors

**Table 2.5** Panel cointegration test, all groups of countries, N2

Pedroni Residual Cointegration Test
Series: GDP_CAPITA NEET P
Date: 05/24/23 Time: 12:39
Sample: 2012 2021
Included observations: 310
Cross-sections Included: 31
Null Hypothesis: No cointegration
Trend assumption: No deterministic trend
Automatic lag length selection based on SIC with lags from 0 to 1
Newey-West automatic bandwidth selection and Bartlett kernel

| Alternative hypothesis: common AR coefs. (within-dimension) | | | | |
|---|---|---|---|---|
| | Statistic | Prob. | Weighted Statistic | Prob. |
| Panel v-Statistic | -2.430814 | 0.9925 | -1.852522 | 0.9680 |
| Panel rho-Statistic | 0.831579 | 0.7972 | 0.438381 | 0.6694 |
| Panel PP-Statistic | -7.661843 | 0.0000 | -6.424287 | 0.0000 |
| Panel ADF-Statistic | -6.874436 | 0.0000 | -6.837115 | 0.0000 |
| Alternative hypothesis: individual AR coefs. (between-dimension) | | | | |
| | Statistic | Prob. | | |
| Group rho-Statistic | 2.783044 | 0.9973 | | |
| Group PP-Statistic | -7.165494 | 0.0000 | | |
| Group ADF-Statistic | -8.426238 | 0.0000 | | |

Source: developed by authors

**Table 2.6** Panel cointegration test, new member states, N1

Pedroni Residual Cointegration Test
Series: GDP_CAPITA EMPL GFCF TO
Date: 05/24/23 Time: 12:41
Sample: 2012 2021
Included observations: 130
Cross-sections included: 13
Null Hypothesis: No cointegration
Trend assumption: No deterministic trend
Automatic lag length selection based on SIC with a max lag of 0
Newey-West automatic bandwidth selection and Bartlett kernel

| Alternative hypothesis: common AR coefs. (within-dimension) | | | | |
|---|---|---|---|---|
| | Statistic | Prob. | Weighted Statistic | Prob. |
| Panel v-Statistic | -0.450956 | 0.6740 | -1.453582 | 0.9270 |
| Panel rho-Statistic | 1.822116 | 0.9658 | 1.813320 | 0.9651 |
| Panel PP-Statistic | -1.947234 | 0.0258 | -1.364377 | 0.0862 |
| Panel ADF-Statistic | -1.903403 | 0.0285 | -1.425241 | 0.0770 |
| Alternative hypothesis: individual AR coefs. (between-dimension) | | | | |
| | Statistic | Prob. | | |
| Group rho-Statistic | 3.585958 | 0.9998 | | |
| Group PP-Statistic | -1.710264 | 0.0436 | | |
| Group ADF-Statistic | -1.350526 | 0.0884 | | |

Source: developed by authors

**Table 2.7** Panel cointegration test, new member states, N2

Pedroni Residual Cointegration Test
Series: GDP_CAPITA NEET P
Date: 05/24/23 Time: 12:44
Sample: 2012 2021
Included observations: 130
Cross-sections included: 13
Null Hypothesis: No cointegration
Trend assumption: No deterministic trend
Automatic lag length selection based on SIC with a max lag of 1
Newey-West automatic bandwidth selection and Bartlett kernel

| Alternative hypothesis: common AR coefs. (within-dimension) | | | | |
|---|---|---|---|---|
| | Statistic | Prob. | Weighted Statistic | Prob. |
| Panel v-Statistic | -0.720975 | 0.7645 | -0.846602 | 0.8014 |
| Panel rho-Statistic | 0.424172 | 0.6643 | 0.364753 | 0.6424 |
| Panel FP-Statistic | -3.564840 | 0.0002 | -3.142812 | 0.0008 |
| Panel ADF-Statistic | -3.746753 | 0.0001 | -3.526962 | 0.0002 |
| Alternative hypothesis: individual AR coefs. (between-dimension) | | | | |
| | Statistic | Prob. | | |
| Group rho-Statistic | 1.812755 | 0.9651 | | |
| Group PP-Statistic | -3.349159 | 0.0004 | | |
| Group ADF-Statistic | -4.185661 | 0.0000 | | |

Source: developed by authors

**Table 2.8** Panel cointegration test, old member states, N1

Pedroni Residual Cointegration Test
Series: GDP_CAPITA EMPL GFCF TO
Date 05/24/23 Time: 12:51
Sample: 2012 2021
Included observations: 140
Cross-sections included: 14
Null Hypothesis: No cointegration
Trend assumption: No deterministic trend
Automatic lag length selection based on SIC with a max lag of 0
Newey-West automatic bandwidth selection and Bartlett kernel

Alternative hypothesis: common AR coefs. (within-dimension)

| | Statistic | Prob. | Weighted Statistic | Prob. |
|---|---|---|---|---|
| Panel v-Statistic | -3.039902 | 0.9988 | -2.129202 | 0.9834 |
| Panel rho-Statistic | 2.147776 | 0.9841 | 1.655662 | 0.9511 |
| Panel PP-Statistic | -6.935967 | 0.0000 | -3.058106 | 0.0011 |
| Panel ADF-Statistic | -3.935686 | 0.0000 | -2.868830 | 0.0021 |

Alternative hypothesis: individual AR coefs. (between-dimension)

| | Statistic | Prob. | | |
|---|---|---|---|---|
| Group rho-Statistic | 3.473956 | 0.9997 | | |
| Group PP-Statistic | -4.226762 | 0.0000 | | |
| Group ADF-Statistic | -2.852044 | 0.0022 | | |

Source: developed by authors

**Table 2.9** Panel cointegration test, old member states, N2

Pedroni Residual Cointegration Test
Series: GDP_CAPITA NEET P
Date: 05/24/23 Time: 12:52
Sample: 2012 2021
Included observations: 140
Cross-sections included: 14
Null Hypothesis: No cointegration
Trend assumption: No deterministic trend
Automatic lag length selection based on SIC with a max lag of 1
Newey-West automatic bandwidth selection and Bartlett kernel

Alternative hypothesis: common AR coefs. (within-dimension)

| | Statistic | Prob. | Weighted Statistic | Prob. |
|---|---|---|---|---|
| Panel v-Statistic | -2.398215 | 0.9918 | -1.374989 | 0.9154 |
| Panel rho-Statistic | 0.713410 | 0.7622 | 0.353970 | 0.6383 |
| Panel FP-Statistic | -6.717437 | 0.0000 | -4.892980 | 0.0000 |
| Panel ADF-Statistic | -5.038423 | 0.0000 | -5.058455 | 0.0000 |

Alternative hypothesis: individual AR coefs. (between-dimension)

| | Statistic | Prob. | | |
|---|---|---|---|---|
| Group rho-Statistic | 1.984530 | 0.9764 | | |
| Group PP-Statistic | -4.997512 | 0.0000 | | |
| Group ADF-Statistic | -6.380404 | 0.0000 | | |

Source: developed by authors

**Table 2.10** Panel cointegration test, candidate countries, N1

Pedroni Residual Cointegration Test
Series: GDP_CAPITA EMPL GFCF TO
Date: 05/24/23 Time: 12:55
Sample: 2012 2021
Included observations: 40
Cross-sections included: 4
Null Hypothesis: No cointegration
Trend assumption: No deterministic trend
Automatic lag length selection based on SIC with a max lag of 0
Newey-West automatic bandwidth selection and Bartlett kernel

Alternative hypothesis: common AR coefs. (within-dimension)

| | Statistic | Prob. | Weighted Statistic | Prob. |
|---|---|---|---|---|
| Panel v-Statistic | -0.267032 | 0.6053 | -0.309369 | 0.6215 |
| Panel rho-Statistic | 0.235336 | 0.5930 | 0.237438 | 0.5938 |
| Panel PP-Statistic | -3.173716 | 0.0008 | -2.792310 | 0.0026 |
| Panel ADF-Statistic | -3.173716 | 0.0008 | -2.792310 | 0.0026 |

Alternative hypothesis: individual AR coefs. (between-dimension)

| | Statistic | Prob. | | |
|---|---|---|---|---|
| Group rho-Statistic | 1.092469 | 0.8627 | | |
| Group PP-Statistic | -3.381169 | 0.0004 | | |
| Group ADF-Statistic | -3.381169 | 0.0004 | | |

Source: developed by authors

**Table 2.11** Panel cointegration test, candidate countries, N2

Pedroni Residual Cointegration Test
Series: GDP_CAPITA NEET P
Date: 05/24/23 Time: 12:55
Sample: 2012 2021
Included observations: 40
Cross-sections included: 4
Null Hypothesis: No cointegration
Trend assumption: No deterministic trend
Automatic lag length selection based on SIC with a max lag of 0
Newev-West automatic bandwidth selection and Bartlett kernel

Alternative hypothesis: common AR coefs. (within-dimension)

| | Statistic | Prob. | Weighted Statistic | Prob. |
|---|---|---|---|---|
| Panel v-Statistic | 0.462930 | 0.3217 | -0.928974 | 0.8235 |
| Panel rho-Statistic | -0.210618 | 0.4166 | -0.170911 | 0.4321 |
| Panel PP-Statistic | -2.195374 | 0.0141 | -3.273268 | 0.0005 |
| Panel ADF-Statistic | -2.206013 | 0.0137 | -3.118695 | 0.0009 |

Alternative hypothesis: individual AR coefs. (between-dimension)

| | Statistic | Prob. | | |
|---|---|---|---|---|
| Group rho-Statistic | 0.766960 | 0.7784 | | |
| Group PP-Statistic | -4.560621 | 0.0000 | | |
| Group ADF-Statistic | -3.975204 | 0.0000 | | |

Source: developed by authors

most cases, so we reject the null hypothesis of no cointegration among variables. There are cointegration relationships between variables (for both N1 and N2).

For the panel of new member states, the probability value is:

- More than 5% in most cases, so we accept the null hypothesis of no cointegration among variables; there is no cointegration relationship between variables (for N1).
- Less than 5% in most cases, so we reject the null hypothesis of no cointegration among variables. There are cointegration relationships between variables (for N2).

For the panel of old member states, the probability value is less than 5% in most cases, so we reject the null hypothesis of no cointegration among variables. There are cointegration relationships between variables (for both N1 and N2).

For the panel of candidate countries, the probability value is less than 5% in most cases, so we reject the null hypothesis of no cointegration among variables. There are cointegration relationships between variables (for both N1 and N2).

A graphical representation of the relationships between the variables was developed in the following (see Fig. 2.5), with data for 2012 and 2021. We created this analysis to see if there is a convergence at the level of EU countries. The relationships considered between variables are EMPL vs TO, GFCF vs TO, GFCF vs P, GFCF vs NEET, and GDP_CAPITA vs P.

According to the graphs above, the following aspects can be observed:

- EMPL vs TO—The same trend is maintained, i.e. a negative slope (downward trendline) in 2021, compared with 2012. A negative slope indicates a negative correlation between the variables. This shows the need for various measures to be implemented, like enhancing the skills and capabilities of workers and businesses to increase export competitiveness. Investing in workforce training and skill development can help companies to meet international standards and expand their market reach.
- GFCF vs TO—The negative slope from 2012 turned positive in 2021, showing the positive correlation between the variables. This is a common-sense result.
- GFCF vs P—In 2012, the horizontal trendline showed little to no correlation between the variables. In 2021, the relationship showed a positive slope, meaning that when one variable increases, the other also tends to increase. Some possible explanations for such a relationship could be the following: in some cases, economic growth driven by GFCF may disproportionately benefit specific segments of the population, leading to increased income inequality. Also, in countries where a significant portion of the economy operates in the informal sector, GFCF may primarily impact formal sectors, leaving informal workers behind and potentially increasing poverty.
- GFCF vs NEET—The negative slope from 2012 turned positive in 2021, showing the positive correlation between the variables. A possible explanation for such a relationship could be that GFCF may create new jobs or demand specific skills that are not readily available in the labour market. Suppose the skills required by

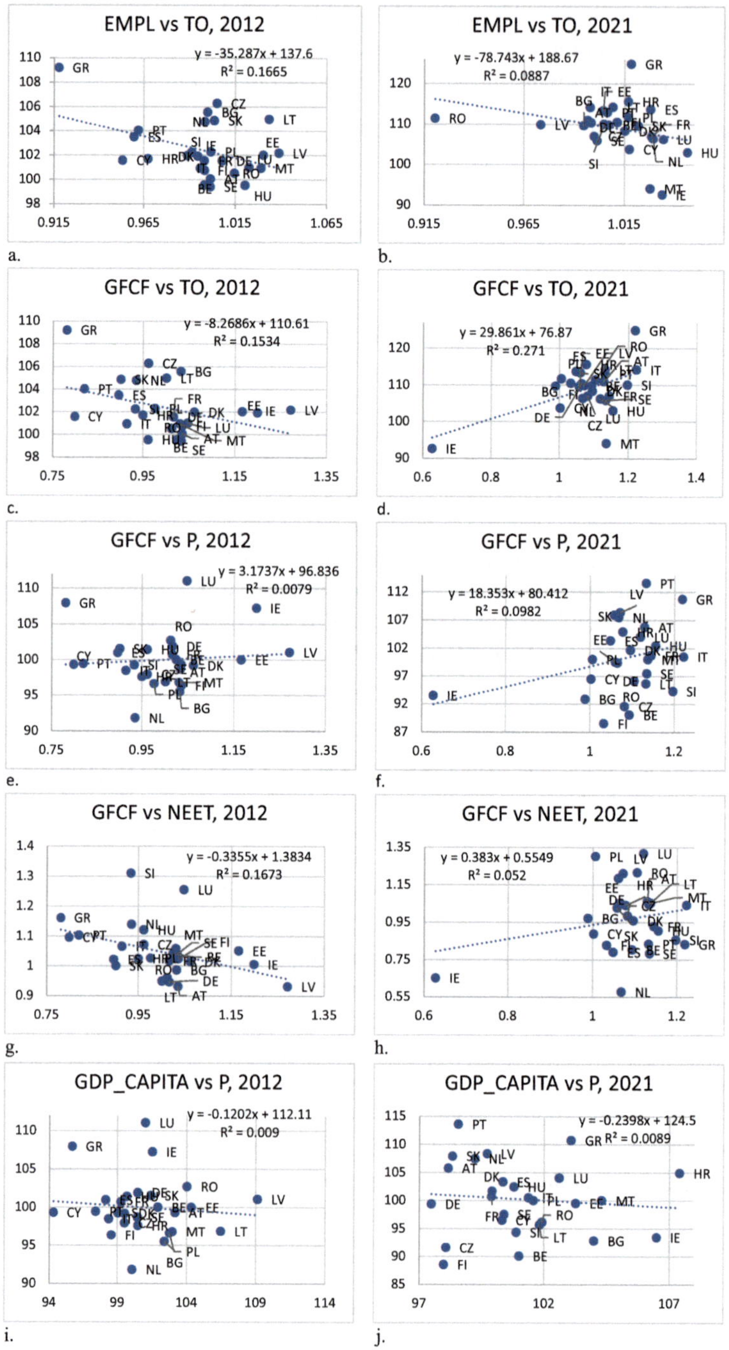


**Fig. 2.5** Scatter plot for selected indicators, 2012 vs 2021 (Source: developed by authors)

employers do not align with the skills possessed by the NEET population. In that case, young people may remain unemployed or not participate in education or training, contributing to a higher NEET rate.
- GDP_CAPITA vs P—In both years, the horizontal trendline shows little to no correlation between the variables. Some measures might envisage investments in education and skill development programmes which can empower individuals with better opportunities for employment and higher-paying jobs, thus reducing poverty. Also, investing in infrastructure, including transportation, energy, and communication networks, can boost economic productivity and create jobs.

## Conclusions

The labour market was significantly affected by both the financial crisis and the pandemic crisis. This study examines the impact of these two crises on several labour market indicators, including the unemployment rate, employment rate, job vacancy rate, and the share of NEETs in the total population.

The study demonstrated the existence of propagated crises with significant and prolonged impacts. The recovery period showed diverse outcomes across countries, highlighting unsustainable rebounds, persistent employment deficits, and instances where the pre-crisis status quo was not regained, signifying the establishment of a "new normal".

The recovery periods for the selected indicators after the financial crisis varied across different EU countries, with some achieving quick recovery within a few years while others taking more than a decade to return to pre-crisis levels. The same development was registered in the case of the pandemic crisis. There are some countries which are still struggling for returning to the pre-crisis levels.

The findings demonstrate the importance of assessing overlapping crises' impact, complexity, and economic resilience. Managing these challenges requires a comprehensive approach to adjustment measures to facilitate a robust recovery rather than focusing solely on quick recovery to avoid adverse effects and negative consequences. Additionally, there is a critical need for risk assessment and preventive measures as fundamental elements of building economic resilience.

In the post-pandemic period, policymakers should strengthen social safety nets by expanding unemployment benefits, providing financial support to vulnerable populations, and retraining and upskilling workers for emerging job opportunities. Investment in infrastructure projects, particularly in areas like renewable energy and public transportation, can create jobs and stimulate economic growth. Addressing inequalities is crucial, and this can be achieved through measures ensuring equitable access to healthcare, education, and economic opportunities, implementing progressive taxation, expanding quality education accessibility, and reducing barriers to economic mobility. Furthermore, enhancing crisis preparedness is essential by investing in research, bolstering healthcare systems, diversifying supply chains, improving disaster response mechanisms, and implementing more efficient early warning systems for potential crises. It's important to note that the specific actions and priorities may vary depending on the unique nature and severity of the crises faced by each country.

To ensure future development, it is crucial to have a clear vision and involve all stakeholders through a community-based road map. Cooperation, partnership, inclusion, and a just transition towards the "new normal" are essential aspects to be considered as emerging outcomes. Crisis management is a shared responsibility of states and local institutions, and national measures and accountability play a vital role. Policymakers should actively support proactive measures.

The lessons learned from past experiences are as follows:

- Fast recovery may not align with resilience; it requires embracing and adapting to the "new normal" rather than returning to the previous state.
- Robust recovery necessitates considering the theory of complexity to achieve favourable outcomes.
- Unidirectional interventions, disconnected from specific local/national realities, can have multiple negative consequences.
- Experiments without proper background assessment and model adoption should be cautiously considered or avoided.

A panel VAR model should be developed for future research and cases lacking cointegration among variables, where the output variable depends on its previous values. Conversely, when cointegration exists among variables, a panel VEC (vector error correction) model should be utilised to understand the dynamics and equilibrium restoration after a shock. Additionally, the impulse response function can demonstrate the impact of a shock on the dependent variable over time.

Future studies should also explore differences by activities and economic sectors and extend the analysis period to understand better the pandemic crisis's impact on the business environment's structure and the business model based on digital transformation, which plays a crucial role in building economic resilience.

## References

American Hotel and Lodging Association. (2020, April 22). *COVID-19's impact on the hotel industry*. https://www.ahla.com/covid-19s-impact-hotel-industry

Böheim, R., & Leoni, T. (2020). *COVID-19 crisis response monitoring: Austria, Johannes Kepler University Linz, Austrian Institute of Economic Research, and IZA, 1-12.*

Cho, Y., & Newhouse, D. (2011). *How did the great recession affect different types of workers? Evidence from 17 middle-income countries*. IZA DP, No. 5681. https://nbn-resolving.de/urn:nbn:de:101:1-201105173175, Last accessed 2022/06/13.

Ciuhu, A.-M., Ghita, S.-I., Vasile, V., & Boboc, C. (2022). Occupational gender disparities–before and after Covid-19. *Romanian Statistical Review, 2*, 31–50. https://www.revistadestatistica.ro/2022/06/romanian-statistical-review-2-2022/

CNN Business. (2020, March 6). *Tens of thousands of airline jobs are at risk as travel plunges*. https://edition.cnn.com/2020/03/06/business/airline-jobs/index.html

Coates, D., Corcoran, D., Cronin, H., Brioscú, A., Byrne, S., Keenan, E., & McIndoe-Calder, T. (2020). *The initial impacts of the COVID-19 pandemic on Ireland's labour market*. Working Paper, Department of Employment Affairs and Social Protection, Central Bank of Ireland.

Cortes, G. M., & Forsythe, E. (2022). Heterogeneous labor market impacts of the Covid-19 pandemic. *ILR Review, 76*(1), 30–55. https://doi.org/10.1177/00197939221076856

Cristea, M. (2020). Labour market: Similarities and differences between the 2020 and 2009 crises. *Business Review*. https://business-review.eu/business/human-resources/labour-market-similarities-and-differences-between-the-2020-and-2009-crises-211553

Dvořák, M., Rovný, P., Grebennikova, V., & Faminskaya, M. (2020). Economic impacts of Covid-19 on the labour market and human capital. *Terra Economicus, 18*(4), 78–96. https://doi.org/10.18522/2073-6606-2020-18-4-78-96

Euromonitor (2020, April 14). *The impact of coronavirus in Brazil: Uneven prospects across industries*. https://blog.euromonitor.com/the-impact-of-coronavirus-in-brazil-uneven-prospects-across-industries/

Eurostat. (2023). *Job vacancy rate by NACE Rev. 2 activity–annual data*. https://ec.europa.eu/eurostat/databrowser/view/JVS_A_RATE_R2/default/table?lang=en&category=labour.jvs

Fiaschi, D., & Tealdi, C. (2022). Young people between education and the labour market during the COVID-19 pandemic in Italy. *International Journal of Manpower, 43*(7), 1719–1757. https://doi.org/10.1108/IJM-06-2021-0352

Fleming, S. (2021). *The pandemic has damaged youth employment: Here's how we can help*. https://www.weforum.org/agenda/2021/07/pandemic-damaged-youth-employment.

Gehrke, B., & Weber, E. (2020). Short-time work, layoffs, and new hires in Germany: how the corona crisis differs from the financial crisis of 2009. *IAB-FORUM* (2020). https://www.iab-forum.de/en/short-time-work-layoffs-and-new-hires-in-germany-how-the-corona-crisis-differs-from-the-financial-crisis-of-2009/?pdf=19577

Hallegatte, S. (2014). *Economic resilience: Definition and measurement*. Policy Research Working Paper Series 6852, The World Bank. https://restoreyoureconomy.org/blog/2022/02/19/community-resilience/the-secret-to-economic-resilience/

ILO. (2020). *The impact of COVID-19 on the tourism sector*. ILO Sectoral Brief. https://www.ilo.org/wcmsp5/groups/public/%2D%2D-ed_dialogue/%2D%2D-sector/documents/briefingnote/wcms_741468.pdf

ILO. (2021, January 25). *ILO Monitor: COVID-19 and the world of work*. Seventh edition, Updated estimates and analysis. https://www.ilo.org/wcmsp5/groups/public/%2D%2D-dgreports/%2D%2D-dcomm/documents/briefingnote/wcms_767028.pdf

ILO-OECD. (2020). *The impact of the COVID-19 pandemic on jobs and incomes in G20 economies*. https://www.ilo.org/wcmsp5/groups/public/%2D%2D-dgreports/%2D%2D-cabinet/documents/publication/wcms_756331.pdf

IMF. (2022). *European Labor Markets and the COVID-19 Pandemic*. Fallout and the Path Ahead, prepared by Sakai Ando, Ravi Balakrishnan, Bertrand Gruss, Jean-Jacques Hallaert, La-Bhus Fah Jirasavetakul, Koralai Kirabaeva, Nir Klein, Ana Lariau, Lucy Qian Liu, Davide Malacrino, Haonan Qu, and Alexandra Solovyeva, DP/2022/004.

Junankar, P.N. (2011). *The global economic crisis: Long-term unemployment in the OECD, IZA DP No. 6057*.

Khanna, A. (2020). Impact of migration of labour force due to global COVID-19 pandemic with reference to India. *Journal of Health Management, 22*(2), 181–191. https://doi.org/10.1177/0972063420935542

La Chaîne Info. (2020, March 15). *Restaurants, cafés et bars fermés: un million de salariés dans l'inquiétude*. https://www.lci.fr/population/coronavirus-restaurants-cafes-et-bars-fermes-un-million-de-salaries-dans-l-inquietude-2148069.html

Lee, S., Schmidt-Klau, D., & Verick, S. (2020). The labour market impacts of the COVID-19: A global perspective. *The Indian Journal of Labour Economics, 63*, 11–15. https://doi.org/10.1007/s41027-020-00249-y

Malik, N., Suliswanto, M. S. W., & Rofik, M. (2021). The unemployment rate amid the COVID-19 pandemic: Propose the best practices policy to maintain labor market stability. *Jurnal Ilmu Sosial dan Ilmu Politik, 25*(1), 48–61. https://doi.org/10.22146/jsp.56450

Mindrican, I. M., & Matei, E. F. (2023). The impact of the Covid-19 crisis on the labour market. Implications of employment policy. *Romanian Statistical Review, 1*, 103–124.

OECD. (2021a). *Fostering economic resilience in a world of open and integrated markets risks, vulnerabilities and areas for policy action, report prepared for the 2021 UK Presidency of the G7.* https://www.oecd.org/newsroom/OECD-G7-Report-Fostering-Economic-Resilience-in-a-World-of-Open-and-Integrated-Markets.pdf

OECD. (2021b). *OECD employment outlook 2021, navigating the COVID-19 crisis and recovery.* https://doi.org/10.1787/5a700c4b-en.

OECD. (2022). *The unequal impact of COVID-19: A spotlight on frontline workers, migrants and racial/ethnic minorities.* https://read.oecd-ilibrary.org/view/?ref=1133_1133188-lq9ii66g9w&title=The-unequal-impact-of-COVID-19-A-spotlight-on-frontline-workers-migrants-and-racial-ethnic-minorities

OECD. (2023). *Economic resilience.* https://www.oecd.org/economy/growth/economic-resilience.htm

Shibata, I. (2020). *The distributional impact of recessions: The global financial crisis and the pandemic recession*, IMF WP/20/96.

Su, C. W., Dai, K., Ullah, S., & Andlib, Z. (2021). COVID-19 pandemic and unemployment dynamics in European economies. *Economic Research-Ekonomska Istraživanja., 35*, 1752. https://doi.org/10.1080/1331677X.2021.1912627

The Guardian. (2020, April 27). *UK tourism hotspots could face worst of post-lockdown job losses.* https://www.theguardian.com/society/2020/apr/27/uk-tourism-hotspots-could-face-worst-of-post-lockdown-job-losses

Verick, S. (2009). *Who is hit hardest during a financial crisis? The vulnerability of young men and women to unemployment in an economic downturn. IZA DP No. 4359.*

Verick, S., & Islam, I. (2010). *The great recession of 2008-2009: Causes, consequences and policy responses.* Employment Working Paper No. 61, ILO.

# Part I
# The Challenges of the Pandemic and the Business Environment. Towards a New Normal?

# Chapter 3
# Digital Transformation: Challenges and Limits for the New Normal

**Razvan Vasile**

**Abstract** The restrictions imposed by the pandemic crisis on economic activity and social interaction determined the forced digitization of households and workplaces. The chapter analyzes to what extent the COVID-19 crisis continued/accelerated the digital transformation of companies and the digital inclusion of individuals and households. Based on the statistical data available for the pandemic period, compared to the pre-pandemic period, it is evident that, at the company level, the digital adaptation was based on minimal, survival components. Thedigital transformation strategy, previously defined, continued only as an exception, the investments in ICT technology being redirected, mainly, to the facilitation of remote work, e-commerce and digital communication. The business environment has changed irreversibly, the work and life model has adapted to remote, flexible, modularized work, with important economic and social implications. At the level of the individual and the household, the effects of forced digitization were different, with the increase in digital discrimination and inequalities for the vulnerable categories and with significantly higher associated costs. Post-pandemic recovery and resilience requires the redefinition of activities and inter-human communication, a new normal, based on the acceptance of digitization as a basic component of work and life in households, at the workplace and in the community.

## Introduction

Information, and, in particular, that in digital format, is becoming more and more important in modern life, human activities being in a higher degree dependent on communication mediated by ICT facilities, whether it is support equipment or communication/information/transmission channels. Human interconnection in the business environment has gradually transformed over the last decades, from face-to-face communication and transmission of documents in an analogy system to digital

R. Vasile (✉)
National Institute of Economic Research "Kostin C. Kiritescu", Bucharest, Romania

 
V. Vasile, E. Bunduchi (eds.), *The Economic and Social Impact of the COVID-19 Pandemic*, Contributions to Economics,
https://doi.org/10.1007/978-3-031-47780-5_3

interaction. Moreover, the restrictions imposed by the pandemic crisis on economic activity and social interaction forced digitization of households and workplaces.

Digital literacy, as the first step in reforming the work content of all workplaces, continued with the digital transformation of jobs for specific professional tasks and digital inclusion in the communication chain, at the company level and with business partners, whether individuals or companies.

The digital transition at the level of the business environment has been uneven, in terms of dynamics and intensity, depending to a large extent on the field of activity and on the content of the work, but equally on the inertia and/or traditions in business, based to a large extent on the physical interaction between individuals.

The digital transformation process of companies was suddenly/brutally implemented due to the pandemic restrictions on communication and direct/physical human interaction, all activities being forced to adapt. The reaction of the companies was different, from closing the business (total and definitive or only temporary) and adaptation (minimal and limited only during the restrictions period) to restructuring/ reinvention (reorganization of jobs, restructuring of employment, change of the model and forms of employment).

Currently, digital connection is no longer just social; it has become a way of doing business or an indispensable facilitator, which has been associated with digital disruption of the workforce capitalization model.

In the post-pandemic stage, a new shock affected the work model, by (re)-organizing work relationships and workplace tasks (or the forms of performing tasks/obligations), the companies' decision on the model of continuing the activity being essential. The experience of the post-pandemic business environment has shown us that, even in the conditions where the decision was to return to the workplace organization model before the Covid-19 crisis, this could not be fully accomplished, components of communication relationships in the system remaining digital, largely due to the positive externalities generated by the saving of time and resources, the facilitation of connectivity and the possibility of operational management to be more efficient and the expansion and speed of information exchange between market actors, on the value chain of production of goods and services, between the producer and the final consumer, regardless of whether this is an individual, household, public institution or private actor in the business environment.

The general scheme of the forced digital transition caused by the pandemic restrictions is limited to the two extremes mentioned below:

1. The lack of or only minimal digital literacy of the workplace in the pre-pandemic period and forced digitization in the pandemic, with a return (but limited) post-pandemic
2. Digital literacy and digital skills associated with the peculiarities of performing the profession in pre-pandemic—the continuation of the digital transition trend and the association with the emphasis on endowments, skills and relationships, associated with the specific measures imposed by the pandemic and, continuing in the post-pandemic with the capitalization of the accentuated dynamics of the

digital transition and the remodelling of jobs, forms of employment, and for the continuation of digitization according to the demands of the 5.0 economy

The variants adopted by the companies, between the two stated limits, were diverse, with an emphasis on optimizing the short-term effects and postponing the digital transformation strategy for post-pandemic, or, on the contrary, supporting the continuation of the digital transformation and, practically, reinventing the business model on all its components, the pandemic restrictions assuming only slight adjustments.

Regardless of the strategy adopted during the pandemic, the work organization model, the redefinition of work tasks, the organization of intra- and intercompany communication relations, in the post-pandemic period has changed, the specialized literature identifying these changes as "the new normal". Practically, we went from digital literacy for survival to digital specialization and innovation of production processes, digital facilities becoming an indispensable component of technological innovation, economic growth, performance and market competitiveness, practically redefining the model of human activity development.

The present chapter analyses to what extent the Covid-19 crisis continued/ accelerated the digital transformation of companies and the digital inclusion of individuals and households.

## Digitization as a Factor in Changing the Content of Work

The forced digitization during the pandemic, has changed the lives of individuals of any age—from young people, who have experienced online education, to active persons who have translated their communication patterns with work colleagues and business partners to online communication and who have learned to carry out their work tasks through various forms of "digital assistance", as well as the elderly, most of them being inactive from an economic perspective; having remodelled their lifestyle and communication style with family, friends, public authorities or others; and having experienced, in various forms, digital literacy or the upgrading of knowledge regarding the interaction in the digital environment. Specialists, more and more, have analysed aspects such as digital literacy, digital specialization, digital disruption, digital innovation for economic growth and digital inclusion, as to mention the most discussed and analysed issues.

We performed a brief analysis of the works published by experts, only from the WoS database (since 1975 until the end of July 2023), which address, in some way or another, the issue of digitalization which are around 800,000, of which in 2020 and after there are 229,000 (i.e. 28.63%).

This indicates our interest and concerns to analyse the dynamics of the digital transformation process of society and its effects. If we narrow the fields of analysis to aspects such as digital innovation, digital literacy, digital inclusion or digital economy, for example, we can observe that expert studies on these aspects have intensified in recent years (Fig. 3.1).

This indicates the interest and concerns of experts to analyse the dynamics of the digital transformation process of society and its effects. If we consider only the limited thematic area that includes the previously mentioned issues and make an integrated extraction from the database (in some articles several of the keywords for which we analysed the separate query may appear together), only for the period 2020 until the date of the analysis, we identify almost 17,600 published works, the interaction of the analysed themes being presented in Fig. 3.2.

So, the effects of digitization forced by the pandemic are multiple, some are still manifest even today, and impact analysis is important because it can better highlight the positive, negative, adverse and contradictory results. As a net effect, it is good to mention that this was positive, in the sense that it reconfirmed the usefulness of digital transformation for increasing the quality of life, but the ways in which this is achieved are different, some even sinuous, which requires a deep reconsideration of the model of work and life. Digital disruption also attracts digital innovation, and the results/effects bring added value in the medium and long term. It is certain that, along with literacy and numeracy, we must also obtain digital literacy (as fundamental knowledge for human development) in order to be able to manage in the present and future society. Even if since 2018 digital competencies were included among the eight key competencies (EC, 2019), only during the pandemic was the need for digital inclusion for all recognized, as a basic requirement for economic, social and cultural survival.

Digitization is changing the world of work, from the sharing of time between work and rest to profound changes in the content of work, even for trades/professions that, by their nature, are related to physical interaction for the exercise of work tasks with other people within and/or outside of the company.

Externalities are both positive and negative; they affect the individual present in the labour market, adjust access and differentiate employment risks, reconsider relations and working conditions, change the employment model and remodel the business environment and the use of the labour factor in production processes. At the same time, it fundamentally changes the mechanisms that influence labour market segmentation—both from the perspective of labour force categories and the impact on economic and social inclusion. The forms of segmentation are varied, from the classic segmentation of professions and trades to the more recent forms related to the effects of pandemic restrictions, when we are witnessing a reconfiguration of the content of work, in which the digital component is quasi-present.

The main changes in the content of work are generated by the adoption of ITC products and technologies that facilitate automation, database management and communication on digital platforms. According to the Eurofound report (Eurofound, 2021), in 2019, 1/3 of workspaces could be considered as "highly digitalized". In 2019, the digital intensity of companies was different according to their size, respectively between highly digitalized, 35% of total large companies (over 250 employees) and 27% of total small companies (with 10 to 49 employees) and high use of robots and limited computer use (40% and, respectively, 17%). Only

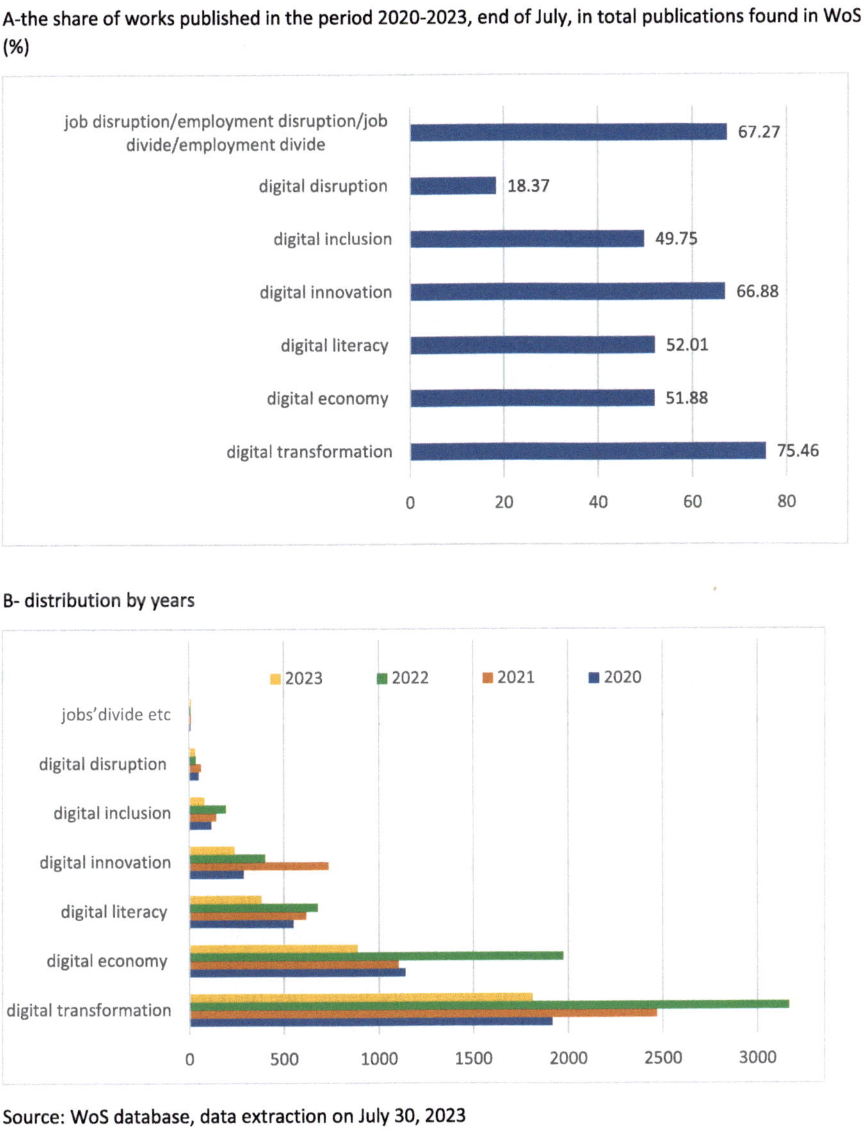


**Fig. 3.1** Experts' interest in the analysis of some aspects of digitization (works published in WoS and distribution over time periods) Source: WoS database, data extraction on July 30, 2023

15% of large companies registered in 2019 limited digitalization as against almost 30% for small ones. The digitalization of the small companies consists mainly in high computer use and limited use of other digital technologies (28% of companies but only 10% of the large ones). So, the diversified digital technologies and the digital intensity are increasing with the size of companies.

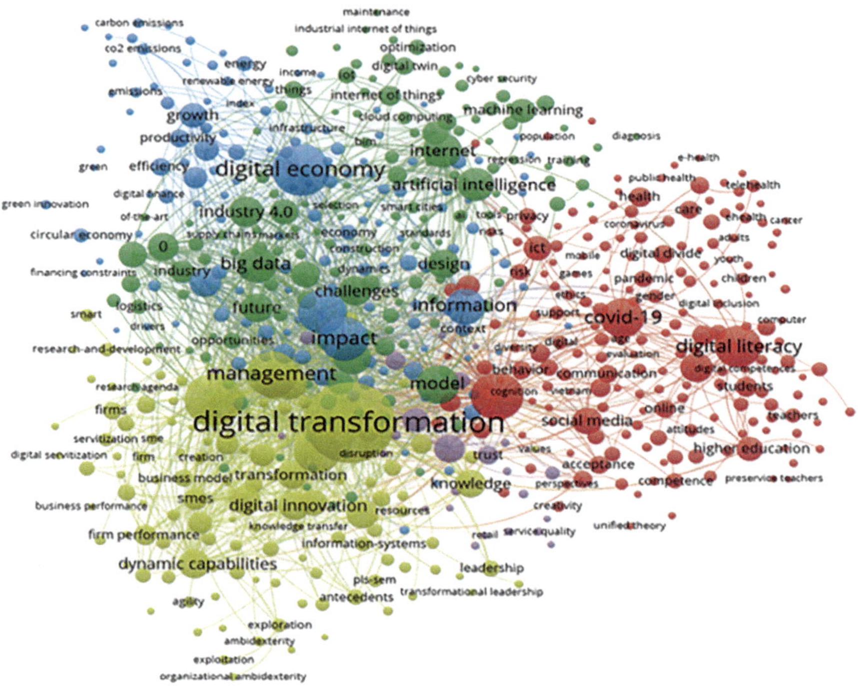


**Fig. 3.2** Thematic distribution of keywords in the works published in the field of digital transformation. Source: WoS database, data extraction on July 30, 2023; (VOSviewer with 25)

According to DESI 2020, before the pandemic, digital changes were made faster and in greater proportion in the fields of activity where information and databases and their management support based on AI were needed. Advanced cloud services were used, for example, in 38.5% of large companies in 2019 but in only 17% in SMEs. Also 32.7% from big companies were using big data analytics in the same year and only 12% of SMEs. Similarly, online sales were used in 39% of large firms and in 17.5% of SMEs (EC, 2020). The same study shows us that the progress in the period before the pandemic was extremely different by country. Among the EU member countries, the best performers were Finland and Sweden, the most dynamic country in the last 5 years before the pandemic was Ireland, and the countries with the worst performances were Bulgaria, Greece and Romania.

After automation processes have eased or replaced physical work, digitization brings new benefits by reducing the time associated with communication and the transmission of information regarding work tasks, their performance and the quality obtained, increasing work productivity and intensifying network communication and access to data. Moreover, the obvious tendency to develop and apply services based on applications, accessible databases and AI raises new challenges in redefining work tasks, evaluating performance and reconfiguring the structure of jobs, but also in the development of technologies associated with digital facilities, for increasing the performance and quality of production processes.

It is widely accepted among specialists that, potentially, digitization supports economic growth in all fields of activity (but in different proportions, depending on the specific attributes of the branch (Chinoracký et al., 2019)) through greater efficiency in production through lower costs and increased productivity.

Digital innovation and the development of technologies assisted by digital transformation redefine the components and attributes of employment and produce changes (redefinition of jobs, creation and destruction of others); the long-term effects on work are ambiguous, as mechanical manipulation should be minimal (Arntz et al., 2016). But it is equally obvious that a broad infusion of digital skills is needed for the entire workforce, without radically changing most trades, professions and jobs. Rather, it completes them; it degrades them from a digital perspective. Moreover, an OECD report from 2018 mentions that automation, robotization and digitization do not consistently threaten the trend of employment expansion and job diversification (Nedelkoska & Quintini, 2018). Studies related to the impact of digitization indicate a heightened dynamic of the creation of new jobs associated with digital transformation and digital innovation (Kvochko, 2013; Katz & Koutroumpis, 2016; Kunming, 2019). Employment is positively influenced by technological transfer (Su et al., 2022), and the digitization of workplaces changes not only the work style but also the execution and managerial processes (Ping & Ying, 2018), diversifying working opportunities (Aly, 2020).

From the perspective of the impact of digital transformation on employment, the effects are different in the short, medium and long term, and their intensity depends on the structure of economic activities and the prevailing employment model. The labour market can be negatively influenced in the short term, especially in less developed economies (Sarabdeen & Hind, 2023), but in the medium and long term, it generates important changes in the structure of the labour supply (digital education of the new contingents of graduates, new specializations or skills associated with the use of ITC facilities, the diversification and flexibility of the forms of employment associated with the reformed digitalized business model). Therefore, the effects of digitization on the labour market are multiple and profound. Some of the already experienced effects of the digitization of the labour market can be listed as follows: the content of work changes, the forms of employment and contractual relationships change, the vulnerability of employment increases, and the fundamentals of the quality of the workplace change. Others, directly related to the limitations imposed during the pandemic period (OECD, 2022) but also to the expansion of facilities offered by the association of some activities with AI, accentuate the asymmetry of the effects on the labour market, such as the reconsideration of the importance of essential jobs/professions in relation to non-essential ones or the redefinition of post-pandemic jobs (new jobs or job's content upgraded). Such examples of labour market segmentation not only induce other forms of discrimination (associated with increasing gaps) but also reconfigure the demand for labour force and skills, profoundly changing the demand for professional training and soft skills.

Pandemic restrictions also transform the digital transition from long-run proofs of business development into an urgent “must to do”, based on faster digital inclusion for all, mainly for solving current problems/tasks, in order to survive in limited freedom of human physical interaction. Since the last decade, the need for employment restructuring associated with the increase in digital intensity in companies has been evident but also for additional labour demand redistribution, polarizing the demand for low-skilled and highly skilled labour, and the demand for middle-skilled labour is diminishing considerably (Acemoglu & David, 2011; Goos et al., 2014; Michaels et al., 2014; Ju, 2014). The Covid-19 crisis, in addition to increasing the need for ITC specialists to ensure the digital transition of managerial communication and, partially, some activities (relations with business partners for contracting and settlement, acquisition of resources for production/services, commercial transactions for products produced/services provided, etc.), requires acquisition of new digital skills by employees, for information, communication, reporting using remote, hybrid work facilities, etc.

The relatively quick reset was necessary, being directed towards digital innovation for smart working, online education, digital payments, online services (i.e. online public services, telemedicine development) and cybersecurity. Many companies, but also households and public authorities, were unprepared, unable to react adequately, despite the existing digital transformation national-level strategies in many developing countries. The pandemic found in many states that public authorities and individual contributors were poorly prepared for a quick transition online, as a result of the distance imposed to reduce the risks of illness. According to the same DESI 2020 report, in the year 2019, 2/3 of Internet users interact with public administration online, submitting forms/documents, the top performers being Estonia, Spain, Denmark, Finland and Latvia. In this context it is worth to underline that Internet used by individuals was only 2/3 in Bulgaria and up to 95% in Denmark, Sweden and Netherlands (i.e. access to social media and entertainment platforms, teleworking, e-commerce and e-government services). It is worth to mention that almost 45% of the EU member state individuals still lack basic digital skills, so the pressure for rapid digitalization was significant, it being necessary to train digital skills both for company personnel and for other categories of the population (workers on own account, young people for online education, elderly people for accessing online services).

The pandemic also highlighted two other aspects of the effects of digitization of jobs, related to the quality of the job, previously less considered, as follows: (a) through remote work associated with the flexibility of working time, the quality of work also improves; and (b) telework is a form of green jobs transformation.

The digitization of work and remote work, accentuated during the pandemic, have reconfigured the sharing of working time and its flexibility, thus reducing the strict boundaries imposed by physical presence at the workplace—the border between the two is diffuse and interrupted (Eurofound, 2022a, 2023). On the one hand, the possibility of personalizing the distribution of the work schedule according to family or social obligations was created, but, on the other hand, a greater dependence on staying connected was created and hence the discussions related to the “right to disconnect". Moreover, working from home has also generated comments and positions from the social partners looking in particular the guarantee of equal pay and access to training for those working remotely, or covering the additional costs incurred by employees for connectivity—broadband access subscription for household, equipment (equipment, furniture or consumables associated with computer work) and logistics costs (electricity, heating, etc.). Also, from the perspective of quality, the risks of working from home related to burnout, physical and emotional exhaustion, or social isolation were analysed.

The company's advantages have been quantified in increases in labour productivity and better management of the deadlines for work tasks but also in reduced operational costs, with the logistics necessary to organize the workplace and maintain working conditions. It is clear that remote work can be considered an alternative with net advantages for both the employee and the employer, but what remains important is to find a balance to optimize the benefits on both sides. The preponderance of advantages compared to disadvantages ultimately depends on the specific employee-employer arrangements, employment relationship and work organization.

Regarding green dividends from telework, experts evaluated, among other aspects, the potential for decreasing carbon footprint, and pandemic time experience revealed a greater acceptance from an organizational perspective (Eurofound, 2022b).

From the employees' perspective, the impact on environmental pollution of the transition from work, with physical presence at the workplace, to telework is highlighted by (a) reduction of pollution due to giving up daily transport to the workplace, alleviating cities' congestions, and (b) the possibility to have housing in rural areas and housing based on green energy and on the adoption of efficient energy consumption models depending on the period of the day or depending on the season (occupancy-based heating, cooling and lighting control and demand-controlled ventilation) (Carbon Trust, 2021). In Ireland, where the increase in the proportion of telework was the highest in the EU countries, relocation of the home associated with the possibility of working even partially in the telework system was the decision of 8.2% of the respondents to the questionnaire applied in April 2021 in the Remote Working National Survey, and another 24% mentioned that they intend to move outside the Dublin capital region (McCarthy et al., 2021; Williamson, 2022). The effects of telework on the environment have been identified both in the short term (Hook et al., 2020; Riley et al., 2021; Tenailleau et al., 2021; Guerin, 2021; Moglia et al., 2021) and in the long term (IEA, 2020).

Moreover, the option for telework, at least a few days a week, associated with the adoption of modern technological systems for transport (the use of electric cars or public transportation instead of personal cars), makes hybrid work attractive even in the post-pandemic period. An important increase in telework was particularly evident in large cities mainly due to the higher share of knowledge-intensive services employment (Sostero et al., 2020) or high-skill service jobs that can be done remotely (Althoff et al., 2022). It is also worth to notice the general benefits from: a) the reducing of the environmental footprint through the incorporation of technological progress and efficiency improvement of Internet, b) online services, c) the use of applications that allow the storage of databases with minimal costs, but also d) reduced energy consumption to an increased traffic of information, etc. (Obringer et al., 2021). The quantification of the global effects is highly difficult to manage. The differentiating factors are multiple: a) from climatic differences and the degree of urbanization to the organization of the work programme in a hybrid system; b) from the average distance for daily commuting to the type of energy sources used in office and residential buildings; c) from the level of development of the country to the structure of the economy and the technologies used for remote work; and d) from the immediate effects on the reduction of emissions (in the estimation made by the International Energy Agency on the reduction of gas emissions by switching to telecommuting 1 day a week, for the EU area, the avoided emissions were calculated to be 3.1 kg CO2 per household in winter and 4.9 kg in summer) to rebound long-term effects (Eurofound, 2022b).

## Digital Skills: Doing Digital vs Being Digital

Pandemic challenges and restrictions create a great opportunity, especially for less developed countries to overcome vulnerabilities by adapting the human factor, upskilling and reskilling for digital interaction.

Digital skills were considered "the backbone of the digital society", which facilitate the appropriate use of digital technologies. The use of the Internet by individuals does not necessarily mean that they have basic digital skills. In 2019, for example, 85% of EU27 citizens used the Internet, but only 58% possessed at least basic digital skills (EC, 2020).

The pandemic not only forced digital literacy for all but also marked the importance of "being digital" instead of "doing digital". The traditional culture of the ITC sector was developed strongly in the pre-pandemic decade and was based on the creation of tools and procedures for digitalization of some information, documents and analysis of some databases. All of these were defined as "doing digital", i.e. performing information/analysis/adjustment tasks using ITC products (programs, algorithms, automatic adjustment methods, etc.). The pandemic has confirmed the usefulness of this direction of development, with substantial benefits in reducing costs, increasing work productivity, changing the employment structure in companies by eliminating jobs involving repetitive activities, etc.

The transition from doing digital to being digital, from the perspective of the workforce, requires a change of mentality regarding the role of the digital transformation of the workplace, requiring the following steps: (a) optimizing the skills to generate reports, documents and databases in digital form; (b) managing the document circuit using digital transmission channels; (c) optimizing communication to business partners or within the company, between employees, according to the information requirements on managerial levels; (d) activating/using the cognitive intelligence to enable continuous improvement in digital task performance, which involves the transition from a simple digital operator to a creator of digital products, including upgrading the applications used to achieve steps a–c; and (e) the interactive use of digital applications for informational support in operational management, which means the association of advanced technologies like AI as a "partner" in work task accomplishment. From a to c, the "doing digital" component was realized, the rest representing the intermediate stages up to fully operational in "being digital".

From the company's perspective, it means investments to ensure flexible digital infrastructure, data and information security and programs for the integrated operation of data and the allocation of two categories of human resources—ITC specialists, who will manage the infrastructure and ensure its smooth operation, and employees, with professions specific to the company's field of activity, with advanced digital skills. For employees, the investment in training becomes two-fold—on the one hand, specific professional training and, on the other hand, advanced digital training, the creation and development of a digital mindset, which ensures interoperability with AI-type technologies, algorithms or other advanced technologies for communication, etc. (Neeley & Leonardi, 2022; Giacosa et al., 2022).

From the simple acquisition of software, licenses and their use in the company, the need arises to customize and develop some applications, customized to the needs of the company, and, from here, collaboration networks develop, IT experts and professionals in the technologies specific to the field of activity, for innovation adapted to performance needs, facilitating the digital transformation of the company's production/management/administrative management processes, i.e. not simply to adapt but to be adaptive. This means that a smart business should include continuing digital changes as a constant, and "doing digital" is no longer optional in a world of competitiveness (Sen, 2023).

If we analyse the concerns of companies to adapt to digital transformation during the pandemic, the need to upgrade digital skills for both ITC specialists and non-ITC employees is clearly highlighted. The companies' efforts were two-fold—on the one hand, training to ensure the operation of the company within the limits imposed by the pandemic restrictions and, on the other hand, the development of the skills necessary to implement the digital transformation objectives non-related to pandemic restrictions. This means that the companies faced two challenges—one, to increase the resilience of the operating company by expanding digital inclusion for its own salaries and, second, to continue, and with what speed, the implementation of the company's digital transformation strategies, started before the pandemic.

An analysis of the companies' initiatives regarding ensuring the training of their own employees, as a requirement associated with the digital transformation of companies shows us their different concerns, depending on the level of skills acquired until 2019 and the policy promoted during the pandemic, respectively a) by the emphasis put only for the minimal additional training necessary for adaptation to the requirements imposed during the pandemic of social distancing or b) to continue the digital reform, and, in addition, the training imposed by the management of the pandemic.

Thus, the theoretically possible situations and training efforts at the company level are presented in the table below (Table 3.1.)

**Table 3.1** The share of companies that provided professional training to their employees during the pandemic (year 2020) and post-pandemic (year 2022), in the total companies, depending on the level of digital intensity and the size of the company (%)

| Firms' digital intensity (2022) | Differences in providing training (% of companies) | | | |
|---|---|---|---|---|
| | ICT/IT specialists | | Other persons employed | |
| | 2022 > 2020 | 2022 < 2020 | 2022 > 2020 | 2022 < 2020 |
| **Small companies (10–49 persons employed)** | | | | |
| Very low | Bulgaria, Latvia, Poland, Lithuania, Hungary, Romania, Slovakia | Croatia | Bulgaria, Hungary, Poland, Romania, Slovakia | Croatia, Latvia, Lithuania |
| Low | EU27 Belgium, Germany, Italy, Estonia, France, Cyprus, Luxembourg, Malta, Austria, Netherlands, Portugal, Slovenia | Czechia, Ireland, Spain | EU27 Belgium, Germany, Spain, Estonia, France, Italy, Cyprus, Austria, Portugal, Slovenia Luxembourg, Netherlands, | Czechia, Ireland, Malta |
| High | Denmark, Finland, Sweden | | Denmark, Finland, Sweden | |
| **Medium (50–249 persons employed)** | | | | |
| Low | Bulgaria, Romania | Slovakia, France | Bulgaria, France, Romania | Slovakia |
| High | EU27 Belgium, Czechia, Denmark, Germany, Italy, Cyprus, Latvia, Lithuania, Luxembourg, Hungary, Malta, Netherlands, Austria, Poland, Slovenia, Finland, Sweden | Estonia, Ireland, Spain, Croatia, Portugal | EU27 Denmark, Germany, Estonia, Spain, Italy, Cyprus, Latvia, Austria, Lithuania, Netherlands, Luxembourg, Hungary, Poland, Slovenia, Finland | Belgium, Czechia, Ireland, Croatia, Malta, Sweden |
| **Large companies (250 and over persons employed)** | | | | |
| High | EU27 Bulgaria, Czechia, Estonia, Spain, Croatia, Italy, Cyprus, Latvia, Lithuania, Luxembourg, Hungary, Malta, Netherlands, Austria, Poland, Romania, Slovakia | Germany, Ireland, Greece, France, Portugal, Slovenia | EU27 Bulgaria, Germany, Estonia, Spain, Italy, Cyprus, Latvia, Malta, Lithuania, Luxembourg, Hungary, Netherlands, Austria, Poland, Portugal, Romania | Czechia, Ireland, Greece, France, Croatia, Slovenia, Slovakia |
| Very high | Denmark, Finland, Sweden | Belgium | Denmark, Sweden | Belgium, Finland |

Note: Digital intensity index (Version 4), data available only for 2022; digital intensity of the company in 2022, by size class by highest share between categories very low, low, high and very high; EU27 from 2020

Source: Eurostat database [ISOC_SKE_ITTS__custom_7223438, ISOC_E_DII__custom_7223506], accessed on July 30, 2023

From the analysis carried out on the basis of the indicators of digital intensity and the provision of professional training for employees, presented in the table above, it is possible to identify a behavioural typology of companies in the pandemic and after the pandemic in relation to their own employees, relatively different from the perspective of ensuring the development/updating digital skills—from continuing the calibration between technology and the level of digital skills for employees by supporting their training to prioritizing ITC specialists or non-specialists, depending on needs and available resources, knowing that compliance with pandemic restrictions determined increases in operational costs, some of which are maintained even in the post-pandemic period. Therefore, according to the size of the company and the digital intensity, we have identified the following situations:

A. During the pandemic, the most vulnerable companies were the small ones, with 10–49 employees, from Bulgaria, Latvia, Poland, Lithuania, Hungary, Romania, Slovakia and Croatia, which recorded a low digital intensity index for most of them, below the EU27 average. As a general characteristic, we can appreciate that these companies, in most member states, made efforts to continue the digital training of employees even in the post-pandemic period, increasing the share of companies that offered training to all employees in 2022 compared to 2020 in 19 of the 27 member countries. However, there were also exceptions, in the sense that the share of companies that offer training to their employees in post-pandemic period in Croatia, Czechia and Ireland decreased.

Some small companies focused on continuing the training even after the pandemic, especially for ITC specialists, and others, on the contrary, continued the training of the other employees, being obvious, on the one hand, that they will continue the digital transition, at least on the components for which the pandemic period demonstrated that it brought beneficial effects for the company's activity. On the other hand, the emphasis on one or another category of staff (ITC specialists or not) indicates the need for continued investments in technology but also the financial limits that lead them to act on the strictly necessary digital transformation components, almost entirely from the category " doing digital". Thus, (a) countries with increasing share of companies that provided professional training to their ICT/IT specialists and with decreased share of companies that provided professional training to their other persons employed (countries with capitalized letters from the table) were Latvia, Lithuania and Malta, and (b) only Spain registered a decreasing share of companies that provided professional training to their ICT/IT specialists and an increased share of companies that provided professional training to their other persons employed (the underlined countries from the table).

B. For medium-sized companies, which, in many countries, have advanced in the digital transition, including during the pandemic, investment in ITC technology remains a continuous challenge, which facilitates not only business development but also increasing market efficiency. For them, the option to quickly adapt to the pandemic and, subsequently, to capitalize on the digital skills acquired by employees represented the most effective way of postcrisis recovery and to become resilient to future similar risks. This digital transformation policy option of medium-sized companies is also confirmed by the results of the current analysis. Thus, for 23 of the member countries, this group of companies was associated with a high digital intensity. For 13 of these, the post-pandemic option was to increase the share of training for all employees—Denmark, Germany, Italy, Cyprus, Latvia, Lithuania, Luxembourg, Hungary, Netherlands, Austria, Poland, Slovenia and Finland. The same option was in the case of Romania and Bulgaria, but we must mention that the majority of medium-sized companies in these countries registered a reduced technological intensity. France and Slovakia are also in the same group of countries with low intensity medium-sized companies, but their behavior was different post-pandemic. In Slovakia, the share of companies that offered training to employees in 2022 compared to 2020 decreased, similar to the share of companies in Ireland and Croatia (but in these countries medium-sized companies with a high digital intensity were predominant). France, after the pandemic, paid more attention to the training of non-specialist employees in ITC, in order to increase the degree of digital inclusion, and in Belgium, Czechia, Malta and Sweden, companies invested more in the training of ITC specialists, as a necessary step for the transition to the upper category of very high digital intensity, also preparing the passage to "being digital".

C. In the analysis of large companies, no situations of low or very low digital intensity were found, which indicates that the digital transition in these companies is advanced in all member states, market competitiveness and capital concentration being factors supporting investments in technology and in the training of its own employees.

For large companies that have a high digital intensity, the trend of professional development of employees continues, with an emphasis on the training of ITC specialists, this being recorded in countries such as Czechia, Croatia and Slovakia. A larger share of companies provided training for other employees in Germany and Portugal. All other states registered the continuation of the trend of increasing the share of companies providing training in 2022 compared to 2020, for all categories of employees, respectively, in 14 of the 27 member states (Bulgaria, Estonia, Spain, Italy, Cyprus, Latvia, Lithuania, Luxembourg, Hungary, Malta, Netherlands, Austria, Poland, Romania), which also defined the overall trend of the EU27. It should be mentioned that, in this group of countries with 250 and over employees, no country recorded a reduction in the share of companies that support the development of the digital skills of all employees, which can be explained on account of the need to correlate the incorporation of technological progress with the latest generation ITC products and services or to finalize the digital transformation efforts on all its components (depending on the specificity of the field of activity and of the employment restructuring policy according to the requirements of the digital transition to the next level defined as very high digital intensity).

In order to maintain the digital intensity and to adapt to the continuous improvement of digital technologies, respectively, to facilitate the adaptation and transition to "being digital", large companies continue to invest in the training of ITC specialists in Denmark and Sweden. After the pandemic, fewer large companies continued their concerns and pace of digital skills training for all employees (in Belgium) or only for other employees (in Finland). For the companies, which are already in the category of very high digital intensity, the digital transformation policies are nuanced, by specializing in the creation of specific applications/adapted to the fields of activity, are innovative and promote working in mixed teams (ITC experts and non-ITC), for the consolidation of the prevailing development towards "being digital".

In this analysis, companies with up to nine employees were not included because in the Eurostat database, there is no information on the efforts of companies to ensure the training of their employees to develop or update digital skills for most of the EU27 member countries. As an exception, for Germany it is indicated that in 2022, 3.3% of the companies with zero to nine employees provided training to ICT/IT specialists to develop their ICT skills, for Portugal, the share for the same year is 1.9% and 2.2% in the pandemic year (2020), and for Spain, the share is 0.4% in 2022 and 0.9% in 2020 (Eurostat, 2023). For the non-ICT specialist staff, the concern of micro-firms was more intense—they provided training for digital skills in Germany, 9.4% of companies (2022); in Portugal, 10% in 2022, up from only 7.9% in 2020; and in Spain, 2.6% of companies in 2022, down from 3.3% in 2020, respectively.

## Some Effects of Forced Digitization During the Pandemic: A Short Quantitative Analysis

The pandemic has changed the way of working for a large part of jobs but also the productivity of work, the employment model and the market competitiveness of companies. Practically, we are witnessing a reskilling revolution that combines the effects of digitization (and, more recently, its forced digitization component from the pandemic) with the current challenges (WEF, 2023) related to the green energy transition, geoeconomic and supply-chain shifts, macroeconomic imbalances from the increase in inflation and the crisis of financial resources for recovery and resilience, etc.

The measurement and analysis of the effects is a difficult approach and involves the association of various quantitative and qualitative methods, from monitoring indicators to specially organized surveys and reports regarding the implementation of economic policy measures during the pandemic period.

The effects of digitization forced by the pandemic are both positive and negative, some of them have not yet been quantified, and many will be defined in the medium and long term. It is certain that the dynamics of development was adjusted by the atypical evolution of the business environment from 2020 to 2021, and the economic recovery is still an ongoing process, with unequal dynamics, by fields of activity and categories of labour market indicators. Moreover, the process of building some mechanisms to ensure economic and social resilience to crises is ongoing; it will require innovative components (tools, statistical indicators and policy measures), including from the perspective of redefinition and reskilling of the workforce, jobs disruption and employment models. Therefore, the following analysis will only highlight some already visible aspects. The available data (new indicators with data only for the post-pandemic period or changes in the methodology of the existing ones) make it possible only to indicate the direction of the transformations and, in some cases, the differences in the intensity of the changes produced. The insufficiency of data for the post-pandemic period or the existence of discontinuous time series (by changing calculation methodologies) limits the applicability of more complex impact analysis methods. Moreover, qualitative analyses, based on surveys/questionnaires, are only a few in the specialized literature and address limited thematic aspects, on geographical areas or groups of countries. However, we were able to identify some surveys that capture a series of effects, for example, the analysis carried out in the Jobs Report for 2023, based on a survey that includes 803 companies that provide employment for 11.3 million workers in 27 fields of activity and 45 countries (WEF, 2023) offering a picture of the changes on the labour market, with an emphasis on employment and the upskilling revolution, but it remains a partial picture, which rather offers a vision of future challenges, jobs disruption and transformation opportunities for business, from the perspective of the organization of jobs, the employment model, etc.

In our analysis, we will measure the gaps recorded for a selection of indicators associated with adaptation, through digitization, from the pandemic period. The aim is to identify the direction and intensity of changes, measured in 2022 (or the last year available), compared to the values of the indicators from 2019 (as a pre-pandemic year), establishing whether the pandemic has adjusted or not and in which direction the gaps between countries regarding digital transformation at the level of individuals, fields of activity and companies. The globalization of markets and the continuous challenge of maintaining competitiveness in the business environment also imply a process of convergence between states, but economic specialization, the dynamics of technological transfer in economic and social activities to maintain comparative advantages and the constraints of resource limits can lead to the increased gaps. In addition, geopolitical trends once again shake the model of labour market transformation, generating adverse effects. Health crisis, labour migration, business reshaping, energy price crisis and the risks of geopolitical instability will affect economic and social convergence, with different emphases on geographic areas. In the analysis, we selected the EU space because the process of complex integration of the economies of the member states represents a common direction at all levels of economic and social development, reaffirmed in the redefined EU strategies for the postcrisis period, especially in the field of the labour market (EC, 2023; CEDEFOP, 2023).

The gaps can be analysed according to different criteria, of which I have selected a few, namely:

– The gaps between countries, in the evolution of some indicators that define the various aspects of digitalization, respectively, social inclusion for all, as an objective assumed to manage the limitation of physical interaction between individuals, including at the workplace
– Gaps in fields of activity, starting from the fact that the pandemic influenced companies differently, depending on the profile of the activities and the nature of the products/services offered

In the analysis, we included only those indicators provided by Eurostat for which we had data available at least for the year before the pandemic, considered to be 2019, and 1 year from the post-pandemic period (2022 or 2021). The digital transformation in the pandemic also allowed the development of new indicators regarding digitalization, which were not calculated for the years before the pandemic, or underwent methodological changes and therefore could not be taken into account in the comparative analysis. Also, the short time interval and the fact that some data are not available annually, but at longer intervals, made the analysis include only the two analysis benchmarks for gaps previously mentioned.

The selected indicators and the results of the analysis allow us to draw a series of relevant conclusions for the topic of digital transformation:

A. There is a convergence in the use of the Internet, more accentuated for the states in the last places in the hierarchy according to the use of the Internet (at least once a week).

The expansion of digital communication represented an important objective for the digital transition of society, and therefore, both individuals and households were concerned about ensuring online access and purchasing specific equipment. Naturally, the diversification and development of communication platforms and online services offered to users have determined the increase in the level of Internet use. During the pandemic, the Internet, along with the telephone, represented the main form of communication.

The progress in the use of ITC technologies by households was modest; on average a gain of 2.8 p.p. was recorded in all member states, the share of households with Internet access being at least ¾ of them. In Romania, the pandemic forced about 6% of households to ensure online access for communication and other services, reaching, in 2022, 89.4% of households, while in Netherlands the share exceeded 98%.

The share of people who used the Internet (at least once a week) at the level of the EU states increased on average by 3.3 percentage points. Bulgaria, located in last place, had an increase of 12 p.p. (approx. 2/3 in 2019 to over ¾ in 2022). For Romania, located below the EU27 average, the increase was from 71.56% in 2019 to 84.05% in 2022, surpassing countries such as Poland, Lithuania and Slovakia. However, the different dynamics in the countries meant that, at the level of 2022, about 14% of individuals have never used the Internet in Greece and only 1.13% in Sweden, the gap between the countries decreasing from 17.6 p.p. to 10.35 p.p (Table 3.2).

**Table 3.2** Internet access for communication, by individuals and households, post-pandemic (2022) compared to the period before the pandemic (1019)

| | | EU27 level | Gap between countries (p.p.) | Maximum level | Minimum level | Romania level |
|---|---|---|---|---|---|---|
| % of households with Internet at home | 2022 | 92.5 | 12.8 | Netherlands 98.3 | Greece 85.5 | 89.4 |
| | 2019 | 89.7 | 23.3 | Netherlands 98.4 | Bulgaria 75.1 | 83.6 |
| | 2022–2019 (p.p.) | 2.8 | x | Netherlands −0.1 | 10.4 | 5.8 |
| % of individuals who have used Internet once a week | 2022 | 87.18 | 17.47 | Denmark 96.44 | Bulgaria 78.97 | 84.05 |
| | 2019 | 83.9 | 28.62 | Denmark 95.46 | Bulgaria 66.84 | 71.56 |
| | 2022–2019 (p.p.) | 3.28 | x | Denmark 0.98 | Bulgaria 12.13 | 12.49 |
| % of individuals who have never used the Internet | 2022 | 6.96 | 12.84 | Greece 13.97 | Sweden 1.13 | 10.35 |
| | 2019 | 10.37 | 22.68 | Bulgaria 24.49 | Sweden 1.81 | 17.66 |
| | 2022–2019 (p.p.) | −3.41 | x | −10.52 | −0.68 | -7.31 |

Source: Eurostat database, Science, technology, digital society (https://ec.europa.eu/eurostat/data/database), accessed on July, 24, 3023

B. The differences between the urban and rural environment are reduced due to a more accentuated dynamics of the rural households.

The increase in Internet access of rural households determined the reduction of gaps between countries from 39 p.p. to almost 25 p.p.. The reduction of the gaps was also registered in urban areas but in much more modest proportions, partly due to the fact that, in 2019, the urban-rural gap was significantly in favour of urban areas. Romania, like other states with lower performances in the pre-pandemic period, recorded a dynamic twice as high as the EU average. If, overall, we can mention a moderate progress, Romania gains three positions in the hierarchy of member states and overtakes Lithuania, Poland and Croatia. Regarding rural households, the progress is modest compared to other countries, in the sense that it gains only one place in the hierarchy in 2022 compared to 2019 (it is ahead of Italy and Croatia but is overtaken by Malta), the causes being multiple—the geographical coverage area, the cost of services, the lack of resources for equipment, especially in poor households, but also the level and access to training for digital skills. However, it is worth mentioning that, for the rural environment, Romania manages to exceed the EU27 average in 2022, by 1.5 p.p., positioning itself on the tenth place in the hierarchy (Table 3.3).

**Table 3.3** Share of individuals (16–74 years old) who have used Internet in the last 12 months, in pre- and post-pandemic, on residential environment (%)

| | | EU27 | Gap between countries p.p. | Maximum level/ minimum level | Romania level |
|---|---|---|---|---|---|
| All | 2019 | 87.4 | 27.1 | Sweden 97.7/Bulgaria 70.6 | 79.7 |
| | 2022 | 91.1 | 15.5 | Luxembourg 98.4/Croatia 82.9 | 88.9 |
| | 2022–2019 (p.p.) | 3.7 | x | 0.7/12.3 | 9.2 |
| Urban | 2019 | 90.5 | 19.7 | Sweden 98.4/Bulgaria 78.7 | 88.8 |
| | 2022 | 93.2 | 11.8 | Luxembourg 99.0/Italy 87.2 | 94.7 |
| | 2022–2019 (p.p.) | 2.7 | x | 0.6/8.5 | 5.9 |
| Rural | 2019 | 83.3 | 39.0 | Netherlands 97.2/Bulgaria 58.2 | 72.3 |
| | 2022 | 87.7 | 25.1 | Luxembourg 97.9/ Greece 72.8 | 83.5 |
| | 2022–2019 (p.p.) | 4.4 | x | 0.5/14.6 | 11.2 |

Note: *p.p.* percentage points
Source: https://digital-agenda-data.eu, accessed July, 24, 2023

C. The pandemic period did not stimulate a significant increase in the use of the Internet for interaction with public authorities, even in countries where online services were less developed.

The EU27 average for the year 2022 remained below 2/3 for the interaction of individuals with public authorities and below ½ for the electronic transmission of some documents, although, in this second category, the progress was double, compared to the first category. It is important to mention that there are significant gaps between countries, of 70–80 p.p., Denmark and Sweden being the countries with the best results. For both analysed indicators, Romania is and remains in the last place, with less than 15% in the share of individuals interacting with public authorities on the Internet and less than 10% in the online transmission of some documents. Moreover, the progress was more modest than that of other countries located in the last places of the hierarchy, which determined the increase of Romania's gaps compared to the EU average (Table 3.4.). The main factors are, on the one hand, the poor development of e-governance and, on the other hand, the lack of trust of Internet users regarding data security, the quality of communication and the efficiency with which citizens' problems are solved, especially by local authorities.

D. During the pandemic, the share of companies that adopted work from home increased, and some of them, post-pandemic, continued with remote work or developed hybrid programmes.

**Table 3.4** Digital interaction of individuals with public authorities (last 12 months), percentage of individuals

| | | EU27 level | Gap between countries (p.p.) | Maximum level | Minimum level |
|---|---|---|---|---|---|
| Interaction with public authorities—all individuals | 2019 | 53.42 | 80.02 | Denmark 91.67 | Romania 11.65 |
| | 2021 | 58.50 | 77.6 | Denmark 92.25 | Romania 14.65 |
| | 2022–2019 (p.p.) | 4.98 | x | Denmark 0.58 | Romania 3 |
| Interaction with public authorities—individuals who used Internet within the last year | 2019 | 61.13 | 79.47 | Denmark 94.08 | Romania 14.61 |
| | 2021 | 64.84 | 76.55 | Sweden 93.27 | Romania 16.72 |
| | 2022–2019 (p.p.) | 3.71 | x | −0.81 | Romania 2.11 |
| Submitting completed forms—all individuals | 2019 | 35.72 | 71.02 | Sweden 76.59 | Romania 5.57 |
| | 2021 | 44.15 | 70.52 | Sweden 79.50 | Romania 8.98 |
| | 2022–2019 (p.p.) | 8.43 | x | Sweden 2.91 | Romania 3.41 |
| Submitting completed forms—individuals who used Internet within the last year | 2019 | 40.88 | 74.28 | Estonia 81.27 | Romania 6.99 |
| | 2021 | 48.94 | 72.54 | Estonia 82.79 | Romania 10.25 |
| | 2022–2019 (p.p.) | 8.06 | x | Estonia 1.52 | Romania 3.26 |

Source: Eurostat database, Science, technology, digital society (https://ec.europa.eu/eurostat/data/database), accessed on July, 24, 3023

The remote access of employees to the work platforms of the companies or the online transmission of some documents has also meant an increase in concerns for data security but also the purchase of Internet services that allow online meetings and increased traffic data and information. The best performing countries are Finland, Malta and Austria and the worst performing are Bulgaria and Hungary. It should be mentioned that, for the indicators presented in Table 3.5, the data are only available for 19 member states, missing Romania, the Czech Republic, Estonia, Ireland, Greece, Spain, France and Croatia. Being a new indicator introduced by Eurostat, the information is partial; they only look at the year 2020 and include as fields of activity only manufacturing, electricity, gas, steam and air conditioning, water supply, sewerage and waste management and remediation activities, excluding micro-enterprises.

**Table 3.5** Enterprises with an increase in the remote access, in 2020

| | | EU27 level | Gap between countries (p.p.) | Maximum level | Minimum level |
|---|---|---|---|---|---|
| During 2020, enterprises have increased the percentage of persons employed having remote access to: | Its e-mail system | 34.9 | 43.6 | Malta 55.8 | Bulgaria 12.0 |
| | The ICT systems of the enterprise, other than e-mail | 34.8 | 44.8 | Malta 54.6 | Bulgaria 9.8 |
| During 2020, the number of remote meetings conducted by the enterprises increased (Skype, Zoom, MS Teams, etc.) | | 51.9 | 70.8 | Finland 89.6 | Bulgaria 18.8 |
| Enterprises with an increase in the remote access, which was fully due to the Covid-19 pandemic: | To the e-mail system of the enterprise | 14.1 | 22.6 | Austria 24 | Hungary 1.4 |
| | To the ICT systems of the enterprise, other than e-mail | 16.3 | 24 | Malta 26.8 | Hungary 2.8 |

Note: Firms with ten or more persons employed in manufacturing, electricity, gas, steam and air conditioning, water supply, sewerage and waste management and remediation activities are included.

Source: Eurostat database, Science, technology, digital society (https://ec.europa.eu/eurostat/data/database), accessed on July, 24, 3023

E. The development of the digital skills of employees who, during the pandemic, worked to a greater extent in remote or hybrid systems was achieved with the support of companies, through training courses, offered both for ITC specialists and for other employees, whose work tasks allowed the transition to online.

There are significant differences between countries and fields of activity, some justified by the field of activity, such as construction, some processing activities, vehicle repairs or transport, etc., but also depending on the degree of digitization from the pre-pandemic period (digital intensity index—DII).

In some activities, post-pandemic (data available for the year 2022), concern for ensuring digital skills has decreased, either through the previous coverage of the needs associated with the requirements imposed by the pandemic or due to the high level of digital intensity of companies or as a result of the return to the model of physical presence at the workplace. If we analyse, from this last perspective, the share of companies that provided training in 2022 compared to 2019, it is found that interest has decreased especially for non-specialist ITC staff, the gaps between countries are increasing, and the countries at the bottom of the ranking have given up or reduced their activities of further training of employees for digital transformation (Table 3.6). If we associate in the analysis the structure of the companies according to the digital intensity and the field of activity, then we find that the performers continue their digital transformation strategy and the less performing states from this perspective return to a greater extent to the pre-pandemic employment models. It can be appreciated that they give up, on the one hand, the gains from the pandemic regarding digital training and remote or hybrid work and, on the other hand, the concerns for the transition from "doing digital" to "being digital", so the continuation of the digital transformation is postponed (partially or totally), for various reasons—financial restrictions, other priorities in the company's development, cost constraints, etc. In this analysis,

**Table 3.6** Share of enterprise that provided training to develop ICT skills, 2019 and 2022, by category of personnel and activities (%)

| | | EU27 level | Gap between countries (p.p.) | Maximum level | Minimum level | Romania level |
|---|---|---|---|---|---|---|
| **Manufacturing** | | | | | | |
| To ICT/IT specialists | 2019 | 10.2 | 14.5 | Austria, 17.3 | Romania, 2.8 | 2.8 |
| | 2022 | 10.8 | 18.2 | Belgium, 21.7 | Romania, 3.5 | 3.5 |
| | 2022–2019 (p.p.) | 0.6 | x | 4.4 | Romania, 0.7 | 0.7 |
| To other persons employed | 2019 | 20.7 | 33.5 | Sweden, 36.5 | Romania, 3 | 3 |
| | 2022 | 18.9 | 33.4 | Finland, 38.3 | Bulgaria, 4.9 | 5.8 |
| | 2022–2019 (p.p.) | −1.8 | x | 1.8 | 1.9 | 2.8 |
| To their personnel | 2019 | 23.3 | 34.5 | Sweden, 38.8 | Romania, 4.3 | 4.3 |
| | 2022 | 21.5 | 35.1 | Finland, 40.6 | Romania, 6.5 | 6.5 |
| | 2022–2019 (p.p.) | −1.8 | x | 1.8 | Romania, 2.2 | 2.2 |
| **Construction** | | | | | | |
| To ICT/IT specialists | 2019 | 3.3 | 8.6 | Ireland, 9.9 | Romania, 1.3 | 1.3 |
| | 2022 | 3.6 | 7.7 | Netherlands, 8.3 | Bulgaria, 0.6 | 3.3 |
| | 2022–2019 (p.p.) | 0.3 | x | −1.6 | −0.7 | 2 |
| To other persons employed | 2019 | 13.3 | 21 | Belgium, 24.6 | Romania, 3.6 | 3.6 |
| | 2022 | 11.3 | 22.2 | Sweden, 24 | Bulgaria, 1.8 | 4 |

(continued)

**Table 3.6** (continued)

| | | EU27 level | Gap between countries (p.p.) | Maximum level | Minimum level | Romania level |
|---|---|---|---|---|---|---|
| | 2021–2019 (p.p.) | −2 | x | −0.6 | −1.8 | 0.4 |
| To their personnel | 2019 | 14.3 | 23.6 | Belgium, 27.4 | Romania, 3.8 | 3.8 |
| | 2022 | 12.5 | 22.1 | Sweden, 24.1 | Bulgaria, 2 | 6 |
| | 2022–2019 (p.p.) | −1.8 | x | −3.3 | −1.8 | 2.2 |
| **Wholesale and retail trade; repair of motor vehicles and motorcycles** | | | | | | |
| To ICT/IT specialists | 2019 | 8.9 | 15.6 | Denmark, 18.5 | Romania, 2.9 | 2.9 |
| | 2022 | 10.2 | 17.5 | Netherlands, 20.6 | Romania, 3.1 | 3.1 |
| | 2022–2019 (p.p.) | 1.3 | x | 2.1 | Romania, 0.2 | 0.2 |
| To other persons employed | 2019 | 21.3 | 33 | Finland, 37.7 | Romania, 4.7 | 4.7 |
| | 2022 | 20.5 | 39.5 | Finland, 45 | Bulgaria, 5.5 | 5.9 |
| | 2022–2019 (p.p.) | −0.8 | x | 7.3 | 0.8 | 1.2 |
| To their personnel | 2019 | 23.6 | 35 | Finland, 40.8 | Romania, 5.8 | 5.8 |
| | 2022 | 23.1 | 41.3 | Finland, 48.4 | Romania, 7.1 | 7.1 |
| | 2022–2019 (p.p.) | −0.5 | x | Finland, 7.6 | Romania, 1.3 | 1.3 |
| **Transportation and storage** | | | | | | |
| To ICT/IT specialists | 2019 | 5.9 | 23.5 | Cyprus, 25.4 | Romania, 1.9 | 1.9 |
| | 2022 | 7.4 | 16.5 | Denmark, 18.5 | Bulgaria, 2 | 3.7 |
| | 2022–2019 (p.p.) | 1.5 | x | −6.9 | 0.1 | 1.8 |
| To other persons employed | 2019 | 15.5 | 30.8 | Cyprus, 33.6 | Romania, 2.8 | 2.8 |
| | 2022 | 15.6 | 26.8 | Cyprus, 31.2 | Lithuania, 4.4 | 5.8 |
| | 2022–2019 (p.p.) | 0.1 | x | Cyprus, −2.4 | 1.6 | 3.0 |
| To their personnel | 2019 | 16.9 | 32.5 | Belgium, 36.5 | Romania, 4.0 | 4.0 |
| | 2022 | 17.3 | 27.4 | Cyprus, 32.9 | Bulgaria, 5.6 | 6.7 |

(continued)

**Table 3.6** (continued)

| | | EU27 level | Gap between countries (p.p.) | Maximum level | Minimum level | Romania level |
|---|---|---|---|---|---|---|
| | 2022–2019 (p.p.) | 0.4 | x | −3.6 | 1.6 | 2.7 |
| **Accommodation and food service activities** | | | | | | |
| To ICT/IT specialists | 2019 | 2.8 | 5.4 | Malta, 6.1 | Romania, 0.7 | 0.7 |
| | 2022 | 2.5 | 6.9 | Cyprus, 7.6 | Ireland, 0.7 | 2.1 |
| | 2022–2019 (p.p.) | −0.3 | x | 1.5 | 0 | 1.4 |
| To other persons employed | 2019 | 10.9 | 23.9 | Cyprus, 25.1 | Romania, 1.2 | 1.2 |
| | 2022 | 8 | 19.5 | Finland, 21.2 | Romania, 1.7 | 1.7 |
| | 2022–2019 (p.p.) | −2.9 | x | −3.9 | Romania, 0.5 | 0.5 |
| To their personnel | 2019 | 11.8 | 24.6 | Cyprus, 25.9 | Romania, 1.3 | 1.3 |
| | 2022 | 8.8 | 20.7 | Finland, 22.7 | Greece, 2.0 | 2.4 |
| | 2022–2019 (p.p.) | −3 | x | −3.2 | 0.7 | 1.1 |
| **Information and communication** | | | | | | |
| To ICT/IT specialists | 2019 | 53.5 | 32.5 | Slovenia, 73.8 | Romania, 41.3 | 41.3 |
| | 2022 | 54.7 | 33.6 | Slovenia, 72.2 | Romania, 38.6 | 38.6 |
| | 2022–2019 (p.p.) | 1.2 | x | Slovenia, −1.6 | Romania, −2.7 | −2.7 |
| To other persons employed | 2019 | 46 | 45.9 | Czechia, 71.1 | Bulgaria, 25.2 | 26.4 |
| | 2022 | 51.1 | 43.9 | Finland, 70.7 | Bulgaria, 26.8 | 30.7 |
| | 2022–2019 (p.p.) | 5.1 | x | −0.4 | 1.6 | 4.3 |
| To their personnel | 2019 | 61.1 | 37.7 | Belgium, 80.8 | Romania, 43.1 | 43.1 |
| | 2022 | 62.9 | 35.9 | Slovenia, 80.1 | Romania, 44.2 | 44.2 |
| | 2022–2019 (p.p.) | 1.8 | x | −0.7 | Romania, 1.1 | 1.1 |

(continued)

**Table 3.6** (continued)

| | | EU27 level | Gap between countries (p.p.) | Maximum level | Minimum level | Romania level |
|---|---|---|---|---|---|---|
| **Administrative and support service activities** | | | | | | |
| To ICT/IT specialists | 2019 | 7.7 | 13.2 | Luxembourg, 16.6 | Slovenia, 3.4 | 4.7 |
| | 2022 | 9.2 | 22.5 | Belgium, 25.1 | Slovakia, 2.6 | 5.9 |
| | 2022–2019 (p.p.) | 1.5 | x | 8.5 | −0.8 | 1.2 |
| To other persons employed | 2019 | 20 | 27.4 | Ireland, 32.8 | Bulgaria, 5.4 | 5.8 |
| | 2022 | 18.6 | 30.8 | Finland, 38.1 | Slovakia, 7.3 | 7.3 |
| | 2022–2019 (p.p.) | −1.4 | x | 5.3 | 1.9 | 1.5 |
| To their personnel | 2019 | 21.9 | 29.9 | Ireland, 36.2 | Romania, 6.3 | 6.3 |
| | 2022 | 20.7 | 31.1 | Finland, 38.8 | Slovakia, 7.7 | 9.8 |
| | 2022–2019 (p.p.) | −1.2 | x | 2.6 | 1.4 | 3.5 |

Note: Enterprises with ten persons employed or more
Source: Eurostat database, Science, technology, digital society (https://ec.europa.eu/eurostat/data/database), accessed on July, 24, 3023

Romania ranks last in most cases both in 2019 and in 2022, which indicates a divergent evolution; the respective efforts are much weaker than those of other countries in similar positions, such as Bulgaria, Slovakia or Lithuania, with which they share the last places.

Regarding Romania's position, it should be mentioned that, in most situations, in 2019 it is in the last place and will remain so in 2022, even if the progress is higher than the EU average. The only exception is the information and communication sector, where the evolution is modest, below the average progress at the EU level, similar to the situation of ITC experts in trade and administrative services. The main reason is the external mobility of ITC experts, for their professional career and much higher earnings from work, the labour market in Romania not being able to attract and retain them in employment.

F. The digital transformation of companies continues to be largely dependent on the field of activity.

In the post-pandemic period, the digital intensity of the forms is defined, for companies with ten and more than ten employees, as predominantly low digital intensity (manufacturing, water supply, trade, administrative services; Table 3.7). The largest share of companies with high digital intensity is found in information and

**Table 3.7** Distribution of companies according to digital intensity (DII) in 2022, by fields of activity and gaps by country, post-pandemic

| Activity | DII | EU27 level | Gap between countries (p.p.) | Maximum level | Minimum level | Romania level |
|---|---|---|---|---|---|---|
| Construction | Very low DII | 43.4 | 58 | Croatia, 73.3 | Finland, 15.3 | 55.5 |
| | Low DII | 42.9 | 33.3 | Denmark, 55.2 | Croatia, 21.9 | 38.1 |
| | High DII | 13.2 | 34.8 | Sweden, 38.9 | Croatia, 4.1 | 6.3 |
| | Very high DII | 0.5 | 2.1 | Belgium, 2.1 | Romania, Bulgaria, 0 | 0 |
| Transportation and storage | Very low DII | 39.6 | 47.9 | Bulgaria, 58.1 | Malta, 15.2 | 51.9 |
| | Low DII | 37.4 | 23.8 | Slovenia, 50.4 | Hungary, 26.6 | 30.8 |
| | High DII | 20.2 | 38.6 | Malta, 47.1 | Bulgaria, 8.5 | 17.1 |
| | Very high DII | 2.8 | 12.4 | Denmark, 12.6 | Romania, 0.2 | 0.2 |
| Accommodation and food service activities | Very low DII | 46.8 | 64 | Greece, 79.7 | Denmark, 15.7 | 47.1 |
| | Low DII | 35.5 | 32.9 | Spain, 47 | Greece, 14.1 | 38.7 |
| | High DII | 15.6 | 30.4 | Sweden, 36.3 | Greece, 5.9 | 13.6 |
| | Very high DII | 2.1 | 7.5 | Finland, 7.8 | Greece, 0.3 | 0.7 |
| Manufacturing, electricity, gas, steam and air conditioning, water supply, sewerage, waste management and remediation activities | Very low DII | **31.2** | 50.1 | Bulgaria, 56.8 | Denmark, 6.7 | 53 |
| | Low DII | 39.6 | 17.9 | Italy, 45.3 | Sweden, 27.4 | 33.5 |
| | High DII | 24.4 | 34.9 | Sweden, 46.8 | Bulgaria, 11.9 | 12.7 |
| | Very high DII | 4.8 | 15.4 | Denmark, 16.2 | Romania, 0.8 | 0.8 |
| Manufacturing | Very low DII | 31.7 | 50.3 | Bulgaria, 57.3 | Denmark, 7.0 | 53.7 |

(continued)

**Table 3.7** (continued)

| Activity | DII | EU27 level | Gap between countries (p.p.) | Maximum level | Minimum level | Romania level |
|---|---|---|---|---|---|---|
| | Low DII | 39.7 | 17.5 | Italy, 45.4 | Hungary, 27.9 | 33.2 |
| | High DII | 23.8 | 34.8 | Sweden, 46.2 | Bulgaria, 11.4 | 12.3 |
| | Very high DII | 4.9 | 15.4 | Denmark, 16.2 | Romania, 0.8 | 0.8 |
| Water supply; sewerage, waste management and remediation activities | Very low DII | 26.8 | 65.2 | Bulgaria, 65.2 | Denmark, 0 | 51.1 |
| | Low DII | 42.0 | 29.5 | Malta, 55.6 | Slovakia, 26.1 | 35.5 |
| | High DII | 29.3 | 53.1 | Sweden, 59.1 | Bulgaria, 6.0 | 13.4 |
| | Very high DII | 1.9 | 13.1 | Denmark, 13.1 | Romania, 0 | 0 |
| Wholesale and retail trade; repair of motor vehicles and motorcycles | Very low DII | 24.9 | 42.1 | Bulgaria, 47 | Finland, 4.9 | 42.9 |
| | Low DII | 38.0 | 23 | France, 45.7 | Sweden, 22.7 | 36.6 |
| | High DII | 30.7 | 36.7 | Sweden, 54 | Bulgaria, 17.3 | 19.2 |
| | Very high DII | 6.4 | 18.3 | Denmark, Finland, 19.4 | Romania, 1.3 | 1.3 |
| Administrative and support service activities | Very low DII | 33.8 | 49.5 | Bulgaria, 58.7 | Finland, 9.2 | 48.7 |
| | Low DII | 38.2 | 30.4 | Germany, 42.5 | Greece, 22.1 | 32.9 |
| | High DII | 24.9 | 36.1 | Finland, 49.6 | Bulgaria, 13.5 | 17 |
| | Very high DII | 3 | 8.3 | Malta, 9.2 | Slovenia, 0.9 | 1.4 |
| Information and communication | Very low DII | 2.4 | 7.9 | Bulgaria, 7.9 | Denmark, Slovenia, 0 | 7.1 |
| | Low DII | 13 | 20.3 | Latvia, 23.5 | Finland, 3.2 | 19.6 |
| | High DII | 71.6 | 20.8 | Luxembourg, 80.7 | Spain, 59.9 | 68.8 |

(continued)

**Table 3.7** (continued)

| Activity | DII | EU27 level | Gap between countries (p.p.) | Maximum level | Minimum level | Romania level |
|---|---|---|---|---|---|---|
| | Very high DII | 13 | 20.6 | Lithuania, 25.2 | Romania, 4.6 | 4.6 |
| Professional, scientific and technical activities | Very low DII | 5 | 22.4 | Hungary, 22.7 | Finland, 0.3 | 18.2 |
| | Low DII | 37.3 | 28.8 | Luxembourg, 46.4 | Denmark, 17.6 | 22.7 |
| | High DII | 54.2 | 37.1 | Finland, 73.1 | Latvia, 36 | 58.3 |
| | Very high DII | 3.5 | 10.4 | Denmark, 11.1 | Slovakia, 0.7 | 0.8 |

Note: DII—digital intensity index (Version 4); firms with ten and more employees
Source: Eurostat database, Science, technology, digital society (https://ec.europa.eu/eurostat/data/database), accessed on July, 24, 3023

communication, professional, scientific and technical activities. Most companies with a very low intensity index are those from construction, transport, storage, accommodation and food services activities.

The specialized literature stated, as early as 2020, that the main benefit of the pandemic was that it accelerated the digital transition, by intensifying online activities and the digital training of employees. There are assessments according to which the digital transition was advanced/was accelerated by the pandemic, especially in small companies, which were left behind in this development process (EIB, 2022; OECD, 2020). On the labour market, the benefits were the flexibility of the forms of employment by increasing the share of employees who work remotely or in the hybrid system and increasing labour productivity. Therefore, it is expected that in the post-pandemic period, the share of people with basic digital skills and above will change significantly. The data provided by Eurostat do not allow us a pre-post-pandemic comparative analysis because the methodology of the indicator has changed while also refining the structure according to digital skills, introducing five component indicators regarding overall digital skills 2.0 and two new groups/categories regarding digital intensity—narrow and limited. A comparative analysis between countries shows Netherlands with over 50% of individuals with above basic overall digital skills, followed by Finland, Ireland, Spain, Denmark, Sweden and Malta with over 1/3 (Fig. 3.3).

In Bulgaria, the share is only 7.8%. The EU27 average is a little over ¼, but the proportion of those with BasicODS is higher, respectively, by 27.4%. Czechia and Slovakia have over 1/3 of individuals with BasicODS, and Romania has the lowest level, at 19%. The most numerous individuals from the LowODS category, an be

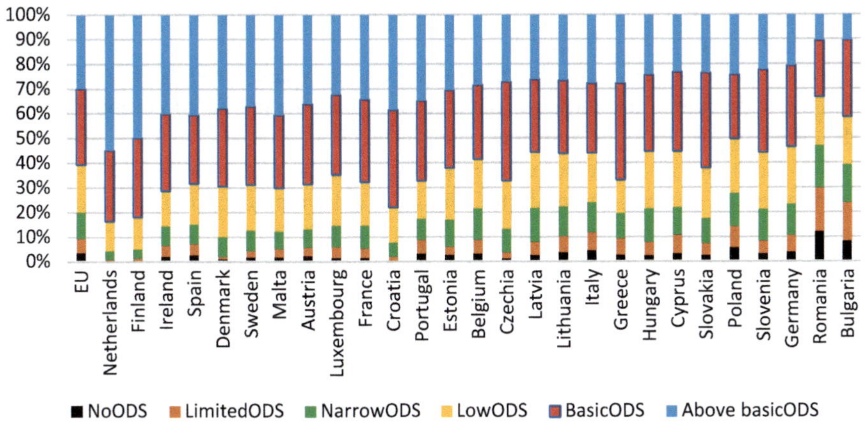


**Fig. 3.3** Share of individuals with overall digital skills (ODS), in EU member state in 2019 and 2021. Source: Eurostat (2023)

found in Germany (with 21.2%) and in Greece, with 10.6%. In the following categories, respectively, NarrowODS and LimitedODS, Romania has the largest share, with 14% in each category, also registering the largest proportion of people without digital skills. This means that the efforts during the pandemic, although some above the EU27 average, failed to substantially improve the level of digital skills of individuals, although from the perspective of access and use of the Internet it has a comfortable weight of 9/10.

## Brief Conclusions and Policy Recommendations

Digital transformation, as a general company modernization process, is ongoing in all companies because digital products and services are increasingly connected with current development, in all human activities. At the company level, the digital transformation is carried out at different speeds and intensities; it influences not only the production processes as such but also the management activity. That's why the need for digital skills differs by job, from the minimum level of communication to carry out current work tasks, which is included in "digital inclusion", up to specialization in the use and development of field-specific digital components of activity, times that redefine work, that make the transition to being digital. AI and big data become true assistants of managerial processes, optimizing working time, more fully substantiating the motivation and content of change measures, feedback and finally the quality of managerial decisions. A distinct but important part of the digital transformation takes into account digital innovation, for information security and the development of new digital technologies (diversification and the possibility of customization to the specific needs of companies, affordability by decreasing costs, rapid technological transfer, etc.).

More and more quickly, digital products and services, through their expansion and the wide ease of use through "open access", become public goods and allow the development of new jobs and new types of business—see the social platforms on which more and more are active companies, from the trade component to content creation to the diversification of the industry of entertainment products, information and interpersonal communication.

In this context of transformation, the pandemic represented a stage that marked several important aspects from the perspective of the formation and use of human capital, among which we mention the following:

- The set of digital skills considered minimal necessary for good and minimal communication with third parties or institutions has been expanded—from the use of mobile phones and the Internet to owning a computer and knowledge of digital programs and products that allow/facilitate information and communication (between individuals, or with public authorities, etc.).
- At the company level, digital skills are included in the job descriptions for almost all jobs, with specific differences, on abilities and competencies, depending on the field of activity and the complexity of the job.
- The digital intensity in companies will increase, with some activities that will radically be transformed, both from the internal perspective, of work organization and management, but also from the external perspective, of the relations between the company and business partners (whether they are public or private, organizations, households or individuals).
- The digital visibility of the company has become an important component of business management, including for activities related to a personal service, which requires physical interaction to achieve it.

If we look at the overall, the digital transformation (as a global factor of the development of the business environment, similar to the green and energy transition and the competitiveness of the company), it is obvious that, in the medium and long term, it is an irreversible process of interconnection, which changes the managerial model and the organization of workplaces and redefines the calculation of labour productivity and the economic performance of the company.

In the current chapter, we have identified some aspects generated by the pandemic, namely, the disruption in the company's digital transformation, especially from the perspective of the human factor of production.

Based on the statistical data available for the pandemic period, compared to the pre-pandemic period, it is evident that (a) the business environment has changed irreversibly, and the work and life model has adapted to remote, flexible, modularized work, with important economic and social implications, (b) at the level of the individual and the household, the effects of forced digitization were different, with the increase in digital discrimination and inequalities for the vulnerable categories and with significantly higher associated costs, and, (c) at the company level, the digital adaptation was based on minimal, survival components.

The digital transformation strategy, pre-pandemic defined, at company level, continued only as an exception, the investments in ICT being redirected, mainly, to the facilitation of remote work, e-commerce and digital communication.

The consumer relationship (as an individual and a household) with the business environment, for current consumer services, has suffered, especially in the case of vulnerable categories of consumers—without access to the Internet, without the financial possibility to purchase minimal digital equipment, without digital education of minimal or low level, which made digital communication difficult. The poor digital endowment of the households of employees, or the lack of it, limited the adaptation to the pandemic conditions of the companies forced to switch to remote work (some companies have invested in facilitating remote work for employees). Digitization efforts were different, depending on the size of the company, the previous level of digitization and, of course, the limits of transferring activities online and performing work tasks remotely.

Post-pandemic recovery and resilience requires the redefinition of activities and inter-human communication, a new normal, based on the acceptance of digitization as a fundamental component of doing more and more tasks/activities in households, at the workplace and in the community. If we summarize the dynamics of the digital transformation of the business and social environment, and the digital intensity of the companies, it is obvious that in nine out of ten of the cases, components were implemented that define the digital transformation of the companies, with different intensities of the process as a whole, in which " technology is fully embedded in business" (Zemmel et al., 2023). In this context, a new repositioning of companies is necessary, in the following directions:

- The inclusion of AI in managerial processes as a tool to facilitate the increase in the work performance of workers who operate with databases, of managers responsible for operational decisions and of those who seek to increase performance in the management of resource flows and results at the company level. The investment effort in AI-related technology and in the upskilling of the employees can be found in the reduction of operating costs and in the increase of EBIT financial results (Chui et al., 2022).
- The metamorphosis of the company from "doing digital" to "being digital"; this means "to build the capabilities to continuously create great customer experiences, lower costs, and build value added", starting from the correct diagnostic analysis of the company's needs to the redefinition/the reconstruction of the operating models of the production and operational management processes up to the construction of the own database (e.g. by using machine learning operations) and the application of our own, high-performance work and analysis methods (Lamarre et al., 2023).
- Redefining work in the company, respectively, the jobs and the skills needed by employees, through the development of mixed teams (technical and nontechnical employees on AI; gender representation; age groups; seniority), whose skills were acquired either through upskilling/reskilling, either by recruiting young graduates from top-tier universities or from other companies in the market, to

build work teams with employees' digital-related skills (Su et al., 2022; EC, 2022; ECLAC, 2021; Konle-Seidl & Danesi, 2022; MIT, 2023, Vasile, 2023).
- Reducing gaps in the employment structure in the company, based on digital skills segmentation criteria, through digital inclusion for all categories of employees and periodic training (digital upskilling) of non-ITC employees.

Finally, we have to realize that digital transformation of the companies is an ongoing process in which we are constantly building new mechanisms to facilitate and increase performance at work, in the conditions where the technologies specific to the field of activity are permanently upgraded, and to which we associate products/services offered by technologies specific to the ITC sector. Therefore, the digitization of the labour force is a parallel process, which produces changes in the employment structure through the continuous process of job destruction-job creation, with the upgrading of the work content, from the perspective of skills, knowledge and finally digital competencies. It is a continuous process of learning and innovation, generating a permanent update of demand and supply on the labour market and the education market (viewed as a lifelong learning process). Moreover, at the level of employees and companies, another language of communication develops, between business partners, between companies and within them, in which digital facilities become common tools both for work and for activities outside the workplace. The permanent demand for updating digital skills from the business environment changes the mechanisms and balances on the labour market, in fact redefining the correlations between the economic optimum (labour productivity) and the social optimum in employment (remuneration and work satisfaction).

## References


Acemoglu, D., & David, A. (2011). Skills, tasks, and technologies: Implications for employment and earnings. In *Handbook of Labor Economics* (Vol. 4, pp. 1043–1171). Elsevier.

Althoff, L., Eckert, F., Ganapati, S., Walsh, C. (2022). The *Geography of Remote Work, NBER Working Paper 29181*, Revised January, https://www.nber.org/system/files/working_papers/w29181/w29181.pdf

Aly, H. (2020). *Digital transformation development and productivity in developing countries: Is artificial intelligence a curse or a blessing? Review of Economics and Political Science*. Available online: https://www.emerald.com/insight/2631-3561.htm.

Arntz, M., Terry, G., & Ulrich, Z. (2016). The risk of automation for jobs in OECD countries: A comparative analysis. In *OECD Social, Employment and Migration Working Papers* (Vol. No. 189). OECD.

Carbon Trust and Vodafone Institute. (2021). *Homeworking report* https://www.vodafone-institut.de/studies/homeworking-report/.

CEDEFOP. (2023). *Future jobs- indicators, Skills intelligence platform*. https://www.cedefop.europa.eu/en/tools/skills-intelligence/future-jobs?year=2022-2035&country=EU27#1

Chinoracký, R., Stanislava, T., & Madlenáková, L. (2019). Does Industry 4.0 have the same impact on employment in the sectors? *Management, (18544223) 14*, 5–17.

Chui, M., Hall, B., Singla, A., & Sukharevsky, A. (2022, December). *The state of AI in 2022—and a half decade in review, QuantumBlack By McKinsey*. https://www.mckinsey.com/capabilities/quantumblack/our-insights/the-state-of-ai-in-2022-and-a-half-decade-in-review
EC. (2019). *Key competences for lifelong learning, European Commission, Directorate-General for Education, Youth, Sport and Culture, Publications Office*, https://doi.org/10.2766/569540
EC. (2020). *Digital economy and society index 2020, Thematic Chapters*. https://digital-strategy.ec.europa.eu/en/library/digital-economy-and-society-index-desi-2020
EC. (2022). *Measuring digital skills across the EU: Digital skills indicator 2.0 JRC Technical Report*, EUR 31193 EN, JRC130341_01.
EC. (2023). *Employment and Social Developments in Europe 2023, Addressing labour shortages and skills gaps in the EU, annual review, Directorate-General of Employment, Social Affairs and Inclusion*, KE-BD-23-002-EN-N.
ECLAC. (2021). *Digital technologies for a new future Economic Commission for Latin America and the Caribbean (ECLAC), (LC/TS.2021/43)*. https://www.cepal.org/sites/default/files/publication/files/46817/S2000960_en.pdf
EIB. (2022). *The 2021/2022 digitalisation in Europe report: The pandemic has made the digital transformation an integral part of European society*, European Investment Bank, 2022–214-EN, https://www.eib.org/en/press/all/2022-214-the-2021-2022-digitalisation-in-europe-report-the-pandemic-has-made-the-digital-transformation-an-integral-part-of-european-society
Eurofound. (2021). *The digital age: Implications of automation, digitisation and platforms for work and employment, Challenges and prospects in the EU series*. Publications Office of the European Union.
Eurofound. (2022a). *Working conditions in the time of COVID-19: Implications for the future, European Working Conditions Telephone Survey 2021 series*. Publications Office of the European Union.
Eurofound. (2022b). *Working conditions and sustainable work Is telework really 'greener'?* An overview and assessment of its climate impacts, Working paper, WPEF22031, https://www.eurofound.europa.eu/sites/default/files/wpef22031.pdf
Eurofound. (2023). *Working conditions and sustainable work*. Job quality is pivotal in addressing today's workplace and societal challenges, https://www.eurofound.europa.eu/publications/blog/job-quality-is-pivotal-in-addressing-todays-workplace-and-societal-challenges
Eurostat. (2023). *Enterprises that provided training to develop/upgrade ICT skills of their personnel by size class of enterprise* Accessed July 30, 2023, from [ISOC_SKE_ITTS__custom_7223438]
Giacosa, E., Culasso, F., & Crocco, E. (2022). Customer agility in the modern automotive sector: how lead management shapes agile digital companies. *Technological Forecasting and Social Change, 175*(2022), 121362. https://doi.org/10.1016/j.techfore.2021.121362
Goos, M., Alan Manning, A., & Salomons, A. (2014). Explaining job polarization: Routine-biased technological change and offshoring. *American Economic Review, 104*, 2509–2526. https://doi.org/10.1257/aer.104.8.2509
Guerin, T. F. (2021). Policies to Minimise Environmental and Rebound Effects from Telework: A Study for Australia. *Environmental Innovation and Societal Transitions, 39*, 18–33.
Hook, A., Court, V., Sovacool, B., & K., and Sorrell, S. (2020). A systematic review of the energy and climate impacts of teleworking. *Environmental Research Letters, 15, no. 9*.
IEA. (2020). *Methane tracker 2020*. IEA. https://www.iea.org/reports/methane-tracker-2020
Ju, J. (2014). The effects of technological change on employment: The role of ICT. *Korea and the World Economy, 15*, 289–307.
Katz, R. L., & Koutroumpis, P. (2016). Assessment of the Economic Impact of Telecommunications in Senegal (2003–2014). In *Columbia Institute for Tele-Information Working Paper*. Columbia Institute for Tele-Information. https://business.columbia.edu/sites/default/files-efs/imce-uploads/CITI/Articles/978-3-319-03617-5_11.pdf
Konle-Seidl, R., & Danesi, S. (2022). *Literature review on digitalisation and changes in the world of work, publication for the Committee on Employment and Social Affairs*, Policy Department

for Economic, Scientific and Quality of Life Policies, European Parliament, https://www.europarl.europa.eu/RegData/etudes/STUD/2022/733986/IPOL_STU(2022)733986_EN.pdf

Kunming, H. W. I. (2019). *Digital industry plays a bigger role in economic growth*. China Daily. Available online: http://www.chinadaily.com.cn/a/201905/23/WS5ce5f791a3104842260bd477.html

Kvochko, E. (2013). *Five ways technology can help the economy*. World Economic Forum. Available online: https://www.weforum.org/agenda/2013/04/five-ways-technology-can-help-the-economy/

Lamarre, E., Smaje, K., & Zemmel, R.W. (2023). *Rewired*, 368 pages, Wiley. https://www.mckinsey.com/featured-insights/mckinsey-on-books/rewired

McCarthy, A., O'Connor, N., Ó'Síocháin, T., & Frost, D. (2021). *Remote Working: Ireland's National Survey–Phase III Report*. NUI Galway Whitaker Institute & Western Development Commission.

Michaels, G., Ashwini, N., & Van Reene, R. (2014). Has ICT polarized skill demand? Evidence from eleven countries over twenty five years. *The Review of Economics and Statistics, 96*, 60–77.

MIT. (2023). *Future of work 2023*, https://www.technologyreview.com/2023/03/14/1069744/the-future-of-work-2023-report/

Moglia, M., Hopkins, J., & Bardoel, A. (2021). Telework, hybrid work and the united nation's sustainable development goals: towards policy coherence. *Sustainability, 13*(16), 1–28.

Nedelkoska, L., & Quintini, G. (2018). *Automation, skills use and training, OECD social, employment and migration Working Papers, No. 202*. OECD Publishing.

Neeley, T., & Leonardi, P. (2022). Developing a digital mindset. *Harvard Business Review, 100*(5–6), 50–55. https://www.hbs.edu/ris/Publication%20Files/Developing%20a%20Digital%20Mindset_81f3f69d-e28d-483e-8d1e-ce0ee159c0bb.pdf

Obringer, R., Rachunok, B., Maia-Silva, D., Arbabzadeh, M., Nateghi, R., & Madani, K. (2021). *The overlooked environmental footprint of increasing internet use*. Resources, Conservation and Recycling 167.

OECD. (2020). *Digital transformation in the age of COVID-19: Building resilience and bridging divides, digital economy outlook 2020 supplement*. OECD. www.oecd.org/digital/digital-economy-outlook-covid.pdf

OECD. (2022). *The unequal impact of COVID-19: A spotlight on frontline workers, migrants and racial/ethnic minorities*. https://read.oecd-ilibrary.org/view/?ref=1133_1133188-lq9ii66g9w&title=The-unequal-impact-of-COVID-19-A-spotlight-on-frontline-workers-migrants-and-racial-ethnic-minorities

Ping, H., & Ying, G. Y. (2018). Comprehensive View On The Effect Of Artificial Intelligence On Employment. *Topics In Education, Culture and Social Development, 1*(1), 32–35. https://doi.org/10.26480/ismiemls.01.2018.32.35

Riley, R., Duffy, A., Foster, S., & Bosredon, M. (2021). Emissions Impact of Home Working in Scotland. *ClimateXchange*. https://doi.org/10.7488/era/1210

Sarabdeen, M., & Hind, A. (2023). Investigating the Impact of Digital Transformation on the Labor Market in the Era of Changing Digital Transformation Dynamics in Saudi Arabia. *Economies, 11*, 12. https://doi.org/10.3390/economies11010012

Sen, V. (2023). *Doing digital, business expert press*. https://learning.oreilly.com/library/view/doing-digital/9781637424100/.

Su, C. W., Xi, Y., Umar, M., & Lobont, O. R. (2022). Does technological innovation bring destruction or creation to the labor market? *Technology in Society, 68*, 101905.

Sostero, M., Milasi, S., Hurley, J., Fernández-Maciás, E., & Bisello, M. (2020). *Teleworkability and the COVID-19 crisis: A new digital divide?* Eurofound and Joint Research Centre.

Tenailleau, Q. M, Tannier, C., Vuidel, G., Tissandier, P., & Bernard, N. (2021). *Assessing the impact of telework enhancing policies for reducing car emissions: Exploring calculation methods for data-missing urban areas–example of a medium-sized European CityUrban climate*, 38.

Vasile, R. (2023). Digital divide and employment: From job disruption to reskilling workers for the future world of work. In L. Chivu, D. L. R. Carmenado, & I., Andrei, J.V. (Eds.), *Crisis after the crisis: Economic development in the new normal . ESPERA 2021. Springer Proceedings in Business and Economics*. Springer. https://doi.org/10.1007/978-3-031-30996-0_22

WEF. (2023). *Future of jobs report* 2023. https://www.weforum.org/reports/the-future-of-jobs-report-2023/

Williamson, H. (2022). *An Evaluation of the Impacts of Remote Working, Department of Enterprise, Trade and Employment.* https://www.enterprise.gov.ie/en/Publications/AnEvaluation-of-the-Impacts-of-Remote-Working.html.

Zemmel, R., Lamarre, E., Smaje, K. (2023). *Author Talks- chat with Rich Tetzeli, Editorial Director, McKinsey Quarterly.* https://www.mckinsey.com/Videos/video?vid=6327832501112&plyrid=IzQolWCsY.

# Chapter 4
# Thinking Beyond COVID-19: What's Next for Romanian SMEs?

**Daniela Antonescu**

**Abstract** In Chap. 4, I looked at the ways on how the pandemic crisis affected Romania's SME sector. I explored the implications of using internet documents and official statistics in research. In addition to posing problems for the medical system, the COVID-19 pandemic has also had an adverse impact on the economic and social systems of the EU member states and the rest of the world. Numerous thousands of lives have been impacted by this urgent global issue which continues to put great strain on financial institutions. Given the circumstances, it is imperative to address economic and social issues as soon as possible and support or push policies that will be advantageous to the several industries affected by the pandemic catastrophe. The SME sector was one of the worst-affected industries when the crisis began to affect Romania, in March 2020. This paper discusses how the COVID-19 crisis affected Romania's SME sector while also seeking to provide advice and recommendations for surviving the crisis and regaining stability following it.'

## Introduction

The COVID-19 pandemic's quick spread created difficulties for the medical, economic and social systems in every member state of the EU, as well as throughout the entire world. Numerous thousands of lives were affected by this disaster, which still has a significant impact on economic systems. In order to manage economic and social problems swiftly, it is also vital to support and promote measures that will help the sectors affected by the pandemic crisis.

The SME sector is one of the most impacted by the pandemic crisis. This sector has a variety of challenges based on the nature of the activities/services it produces, but it is mostly affected by a shortage of financial reserves needed to cover fixed costs (particularly staff salary and office rent).

D. Antonescu (✉)
Institute of National Economy - Romanian Academy, Bucharest, Romania



V. Vasile, E. Bunduchi (eds.), *The Economic and Social Impact of the COVID-19 Pandemic*, Contributions to Economics,
https://doi.org/10.1007/978-3-031-47780-5_4

The goal of this chapter is to document the immediate impact of the sanitary crisis on the entrepreneurial sector in the European Union and in Romania, as well as the steps taken to lessen such effects. The specific indicators of the entrepreneurial sector analysed correspond to the SARS-CoV-2 pandemic (2019–2022) as supplied by the National Trade Register Office. Finally, adequate palliative measures are analysed along with future actions for managing the causes/factors, possible solutions and financing sources for the SME sector on medium and long term.

## Literature Review

After the emergence of the sanitary crisis, a large volume of specialised studies (economic, social, demographic, medical, etc.) intended to approach theoretical-methodological elements that would put their mark on the dynamic and static models characterising the SME sector during crises. Thus, Bloom et al. (2021) analysed data obtained by a survey on a number of 2500 small-sized enterprises from the USA, with the purpose of evaluating the impact of COVID-19 restrictions on small firms. The results showed that, during the pandemic, the volume of direct sales of small companies dropped by about 40%, whereas online sales of large companies fell by less than 10%.

The idea of resilience received a lot of attention in the specialised literature during this period of economic activity slowdown and significant financial losses.

Hence, the specialised literature focused its attention on the concept of resilience, seen as the ability to regain power and vitality during and after the emergence of disasters, failures and traumas and to return to some normality or to an initial state. In the context of leadership, resilience is perceived as an essential characteristic of the leaders that can take responsibility for maintaining the energy of their team members. This is associated frequently with the capacity of a team to re-establish and achieve high levels of energy when faced with conflicts, professional situations and labour relations.

During the crisis, leaders who have resilience capacities are associated with various difficult instances they must face. At the same time, employees' resilience is described as their capacity of adjusting and prospering continuously, even when faced with certain challenges.

The adaptable management of a business in the face of a crisis (be it a pandemic) is seen in a broader framework that includes recuperation, strengthening and assuring persistent and coherent measures. Organisations must be able to function in unpredictable environments in order to survive and to operate successfully in the future. Companies need to build resilience capabilities that would enable them to quickly and adequately respond to unforeseen occurrences that could endanger their continued existence (Lengnick-Hall et al., 2011; Walker et al., 2003).

The concept of resilience is different from other concepts such as flexibility, mobility or power. Some characteristics of these concepts tend to be different, even though others, such as flexibility (the ability to adjust rapidly to environmental changes) and mobility (the ability to rapidly identify opportunities, to change direction and avoid collisions), share several common elements with resilience. While flexibility and mobility are required for approaching challenges and changes on a daily basis, resilience is the action to mitigate (resist) unexpected threats and crises (Lengnick-Hall et al., 2011).

Resilience is also associated with an activity of adjustment that allows organisations to overcome the crisis by a "leap" from a weaker position to a better one, or to a more advanced stage in the framework of a dynamic development process. This quality distinguishes resilience from other concepts. Moreover, resilience is not regarded as a final state, but rather as a progressive and developmental process in a hazardous (or uncertain) environment over a period of time, or over a cycle.

From the perspective of a firm, organisational resilience is defined as its capacity to master and efficiently develop answers for a specific situation and, finally, commit to transformative activities with the purpose of taking advantage from the existing uncertainties and of survival.

According to the studies in the field, resilience research in the field of business and management is fragmented on several flows of activities (Zaman & Vasile, 2014):

1. The activity as reaction of the organisation (firm) to a series of external threats
2. The action regarded as that model of business' adjustability based on the design principles that reduce vulnerabilities on the supply chain

The definitions and particular concepts were developed as a result of the research findings. In this regard, the goal was to create five different types of responses: (1) preventive control (risk management, removing physical barriers, coping operational systems, standardising procedures, etc.); (2) conscious action (detecting threats and providing effective solutions to new or difficult situations); (3) productivity optimisation (improving and extending existing competencies, modernising working methods and utilised technologies, etc. for supplying customers and the market of reference); (4) applying innovation (development, innovating and exploring the unknown, new markets and technologies); and (5) paradoxical thinking (combines the four stages and takes into account the character and needs of the activities specific to the organisation).

In addition, Denyer (2017) identified two key aspects of organisational resilience, namely, the protective aspect and the progressive one, as well as two key features for enhancing resilience, namely, consistency and flexibility. All of these aspects are combined into a holistic system that needs integration, balance and relevance (in accordance with the intended purpose).

Organisational resilience occurs at several levels, being correlated with resources, routine and the process in itself. Organisations have built their resilience by the complex interaction of several factors at individual, group and organisational level.

These differences of attitudes and behaviours cause several disagreements or misunderstandings at firm level, and, consequently, it is not surprising that managers want to achieve or increase resilience.

Regarding organisations, resilience depends on the nature of the firm, on its activity and on the industry in which it operates but also on the uncertainty level and the development rate of the competing industries (rate of technological changes, regulations and market).

When the resilience of a firm is seen from the procedural viewpoint, we identify three stages: (1) anticipation, (2) overcoming and (3) adjustment.

The activities of the past (reactive action), the present (parallel action) and the future (active action) are all mitigated by resilient organisations. The resilience process' ad hoc organisational structure is connected to crisis management strategies.

Adjustment might assist organisations in avoiding the negative effects of unexpected events or mitigating them in two ways: by reflection and learning and by using the opportunities in organisational change. Firms must, on the one hand, be able to analyse a problem and assimilate learned information into their own knowledge base. They should, however, take action based on their knowledge and bring about change.

Firms are better able to adapt to change and maintain coherence when they foster strong and pleasant relationships with their workforce. A stronger sustainability potential helps organisations handle unforeseen problems and meet future difficulties more successfully. Entrepreneurs must also remember to be innovative and competitive within their own company.

Researchers all over the world were actively involved in evaluating the implications of COVID-19 on firms and markets. Some studies laid more emphasis on the importance of medical issues and others on the psychosocial ones and on the need for clearer communication with the public, for information and communication and for enabling teleworking technologies, whereas other researchers modelled development scenarios of countries during and after the pandemic. Thus, the effects of the pandemic on health, public policies and economic strategies were broadly examined. In the case of crises, state intervention in the functioning of firms by suspending some activities or providing some services is not a new phenomenon, but it turned into a global phenomenon in the context of the global pandemic.

The concept of resilience is used in several fields: medicine, psychology, ecology or engineering, being increasingly more used in economy, or at firms' level as well. It is defined as the capacity of recovering rapidly or of adjusting to adverse situations or changes and might be defined as organisational resilience. Some authors consider that it is better to define organisational resilience by using the term "antifragile". Irrespective of the definition, resilience implies the capacity of an organisation to resist shocks by attempting to adjust to changes (Zaman & Vasile, 2014; Zaman at al., 2020).

Increasing economic resilience to shocks became the core of several economic policies within the EU. This fact is due to the negative effects of economic, financial, social and political nature generated by the current sanitary crisis. Next to resilience, we might also identify other core objectives of the EU policy: the fourth industrial revolution, the need to mitigate extreme climate change, etc.

The European Commission defines economic resilience as the capacity to withstand shock and return rapidly to the state of economic growth prior to the crisis or recession.

Firms need to be able to analyse crises and add new knowledge to their existing knowledge bases. On the other hand, they must make changes and act in accordance with their knowledge.

Various types of policies and their combination might be employed for strengthening the concept of economic resilience: preparation, prevention, protection, promotion (change) and transformation policies are stages of these combinations.

There are several approaches to achieving economic resilience, each with a unique impact on the welfare of various societal groups. The level of stability, certainty and balance of job and income prospects has a significant impact on the welfare of workers and residents. Consequently, the policies promoting both economic resilience and employment should be regarded as priority. Last, but not least, those policies should be promoted which support the capacity of the labour market to handle economic shocks with limited losses for the welfare of the workers. A high proportion of precarious (atypical) positions in the overall number of jobs created demonstrates that resilience, the economy and the labour market are not always mutually exclusive. A certain calibre of labour may be seen as a factor in accelerating the development of resilience by lowering its particular vulnerability.

Social sustainability was threatened by increased inequalities in opportunities and neglect of certain economic sectors. A higher inequality means, at the same time, higher vulnerability to shocks and this affects resilience.

Regarding the idea of resilience, the responses of European nations throughout the recent crises varied. While domestic GDP declined severely in almost all member states, the economic and social effects of the crisis varied from one member state to the next. During the sanitary crisis, there were numerous instances of severe job losses and the closure of numerous small businesses.

The current crisis has had an impact on the EU, and many of its member states have temporarily shut down their economies. Even though most nations temporarily relaxed the limitations and reopened their stores and retail operations, the uncertainty surrounding the virus' potential future evolution still dominates discussions and studies.

A significant economic and social variance is possible due to the wide variations in member states' risk levels and current mitigation strategies. It is crucial that European nations and regions develop some level of resilience and resistance in this situation. This fact will result in a quicker recovery and a greater ability to manage upcoming difficulties.

## The General Economic Background in the European Union During the COVID-19 Pandemic

At the EU level, in the first phase, the pandemic crisis had a particular characteristic: a high number of infections concentrated in a relatively small number of regions (World Bank, 2021). Moreover, in the countries where a very high number of SARS-

CoV-2 infections were recorded, such as Spain and Italy, there were regions without a high incidence of the disease. At the same time, at subregional level, the same characteristic could be observed. For instance, three Slovenian municipalities which together represent 1.5% of the population registered 66% from the total COVID-19 cases at national level (European Commission, 2021a, b).

The following characteristics describe the COVID-19 pandemic's subsequent regional evolution:

- The availability of intensive care beds was crucial and maintained the ability to quickly contain emerging infection outbreaks; in relation to a population of 100,000, Portugal had the fewest beds (4.2), and Germany had the most (29.2).
- The number of employees in the health system determined the obvious territorial models; generally, higher proportions of foreign workers in the total workforce are concentrated in northern European nations and in the smaller states.
- The nature of containment measures varied greatly among EU countries, ranging from complete lockdown to freedom of movement.
- The level of digitalisation (IT infrastructure, internet connection, IT specialists).
- The pandemic and the response actions caused a wide range of distinct (positive and/or negative) effects at territorial level. Overall, we may argue that most consequences for the labour market were negative.

As a result, in the early stages of the pandemic, it was necessary to take steps to keep the workforce afloat (e.g. spaces and working conditions for telework and work from home were established). In contrast to the rest, employees with tertiary degrees used the new telework programmes more readily. Increased social and territorial inequality, as well as social exclusion, resulted from this fact, particularly in areas where the labour force has less professional expertise.

As a conclusion, we can argue that the sanitation-pandemic issue has, by a wide margin, favoured digitalisation-based enterprises and areas with adequate infrastructure, particularly knowledge zones. It was discovered that areas with poor broadband infrastructure, limited internet access and less familiarity with "digital life" among the populace, as well as those with higher proportions of elderly people and other areas based on a single industry (such as tourism, etc.), were also affected.

## *Gross Domestic Product*

The comparative analysis of real GDP growth rates is presented below for 2 years, 2019 and 2022, in order to see which of the countries has reached a level of resilience.

1. At the EU-27 level, the real GDP growth rate in 2022 was 3.5%, compared to 1.8% in 2019, which indicates that the growth process is resilient.
2. The following countries have reached the level of real growth rate existing before the start of the pandemic crisis: Germany (+1.8% as compared to 1.2%), Finland (+2.1 as compared to 1.2%), Sweden (+2.6% as compared to 2%), Latvia (+2.8%

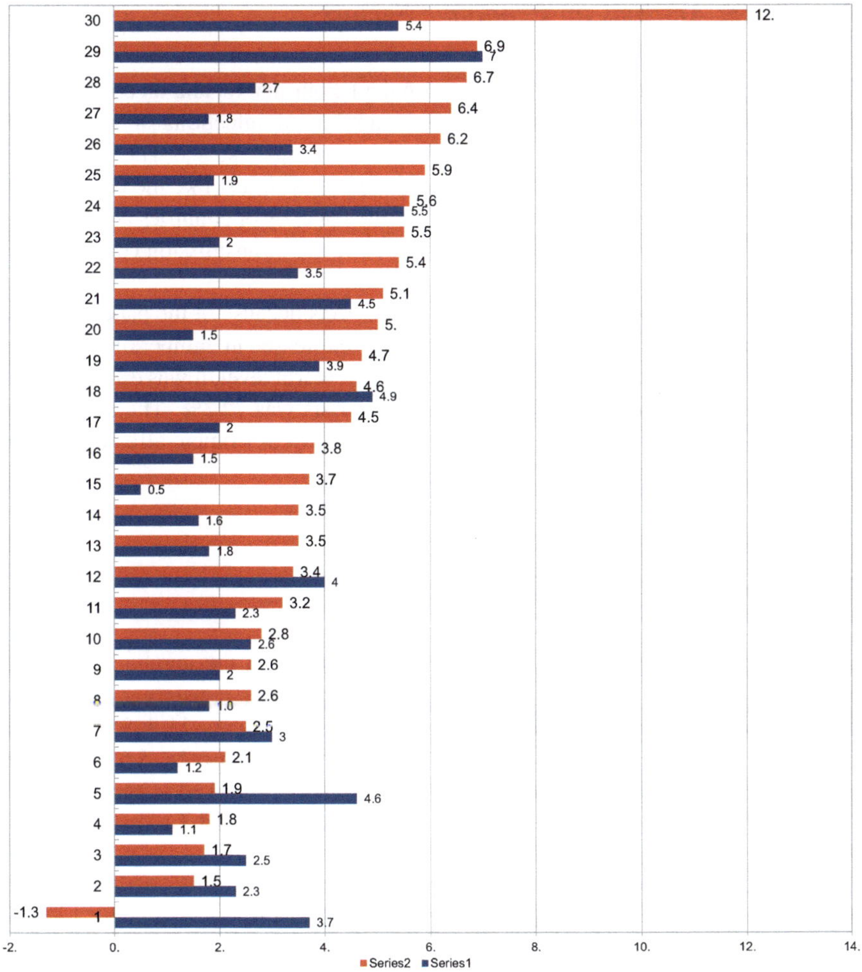


**Fig. 4.1** Gross domestic product in EU-27—real growth rate, 2022 and 2019. Source: Based on Eurostat, 2023

as compared to 2.6%), Belgium (+3.2% as compared to 2.3%), Denmark (3.8% vs. 1.5%), the Netherlands (4.5% vs. 2%), Romania (+4.7% vs. 3.9%), Austria (+5% vs. 1.5%), Poland (+5.1%), Slovenia (+5.4%), Spain (+5.5%), Cyprus (+5.6%), Greece (+5.9%), Croatia (+6.2%), Island (+6.4%), Portugal (+6.7%) and Ireland (+12%).

3. The following countries failed to reach the level of 2019: Estonia (−1.3%), Luxembourg (+1.5% vs. 2.3%), Slovakia (+1.7% vs. 2.5%), Lithuania (+1.9% vs. 4.6%), the Czech Republic (+2.5% vs. 3%) and Bulgaria (+3.4% vs. 4%) (Fig. 4.1).

## Workforce: Analysis on Economic Sectors

The sanitary crisis had a particular impact on the labour market and on employment. Thus, by the beginning of June 2020, the number of infections at world level exceeded 7.3 million cases, affecting almost all member states. The number of cases and the fear of infection spread at community level, just like the containment measures. From facilities to physical distance, the majority of countries adopted total or partial lockdown in taking measures against infection transmission (International Labour Organization, 2020).

While household workers suffered various impacts because of the pandemic, one of its main impacts was the diminished workload (expressed in number of hours) and the loss of jobs. At the same time, in a first stage, at world level, it was estimated that the share of employees affected by the sanitary crisis was 72.3%. The analysis on gender groups indicates that the number of employed women affected by the pandemic increased (from 32% to 49%).

## Agriculture, Forestry and Fishing

In the entire EU, a decrease by −2.07% was registered in the number of worked hours in 2020 as compared to the year 2019. The countries registering the highest decreases for this indicator are Estonia (−12.13%), Lithuania (−11.84%), Slovakia (−5.87%), Romania (−5.69%) and Germany, with a decrease by 5.63%. At the same time, increases were reported for the number of hours worked in agriculture for Austria (+5.84%), Poland (+3.91%), Denmark (+2.77%) and Croatia (+2.31%) (Fig. 4.2).

In 2022, the following countries managed to reach the level recorded before the pandemic (2022 vs. 2019): Poland (+5.25%), Austria (+4.61%), Greece (+11.88%), Croatia (+14.06%) and Luxembourg (0.53) (from 18,356,498 hours worked in 2019 to 17,716,817 hours worked in 2022).

Even at the EU-27 level, resilience in terms of employees (hours worked) was not reached in 2022.

## Industry

In the industry, the situation was somewhat more difficult as compared with the one in agriculture, the decrease in the number of hours being by 6.79% at EU level, the majority of countries registering losses (2020 vs. 2019). The only country recording a relatively low growth was Ireland, with a percentage plus by 0.4%. The most significant decreases were reported in Hungary (−12.1%), Italy (−11%), Slovakia (−10.3%), Spain (−10%), Czech Republic (−8.1%), Portugal (−7.9%) and France

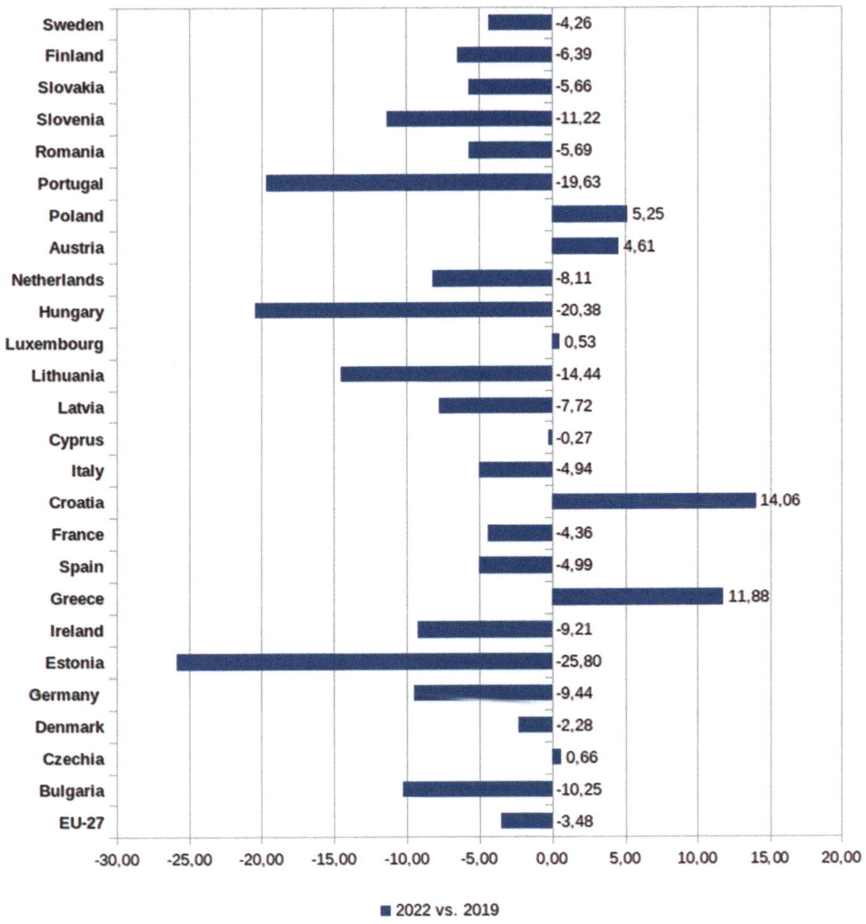


**Fig. 4.2** Employment in agriculture, forestry and fishing (hours worked) (2022 vs. 2019) (%). Source: Based on Eurostat, 2023

(−7.5%). Romania had a decrease by −5%, being placed in the lower part of the ranking.

In the year 2022, there was not a resilience compared to the year 2019 (−2.82), although there are some exceptions (ten countries: Ireland, Estonia, etc.).

The number of hours worked decreased from 57,039,165 hours worked in 2019 to 55,428,004 hours worked in 2022 (Fig. 4.3).

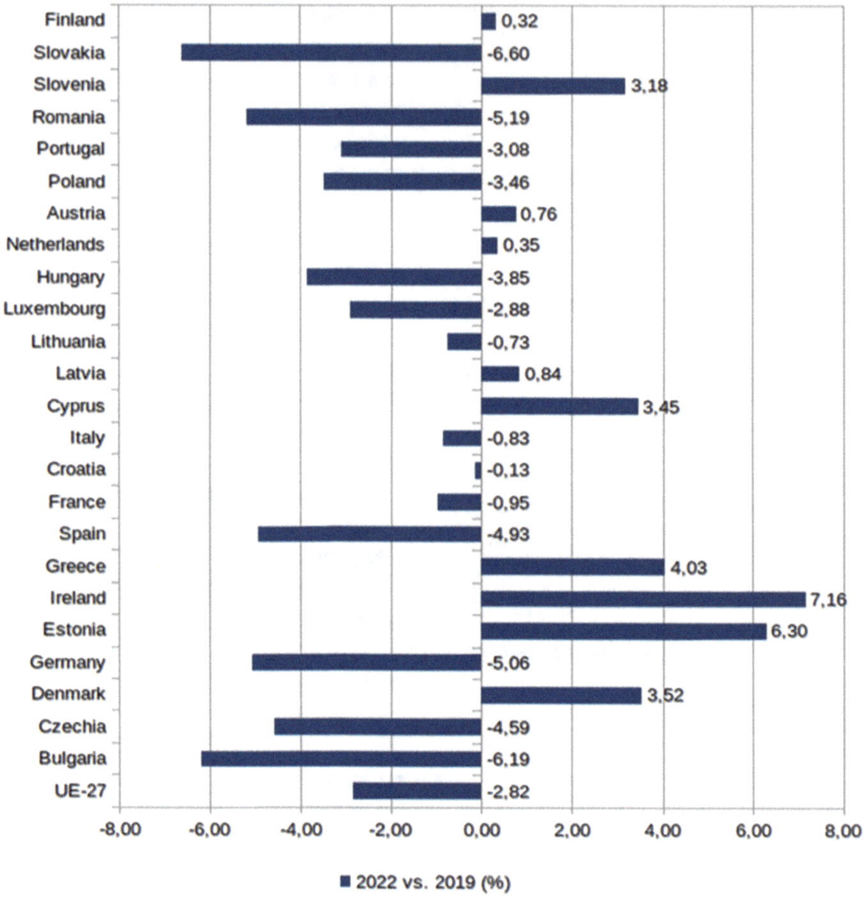


**Fig. 4.3** Employment in industry, in EU-27 (number of hours worked)—2022–2019 (%). Source: Based on Eurostat, 2023

## *Constructions*

The construction sector underwent a decrease by 4.45% for the number of hours worked by employees, lower than in industry but higher than in agriculture. The highest decreases were reported in Spain (−11.88%), Greece (−10.12%), Luxembourg (−9.86%), Italy (−8.95%), Ireland (−8.38%), Iceland (−8.26%) and Slovakia (−7.99%). Even though national economies were closed, increases were reported in the number of hours worked for Romania (+3%), Denmark (+1.72%), Hungary (0.53%) and Croatia (+0.06%) (2020 vs. 2019).

In the year 2022, there is a resilience compared to the year 2019 (+4.9%), although there are some exceptions (Latvia, Spain, Slovakia, Bulgaria) (Fig. 4.4).

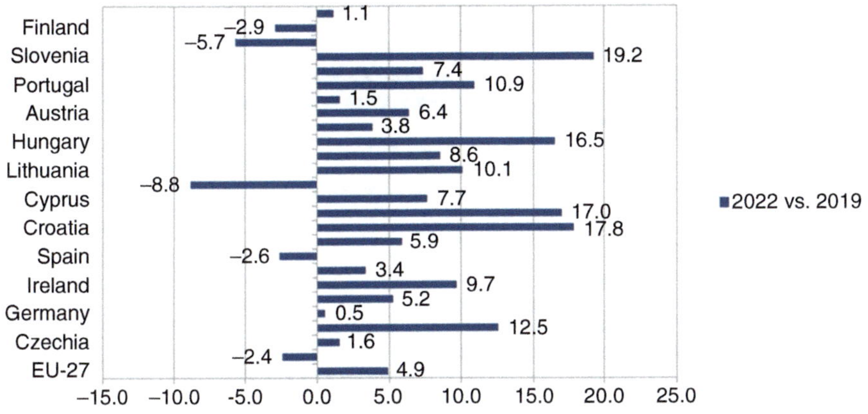


**Fig. 4.4** Evolution in the number of employees in construction sector (number of hours worked)—2022–2019 (%). Source: Based on Eurostat, 2023

The number of hours worked increased from 24,310,324 hours worked in 2019 to 25,503,319 hours worked in 2022.

### Wholesale and Retail Trade, Transports, Accommodation and Catering

The services sector of the economy (trading, transport and HoReCa) was one of the worst hit during the pandemic. Thus, in the year 2020, at EU-27 level this sector recorded the highest decrease, by −11%. This was one of the industries most impacted by the sanitary crisis.

In 2022, most of the member states did not reach the value of the indicator registered in 2019. Romania is in the top of the countries that have recovered, occupying the second place in the EU ranking (Fig. 4.5).

The number of hours worked decreased from 85,231,791 hours worked in 2019 to 86,324,512 hours worked in 2022.

## Regional Impact (EU-27–NUTS 2 Regions)

According to annual statistics, 169 out of 240 NUTS 2 areas' employment rates for workers aged 20 to 64 declined between 2019 and 2020 (by 70.41%). However, 61 regions (25.42%) saw an increase in employment rates, while 10 regions saw no changes at all.

In 2022, there were 193,458 employees in the EU-27, with 3294 more employees than in 2019. Thus, at the EU level, a process of resilience can be observed from the employment perspective, with relatively large differences from one country to

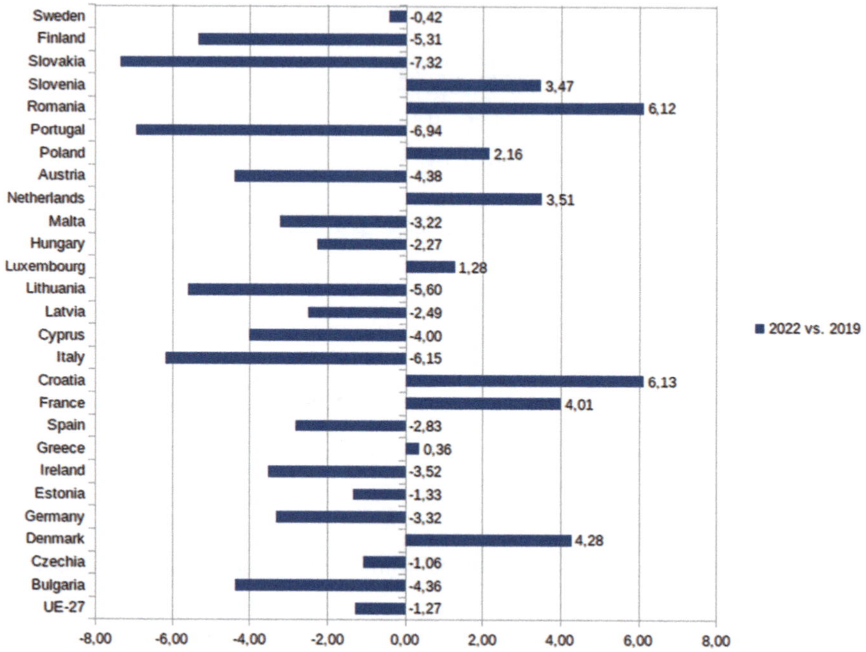


**Fig. 4.5** Wholesale and retail trade, transport, accommodation and catering (%), 2022 vs. 2019. Source: Based on Eurostat, 2023

another. The highest resilience was found in countries such as Malta and Ireland and the lowest in Latvia and the Czech Republic (Fig. 4.6).

In the areas regarded as the primary vacation destinations, the employment rate fell rapidly. Thus, between 2019 and 2020, Notio Aigaio and Kriti (both in Greece) saw employment rates decline by 7.3 p.p. and 5.1 p.p., respectively, while Illes Balears and the Canary Islands (both in Spain) had losses of 6.1 and 4.3 percentage points, respectively.

In response, the majority of Poland's regions saw an increase in employment rates for the regional workforce (2019 vs. 2020), with Lodzkie and Swietokrzyskie in the centre of the country recording gains of more than 2 p.p. The largest gains were seen in Corse and Languedoc- Roussillon (southern France), where the employment rates increased by 4.5 percentage points and 3.1 p.p., respectively.

The comparative analysis of the 2 years, 2019 and 2022, shows that most states managed to achieve resilience, with the exception of Cyprus (Fig. 4.7).

The youth, temporary and seasonal workers, and those employed in the leisure, hotel and transportation industries, were particularly impacted by the crisis.

Compared to 2019, the overall workload (the number of hours worked) declined by −6.76% across the entire EU in the year 2020. With a reduction of only −4.6, Romania had a considerably smaller decline than the rest of the EU.

While 12 regions (5% of the total) had a workload increase, nearly 94% of the regions witnessed a decrease in the effective hours worked.

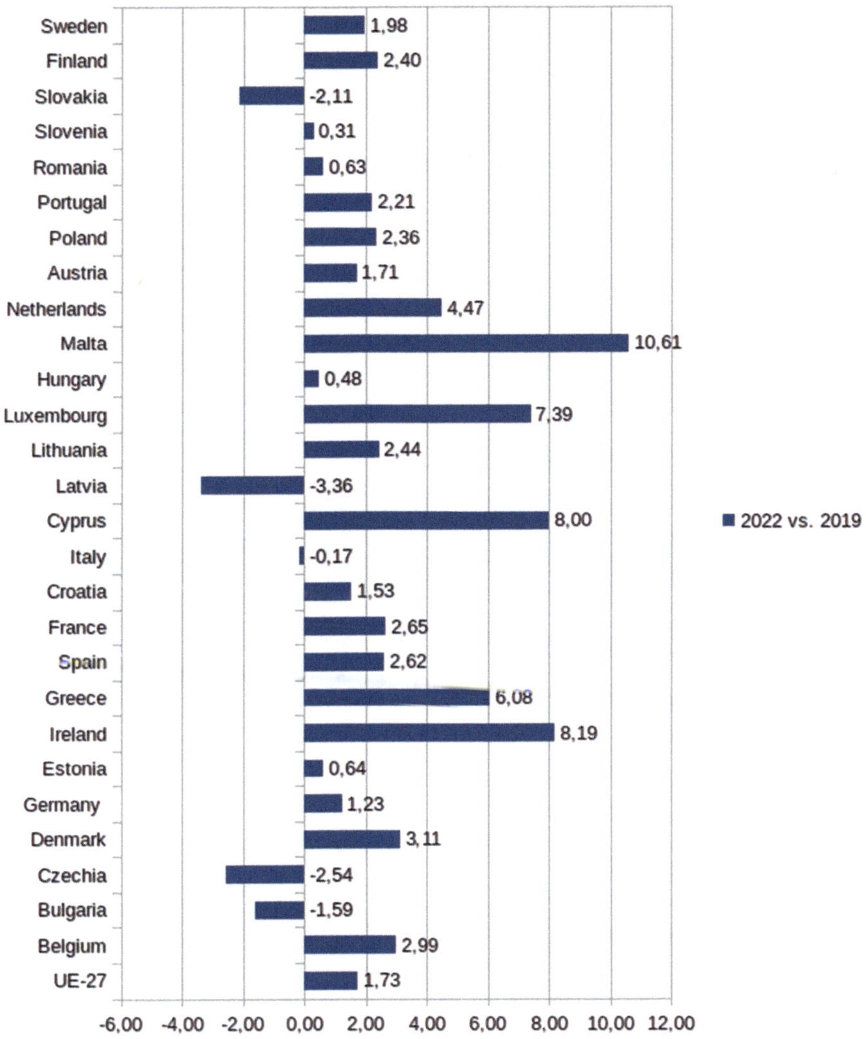


**Fig. 4.6** Resilience of employment at EU-27 level, 2022 vs. 2019 (%). Source: Based on Eurostat, 2023

The southern regions were more affected by the pandemic's effects on the number of hours worked effectively (2020 vs. 2019), while the northern and eastern regions were generally less affected. While the northern and eastern regions were, on average, less affected, the pandemic had a bigger impact on the number of hours worked effectively in the southern regions (2020 vs. 2019).

In 2022, the effects of the crisis seem to have diminished, registering a slight process of resilience (Table 4.1).

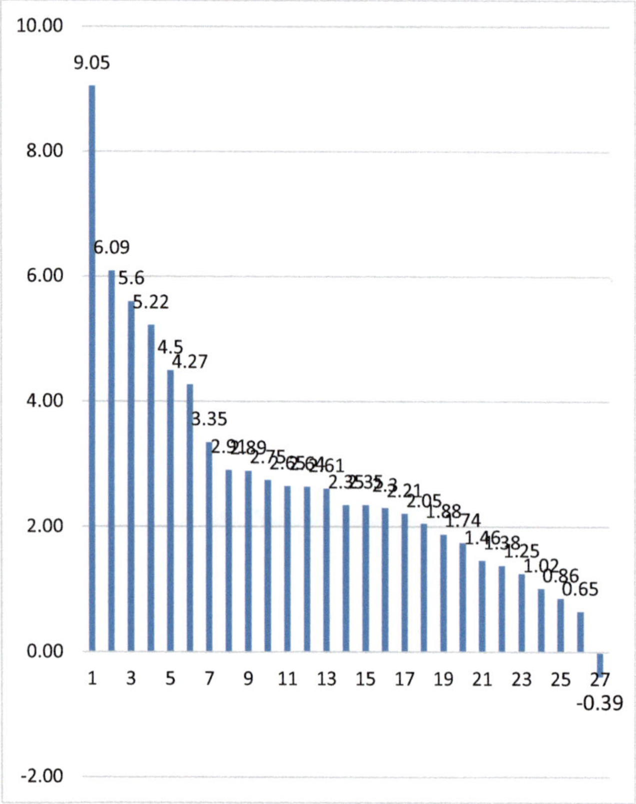


**Fig. 4.7** Employment rate—2022 vs. 2019 (%). Source: Based on Eurostat, 2023

**Table 4.1** Total employment in EU-27 and Romania (thousand hours worked; %)

| | 2019 | 2020 | 2021 | 2022 | 2022 vs. 2019 (%) |
|---|---|---|---|---|---|
| EU-27 | 339,986,506 | 317,006,896 | 333,332,336 | 342,809,833 | 0.83 |
| Romania | 15,596,019 | 14,879,402 | 15,565,947 | 15,615,718 | 0.13 |

Source: Based on Eurostat, 2023

Businesses were forced to adopt temporary layoffs during the pandemic, which affected 2.8% of the workforce (2020). One in ten employed individuals was temporarily laid off in the Canary Islands, Illes Balears (Spain), Notio Aigaio and Ionia Nisia (Greece), with a high loss of 14.5% in the Canary Islands, Canarias. These were supplemented by a few additional tourist hotspots, including Cataluña (Spain), Cyprus, Madeira and the Algarve in Portugal, which were all hit by temporary workforce reductions.

The percentage of layoffs caused by an employee's personal illness or disability remained stable (2.1% in 2019 and 2.2% in 2020). The greatest value for this indicator, 8.0%, was recorded in the Spanish province of Ceuta, while the value was lower in certain other Spanish and French regions.

One of the pandemic's important characteristics was the home-based employee. Thus, compared to 2019, when 1 in 20 employees (or 5.5%) worked from home, this proportion increased to 12.4% in 2020. This indicates a 140% rise above pre-pandemic values. About 9% of employment in Europe was remote as of February 2022. This is down from a peak of around 20% which occurred 4 months earlier, in October 2021, and lasted for about 1.5 years, from October 2020 to March 2022 (European Commission, 2021a, b).

In contrast to the 134 regions with fewer shares than the average, 94 NUTS 2 regions reported a workforce that worked from home at a rate that was higher than the EU average in 2020. A few capital regions had weights that were substantially higher than the mean for the area. As a result, Helsinki, the capital of Finland, had more than 37.0% of all employed people in the EU in 2020 who did their jobs from home.

In this regard, it is also necessary to note the regions of eastern and central Ireland (24.7%), Wien (24.2%), Hovedstaden (23.6%) and Île-de-France (23.4%). The regions of eastern and central Ireland account for 24.7%, Brussels for 25.7% and the Brabant Wallon region (Belgium) for 26.5%. At the same time, it was discovered that at least one-fifth of the workforce worked from home in eight EU regions, most of which were urban. There were fewer people who worked from home in the southernmost parts of the EU.

According to a study on residential areas, the capital regions and urban areas had a larger percentage of employed people who worked from home. In the EU, the average number of people working from home in 2020 was 12%, with higher figures than in the aforementioned regions. The rise in the number of people working from home reflects, at least in part, the economic characteristics of those locations that offer greater employment chances for individuals working in specialised fields like finance, Information and Communication Technology (ICT), education, some government structures, etc. There were fewer opportunities for people in manual occupations like agriculture, manufacturing, distribution, etc. to work from home.

Regarding the evolution of unemployment throughout the pandemic, there were 15 million unemployed people (15–74 years old) at the level of the EU–27 areas, with an unemployment rate of 7.1% in 2020 compared to the average of 6.7% in 2019. This rate had its first spike (after 2013) following 6 years of declining unemployment. The unemployment rate rose to 6.2%, the same level as the EU-27, 2 years following the health crisis. The EU's southernmost and most remote regions had the highest unemployment rates, while a cluster of areas in southern Germany, the Czech Republic, western Poland and Hungary had the lowest rates.

In 2020, 11 of Greece's 13 regions (Peloponnisos and Athens being the exceptions) had unemployment rates of 16%, as did 5 regions in southern Spain, 2 region islands, 4 ultra-peripheral areas of France and 3 regions in southern Italy. The lowest unemployment rates (1.8%, 1.9% and 2.0%, respectively) were recorded in Wielkopolskie, Poland; St. Ednechy, Czech Republic; and Jihozápad, Czech

Republic. In three German states, Niederbayern, Unterfranken and Trier (2019), there was a 2.0% unemployment rate.

One hundred sixty NUTS 2 regions (66.66%) in the EU reported greater unemployment rates and a dramatic decline in the labour market situation, and the most affected regions were those that were recognised as based on tourism. The unemployment rate decreased in some regions in 2019 and 2020, including the Dytiki Makedonia region of Greece (down 4.9 percentage points), three ultra-peripheral regions of France (La Réunion, Guyenne, Guadalupe) and the Ciudad de Melilla region of Spain (down 3.3 percentage points).

Unemployment among youths (15–24 years of age) was on a decreasing trend, from 33.5% in 2019 to 31.5% in 2020 and to 32.7%, and increasing to 34.7% in 2022.

Another statistic is the youth unemployment rate, which follows the same logic as the unemployment rate among people of working age (albeit not all young people are employed). As a result, it's probable that there is some mistake in the youth unemployment rate. For instance, if the unemployment rate for young people is 25%, it does not necessarily follow that 25% of all young people are unemployed. Instead, just 25% of young people in the workforce are unemployed (and 75% are in jobs), while those who are not in the workforce sector may still be engaged in other areas, such as education.

The southern regions of Europe had the highest concentration of youth unemployment rates. Thus, more than 40% of the young workforce (15 to 24 years old) was unemployed in 22 regions (2020). This group contained three ultra-peripheral regions of France, Spain, Italy and Greece. Additionally, five regions were discovered, most of which were peripheral, where the unemployment rate for young people was above 50.0%. These territories were Mayotte (France), Sterea Ellada (Greece), Canarias (Spain) and Ciudades Autónomas de Ceuta (two regions).

## The COVID-19 Crisis' Effects on Romania's Sector

The COVID-19 issue had a big impact on entrepreneurship in March 2020, with drops as high as 74% compared to the previous year. Romania's business environment saw a sharp decline in the number of newly founded firms (National Trade Register Office). Also, a million people officially lost their jobs, 35,000 hospitality enterprises closed their activity, whereas enterprises lost 22.5 billion euros in income.

### *Small- and Medium-Sized Companies with Romanian Capital*

NTRO reports that the overall number of registrations decreased from 42,034 enterprises to 27,129 firms, with a negative dynamic of −35.46% throughout the period from January 1 to March 31, 2020, compared to the same period in 2019. The number of limited liability company registrations decreased by 49.8%, from 8434 in the year 2019 (same period) to 4238 in the year 2020 (in the period of 1 January–31 March 2020). Authorised natural persons registered a negative dynamic by 55.79% (from 2843 to 1257) over the same period. At territorial level, counties were impacted to various shares; the most affected regarding the number of total firm registrations were Dambovita, Ialomita, Salaj, Mehedinti, Gorj and Arges, and at the opposite pole were ranked Bucharest, Ilfov, Covasna, Cluj, Iasi and Botosani (Table 4.2).

Among the fields impacted by the COVID-19 crisis, we can mention agriculture, the extractive industry, entertainment, cultural and recreational activities, the manufacturing industry and private households' activities as household personnel employers (Table 4.3). A particular aspect that might be mentioned in this first stage is represented by the growth by about 33% in the number of registrations for firms in the field of thermal/electric/gas/warm water generation, compared to the same period of the previous year.

In Romania, the number of enterprises that dissolved decreased during the pandemic from 7958 to 7294 (in the period 1 January 2020–31 March 2020, compared to the same period in the previous year), with a negative dynamic of 8%. The most impacted counties, with the highest negative dynamics, were Caras-Severin, Vaslui and Bistrita-Nasaud but also Olt, Calarasi, Valcea, Giurgiu and Dambovita. On sectors of activity, the evolution in the dynamics of firms' dissolution is as follows (NACE – version 2008): electric and thermal power generation and supply, gas, warm water and air conditioning (−66.67%); trade; motor vehicles/motorcycle repairs (−16.37%); administrative services activities and support services activities (−11.85%); and agriculture, forestry and fishing (−14.35%) (Table 4.4).

There were unfavourable trends even when businesses were suspended. As a result, there were 709 suspensions throughout March 2020, as opposed to 1393 in March 2019 (a negative dynamic of 49%). Businesses and organisations in Romania had to pause activities in order to stop operations at this time due to a number of legislative actions taken to combat the effects of the COVID-19 pandemic. Mehedinti, Satu Mare, Calarasi and Vrancea had the worst situations, with scores of −91.67%, −76.47% and 50%, respectively. At the level of the Bucharest municipality, there were fewer suspensions: from 146 in March 2019 to 76 in March 2020 (a drop of 47.95%). The three industries with the most suspended companies are trade (973 companies, or 29% of the total), professional activities (287 companies, or 8.6% of the total) and manufacturing (247 companies, or 7.4% of the total).

When comparing March 2020 to March 2019, there was a dynamic in the process of writing off companies of about +89.67% (from 3739 to 36,195 companies). However, it should be noted that the right to object to a company's dissolution was suspended as a result of the emergency declaration, and because the write-off state is a stage after dissolution, the procedures were suspended in practice until the state of emergency was lifted. As a result, since the dissolution procedure cannot be completed, neither can the write-off operation.

**Table 4.2** The variations in the number of registrations completed between January 1 and March 31, 2020, at counties level (%)

| −50% and −60% | −49% and −45% | -44% and −40% | −39% and −35% | -34% and −30% | −29% and −20% | −18% | Under −3% |
|---|---|---|---|---|---|---|---|
| Dambovita | Prahova | Hunedoara | Vaslui | Constanta | Botosani | Covasna | Ilfov |
| Ialomita | Suceava | Galati | Satu Mare | Neamt | Iasi | | Bucharest |
| Salaj | Vrancea | Bihor | Mures | Braila | Cluj | | |
| Mehedinti | Alba | Bistrita-Nasaud | Arad | | | | |
| Gorj | Olt | Buzau | Tulcea | | | | |
| Arges | Teleorman | Bacau | Sibiu | | | | |
| | Caras-Severin | Dolj | Giurgiu | | | | |
| | Maramures | Brasov | | | | | |
| | | Valcea | | | | | |
| | | Harghita | | | | | |
| | | Timis | | | | | |
| | | Calarasi | | | | | |

Source: Based on National Institute of Statistics, 2023; National Trade Register Office, 2023

**Table 4.3** Evolutions of registrations made over the period 1 January 2020–31 March 2020 compared with the same period of the previous year (%)

| Fields | (%) |
|---|---|
| Production, supply of electricity, heat, gas, hot water and air conditioning | +33% |
| Transport and storage | −4% |
| Real estate transactions | −9% |
| Information and communications; constructions; financial intermediation and insurance | −23% -- 25% |
| Education | −27% |
| Other services activities; public administration and defence; social security in the public system | −33% |
| Wholesale and retail trade; repair of motor vehicles and motorcycles | −34% |
| Administrative and support services activities; professional, scientific and technical activities | −35% |
| Hotels and restaurants; health and social work | −42% |
| Water distribution; sanitation, waste management, decontamination activities | −45% |
| Agriculture, forestry and fishing; extractive industry | −48% |
| Entertainment, cultural and recreational activities | −57% |
| Manufacturing industry | −64% |
| Activities of private houses that involve hiring domestic help; activities of private households that involve creating commodities and services for their own purposes | −100% |

Source: Based on National Trade Register Office, 2023

In 2020, many firms accumulated debts and rolled over their debts. Many of them attempted to reinvent themselves, but the crisis also impacted fields like trade, HoReCa and the events industry. The last data (2021) show that SMEs will have to find solutions for paying outstanding debts, postponed from the past year. In Romania, the estimated number of firms in the insolvency risk area was 60,000.

Over the period 1 January 2021–31 October 2021, a number of 4,777 firms went into insolvency, most from the manufacturing industry, 7.7% more than for the same period of 2020. In the month of October, 550 firms went into insolvency (Table 4.5).

In 2021, firms aiming to overcome the crisis should have been prepared to anticipate changes and invest in solutions that would have helped them in better managing risks.

In 2021, the financial effects of the sanitary crisis began to take shape, effects that were postponed from the year 2020 due to fiscal facilities granted, and to the fact that the obligation of the debtors to open the insolvency procedure was suspended, even though they were in such a situation.

Insolvency and restructuring prove to be the most efficient methods for the recovery of companies in difficulty. There are solutions aiding to protect companies in times of crisis, irrespective of the crisis' nature.

In 2020, on average seven companies with impact on a monthly basis (the ones with assets of over 1 mill. euros) went into insolvency and restructuring, a bit over half of the number registered for the previous year, 2019.

**Table 4.4** Dissolutions from 1 January 2020 to 31 March 2020, relative to the same time in the previous year (%)

| Between −50 and − 55% | Between −49 and −40% | Between −39 and −30% | Between −21 and −11% | Between −9 and −5% | Between −4 and 0% | Between +3 and +8% | Over +20% |
|---|---|---|---|---|---|---|---|
| Caras-Severin | Olt | Teleorman | Tulcea | Gorj | Braila | Constanta | Hunedoara |
| Vaslui | Calarasi | Harghita | Botosani | Vrancea | Ilfov | Galati | Covasna (+46%) |
| Bistrita-Nasaud | Valcea | Arad | Ialomita | Alba | Bacau | Sibiu | Brasov (+72%) |
| | Giurgiu | Bihor | Dolj | Cluj | Mehedinti | Prahova | |
| | Dambovita | | Maramures | Bucharest | Mures | Arges | |
| | | | Salaj | Buzau | | Neamt | |
| | | | | Iasi | | Suceava | |
| | | | | Timis | | Satu Mare | |

Source: Based on National Trade Register Office, 2023

**Table 4.5** Professionals gone into insolvency over 1 January 2021–31 October 2021 (no., %)

| | No. of professionals gone into insolvency over the period 1 January–31 October 2021 | No. of professionals gone into insolvency over the period 1 January–31 October 2020 | (%) 2021 vs. 2020 | No. of professionals gone into insolvency over the period 1 October 2021–31 October 2021 |
|---|---|---|---|---|
| Administrative services activities and support services activities | 224 | 179 | 25.14% | 28 |
| Entertainment, cultural and recreational activities | 63 | 54 | 16.67% | 5 |
| Professional, scientific and technical activities | 222 | 239 | −7.1% | 24 |
| Public administration and defence; public system social insurances | 1 | 2 | −50.0% | |
| Agriculture, forestry and fishing | 207 | 178 | 16.29% | 21 |
| Other services activities | 87 | 74 | 17.57% | 8 |
| Wholesale and retail trade; motor vehicles and motorcycle repair | 1423 | 1356 | 4.94% | 163 |
| Constructions | 816 | 734 | 11.17% | 97 |
| Water distribution, sanitation, waste management, decontamination activities | 50 | 46 | 8.70% | 3 |
| Hotels and restaurants | 404 | 348 | 16.09% | 42 |
| Extractive industry | 17 | 20 | −15.00% | 4 |
| Manufacturing industry | 605 | 550 | 10.00% | 72 |
| Information and communications | 100 | 93 | 7.53% | 9 |
| Financial intermediation and insurances | 17 | 23 | −26.09% | 1 |
| Education | 25 | 16 | 56.25% | 5 |
| Electric and thermal energy | 15 | 25 | −40.00% | 2 |

(continued)

**Table 4.5** (continued)

| | No. of professionals gone into insolvency over the period 1 January–31 October 2021 | No. of professionals gone into insolvency over the period 1 January–31 October 2020 | (%) 2021 vs. 2020 | No. of professionals gone into insolvency over the period 1 October 2021–31 October 2021 |
|---|---|---|---|---|
| generation and supply, gas, warm water and air conditioning | | | | |
| Health and social assistance | 17 | 22 | −22.73% | 1 |
| Transport and warehousing | 423 | 412 | 2.67% | 59 |
| Real estate transactions | 61 | 64 | −4.69% | 6 |
| Total | 4777 | 4435 | 7.71% | 550 |

Source: Based on National Institute of Statistics, 2023

The sectors of activity with most companies of impact gone into insolvency and restructuring are industry (26%), trade (14%), energy (10%) and agriculture (10%).

According to an analysis on 100 companies in insolvency, about 57% of the companies in difficulty have postponed accessing this procedure for 3 years on average. This aspect occurs in the context in which 73% of the entrepreneurs say that they became better managers as result of the experience from the period of recovery by insolvency, which includes an important component of restructuring and negotiation.

In general, in Romania, companies postpone going into insolvency because of the fear of failure, the difficulty to begin a new business for 3 to 4 years, so that obviously the phenomenon diminishes the rate of debts' collection and increases the costs of recuperating them.

Reorganisations evolved from about 1% in the number of insolvencies in 2008 to about 6%. In the EU, 600 firms go into bankruptcy on a daily basis, and 200,000 firms exit the economy yearly (1.7 mill. lost jobs), while 3 million new jobs could be created by providing a second chance.

The Directive regarding restructuring and insolvency is applied in the EU, in versions adapted to the sociocultural and economic context specific to each member state. The Netherlands is the first state of the EU that enforced this Directive by introducing for the first time in the legal history of the country a restructuring mechanism similar to the ones from the UK and the USA.

Under the COVID-19 pandemic, a number of analyses and ad hoc statistical studies were carried out, specifically focusing on managers of businesses in the manufacturing, construction, trade and services industries regarding their perception of the evolution of perspectives in the activity of the business they manage.[1] The main perception at this first stage was that in April 2020, almost 21.2% of the economic agents could not predict how their enterprises would develop.

## *Small- and Medium-Sized Companies with Foreign Capital*

Foreign direct investments are correlated directly with a series of positive and favourable effects for the countries where they set up their activity. Thus, the foreign investment is regarded as an essential engine of the strategy for economic development and modernisation, of increasing incomes and jobs.

Foreign direct investments are preferable to other sources of capital, as they answer to both the specific interest of the investor and of the state that pursues economic growth. Of importance are also the indirect effects that are shown by the FDIs (foreign direct investments) in the framework of a local economy, for instance, driving the formation of human capital, technological externalities and access to external markets.

In the year 2021 (October), 235,702 firms with foreign capital were registered on Romanian territory, 2.05% more than in 2020 (a number of 4726 additional firms). The value of subscribed capital was 49,459,377.8 euros, a decrease by 2.3% compared to the year 2020 (Table 4.6).

Most FDIs are from Italy (2021), about 21.35%, followed by those from Germany (10.18%), Turkey (7.07%) and Hungary (6%).

Regarding the structure of fields, most FDIs are found in professional, administrative, scientific and technical activities (26.33%), followed by those in trade (25.27%), constructions (13.7%) and the extractive and manufacturing industry (6.58%).

Following the subscribed share capital, the wholesale and retail trade, automobile and motorcycle repair sectors (47.89%), the extractive and manufacturing industries (21.45%) and financial intermediation (16.47%) are where the SMEs are found.

The evaluation according to the ranking on countries of residence of the investors in companies with foreign participation to the shared capital, on 31 October 2021, shows that from the numerical viewpoint, most companies originate from Italy (21.35%), followed by those from Germany (10%), Turkey (7%) and Hungary (6%).

Regarding subscribed capital (thousands of euros), the countries that invested most in Romania are the Netherlands (20%), Germany (11%) and Austria (10%).

With respect to the value of the capital subscribed by the foreign companies, a 0.1% decrease was recorded, while numerically a 1.6% increase was registered.

[1] NIS Survey 2020

**Table 4.6** Number of companies with foreign participation to capital and subscribed shared capital – balance (no., %)

| Balance on | Companies | | Value of subscribed share capital | | | | | |
|---|---|---|---|---|---|---|---|---|
| | | | Total | | Total | | Total expressed in hard currency equivalent | |
| | No. | % | k RON | % | k USD | % | k EUR | % |
| 31 October 2021 | 235,702 | 102.0 | 183,007,025 | 99.6 | 64,500,240 | 99.7 | 49,459,377.8 | 99.7 |
| 31 December 2020 | 230,976 | 100.0 | 183,756,816 | 100.0 | 64,682,942 | 100.0 | 49,611,302.7 | 100.00 |

Source: Based on National Trade Register Office, 2023

## *Restrictions and Opportunities for SMEs*

Prior to relaunching consumption in order to overcome this crisis, production must be restarted to ensure opportunities in the current situation. In reality, the programme SME Invest, which seeks to revive industry with those who choose to participate and who have the necessary skills, is founded on this component. This programme fosters public-private cooperation that ought to have positive effects on protection while simultaneously highlighting home-grown goods.

The financial system is not experiencing a capital shortage. Entrepreneurs must therefore make a variety of investment plans. Even in some industries that have been significantly damaged by the crisis (restaurants due to the lockdown, etc.), there are entrepreneurs looking for innovative methods to react. The state should prioritise systemic investments, support-type investments and value chain support to increase consumption.

Another option is to advertise new products and find creative solutions that might be used to treat COVID-19 patients directly or indirectly, in addition to ensuring the needs of hospitals and healthcare facilities based on creative solutions that may be put forth by some businesses, particularly SMEs, in the fields of medical devices, biotechnology, drugs, etc.

The IT sector is experiencing an enormous momentum because it has the chance to create goods and services that make people's lives easier, providing the necessary motivation for the technological revolution to advance to the next stage of development.

The telecoms sector is also one of the biggest winners because there is now a greater than ever demand from the public for high-speed internet access.

Large cities with little traffic also contribute to a greater understanding of the advantages of clean air. The quality of air and water, as well as the production of food, beverages, personal care products and cosmetics, among other things, will all benefit from an increase in concern for sustainability and clean business practices over the medium term.

The race to develop a treatment for the coronavirus coincided with pharmaceutical companies engaged in research and development receiving significant capital infusions or increases in the value of their stock on the stock exchange, while generic drug manufacturers saw very strong sales.

For technological companies that provide online services, there is long-term potential. Large firms' perspectives on work-from-home policies will shift as a result of this crisis. The same might be said for consumer mindsets, who will access more services online, shop online and have packages delivered, among other things. After this crucial period, or possibly sooner, it seems extremely likely that we will observe the first steady increases in this regard. In addition to the many constraints, the COVID-19 economic phenomenon also created a number of opportunities for numerous enterprises.

## *Evolutions and Forecasts*

Forecasting is a complex and multilateral estimation activity based on several alternatives or instances regarding the past evolution and future perspectives, while making use of the possibilities provided by economic research, by the methods and techniques with the aid of which economic forecasts might be realised.

In this chapter we used the method of extrapolation based on the FORECAST functions of Excel, under the condition that all other economic conditions remain constant (inflation, exchange rate, etc.).

The indicators for which forecasts were made are the ones specific to the SME sector.

The forecasts were made for a confidence interval with a probability of 95% based on the statistical data series in the Tempo-online database for the period 2000–2019 (or 2020). The results are presented as graphics.

The forecasts presented hereunder consider the trends that, according to our assumptions, will be taken by the SME sector.

Taking into account the evolution of the sector as of 2000, and up to 2019 (the last year for which there are official statistics), we identified three possible variants: optimist, pessimist and average. These are presented under the form of graphics in the following (Fig. 4.8):

## Proposed Measure for Recovery and Resilience

The first measures as recommendations for supporting SMEs were already taken at the European Union level by March 2020. Among these, we mention the following:

- In order to take practical actions, it was necessary to identify the most risky and vulnerable industries and take the additional support, in parallel with monitoring the effects on less directly impacted industries (the first most impacted industries were healthcare, transportation, hospitality, retail trade for non-food goods, etc.).
- It was suggested that certain programmes be used to support SMEs and maintain employment through statutory wage plans. The avoidance of layoffs of workers on permanent contracts is deemed crucial.
- It was proposed that payments from the public sector to private contractors and suppliers be made more swiftly, especially when they are from the SME sector, in addition to postponing taxes on properties in the industry's most risk-prone areas. However, this recommendation may be extremely burdensome for those in the retail and HoReCa industries. Local governments benefit from fiscal incomes, so the national governments are responsible for paying for issued losses. For this purpose, plans are put out for delaying rent and mortgage payments.
- The SME sector is supported through ongoing payments more than through loans or loan guarantees. When SMEs resume their previous activities, they can find themselves in a situation where they are unable to pay off new loans.

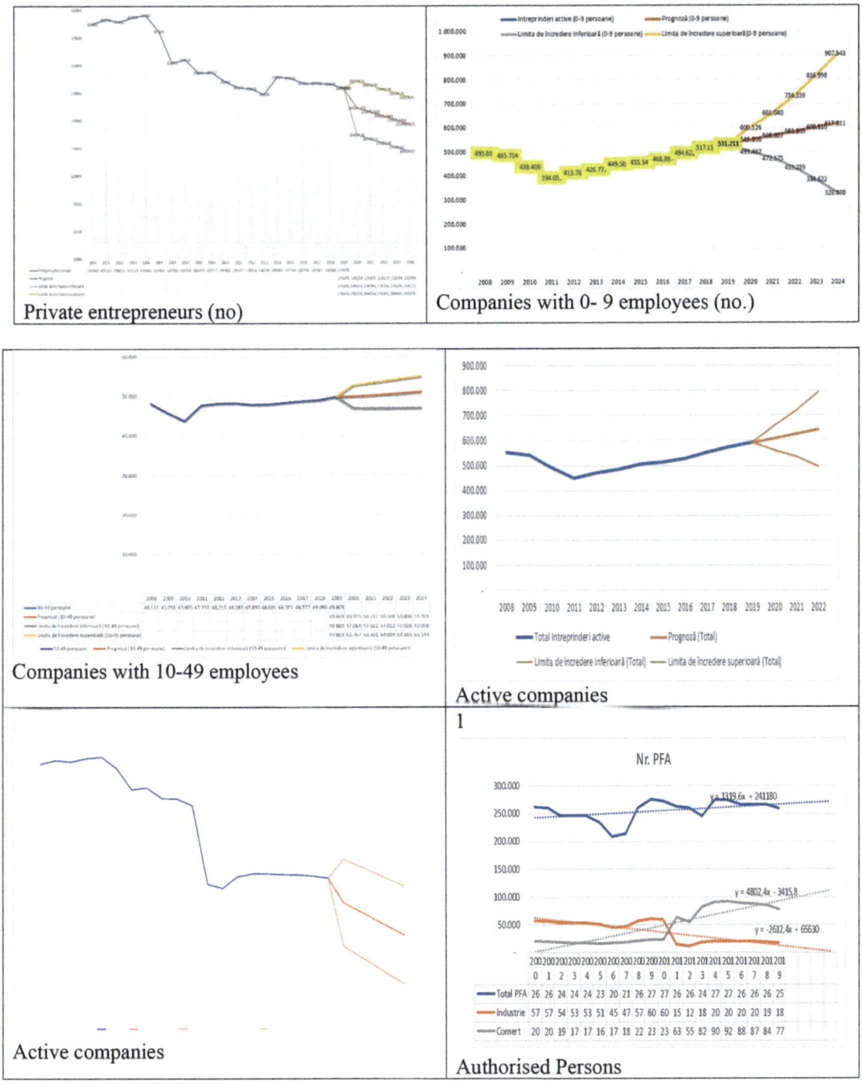


**Fig. 4.8** SME forecasting (private entrepreneurs, companies, authorised persons). Source: Author's computations

- To lessen the effects of COVID-19, the establishment of a European Investment Fund was suggested, with a focus on supporting SMEs.
- The inversion of the import borders will be pursued, export prohibitions and export restrictions to prevent harm to the single market's supply chain.
- Extending the period and deadlines for financial reports and simplifying (temporary) requirements in the legislation specifically devoted to SMEs.
- Postponement of payments and financial obligations such as social insurance contributions and payments, as well as extending the time needed to file financial

statements, eliminating some administrative penalties for late filing or payment in the event that the issue was brought on by real financial difficulties brought on by COVID-19.

- Last but not least, it is advised that best practices be exchanged while also keeping an eye on the actions taken in other European nations.

The following are the specific fields that were targeted by the EU's proposed packages of measures:

The national policies for the medical equipment and pharmaceutical industries must foster European solidarity and collaboration. The Commission works to make sure there is a sufficient supply of medications and safety gear on the market in the community.

The tourism industry is under unprecedented pressure in the EU and its member states. It is dealing with a significant drop in foreign arrivals. The slowdown in domestic travel is also affecting the tourism industry, mostly as a result of citizens' rising unwillingness to travel and the preventative safety measures. SMEs in the sector are particularly impacted by this broad decline in travel for leisure or commercial objectives. By the end of February, travel disruptions on domestic soil and within the EU (representing 87% of all tourist arrivals) had worsened the situation.

Because European supply networks are so intertwined, the transportation industry is one of the most severely impacted by the pandemic. These connections are maintained through a wide network of goods delivery services. Significant economic harm resulted from interruptions in these goods flows. The pandemic also had a significant impact on the aviation sector at the same time. The Commission has put out specific legislation that would temporarily exclude air companies from the requirement to employ hourly slots in accordance with legislation.

Furthermore, the adoption of entrance prohibitions on land borders and the restrictions placed on drivers of moving vehicles passing through member states had a significant negative impact on land-based supply chains. All items are impacted by this fact, but perishables and vital supply materials are particularly affected, and as SMEs make up the large majority of businesses in this industry, the repercussions are both rapid and severe.

In order to provide state aid, the EU and European Investment Bank must mobilise their budgets to help the SME sector while simultaneously ensuring the banking industry's liquidity and greater flexibility within the European budgetary framework. We include the following as some of the methods to provide liquidity to SMEs impacted by the pandemic crisis (Eurofound, 2020):

1. The European Fund for Strategic Investment (EFSI) will receive one billion euros from the European Investment Fund (EIF) to guarantee the EU budget. At least 10,000 SMEs will benefit from this initiative.
2. Postponement the credits (delayed loan repayments) for SME victims of the crisis.
3. To combat issues brought over by COVID-19, the European Structural Investment Fund (ESIF) has provided 37 billion euros. The initiative presumptively waives the requirement to request the ESIF prefinancing reimbursement for this

year. It comes from the EU budget in the amount of 7.9 billion euros, which the member states can use to add to the 29 billion euros already designated for structural financing. The investment for 2020 will essentially increase as a result.

4. A proposal was made to include the consequences of the public health issue in the European Union Solidarity Fund's application area at the local level. For the year 2020, the health sector had access to up to 800 million euros.
5. The member states' national budgets will serve as the primary source of the fiscal response. The EU's rules on state aid give member states the freedom to act quickly and effectively to help their people and businesses, especially SMEs, who are struggling financially as a result of the pandemic.
6. In the event of negative growth or significant decreases in activity, the fiscal efforts necessary from MS are adjusted. The activation of the general crisis clause by European institutions in order to receive more widespread fiscal policy help is suggested to the Council.
7. In order to prevent long-term consequences, the promotion of policies that safeguard employees from losing their jobs and income is advisable. Special attention is given to short-term employment programmes, or programmes for professional development and reskilling, which have previously demonstrated their effectiveness.
8. In accordance with the terms of the current and future regulations, it may also be possible to mobilise the European Globalization Fund (EGF) to assist workers who have been laid off and workers who are starting their own independent businesses. In 2020, up to 179 million euros were made available for battling the coronavirus-caused crises' impacts. To support the SME sector, which was severely impacted by the sanitary crisis, Romania adopted and put into practice several of these proposals.

## Sources and Tools for SME Support

To strengthen the SME sector and stop its total collapse due to the sanitary crisis, a number of programmes were advocated at the national level. Payment delays, non-reimbursable financial state help, favourable bank loans and national and European programs are a few of these attempts.

Therefore, delaying utility payments and forgoing rent payments for properties serving as headquarters were the first steps taken to support SMEs during the medical crisis.

The notary public, attorneys, judicial executors and other professions that provide services of public interest were likewise covered by these regulations. For other contracts SMEs had in development, force majeure may only be invoked against them after the parties have made an effort to communicate with one another, as evidenced by writs by any means, including electronic ones, to renegotiate the contract and adjust its clauses in light of the exceptional circumstances brought on by the emergency state. The declaration of the lone beneficiary was extended by

3 months to complete this payment delay (as it had been suspended throughout the emergency state's duration).

The SME Invest Romania programme was a tool that was especially helpful for businesses. Through this programme, the state provided guarantees for beneficiaries listed on the website for the following credit types: one or more working capital credit lines or loans, each with a weighted average value of up to 80% of the financing value (not covering interest, fees and bank charges).

The Military Ordinance No. 3 from 24 March 2020 regarding the measures to prevent the spread of COVID-19 (the Official Bulletin No. 242 from 24 March 2020) was put into effect, and the Military Ordinance No. 3's implementation period began on that date. This period of time runs through 31 March 2021.

A normative act with the force of law is used each year to approve interest subsidisation for the first year and for the following 2 years only if the economic growth predicted by the National Commission for Strategy and Forecast is below the rate observed in the year 2020.

For loans or lines of credit used for investments, the maximum term is 120 months, while for working capital, the maximum term is 36 months. After the last year of extension, the working capital credits or lines of credit may be extended for a total of 36 months, with repayment terms determined by the enforcement of the emergency ordinance's procedural standards.

In addition to the credits mentioned above, the state budget included engagement credits totalling one billion lei for the Program Start-Up Nation 1 in 2020. These credits could support about 5000 businesses, which are two times less than the programme's previous goal of supporting 10,000 companies.

There are a series of programmes which are financed by the state budget targeting the sectors that were affected strongly by the crisis. One of the fields is industry, and the instrument called Programme of Micro-industrialisation 2020 has an allocation of 65 million lei in engagement credits and 65 million lei in budgetary credits. This programme operated also in the year 2018, when 247 firms were financed and obtained non-reimbursable funds of up to 450,000 lei each. The majority of the companies asked for the maximum sum of 450,000 lei. The government released the Micro-industrialization Program's organisational structure in 2019 but no longer held opening sessions. The micro-industrialisation initiative is run by the Ministry of Economy.

Next to industry, the trade sector was impacted considerably by the sanitary crisis. This sector was supported by the Programme Trade 2020 aimed at developing e-commerce services, with a financial allocation by 40 mill. lei in engagement credits and 40 mill. lei in budgetary credits. The programme Internationalisation 2020, which had a budget of 10 mill. lei in engagement credits and 10 mill. lei in budgetary credits, supported businesses operating in industries (food industry, furniture manufacturing, etc.).

Prior to this initiative, private Romanian businesses could get up to 25,000 lei in non-reimbursable state funding apiece to attend international trade shows and fairs. For instance, the Ministry of Economy organised the selection of such businesses in

2018 and offered precedence to companies that opted to focus on markets outside the European Union.

The programme Women Entrepreneurs 2020 was one unique tool used to encourage female entrepreneurs in the small- and medium-sized business sector. In previous iterations, this initiative allowed 80 Romanian businesswomen to enrol in entrepreneurial training programs both domestically and abroad.

For a limited time, wage subsidies of up to 50% of the salary costs from public funds were offered for SME sector employees who were experiencing technical unemployment. The subsidy may be used to offset social contributions, wage taxes, and help from the SURE fund.[2]

Next to the national financing sources, we might also mention allocations from European funds[3] which have the ceiling of 1 billion euros and that are distributed as follows: 300 million euros for grants, 500 million euros for vouchers and 200 million euros in investments for medical and protection equipment, or equipment regarding specific interventions in the sanitary crisis, etc.

The community funds allocated by ROP Priority Axis 2.2, which are specifically targeted at microenterprises, are one such category. Under certain conditions, these businesses are eligible to receive European funds worth between 200,000 and 1 million euros (projects may be submitted using the electronic app MySMIS). Small textile manufacturers, computer repair shops, software editing companies, video production companies, etc. can all apply for European grants and use the money to invest in developing the infrastructure for online commerce.

With the exception of Bucharest-Ilfov, which was ineligible, the 68 million euro budget given to this axis is intended for the developing regions where money from the 2016 tender is still waiting to be spent. The following regions are eligible for the project call:

- North-east region with a total budget of 31.4 million euros
- West region with a total budget of 36.6 million euros

For the actual programming period, SMEs have available regional and sectoral operational programmes: eight regional operational programmes and Smart Growth and Digitalisation Programme.

Grants in set amounts based on turnover that are intended to provide working capital for the firms' ongoing operations are one of these supports. The 10% share between the grant's worth and the turnover's value is taken into consideration while allocating these grants. The targeted operations (stocks of raw materials, essential materials, ware stocks, etc.) have an indirect effect on boosting domestic demand. In addition to this funding, the Regional Operational Programme (ROP), the SME

[2]SURE is a 100 billion euro solidarity tool that will support businesses so they can survive and assist workers in maintaining their salaries. Additionally, farmers, fishermen and the most vulnerable people will benefit from this support.

[3]For some financings, the project applications are already open, and for others the sessions were budgeted to prepare the launching of new calls.

Initiative's axis provided loans with European guarantees for SMEs. The ROP financing line has available a total of 250 million euros.

Last but not least, the European Union has been supporting Romanian investment funds for risk capital financing over the past few years. These funds provide funding ranging from 25,000 euros to 5 million euros through companies (GapMinder, Morphosis Capital, etc.).

According to all the measures and funding options discussed above, it is predicted that the set-amount grants and consumption vouchers will be the easiest to implement, while the investments will be the most challenging. Due to the lack of project analysis expertise and the volume of applications, as well as from the perspectives of financial viability, market success and outlooks for relaunch and recovery, among other factors, the evaluation of the projects submitted by SMEs for consideration by management authorities or by other financiers will be a relatively challenging process.

## Conclusions

The end of the sanitary crisis is not easily foreseeable, and therefore, next to the very useful financing sources for supporting the SME sector, we propose a series of additional actions for complementing the ones existing already. Thus, it would be useful to support industrial parks and business incubators by means of European funds (as these were financed by community funds in the previous programming periods), at regional/local level.

In order to do this, we advocate cutting red tape (bureaucracy) and extending the implementation term of projects being developed with European money beyond the initial maximum duration anticipated.

We also suggest funding some projects aimed at skilling, reskilling and improving the labour force, as well as providing them with the tools and materials they need to advance their activities under the programs, establishing some regional support centres that would provide free services to businesses that are necessary and helpful, designating some disadvantaged areas as redevelopment priority areas in accordance with Emergency Ordinance No. 124/1998.

For relaunching tourism, which was impacted severely by the COVID-19 crisis, we propose promoting vacation vouchers but also returning sums paid in advance by the tourist who could not benefit from the tourist services (European funds for recovery and resilience).

Some of the negative effects were distancing and compliance with some rules by which people had to avoid contact as to hinder virus outspread. This aspect contributed to implementing work from home/online work (product sales, payment of taxes and duties, etc.). Therefore, we suggest digitalisation measures for the Romanian public administration, mainly with the help of Romanian firms (concept, services), that would support the two new forms of work.

Firms in the agricultural sector were also impacted by the sanitary crisis; therefore it is important to pay attention also to them by advance payments of the subventions for agriculture, investments for rendering operational again the irrigation systems existing before 1989 in Romania, irrespective of their subsequent classification. In addition, subsidies may be considered (even partially) for the cost of the electric energy used to pump water for steep irrigations, the continuation and expansion of programs to build forest curtains to protect agricultural crops from droughts, loans with subsidised interest rates for processing plants for Romanian-grown fruits and vegetables, support programs for farmers, etc.

All these measures might contribute to the recovery/relaunch of the SME sector in Romania and to diminishing the effects of the current sanitary crisis.

In conclusion, both in Romania and globally, the COVID-19 issue had a significant influence on the SME sector.

Following the assessments carried out in this chapter, we may conclude that the sanitary crisis had the following effects on the SME sector: the number of businesses established decreased by 31% (2020 vs. 2019), while the number of legal company registrations, suspended businesses and insolvency firms increased.

All states impacted by the COVID-19 pandemic took measures for supporting and recovering in the SME sector. Some of the member states provided new credits in concession conditions and others granted support to small entrepreneurs, the unemployed and other affected social categories and changed the bankruptcy law, the insolvency law, the regulations for restructuring the business, etc (Friedrich Naumann Foundation, 2020).

The Association of Financial-Banking Analysts reports that three out of ten businesses in Romania, employing a total of 850.000 people (or one fifth of all private sector workers), are in the risk category, with larger expenses than incomes.

All available resources (national and EU) should be included in the packages of actions aimed at SMEs affected by the COVID-19 situation. Some prominent Romanian economists believe that preserving SMEs and social protection are the most crucial policies to implement. Despite financial and legislative efforts, there is no way to provide limitless protection. Up to this point, costs of over 10 billion euros associated with the COVID-19 problem have been estimated. The implications of the current crisis, which is thought to be more severe than the one in 2009, are difficult to predict.

## References

Bloom, N., Davis, S. J., & Zhestkova, Y. (2021). COVID-19 shifted patent applications toward technologies that support working from home. *AEA Papers and Proceedings, 111*, 263–266.

Denyer, D. (2017). *Organizational resilience*. BSI and Cranfield University. https://doi.org/10.1201/b14838.

Eurofound. (2020). *Regulations to address work–life balance in digital flexible working arrangements*. https://www.eurofound.europa.eu/sites/default/files/ef_publication/field_ef_document/ef19046en.pdf

European Commission. (2021a). *New cohesion policy.* https://ec.europa.eu/regional_policy/en/2021_2027/
European Commission. (2021b). *Winter 2021 economic forecast.* Available at: https://ec.europa.eu/commission/presscorner/detail/en/ip_21_504
Eurostat (2023). https://ec.europa.eu/eurostat
Friedrich Naumann Foundation (2020). Romania's SMEs resilience in crisis times. https://www.freiheit.org/romania-and-republic-moldova/smes-resilience-crisis-times
International Labour Organization. (2020). *Cooperatives and wider SSE enterprises respond to COVID-19 disruptions, and government measures are being put in place.* https://www.ilo.org/global/topics/cooperatives/news/WCMS_740254/lang-en/index.htm
Lengnick-Hall, C. A., Beck, T., & E., Lengnick-Hall, M. L. (2011). Developing a capacity for organizational resilience through strategic human resource management. *Human Resource Management Review, 21*(3), 243–255. https://doi.org/10.1016/j.hrmr.2010.07.001
National Institute of Statistics (2023). www.insse.ro
National Trade Register Office (2023). www.onrc.ro
Walker, W. E., Harremoës, P., Rotmans, J., van der Sluijs, J. P., van Asselt, M. B. A., Janssen, P., & Krayer von Krauss, M. P. (2003). Defining uncertainty: A conceptual basis for uncertainty management in model-based decision support. *Integrated Assessment, 4*(1), 5–17. https://doi.org/10.1076/iaij.4.1.5.16466
World Bank. (2021). *Global Economic Prospects*. World Bank.
Zaman, Gh. et al. (2020). *Rolul statului-natiune in gestionarea crizei SARS-COV 2 din Romania.* Politici de combatere, recuperare şi rezilienţă în domeniul economiei, Studii ale cercetatorilor Academiei Romane, Volumul 1, Pagini 101, Editor: Editura Academiei Romane, https://acad.ro/SARS-CoV-2/doc/d10-RolulStatului-Natiune.pdf
Zaman, G., & Vasile, V. (2014). Conceptual framework of economic resilience and vulnerability at national and regional levels. *Romanian Journal of Economics, 39*(2), 5–18. http://www.revecon.ro/articlcs/2014-2/2014-2-1.pdf

# Chapter 5
# Distortions and Gains in the Foreign Trade Activity During the Post-pandemic Era

**Elena Banica and Artur Emilian Simion**

**Abstract** In 2020, there was a notable decline in the volume of global international trade, potentially one of the most significant since World War II. Drawing from the most recent statistical data on Romania's foreign trade in goods and partners, and examining the economic landscape shaped by the conditions brought about by the COVID-19 pandemic, this section focuses on international trade activities in 2020 at the global, regional/European and national level.

Worldwide, the trade in services saw a steeper decline, and its post-lockdown recovery has been more sluggish compared to the trade in goods. The drop in global trade in 2020 was less severe than during the global financial crisis of 2008–2009. However, the influence of COVID-19 was characterised by the variability in specific goods and trading partners. The composition of foreign trade by product category underwent changes due to significant disruptions in the international transportation sector.

The unparalleled variability in the pandemic's impact on trade witnessed in 2020 underscores the need for adaptability. It's essential to pinpoint action plans and strategies to mitigate risks at both the corporate and governmental levels.

## State of the Art

On May 5, 2023, the General Director of the World Health Organization declared the end of the Public Health Emergency of International Concern for the disease caused by the coronavirus SARS-CoV-2 (World Health Organization, 2023). The COVID-19 pandemic caused the deterioration of most macroeconomic indicators through the measures taken by countries to combat the effects of the pandemic, leading to significant reductions in most economic domains, job losses, disruption of

E. Banica (✉)
Institute of National Economy - Romanian Academy, Bucharest, Romania

A. E. Simion
National Institute of Statistics, Bucharest, Romania

 
V. Vasile, E. Bunduchi (eds.), *The Economic and Social Impact of the COVID-19 Pandemic*, Contributions to Economics,
https://doi.org/10.1007/978-3-031-47780-5_5

international trade and problems in the educational system. The virus, which has led to millions of deaths at global level, strongly marked daily life and manifested itself at a time when the global economy was in decline because of trade disagreements between countries and political uncertainties, climate risks, poverty and inequality rates in emerging economies (World Bank, 2022).

Global trade decreased during the pandemic, but its effects varied depending on the type of goods, services and main trading partners. The uncertainties that characterised the world market led to urgent measures for the support of companies and for the adoption of new strategies to combat the effects of the pandemic (Arriola et al., 2021).

The measures taken by the states of the world to slow down the spread of the virus generated the COVID-19 crisis. Therefore, the temporary closure of borders during the lockdown period led to the collapse of global trade.

The existing literature on the effects of COVID-19 on international trade is diverse. There are studies focused on the shock caused by COVID-19, although they were made at country level. For example, the analysis carried out for Switzerland (Büchel et al., 2020) revealed that during the lockdown period in 2020, when the economic activity was stopped, the value of trade decreased by 11% as compared to the same period of 2019, this shock being stronger than the one in 2009. On the other hand, the decline in Swiss exports was linked to the amplitude of COVID-19 diseases in partner countries, whereas Swiss imports were linked to the degree of restriction measures taken in the exporting state. Last but not least, at the level of traded goods, only pharmaceutical and chemical products were not negatively affected, as the crisis affected the supply and demand in external trade (Liu et al., 2021). In the case of Spain (De Lucio et al., 2020), the analyses revealed that for the first half of 2020, the severity of the measures in the destination countries directly affected the external transactions and reduced the exports, while the imports of goods decreased less. The analyses also showed a sharper decline in export and import of services, as tourism is a very important economic domain in Spain.

There are also different studies based on the analysis of EU member states' trade data that prove the effects of the crisis (Kejzar & Velic, 2020). As the pandemic spread and the protection measures became stricter, the demand on the European market decreased steadily at the same time with the reduction of the labour force capacity and the cessation of industrial production (Espitia et al., 2021). COVID-19 has had a negative impact on trade growth for all EU member states, as well as their trading partners. Studies have suggested that COVID-19 has affected trade growth by reducing countries' share in the global value chains from the beginning of the pandemic to June 2020 (Hayakawa & Kohei, 2021).

The states' degree of development represented an important factor in establishing the anti-crisis measures. The costs of international trade transactions are strongly related to countries' economic policy (WTO, 2021). Thus, for developed countries, whose incomes are higher, the costs generated by the activity of marketing and transporting goods are particularly important, while commercial tariffs are less relevant in the context of COVID-19 (Anderson & Van Wincoop, 2004). Moreover, the type of goods produced and traded is important, given that developed countries have increased skills in organising production, which leads to an increased complexity of traded goods compared to less developed countries (Minondo & Requena-Silvente, 2013).

States' involvement in international trade has different motivations, depending on the level of income. Developed countries aim to ensure the sustainability of production and trade, while lower-income states want to attract investment mainly for economic modernisation and development (World Bank Group, 2017). Based on the studies carried out so far, it can be stated that countries with lower incomes were more vulnerable from the perspective of the organisation of the labour market under the conditions of the pandemic and the economic blockade, having fewer jobs that can be performed from home (McMahon et al., 2020).

During the pandemic, while some economic fields registered a significant decline, others experienced significant growth, even stimulated by the measures to stop the effects of the virus. This is the case for the production of medical goods and equipment and information technology products, necessary for working from home. Regardless of the sector, both the population and the companies had to adapt to the new conditions. The most sustainable change imposed during the pandemic has been the transition to e-commerce, which represented, for most companies, the key element of survival on the market by meeting the demands and developing the customer portfolio (FedEx, 2021).

In the context of the global COVID-19 pandemic, e-commerce became a lifeline even for the most inexperienced of online shoppers and determined a large part of consumers to resort to e-commerce and others to purchase new categories of products online. At the same time, the value of the goods traded electronically seemed to be directly proportional to the risk posed by the COVID-19 pandemic in that country, meaning that the higher the number of diseases in each country, the higher the probability of the consumer opting for e-commerce (Sturza & Ivanov, 2021).

Companies in Romania were also affected by the COVID-19 crisis, being forced to adapt their activity and market behaviour under conditions of restrictions, lockdown and changing rules.

## Impacts on World International Trade of the COVID-19 Pandemic

The COVID-19 pandemic and associated policy measures had strong economic consequences in 2020. The 10% decline in the volume of international trade in goods and services in 2020 marked one of the largest reductions in international trade since the end of World War II (OECD, 2022), with trade in services being considerably more affected than trade in goods (UNCTAD, 2021). According to a report by UNCTAD, the global trade in goods recorded a reduction of 7.4% in 2020 as compared to 2019. This was the biggest annual reduction in international trade transactions since the crisis in 2009, when trade contracted by around 22% (UNCTAD, WEF, 2021). Global trade in services recorded a decline of more than 20% in 2020 (WEF, 2021).

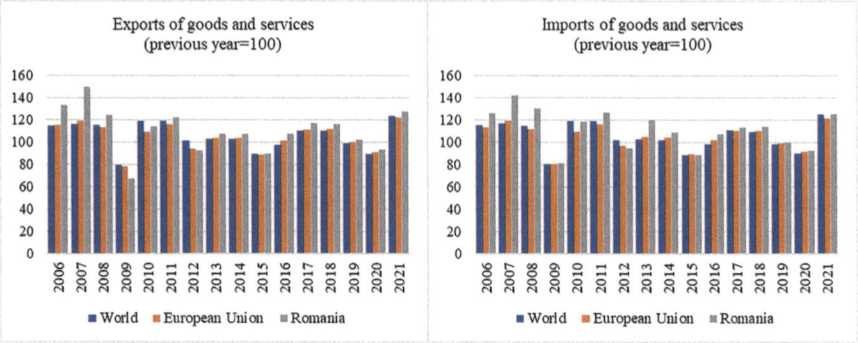


**Fig. 5.1** Trade in goods and services in total worldwide, in EU27 and Romania, previous year = 100 (Source: UNCTAD STAT database https://unctadstat.unctad.org/wds/TableViewer/tableView.aspx, Goods and Services (BPM6): Exports and imports of goods and services, annual. Data extracted in May 2023. EU structure on 2020 level)

The economic effects of the global financial crisis of 2008–2010 and those of the COVID-19 pandemic on international trade are often compared, even if the origins of crises, policy measures and economic adjustment mechanisms were different. The great financial crisis originated in the financial sector and was characterised by a sharp decline in commercial transactions in several countries and at the level of several goods, based on the reduction of firms' confidence in international markets (Baldwin, 2020); at the same time, a drastic reduction of trade finance took place (OECD, 2010). The COVID-19 pandemic has its origins outside the economic system and has forced leaders of the countries around the world to implement significant measures to isolate the virus and provide support to companies, with a strong and long-term influence on human behaviour and relationships. Altogether, these factors have led to strong and heterogeneous effects on demand, supply, domestic markets and international trade (Fig. 5.1).

The changes that occurred in 2020 in the global demand and supply of goods and services have created significant pressures on international trade. The restrictions and the costs involved in temporarily closing borders, reducing passenger travel opportunities and transport disruptions, have also had an impact on international trade transactions. In some cases, they revealed vulnerabilities such as the supply of materials, parts and components, but also the existence of unexpectedly large stocks, as the demand for them decreased.

The impact of the COVID-19 crisis on foreign trade was less severe than the one of the 2008–2009 economic and financial crisis. At global level, the economic crisis of 2008–2009 led to a reduction of about 20% in the volume of trade transactions (20.1% for exports and 19.8% for imports of goods and services, respectively), while the pandemic of COVID-19 affected international trade by about 11% (11.0% on exports and 11.2% on imports of goods and services). At the EU level, the same negative evolution is observed, respectively, a reduction in the period 2008–2009 of about 21% (21.9% in exports and 19.9% in imports) while in 2020 of less than 10% as compared to 2019 (10.3 in exports and 9.1 in imports of goods and services).

Romania was more affected from the perspective of exports during the economic crisis of 2008–2009 (−32.7% in 2009 compared to 2008) than from that of imports (which decreased by 19.2%), indicating a cyclical demand on foreign markets for goods from Romania. During the pandemic crisis, Romania was much less affected than the EU average, the exports of goods and services falling by 6.5% and imports by 8% in 2020 compared to 2019 (Fig. 5.2).

The declines in international trade in 2020 took place in the context of a reduction trend of trade transactions since 2019 (exports and imports of goods and services worldwide decreased by about 1.6% in 2019 compared to 2018). The growth of world trade in goods slowed at the end of 2018 and became negative in 2019 (about −3% for both global exports and imports). Probable factors behind this slowdown have included growing economic policy uncertainty, rising trade policy tensions (WTO, OMC, 2020) and declining expansion of international supply chains (Arriola et al., 2020) (Table 5.1).

The social distancing requirements due to the COVID-19 pandemic have greatly influenced the provision of services, which are based on human contact rather than trade in goods. Thus, trade in services was affected much more than international trade in goods, given that the downward trend in 2019/2018 did not manifest itself for international services, but only for goods. At EU level, closing of borders and partial cessation of goods production have led to a reduction in mainly transport services (−28% in the second quarter of 2020 compared to the second quarter of 2019 at EU level) and tourism (−88% in second quarter of 2020 compared to the second quarter of 2019 at EU level). These are the two major categories of internationally traded services and the ones that have suffered the most from COVID-19 restrictions at international travel. Other types of services with significant shares in the structure of exports, which decreased during the pandemic, are construction services, telecommunications services or other business services, such as researching, management consulting or trade-related services (Fig. 5.3).

The recovery of trade in services since Q3 2020 has been slow, the value of EU exports of services reaching the level of Q2 and Q3 2019 only in Q3 2021. In Romania, the available data show an evolution similar to the EU average, total exports of services being reduced by 24% in the second quarter of 2020 compared to the second quarter of 2019 amid declines in transport exports (−30.7%), tourism (−86.3%), construction (−19.8%) and other business services (−7.7%).

## Changes in the Geographical Orientation of Foreign Trade in Goods

The reduction in international trade in goods and the subsequent recovery were determined by the rate of geographical spread of the SARS-CoV-2 and the timing of the introduction and the degree of restriction measures for isolation of the virus. Thus, in 2020, changes in the evolution of trade in goods have been less geographically synchronised between the states of the world compared to the evolution during the economic and financial crisis of 2008–2009. Figure 5.4 shows the evolution of

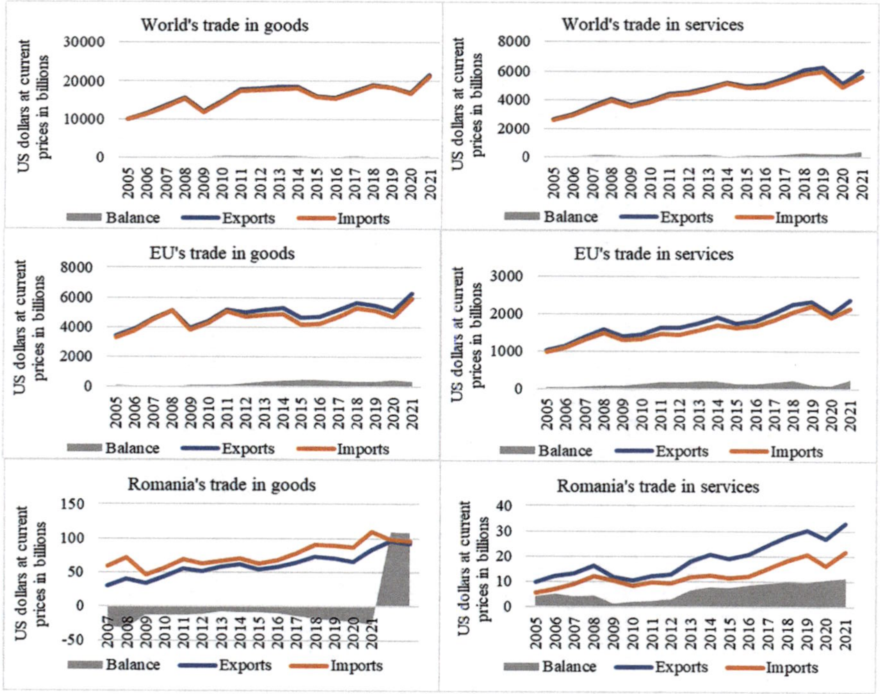


**Fig. 5.2** International trade in goods vs international trade in services (Source: UNCTAD STAT database https://unctadstat.unctad.org/wds/TableViewer/tableView.aspx, Goods and Services (BPM6): Exports and imports of goods and services, annual. Data extracted in May 2023. EU structure on 2020 level)

**Table 5.1** Dynamics of foreign trade flows during crisis

| | Trade in goods (%) | | | Trade in services (%) | | |
|---|---|---|---|---|---|---|
| | 2009/2008 | 2019/2018 | 2020/2019 | 2009/2008 | 2019/2018 | 2020/2019 |
| World's exports | 77.8 | 96.9 | 91.7 | 89.7 | 102.3 | 80.0 |
| World's imports | 77.3 | 97.2 | 92.3 | 89.9 | 102.7 | 78.7 |
| EU's exports | 77.6 | 97.0 | 93.8 | 88.0 | 101.9 | 83.9 |
| EU's imports | 75.1 | 96.3 | 92.4 | 87.7 | 105.3 | 83.5 |
| Romania's exports | 84.4 | 96.7 | 93.1 | 72.1 | 107.9 | 89.4 |
| Romania's imports | 64.0 | 99.4 | 96.7 | 87.0 | 113.1 | 79.3 |

Source: UNCTAD STAT database https://unctadstat.unctad.org/wds/TableViewer/tableView.aspx, Goods and Services (BPM6): Exports and imports of goods and services, annual. Data extracted in May 2023. EU structure on 2020 level (EU27)

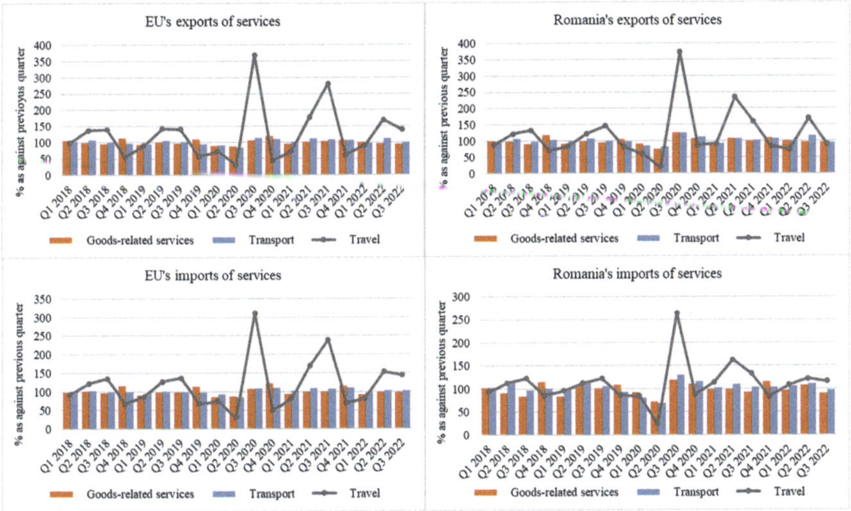


**Fig. 5.3** Dynamics of international trade in services by main categories, for EU and Romania (Source: UNCTAD STAT database, https://unctadstat.unctad.org/wds/TableViewer/tableView.aspx Services (BPM6): Trade and growth by main service-category, quarterly. Data extracted in May 2023. EU structure on 2020 level)

Romania's exports compared to the main trading partners, namely, Germany and Italy, during the two periods of crisis.

The analysis of the monthly data available in Eurostat revealed that Romania's export flows are strongly synchronised with the evolution of exports of the main partner countries, Germany and Italy. Both the 2008–2009 financial crisis and the COVID-19 pandemic affected Romania's foreign trade to a lesser extent than Italy's, but in the case of Germany, the impact of the 2020 lockdown on exports was lower.

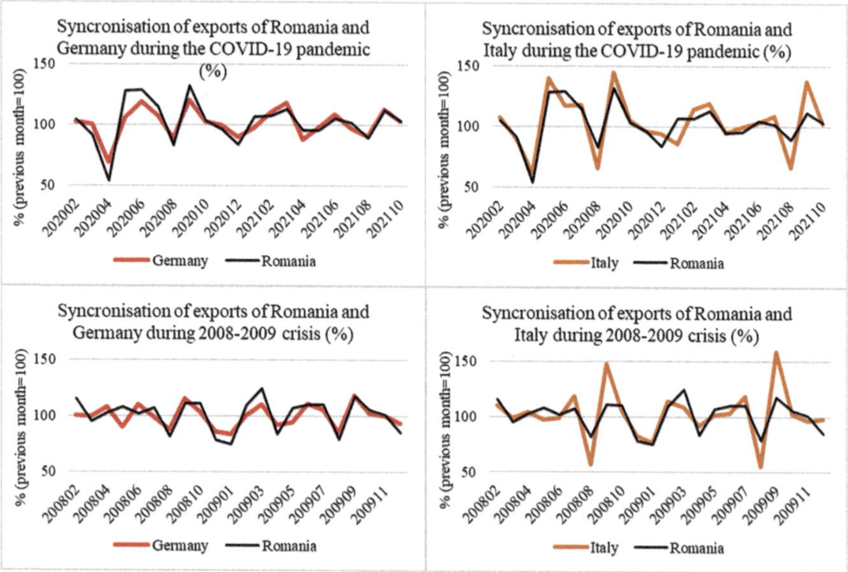


**Fig. 5.4** Synchronisation of Romania's exports of goods with main partner countries (EU structure on 2020 level. Source: Calculations based on Eurostat Comext database, data extracted in May 2023)

There are two fundamental aspects with strong impact on the analysis and its results: (a) Romania is part of the EU and (b) international globalisation. The European single market is the catalyst for stimulating foreign trade transactions of the member countries, both within the EU and with non-member countries. At the same time, it leads to an increase in the capacity for innovation, production and efficiency, as a consequence of an enlarged number of national markets in which EU companies perform trade operations and the increase in the resources to which they have access (Fig. 5.5).

The assessment of the impact of the COVID-19 crisis takes into consideration the important aspects of the Romanian and European economy from the last months of 2019 and the beginning of 2020. Taking into consideration the important degree of trade openness of Romania (64,5% in 2019 and 68,7% in 2021 in case of goods), the impact of COVID-19 in Romania's main partner countries has been reflected in the national economy. The international crisis of 2008–2009 has shown a strong synchronisation of business cycles at European Union (EU) level. The economic and financial crisis has affected the old EU member states at the same time, and it has been felt in the new member states with only a small delay (Tatomir & Popovici, 2013).

The analysis of the evolution of monthly exports (% as compared to the previous month) shows a strong synchronisation at the regional level of export flows, as shown by the information presented in Fig. 5.6. The two macroeconomic shocks, namely, the economic crisis of 2008–2009 and the health crisis in 2020, affected the foreign trade of the countries of south-eastern Europe at a similar level, although we appreciate that the high degree of correlation of export flows is the influence of EU membership, rather than geographical location (Fig. 5.7).

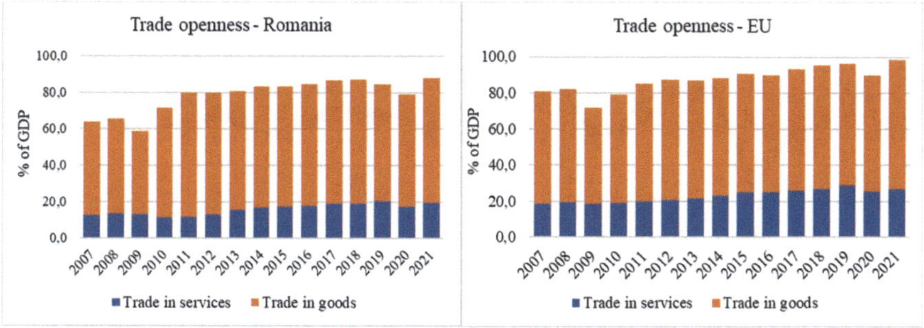


**Fig. 5.5** Trade openness, % of GDP (EU structure on 2020 level) (This table shows the sum of exports and imports of goods/services as percentage of nominal gross domestic product. Source: UNCTAD STAT database https://unctadstat.unctad.org/wds/TableViewer/tableView.aspx, Goods and services (BPM6): Trade openness indicators, annual. Data extracted in May 2023)

The two macroeconomic shocks have had important effects on Romania's international economic relations but without a significant difference from the point of view of the partner countries in relation to which the export was lower than the import. In the top ten partner countries with which Romania registered trade deficits in 2009 and 2020, there were six EU member states and four third countries (outside of EU). This is a proof of the international nature of the crises and their impact on global supply and demand. It should be noted that between 2020 and 2009, the top countries with deficits did not change substantially, only two countries being replaced by others (the Czech Republic and Brazil were replaced in 2020 by Turkey and Belgium), which proves the stability of traditional trade relations, despite the external factors.

The top partner countries for which Romania registered trade surpluses in 2009 and 2020 are characterised by heterogeneity. There are several states from the Middle East with which Romania has developed and maintained bilateral relations, obtaining important trade surpluses. The trade relations of Romanian companies on non-EU markets through exports of goods have a positive impact on the national economy, and further expansion in these areas can help Romanian economy by reducing the dependence on EU partners.

The importance of traditional trade relations is also highlighted by the evolution of transactions with the United Kingdom. The positive trade balance was maintained during the years of crisis. Exports from Romania to the United Kingdom were not affected by the Brexit phenomenon, which overlapped with the COVID-19 pandemic. Moreover, the trade surplus doubled in 2021 as compared with 2020. The introduction of customs duties on imports of goods from the United Kingdom led to a drastic reduction in Romanian imports from the United Kingdom while maintaining exports at a high level; this is a picture of the sustainable trade relations by the export of Romanian goods on the UK market, especially the medium-tech ones, which also incorporate a high- and medium-skilled workforce.

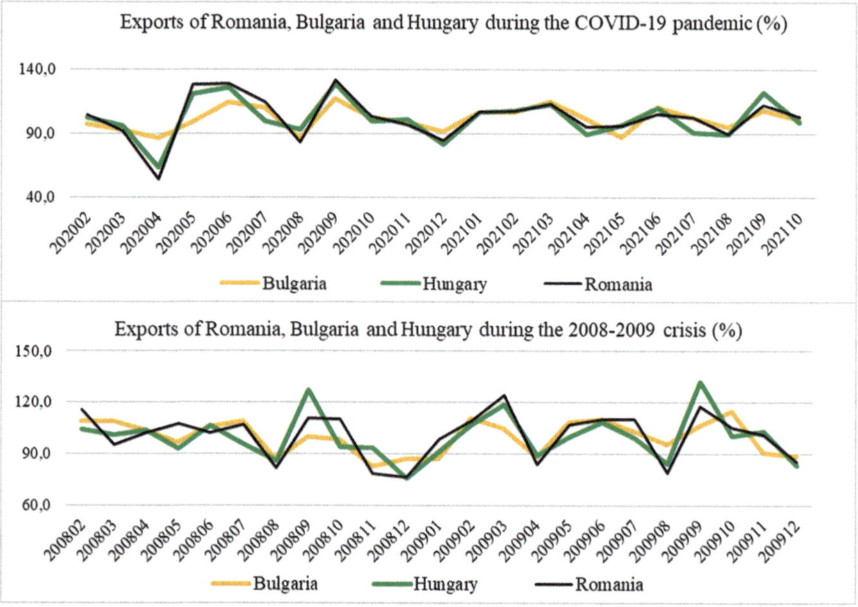


**Fig. 5.6** Synchronisation of Romania's exports of goods with neighbouring countries (EU structure on 2020 level. Source: Calculations based on Eurostat Comext database, data extracted in May 2023)

Annex 5.2 presents the trade balances registered by Romania in relation to the countries included in Figs. 5.7 and 5.8 before and after the crisis periods (2009–2010 and 2019–2022, respectively).

## Changes in the Structure of Foreign Trade in Goods

International trade played an important role in addressing the supply shortage of pandemic goods, such as pharmaceuticals, personal protective equipment, surgical masks and electronics. The effects of crisis periods on foreign trade activity are characterised by heterogeneity in the level of traded products. The analysis of the similarity index of Finger-Kreinin exports calculated for exports shows that in 2020 the structure of foreign trade transactions is considerably different from that of 2019 (Fig. 5.9).

To calculate the Finger-Kreinin index of similarity of export and import structure across two-digits CN product categories, the following formula was used:

$$\text{The index formula}: \text{FKI}_{t,t-n} = \sum min \ \{x_{\text{i}t}/\text{X}_t, x_{\text{i}t-n}/\text{X}_{t-n}\}$$

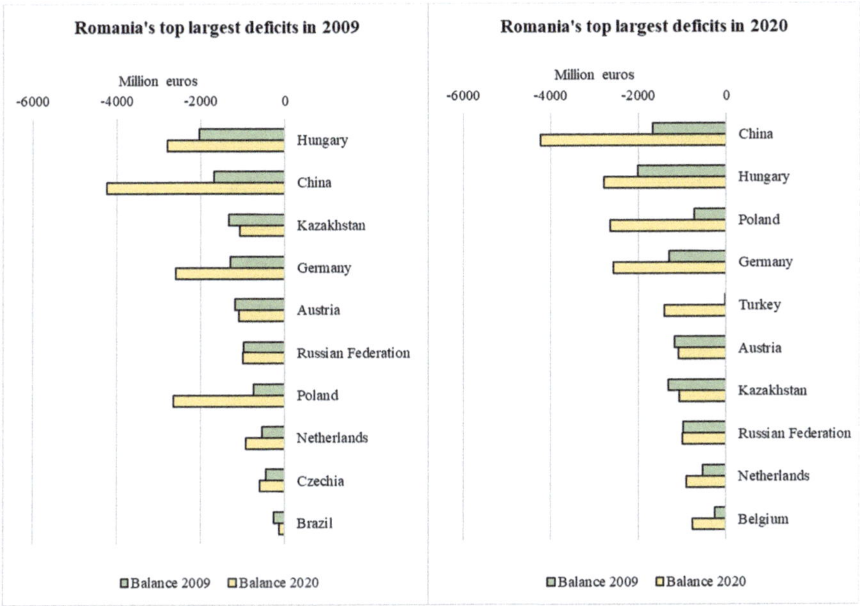


**Fig. 5.7** Romania's top largest deficits in 2009 and the change in 2020, million euro (Source: Calculations based on NSI's foreign trade database, data extracted in May 2023)

where $x_{it} / X_t =$ share of exports/imports of merchandise I in RO's total exports/imports at time t and $x_{it-n} / X_{t-n} =$ share of exports/imports of merchandise i in RO's total exports/imports at the reference period *(t-n)*.

The value of 100 of the index means the export/import shares of two-digits CN goods categories in a period are identical to those in the reference period. On the contrary, the value of 0 means the export/import shares of two-digits CN goods categories over a period are entirely different to those in the reference period. A value of 50% can be interpreted as representing a 50% overlap in export/import structures between the two periods.

The Combined Nomenclature is the relevant nomenclature for foreign trade statistics purposes and is the base for EU customs tariff. The eight-digit sub-headings in the nomenclature are used in export/import declarations for extra-EU trade and in statistical declarations on intra-EU trade. There are changes to the nomenclature every year, but the structure on two-digits CN level provides the most stable base for long data series.

In the years before the COVID-19 pandemic, the structure of exports of goods at the two-digits CN level was relatively constant from year to year, but 2020 marked a deeper change than the one observed in 2007 and 2008, both compared to the year before and compared to 2009. In 2020, the demand sharply fell in partner countries, and Romanian exports decreased consequently. After the lockdown period, the

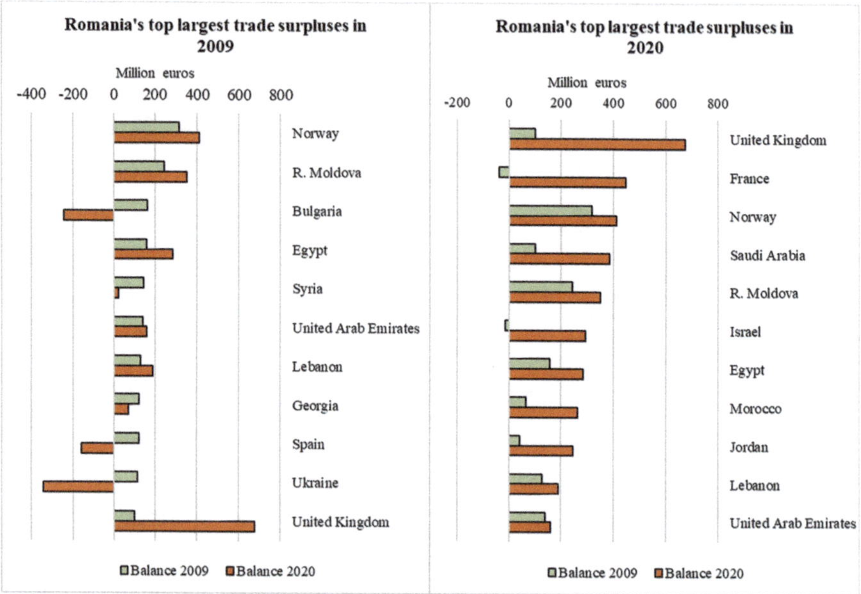


**Fig. 5.8** Romania's partner countries—larger surpluses in 2020 and 2009 (Source: Calculations based on NSI's foreign trade database, data extracted in May 2023)

export flows did not recover immediately because the restrictions in movement of goods and people were still in force.

With regard to imports, the structure at the level of goods according to two-digits CN was affected to a lesser extent than exports, suggesting that the domestic demand remained at high level and the lockdown period did not affect the imports of goods in a significant way. Against the background of the restrictions imposed at national level, the demand for consumer goods, especially food products and medical devices, was high, and imports ensured the balance of supply, covering the growing need for various goods. Figure 5.10 shows the main goods exported and imported in 2009 and 2020.

The structure of Romania's foreign trade did not change substantially in the crisis years, 2009 and 2020, a continuity in the main type of goods traded by Romania on foreign markets being noticed, both for export and import. Thus, both exports and imports consist mainly of electrical machinery, mechanical devices and vehicles. These three categories of goods accounted for 40% of Romania's exports of goods in 2009 and 47% in 2020, respectively. The share of mineral fuels decreased from 6% in total exports in 2009 to 2% in 2020, because of the partial stoppage of economic activity in the pandemic: the reduction of the activity of production and transport of goods affected these categories of goods. In terms of imports, the three categories of goods accounted for 34% in 2009 and 37% in 2020. The important share of the top three chapters in exports and imports is mainly determined by the car manufacturing industry, an activity with a long tradition in Romania, which developed mainly after

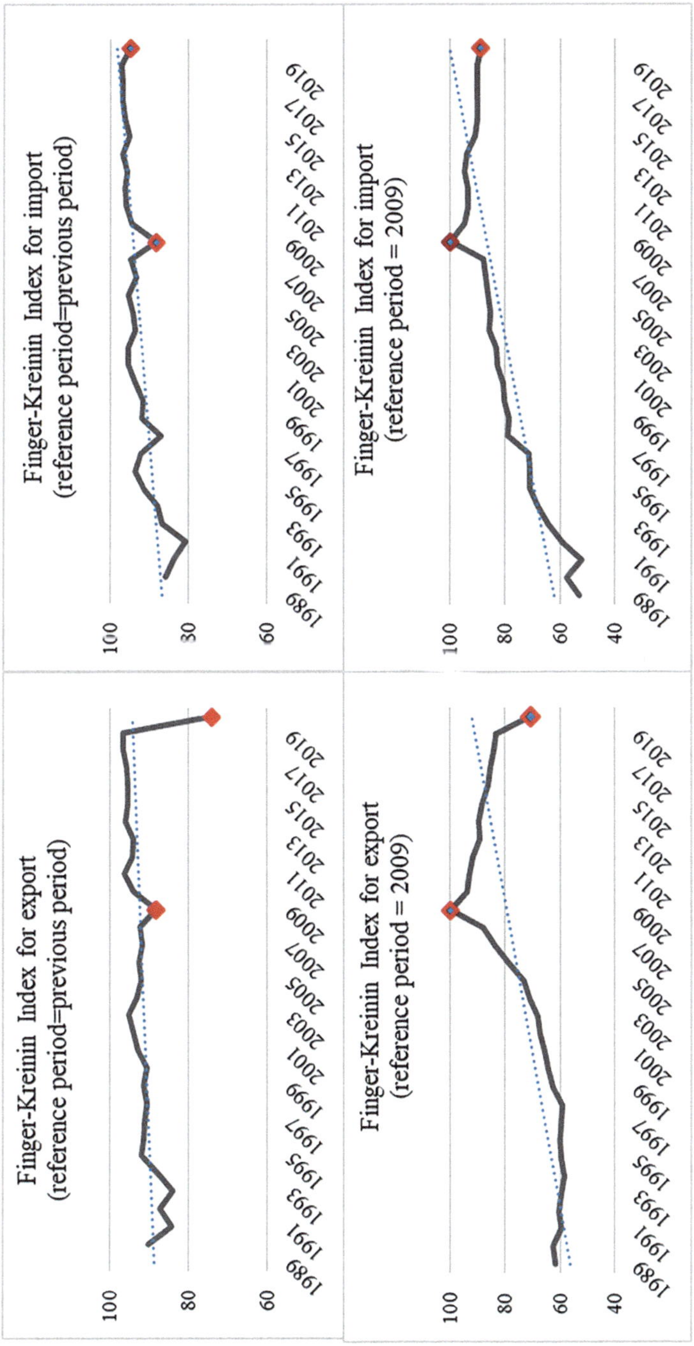


**Fig. 5.9** Finger-Kreinin index of similarity of export and import structure across two-digits CN product categories (Both figures in Fig. 5.9 show the Finger-Kreinin index, which measures the degree of similarity of Romania's export and import structure on two-digits CN level in a period as compared to the (**a**) previous period and (**b**) year 2009. The year 2009 was the year of maximum impact of the economic crisis. Source: Calculations based on NSI's foreign trade database, data extracted in May 2023)

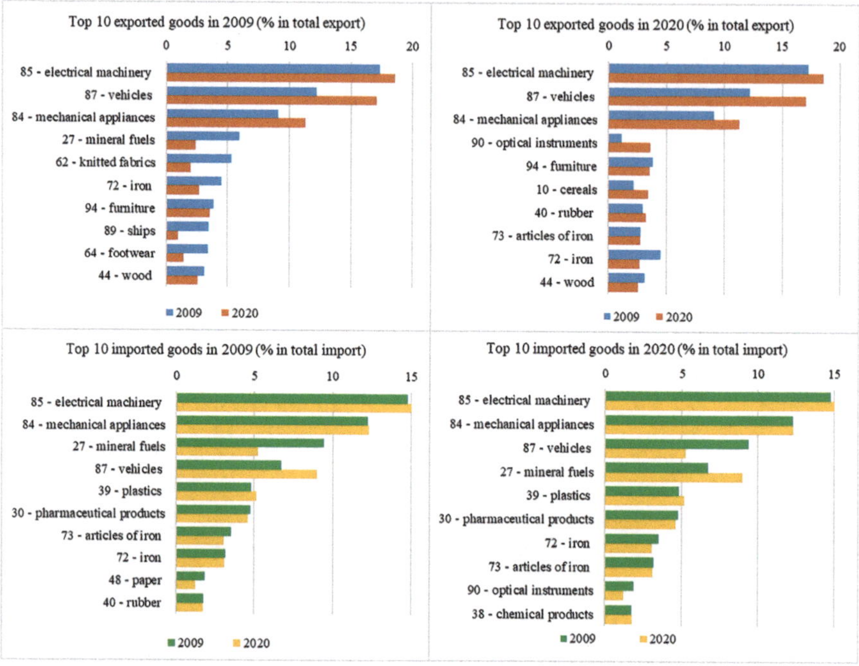


**Fig. 5.10** Changes in trade of ten most traded products in 2009 and 2020 (Source: Calculations based on NSI's foreign trade database, data extracted in May 2023)

Romania's accession to the EU. Exports of Romania on external markets consist of final goods (vehicles), subassemblies and spare parts for the European car market, especially Germany. The integration on the international value chains and the high share of three products in total export and import lead to a high degree of dependence on the commercial partners, especially those from the EU market. Any change of the economy of the partner countries has an impact on the Romanian economy, especially on the foreign trade transactions (Fig. 5.11).

An important category of goods for export is furniture, because it is an industry in which the raw material is intensely processed and the export is represented by final goods, with high added value. The export of such final goods originating from Romania contributes to the sustainable economic development through competitive exports and the contribution of a medium and highly qualified labour force.

Economic policies in the field of foreign trade in Romania should be oriented towards the promotion on external markets of those goods that incorporate medium- or high-technology as well as skilled labour. Romania has the largest deficits in trade in high- and medium-technology goods (electrical machines, pharmaceuticals, mechanical appliances); at the same time, the most important trade surpluses are found in basic goods and natural resources (cereals, wood, oil, live animals) as well as in low value-added goods, such as clothing or footwear. In the top trade surpluses, there are few categories of goods with high added value, such as furniture and

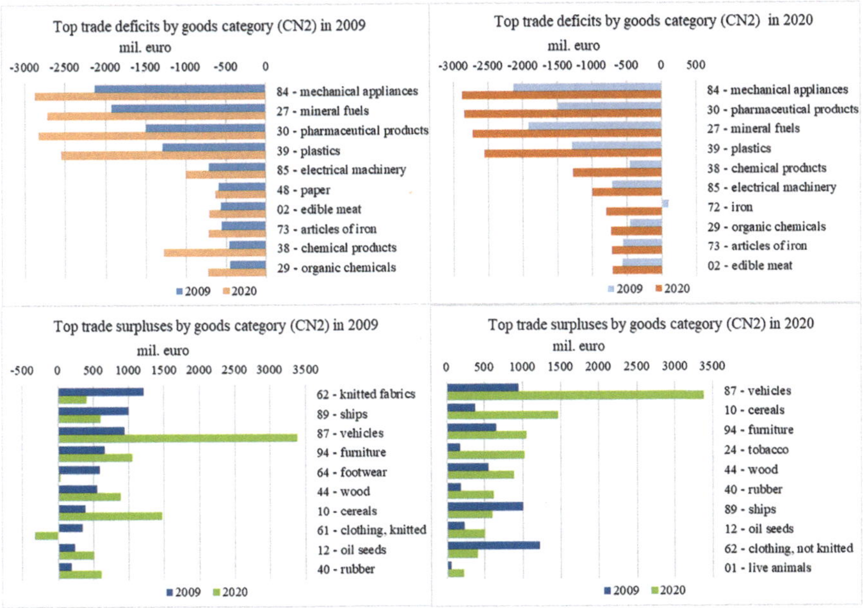


**Fig. 5.11** Product categories with highest and lowest trade balance in 2009 and 2020 (Source: Calculations based on NSI's foreign trade database, data extracted in May 2023)

maritime ships. The activity of processing goods by importing raw materials and exporting final products (the former *lohn* system) is still carried out in the national economy; because of the application of European regulations in the field of taxation and registration in national statistics, the current records in statistics do not allow this phenomenon to be accurately reflected (Fig. 5.12).

The magnitude of the changes in Romania's export structure reflects the considerable heterogeneity of the effects of the two crises on foreign trade by product category. Domestic demand has increased for certain categories of goods, such as protection and pharmaceuticals, foodstuffs and small and large appliances (e.g. electrical and electronic appliances).

For other categories of goods, demand has seen significant declines in periods of isolation and/or teleworking, such as clothing and textiles (excluding masks and other protective equipment) or durable goods for which demand usually falls during periods of crisis.

For example, trade in manufactured textiles—a category that includes masks and other textile-based protective equipment—increased by almost 60% in 2020 compared to 2019, while trade in pharmaceuticals increased by 9%. High growth rates were also recorded for various foodstuffs, such as meat products (+ 8%), fruits (+ 10%) and dairy products (+ 8%), but also for various chemicals (+ 18%). Simultaneously with these increases, fuels and mineral oils decreased in share in total foreign trade (−38%) as well as other goods used in production: silk (−34%),

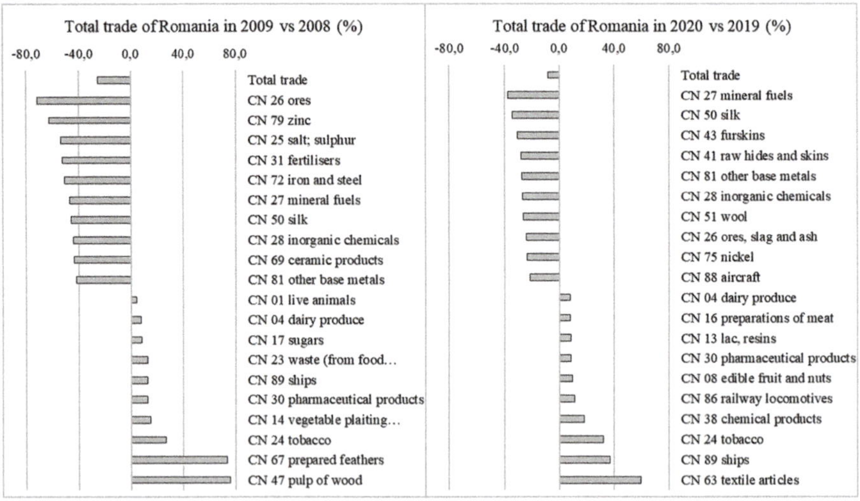


**Fig. 5.12** Main changes in trade (export+import) during crises periods (Total trade refers to export +import; *CN* Combined Nomenclature. Source: Calculations based on Romanian National Institute of Statistics data, data extracted in May 2023)

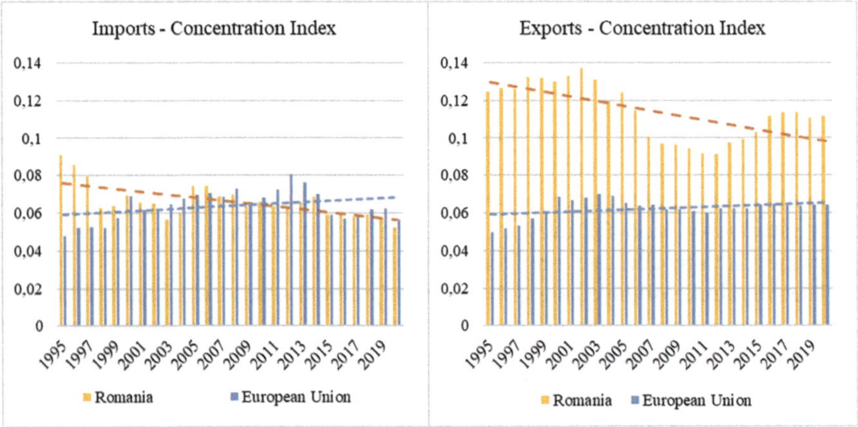


**Fig. 5.13** Concentration index for Romanian exports and import (EU structure on 2020 level. Source: UNCTAD STAT database https://unctadstat.unctad.org/wds/TableViewer/tableView.aspx, data extracted in February 2022)

raw hides and skins (−28%), wool (−26%), ores (−24%) and nickel (−24%) (Fig. 5.13).

The concentration index for export and import (Herfindahl-Hirschman Index (HHI)) reflects the degree of product concentration for export or import. The following HHI formulae was used (the value of HHI is between 0 and 1):

$$H_j = \frac{\sqrt{\sum_{i=1}^{n}\left(\frac{x_{ij}}{X_j}\right)^2} - \sqrt{1/n}}{1 - \sqrt{1/n}}$$

where:

$H_j$ = country or country group index$x_{ij}$ = export/import for country $j$ and product $i$

$$X_j = \sum_{i=1}^{n} x_{ij}$$

where:

$n$ = number of goods (SITC Rev. 3 at three-digit level)

When trade transactions of a country are concentrated on a limited number of products, the index value is closer to 1. The index will be closer to 0 when export and import transactions refer to as many goods.

Using statistical data on foreign trade in goods at the level of 2022, the following aspects should be noted regarding the concentration of imports and exports of goods in Romania:

- The top ten partners with which Romania has developed international trade relations represent 62% of export of goods and 69% of the import of goods.
- The first two partner countries have significant shares in Romanian foreign trade: Germany holds about 18% of imports and 20% of total exports of goods, and Italy accounts for more than 10% of exports of goods and more than 8% of imports of goods.
- China and Turkey are among Romania's main non-EU trading partners, about 11% of imports of goods originating from these countries and more than 4% of national exports having as destination one of these two states.

In Romania, imports and exports of goods are highly concentrated on a few destinations and origin countries. However, there is a trend to reduce the concentration degree for both exports and imports, especially during periods of major crises.

## Conclusions

The changes in the evolution of international trade in 2020 were deep but, globally, trade has contracted less than during the period of economic and financial crisis in 2008–2009. The recovery of exports and imports from the second half of 2020 suggests that the duration of the health crisis was short and did not produce significant long-term changes. However, the measures taken by governments to protect the population continued even in the years 2021 and 2022, mainly affecting tourism, which further prolonged the constraints on trade in goods and services.

Structural changes in international trade have meant high uncertainty and adjustment costs for both world governments and companies. Based on the experience gained during the pandemic, companies can adopt new strategies on the markets, especially because of the probability of new pandemics/crises in the future. Firms could act more cautiously, in order to mitigate business risks, and give up part of the human workforce by further automating production processes, creating additional stocks to ensure greater resistance to possible disruptions of the supply chains.

In the short term, the reduction of the population's income due to the partial stoppage of economic activity led to the reduction of the demand for goods with immediate effects on the supply. Although the lockdown period was short, the behavioural pattern of consumers has changed due to the need to reduce spending and adopt a more restrained behaviour in consumption.

The economic recovery is conditioned by addressing the interdependent economic risks posed by the crisis. World governments need to address issues such as financial instability, reduced access to credit or external debt. In addition to these domestic financial and economic issues, the outlook for post-pandemic recovery is influenced by events in the global economy, such as the price of primary goods, especially fuels. These global developments expose both households and companies and governments alike to a number of risks for the economic recovery.

Along with the necessity to address the risks posed by the pandemic, opportunities for the sustainable development of the economy must be seized. Climate change poses a major risk to the world economy. In this context, the European Commission has included in the budget plan 2021–2027 an important component, called the Next Generation EU, intended for the economic recovery from the pandemic. The budget plan was created around the European Green Pact, launched at the end of 2019 with the aim of reducing pollution, so that Europe may become climate neutral by 2050.

In Romania, financial funds are needed to stimulate companies and support their activity, especially those with Romanian capital. In addition, actions to protect the local workforce are needed in order to reduce the phenomenon of migration as well as the unemployment rate.

National production must be encouraged in order to develop those sectors where there is important potential for development but also a waste of added value. This is the case of the export of raw materials with low impact on the trade balance, along with the import of finished products or even cheaper raw materials than those available on the Romanian market. This practice, which is particularly prevalent in the case of agricultural raw materials (e.g. cereals) and timber, should be reduced in order to encourage the development of the processing capacity for achieving competitive goods for exports.

To reduce the dependence of the national economy on large multinational companies, there is a need to support the development of Romanian-owned companies, and this aspect has to be treated as a priority at the level of national policies and strategies. Last but not least, financing national research and development by allocating funds to the companies for this purpose could help reduce imports of goods and develop national production for meeting the growing needs of the population and firms.

## Annexes

**Annex 5.2** Romania's trade balance evolution for selected countries (million euro)

| | Balance 2009 | Balance 2010 | Balance 2019 | Balance 2020 | Balance 2021 | Balance 2022 |
|---|---|---|---|---|---|---|
| Total balance | −9869 | −9509 | −17,295 | −18,388 | −23,698 | −34,101,2 |
| Austria | −1185,0 | −1047,7 | −1181,0 | −1089,3 | −1254,6 | −1784,9 |
| Belgium | −248,8 | −270,8 | −823,3 | −782,6 | −837,2 | −1138,4 |
| Brazil | −261,7 | −241,1 | −160,5 | −128,3 | −193,5 | −263,0 |
| Bulgaria | 163,7 | −98,3 | −116,8 | −244,9 | −1129,2 | −5234,1 |
| China | −1689,4 | −2245,9 | −3783,4 | −4235,1 | −5070,6 | −6295,0 |
| Czechia | −438,3 | −545,5 | −467,6 | −598,8 | −477,4 | −737,4 |
| France | −38,1 | 342,3 | 511,6 | 453,3 | 617,0 | 634,1 |
| Germany | −1300,6 | −1087,4 | −1900,8 | −2584,3 | −4271,7 | −4179,9 |
| Hungary | −2026,8 | −2253,9 | −2766,6 | −2792,4 | −2560,8 | −1399,6 |
| Israel | −13,0 | −2,3 | 310,3 | 292,2 | 406,6 | 596,9 |
| Jordan | 43,2 | 55,7 | 211,9 | 245,1 | 399,4 | 568,8 |
| Lebanon | 129,4 | 152,2 | 269,7 | 189,1 | 140,3 | 197,3 |
| Morocco | 66,7 | 69,6 | 384,9 | 263,3 | 309,8 | 360,2 |
| Netherlands | −545,4 | −630,3 | −1269,8 | −927,8 | −1322,8 | −1789,1 |
| Norway | 315,8 | 225,0 | 341,4 | 410,3 | 468,0 | 262,4 |
| Poland | −737,0 | −764,0 | −2729,4 | −2648,5 | −3171,6 | −3938,5 |
| Saudi Arabia | 101,8 | 144,6 | 239,7 | 383,7 | 276,4 | 200,9 |
| Spain | 122,7 | 136,7 | −310,9 | −153,4 | −232,5 | −371,4 |
| Syria | 145,8 | 153,2 | 43,9 | 21,6 | 14,6 | 7,1 |
| United Arab Emirates | 140,4 | 197,7 | 172,8 | 160,5 | 193,9 | 334,6 |
| Turkey | −10,3 | 885,1 | −1618,8 | −1417,2 | −1791,4 | −3226,7 |
| Egypt | 158,6 | 152,9 | 581,4 | 284,5 | 550,3 | 329,8 |
| United Kingdom | 101,9 | 288,0 | 924,2 | 669,6 | 1262,0 | 1646,7 |
| Georgia | 122,8 | 142,9 | 182,0 | 71,2 | 110,1 | 262,5 |
| Kazakhstan | −1328,3 | −1271,7 | −1603,6 | −1077,2 | −1457,7 | −3169,1 |
| Rep. of Moldova | 243,2 | 324,3 | 494,6 | 349,4 | 579,7 | 1153,4 |
| Russian Federation | −987,7 | −1211,6 | −2083,3 | −992,8 | −2140,8 | −3481,0 |
| Ukraine | 113,8 | −11,4 | −314,8 | −346,9 | −617,7 | −655,5 |

## References

Anderson, J. E., & Van Wincoop, E. (2004). Trade costs. *Journal of Economic Literature, 42*, 691–751. https://doi.org/10.1257/0022051042177649

Arriola, C., Kowalski, P., & Tongeren, F. (2021). The impact of COVID-19 on directions and structure of international trade. *OECD Trade Policy Papers*. https://doi.org/10.1787/0b8eaafe-en

Arriola, C., et al. (2020). *Efficiency and risks in global value chains in the context of COVID-19, OECD Economics Department Working Papers, No. 1637*. OECD Publishing. https://doi.org/10.1787/3e4b7ecf-en

Baldwin, R. (2020). *The greater trade collapse of 2020: Learnings from the 2008–09 great trade collapse*. https://voxeu.org/article/greater-trade-collapse-2020

Büchel, K., Legge, S., Pochon, V., & Wegmüller, P. (2020). Swiss trade during the COVID-19 pandemic: An early appraisal. *Swiss Journal of Economics and Statistics, 156*.

De Lucio, J., Minguez, R., Minondo, A., & Requena, F. (2020). *The impact of COVID-19 containment measures on Trade*. Department of Applied Economics II, Universidad de Valencia. https://www.emerald.com/insight/content/doi/10.1108/AEA-11-2020-0156/full/html

Espitia, A., Mattoo, A., Rocha, N., Ruta, M., & Winkler, D. (2021). Pandemic Trade: Covid-19. *Remote Work and Global Value Chains, 45*, 561. https://doi.org/10.1111/twec.13117

FedEx. (2021). *Raportul FedEx privind tendințele în comerț în anul 2021–Identificarea oportunităților în perioadele de incertitudine*. https://www.fedex.com/content/dam/fedex/eu-europe/campaigns/h1-2020/trends-report/fedex_trade_trends_report_ro-ro.pdf

Hayakawa, K., & Kohei, I. (2021) *Who sends me face masks? Evidence for the impacts of COVID-19 on international trade in medical goods*, Institute of Developing Economies, Japan External Trade Organization (JETRO) https://onlinelibrary.wiley.com/doi/epdf/10.1111/twec.13179

Kejzar, K. Z., & Velic, A. (2020). Covid-19, trade collapse and GVC linkages: European experience. *Covid Economics*, 222–244. https://www.econbiz.de/Record/covid-19-trade-collapse-and-gvc-linkages-european-experience-zajc-kej%C5%BEar-katja/10012384045

Liu, X., Ornelas, E., & Shi, H. (2021). *The trade impact of the covid-19 pandemic, CEPR WP 16201*. https://cep.lse.ac.uk/pubs/download/dp1771.pdf

McMahon, D. E., Peters, G. A., Ivers, L. C., & Freeman, E. E. (2020). Global resource shortages during COVID-19: Bad news for low-income countries. *PLoS Neglected Tropical Diseases, 14*(7), e0008412. https://doi.org/10.1371/journal.pntd.0008412. https://journals.plos.org/plosntds/article?id=10.1371/journal.pntd.0008412

Minondo, A., & Requena-Silvente, F. (2013). Does complexity explain the structure of trade? *Canadian Journal of Economics/Revue canadienne d'économique, 46*, 928–955. https://doi.org/10.1111/caje.12033

OECD. (2010). *Trade and economic effects of responses to the economic crisis, OECD trade policy studies*. OECD Publishing. https://doi.org/10.1787/9789264088436-en

OECD. (2022). *OECD Economic Outlook No 109 (Edition 2021/1), OECD Economic Outlook: Statistics and Projections (database)*, Accessed Feb 21, 2022, from https://doi.org/10.1787/4229901e-en.

Sturza M., & Ivanov R., (2021). *Impactul pandemiei de COVID-19 asupra comertului electronic*. https://vdalegal.com/impactul-pandemiei-de-covid-19-asupra-comertului-electronic/

Tatomir C., & Popovici O., (2013). *Sincronizarea ciclurilor de afaceri la nivelul Uniunii Europene: Deziderat sau realitate?* http://store.ectap.ro/articole/878_ro.pdf

UNCTAD. (2021). *Global merchandise trade exceeds pre-COVID-19 level, but services recovery falls short | UNCTAD*. Accessed May 20, 2023.

UNCTAD. (2022). *Key statistics and trends in international trade 2021–The effects of the COVID-19 pandemic on international trade*. https://doi.org/10.18356/9789210015356.

WEF (World Economic Forum). (2021). *How has the COVID-19 pandemic affected global trade? | World Economic Forum*. Accessed May 20, 2023.

World Bank. (2022). *World development report, finance for an equitable recovery*. https://openknowledge.worldbank.org/bitstream/handle/10986/36883/9781464817304.pdf

World Bank Group; IDE-JETRO; OECD; UIBE; World Trade Organization. (2017). *Global Value Chain Development Report 2017: Measuring and Analyzing the Impact of GVCs on Economic Development*. World Bank. © World Bank. https://openknowledge.worldbank.org/handle/10986/29593 License: CC BY 3.0 IGO.

World Health Organization. (2023). *Statement on the fifteenth meeting of the IHR (2005) Emergency Committee on the COVID-19 pandemic*. Statement on the fifteenth meeting of the IHR (2005) Emergency Committee on the COVID-19 pandemic (who.int)

WTO. (2021). *Trade cost index: Evolution, incidence and determinants: Background note*. http://tradecosts.wto.org/docs/Trade_Cost_Index_Background_Note_24-03-2021.pdf

WTO, OMC. (2020). *Report on G20 trade and investment measures*, mid-October 2019 to mid-May 2020, https://www.wto.org/english/news_e/news20_e/report_trdev_nov20_e.pdf

# Chapter 6
# Tax Burden During the Pandemic: Lessons Learned and Challenges

**Marius-Răzvan Surugiu, Raluca Mazilescu, and Camelia Surugiu**

**Abstract** This chapter delves into the challenges and strategies employed within the realm of taxation by European Union countries to alleviate the impact of the COVID-19 crisis. Furthermore, it scrutinises the effects of various variables on indirect tax revenues, focusing on Romania as a case study. The analysis is based on quarterly data between 2009 and 2021. The findings indicate that three of these variables exhibit statistically significant impacts on indirect tax revenues, namely, the unemployment rate, inflation rate and the disease-related dummy variable.

## Introduction

The COVID-19 crisis was harming employment, trade and budgets. Countries' budgets have seen a reduction in tax revenues during this pandemic. Governments have taken various tax measures to help taxpayers fight the pandemic's adverse effects, mainly aimed at relaxing taxation. These measures are tailored to economic challenges and those in the health system.

The measures adopted have a substantial impact on the economy but also with some costs. The labour market has been affected, with job losses and the worsening situation of employers who went bankrupt. The policymaker has adopted tax exemptions and deferrals, which has increased the budget deficit.

In the future, the policymaker may take steps to reduce it, focusing on an increase in taxation or a reduction in spending. Both types of measures are not well received by taxpayers, raising taxes being a measure that can stimulate noncompliance (taxpayers will try to identify new ways to hide revenue), and reducing government

---

M.-R. Surugiu (✉) · R. Mazilescu
Institute of National Economy - Romanian Academy, Bucharest, Romania

C. Surugiu
Faculty of Administration and Business, University of Bucharest, Bucharest, Romania



V. Vasile, E. Bunduchi (eds.), *The Economic and Social Impact of the COVID-19 Pandemic*, Contributions to Economics,
https://doi.org/10.1007/978-3-031-47780-5_6

spending will negatively affect the taxpayer-government relationship, mainly because of reducing public goods and services supply.

## Literature Review

The literature highlights the various COVID-19 crisis effects on the economy and the importance of the multiple measures which governments can take. Ţibulcă (2021) estimated tax revenues for EU27 Member States in the period 2020–2022, the results indicating that tax revenues in most EU countries declined in 2020 and 2021, with a slight recovery in 2022. The authors recommend that measures be taken to improve the tax revenue level, such as the introduction of progressive taxation, common legislation on the taxation of the profit of multinational companies and the digitalisation of tax systems.

Almeida et al. (2021) analyse the COVID-19 crisis impact on EU households' incomes and highlight that the pandemic can significantly affect disposable income, with lower-income households being affected to a greater extent. According to the authors, the impact of the crisis is expected to be similar to that experienced during the financial crisis, with the tax measures taken having a significant role in mitigating the adverse effects on income.

Sobolevschi David et al. (2021) analysed the pandemic impact on the Romanian business environment. They underlined the importance of increasing the digitalisation of the administration and reducing bureaucracy, as well as tax measures adopted by the state, followed by financial measures adopted at the level of companies, respectively, reducing costs and delaying payment of the suppliers. According to the authors, measures adopted to fight crisis effects must be limited in time to prevent unethical behaviour.

Among the most important obstacles faced by Romanian entrepreneurs who wanted to start a new business during the COVID-19 pandemic crisis are bureaucracy, instability or lack of clarity of legislation, sometimes difficult relationships with state authorities, excessive taxation and corruption (especially within the institutions), but the SMEs benefited from various support measures taken by the authorities, which mitigated the shock of the pandemic crisis (Prelipcean et al., 2021).

The effects of the pandemic on companies from Romania include technical unemployment, a shortage of supply and demand, reduced investment, layoffs and employee departures. The government has adopted measures to help companies overcome the turmoil, and it was also necessary for companies to adopt reorganisation and reorientation measures to cope with market pressures (Morosan-Danila & Bordeianu, 2021).

The impact of COVID-19 on health expenses was studied in the literature, highlighting the high degree of centralisation of the Romanian healthcare system, and the analysis confirmed the health-led growth hypothesis (Onofrei et al., 2021).

According to the authors, increasing health spending and unifying health insurance schemes could help improve health services and economic performance.

The study conducted by Popa (2021) shows that after the first year of the pandemic, among the demand-side components of GDP, private consumption contributed to the greatest extent to the contraction of this indicator in the case of Romania. On the other hand, among the components related to the supply, the most affected types of services were trade, transport, hotels and restaurants and cultural, recreational and entertainment activities.

## Challenges and Measures Adopted in the Area of EU Taxation Mitigating COVID-19 Crisis Impact

The onset of the pandemic impacted the application of customs duties provisions in decision-making, procedures and formalities (Taxation and Customs Union, 2020a). Given the global situation at the time, goods brought into EU customs territory to counteract COVID-19 crisis effects, such as ambulances or medical equipment, could be declared for temporary admission, with total relief from customs duties. The same approach could be applied to the provisional admission of surgical and laboratory equipment.

The European Commission, through Decision (EU) 2020/491 of 3 April 2020, has decided to assist affected Member States by temporarily suspending customs/VAT on protective gear, test kits and medical devices. This measure addresses the import of medical equipment from third countries (Taxation and Customs Union, 2020b). The action facilitated medical equipment access for healthcare personnel and patients.

According to the Commission Decision (EU) 2020/491 of 3 April 2020, goods made available to persons affected/at risk of disease as a result of COVID-19/ engaged in combating COVID-19 outbreak are customs/VAT exempted, and the goods are (Taxation and Customs Union, 2020c) medical devices (fans, artificial respirators; monitors; pumps (nutrition pumps, drug infusion pumps, suction pumps, suction probes); helmets; suction systems); medical supplies (intubation kits, syringes, etc.); monitoring stations and patient monitoring devices; portable ultrasound scanners; computed tomography systems/scanners; paper surgical masks; liquid thermometers, digital thermometers or infrared thermometers for forehead placement; hand washing soap; wheelchairs for people with disabilities and stretchers for transporting patients in hospitals and clinics; COVID-19 test sets; hospital beds; various drugs; and medical, surgical or laboratory sterilisers. Importation without customs/VAT was applied to state organisations (including hospitals, government organisations, etc.) and charities (Taxation and Customs Union, 2020b).

The COVID-19 crisis significantly impacted the economy. Businesses face various problems during this period, such as supply chain disruptions and reduced labour mobility. To find solutions to this crisis, states are taking steps to support households and businesses. Countries have adopted various measures, such as restrictions on the free movement of people and goods, closing a large part of the economy (Saint-Amans, 2020). The result highlights a decline in economic activity in many countries. Measures taken by various countries include:

- Temporary provision of social assistance to individuals and workers, including through benefits provided by the tax system. This includes access to unemployment benefits or sick leave.
- Waiving or postponing social security contributions of employers, self-employed workers and payroll taxes. Vulnerable sectors would benefit from this measure to reduce labour costs.
- Tax exemptions for health workers and other sectors related to the management of emergencies.
- Postponement of VAT and customs/excise duties for imports (food, medicine).
- Extension of payment terms.
- Suspension of debt recovery.

During this crisis, various economic sectors were affected, requiring investments in the health sector, social protection, etc. Tax policy plays a vital role through the measures adopted by different countries, which aim to relax taxation for individuals and businesses. According to the IMF (2020), the principles of tax law design should be observed, such as:

- The use of secondary instruments (such as regulations) or administrative actions (like guidelines) to implement measures instead of changes to existing laws or the adoption of new laws
- Halting reforms during the crisis to preserve system integrity

The analysis of the measures taken by various EU countries highlights the following issues:

- Belgium—automatic extension of the deadline for personal income tax payment. Company tax and social security contributions payments can be deferred. One measure is to provide support for communes that decide to suspend taxes. Among the measures adopted are those related to tax deferrals, such as the suspension of the municipal tax (tax on the hotel sector) and the tax on taxi activities (Anderson et al., 2020). Tax exemption measures have been announced (KPMG, 2020m), and measures have been taken to prolong the due dates for filing corporate and non-resident income tax returns (CIAT/IOTA/OECD, 2020). The payment period is also extended for excise duties on alcohol and all beverages.
- Denmark—postponement of payment for VAT, social security contributions and labour taxes (Anderson et al., 2020). Companies with losses can receive a tax credit for their research and development costs (KPMG, 2020f). Another measure concerns temporarily postponing VAT payments (CIAT/IOTA/OECD, 2020). Thus, the companies paying monthly VAT have a 1-month deferral of VAT payment. There is also a postponement of the payment of taxes due by self-employed workers.

- France—delaying direct taxes and contributions for companies and self-employed individuals (Anderson et al., 2020; CIAT/IOTA/OECD, 2020). Exemptions have been adopted in the case of the payment of tax for businesses and employees (KPMG, 2020e, 2020j). Tax exemption provisions offer 5.5% VAT (reduced from 20%) for face masks and hand sanitisers.
- Germany—indirect taxes and social contributions deferrals (Anderson et al., 2020).
- Greece—tax deferrals, subsidy of self-employed, small business owners and employees' contributions (Anderson et al., 2020). The measures also targeted tax exemptions (KPMG, 2020h, 2020k): tax exemption for businesses and self-employed workers; tax exemption for individual taxpayers; exemptions from paying social security; and a 25% reduction in taxes due (excluding VAT and withholding taxes). A measure has been adopted for SMEs and large enterprises to extend tax return filing and debt payment deadlines (CIAT/IOTA/OECD, 2020).
- Hungary—the cancellation of taxes and social security for various activities; cancellation of the tourism development tax; and cancellation of taxes for small businesses (Anderson et al., 2020). One measure aims at faster VAT refunds for SMEs (KPMG, 2020b). A postponement of tax payments is granted upon fulfilment of specific requirements (CIAT/IOTA/OECD, 2020).
- Italy—reduction of taxes and contributions for companies in the severely affected sectors (tourism, transport, restaurants, culture, sports, education, events), which include (a) suspension of VAT and contributions payment, (b) reduction of tax for income from rents, (c) reduction of the tax on sanitation costs, (d) deductibility of donations for COVID-19 and (e) suspension of tax payment and filing tax returns, and deferrals of taxes and contributions payment (Anderson et al., 2020). Various measures refer to tax exemptions with extended payment deadlines (KPMG, 2020i). There has been a measure to suspend the payment of taxes owed by individuals, businesses and resident professionals in the area subject to a complete lock due to the pandemic (CIAT/IOTA/OECD, 2020). Companies and professionals who did not work anymore due to the pandemic, such as shops, theatres, restaurants, hotels, etc., were subject to a suspension of VAT payments, withholding taxes and social security contributions.
- Netherlands—postponement of tax payments (VAT, income tax, payroll tax and corporate tax) (Anderson et al., 2020; CIAT/IOTA/OECD, 2020). Other measures included offsetting a loss on the previous year's profit or exempting from paying taxes excluding VAT (rescue materials and equipment) and postponement of energy tax and surcharge payment (KPMG, 2020a, 2020g).
- Spain—postponement of the payment of taxes for SMEs and self-employed workers (Anderson et al., 2020).
- UK—postponement of VAT payment (Anderson et al., 2020).
- USA—a tax credit for retaining employees for companies forced to suspend operations or which had gross revenues 50% lower than the previous year and postponement of contributions and payroll tax for employers (Anderson et al., 2020).

- Luxembourg—an extension of companies' and individuals' tax return deadlines; extension of companies' direct and self-employed tax payment deadlines; and removal of VAT returns late submission penalties (Deloitte Luxembourg, 2020).
- Portugal—postponement of transfer pricing documentation submission deadline (KPMG, 2020c).
- Czech Republic—an option proposed in income tax allowing taxpayers to use tax losses retroactively as a tax exemption measure (KPMG, 2020d, 2020n). The tax return filing and payment deadline for personal and corporate taxes has been extended (CIAT/IOTA/OECD, 2020).
- Poland—the deadline for submitting the transfer pricing report being extended (CIAT/IOTA/OECD, 2020). Regarding corporate tax, the deadline for annual tax return filing and payments has been extended. Tax exemptions include extended deadlines for corporate tax returns and waivers for corporate tax payments. Employers can also be exempted from social security contributions under specific conditions (KPMG, 2020l).

The COVID-19 crisis has significantly impacted the activity of companies and the financial situation of many people, who may, for example, be fired or on unpaid leave. For many businesses, especially small businesses and the self-employed, the reduction in economic activity will also have severe consequences as the number of customers decreases significantly, contracts are terminated, supply chains are disrupted, and so on. At the same time, these businesses have certain expenses generated by renting space for business, utility bills, salary costs, etc. Thus, companies may have problems with cash flow, which also affects the suppliers.

Attempts have been made to change tax policy in various countries by adopting measures to assist taxpayers and reduce the tax burden by postponing/suspending the due tax payments. During this period, the public debt of EU countries increased significantly. In the Eurozone, public debt as a proportion of GDP rose from 83.6% (late 2019) to 97.3% (late 2020) and then fell to 91.6% (in 2022). In the EU, the share increased from 77.2% to 90.1% in 2020, falling to 84.0% in 2022 (Table 6.1).

In December 2021, a European Commission proposal emphasised the importance of three new taxes that could be used at the EU level to help repay the joint government loans for the COVID-19 Recovery Fund. The first measure will introduce a tax on CO2 emitted by fuels and apply it to buildings and cars. A quarter of such revenue from CO2 taxation, which now is revenue for governments, would be for the EU budget in the future. The second tax is on carbon for imports of goods from countries with lower CO2 emissions standards, and three-quarters of that revenue will be for the EU budget. The third tax provides the EU budget with a 15% share of residual profit from large multinational companies that will be re-domiciled in EU countries. These proposals were to be negotiated by the European Parliament and EU countries (Strupczewski & Abnett, 2021).

On May 18, 2021, the European Commission issued the Communication on Business Taxation for the 21st Century. This communication outlines EU tax policy to aid Europe's recovery from the COVID-19 crisis. The proposals aim to improve domestic tax relief for losses, tackle aggressive tax planning linked to shell

**Table 6.1** General government gross debt in EU, 2019, 2020 and 2022, % of GDP

| Country/area | 2019 | 2020 | 2022 | Country/area | 2019 | 2020 | 2022 |
|---|---|---|---|---|---|---|---|
| Euro area—19 countries (from 2015) | 83.6 | 97.3 | 91.6 | Cyprus | 91.1 | 115.3 | 86.5 |
| Euro area—18 countries (2014) | 83.8 | 97.6 | – | Latvia | 36.7 | 43.2 | 40.8 |
| European Union—27 countries (from 2020) | 77.2 | 90.1 | 84.0 | Lithuania | 35.9 | 46.6 | 38.4 |
| Belgium | 97.7 | 112.8 | 105.1 | Luxembourg | 22.3 | 24.8 | 24.6 |
| Bulgaria | 20.0 | 24.7 | 22.9 | Hungary | 65.5 | 80.1 | 73.3 |
| Czechia | 30.0 | 37.7 | 44.1 | Malta | 40.7 | 53.4 | 53.4 |
| Denmark | 33.6 | 42.1 | 30.1 | Netherlands | 48.5 | 54.3 | 51.0 |
| Germany | 58.9 | 68.7 | 66.3 | Austria | 70.6 | 83.2 | 78.4 |
| Estonia | 8.6 | 19.0 | 18.4 | Poland | 45.6 | 57.4 | 49.1 |
| Ireland | 57.2 | 58.4 | 44.7 | Portugal | 116.6 | 135.2 | 113.9 |
| Greece | 180.7 | 206.3 | 171.3 | Romania | 35.3 | 47.4 | 47.3 |
| Spain | 95.5 | 120.0 | 113.2 | Slovenia | 65.6 | 79.8 | 69.9 |
| France | 97.5 | 115.0 | 111.6 | Slovakia | 48.1 | 59.7 | 57.8 |
| Croatia | 71.1 | 87.3 | 68.4 | Finland | 59.5 | 69.5 | 73.0 |
| Italy | 134.3 | 155.6 | 144.4 | Sweden | 34.9 | 39.7 | 33.0 |

Source: Eurostat (2023)

companies, require companies to disclose effective tax rates and more. A new corporate taxation framework is envisioned to reduce administrative burdens, eliminate tax barriers and foster a more business-friendly atmosphere in the EU (Deloitte Luxembourg, 2021).

## Tax Measures Adopted During the Pandemic in Romania

With the pandemic's beginning, numerous countries took action to combat its adverse effects, including restrictions on movement and trade. The economy suffered significantly, with sudden declines in economic activity and eroding global trust (Saint-Amans, 2020). Romania also implemented several measures, such as waiving interest and penalties for tax non-payment, suspending enforcement actions on budget receivables and extending deadlines for building, land and transport taxes (KPMG, 2020o).

In Romania, measures were implemented to defer tax payments and exemptions, introduce flexible work schedules and facilitate social contributions payments. These measures (including reductions, deferrals and tax exemptions) were as follows (KPMG, 2020p):

- Discounts for timely corporate/micro-enterprise tax payments
- Exempting customs duties on emergency medical stocks
- Postponed VAT for imported COVID-19 prevention goods

Other adopted measures were the following:

- Benefits for employees amounting to 75% of the basic salary if they had a temporary suspension of employment contract. Eligible individuals on sick leave, paid parental leave or technical unemployment or with contract suspension were guaranteed the insertion incentive for 90 days (GEO no. 30 of March 18, 2020 for the modification and completion of certain normative acts, a Government Emergency Ordinance / OUG nr. 30 din 18 martie 2020 pentru modificarea şi completarea unor acte normative).
- Activity-specific tax was exempted when activities were suspended. VAT on the import of denatured ethyl alcohol for COVID-19 products was postponed (GEO no. 48 of April 9, 2020 regarding certain financial and tax measures / OUG nr. 48 din 9 aprilie 2020 privind unele măsuri financiar-fiscale).
- Five per cent bonus for income tax payments and contributions and e-filing of tax returns and, from 2021, up to 10% bonus for income tax and contributions payments (GEO no. 69 of May 14, 2020 for the amendment and completion of Law no. 227/2015 on the Tax Code, as well as for the establishment of certain tax measures / OUG nr. 69 din 14 mai 2020 pentru modificarea şi completarea Legii nr. 227/2015 privind Codul fiscal, precum şi pentru instituirea unor măsuri fiscale).
- Exemption for 90 days in 2020 for the activity-specific tax and 10% bonus for on-time corporate/micro-enterprise tax payments (GEO no. 99 of June 25, 2020 regarding certain tax measures, the modification of certain normative acts and the extension of certain deadlines / OUG nr. 99 din 25 iunie 2020 privind unele măsuri fiscale, modificarea unor acte normative şi prorogarea unor termene).
- Two per cent to 10% reduction in corporate/micro-enterprise/activity-specific taxes and deadline extension for tax return filing and corporate/micro-enterprise/activity-specific tax payments (GEO no. 153 of September 3, 2020 for the establishment of tax measures to stimulate the maintenance/increase of own capital, as well as for the completion of certain normative acts / OUG nr. 153 din 3 septembrie 2020 pentru instituirea unor măsuri fiscale de stimulare a menţinerii/creşterii capitalurilor proprii, precum şi pentru completarea unor acte normative).

Some of the measures adopted for social protection were as follows (KPMG, 2020p):

- Support for employers in hiring individuals over 50 with full-time contracts (GEO no. 92 of May 28, 2020 for the establishment of active support measures for employees and employers in the context of the epidemiological situation determined by the spread of the SARS-CoV-2 coronavirus, as well as for the modification of certain normative acts / OUG nr. 92 din 28 mai 2020 pentru instituirea unor măsuri active de sprijin destinate angajaţilor şi angajatorilor în contextul situaţiei epidemiologice determinate de răspândirea coronavirusului SARS-CoV-2, precum şi pentru modificarea unor acte normative).

- Fifty per cent of the employee's salary for the employer (12 months), capped at 2500 lei (516 euros)/month/person employed.
- Employees facing reduced work schedules were granted an allowance of 75% of the salary difference resulting from the reduction.
- Employers with fixed-term contracts for employees of up to 3 months received in 2020 a state payment of 41.5% of employees' salaries, capped at 41.5% of the gross average salary.
- One-time financial support of 2500 lei for employers (516 euros); the amount was offered for each employee working remotely for at least 15 working days; this support aimed to facilitate the purchase of technological goods and services.

In the first half of 2019, state budget revenues accounted for 7.6% of GDP; in the first half of 2020, they reached 6.8%. The most significant contribution to the state budget revenues is VAT, with a share of 3.0% in the first half of 2019 (2.4% in the first half of 2020), followed by excise duties (1.4% in the first half of 2019 and 1.3% in the first half of 2020) and income tax (1.1% in the first half of 2019 but also the first half of 2020).

During January–June 2019, the share of revenues to the state social insurance budget in GDP was 3.3%, the ratio decreasing to 3.1% of GDP in the first half of 2020. The budget revenues of the National Health Insurance Fund were 1.6% in the first half of 2019, with the ratio falling to 1.5% in the first half of 2020. Unemployment insurance budget revenues accounted for 0.1% of GDP in the first half of 2019 and the first half of 2020.

Throughout the first 6 months of 2019, the revenues raised to the budget increased by 14.1% compared to the level recorded in the first half of 2018. In the first half of 2019, the degree of voluntary compliance at declaration was 94.8% (decreasing to 92.6% in the first half of 2020), and the voluntary compliance at payment was 86% (compared to 78.4% in the first 6 months of 2020 (ANAF, 2019, 2020, 2020b). In the first 6 months of 2019, voluntary compliance at payment dropped to 86% (Table 6.2). Nonetheless, most regional directorates witnessed a rise in this indicator's value (ANAF, 2019). In 2019, the degree of voluntary filing of tax returns was 94.7%, and compared to 2018, there is an increase of 0.3 pp. The degree of voluntary compliance at payment was 86.6% in 2019, and compared to 2018, there is an increase of 0.2 pp. (ANAF, 2020). In the first half of 2021,

**Table 6.2** Voluntary compliance degree, %

| Indicator | 2018, semester I | 2018 | 2019, semester I | 2019 | 2020, semester I | 2021, semester I | 2022, semester I |
|---|---|---|---|---|---|---|---|
| Degree of voluntary compliance at the declaration | 94.1 | 94.4 | 94.8 | 94.7 | 92.6 | 94.3 | – |
| Degree of voluntary compliance at payment | 86.3 | 86.4 | 86.0 | 86.6 | 78.4 | 85.5 | 86.9 |

Source: ANAF (2019, 2020, 2020b, 2021, 2022)

voluntary compliance at payment stood at 85.5%, and it rose to 86.9% in the first 6 months of 2022, compared to the first 6 months of 2019 (86%) (ANAF, 2021, 2022). Voluntary compliance at payment is determined by dividing receivables by declared amounts. Voluntary compliance at declaration is calculated by dividing the number of taxpayers with timely tax return submissions by the estimated number of total taxpayers. The degree of electronic filing of tax returns (Table 6.3) increased in 2019, compared to 2018, by 1.9 pp. (ANAF, 2019, 2020, 2020b).

During the pandemic, the policymaker adopted measures to sustain income, maintain employment and support businesses. New ways of using taxes to help the economy overcome the challenges posed by the pandemic were considered. This situation could provide an opportunity to use taxes in various ways. The new changes to the tax legislation should be adapted to the current status of the economy and society, heavily shaped by the challenges of the pandemic (Fig. 6.1).

**Table 6.3** Degree of electronic filing of tax returns, %

| Indicator | 2018, semester I | 2018 | 2019, semester I | 2019 |
|---|---|---|---|---|
| Degree of electronic filing of tax returns | 93.9 | 95.2 | 97.0 | 97.1 |

Source: ANAF (2019, 2020, 2020b)

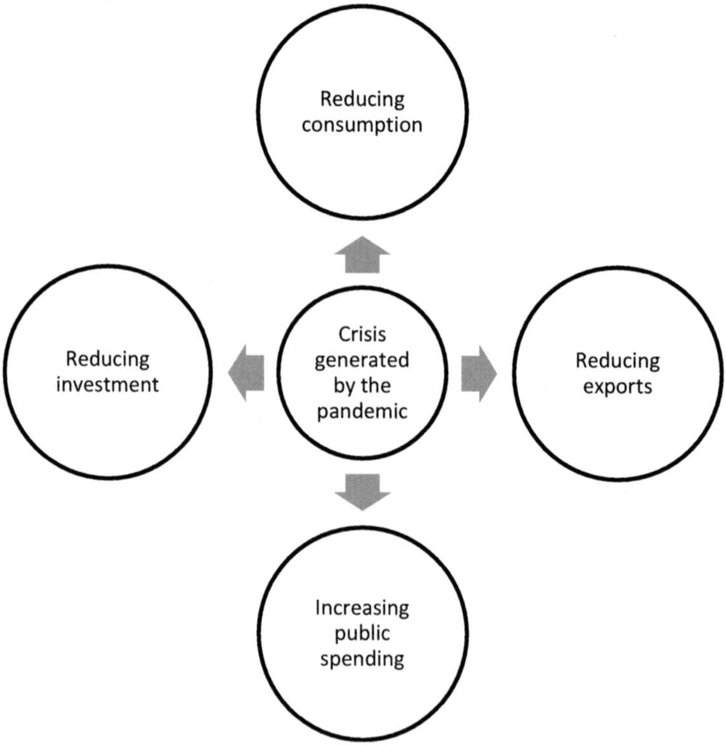


**Fig. 6.1** COVID-19 impact on the economy (Source: developed by the authors)

**Table 6.4** Budget revenues in Romania, % in GDP

| Name of the budget/ tax | 2018, semester I | 2018 | 2019, semester I | 2019 | 2020, semester I | 2021, semester I | 2022, semester I |
|---|---|---|---|---|---|---|---|
| Total revenues—ANAF/NAFA[a] | 11.9 | 25.9 | 12.6 | 26.1 | 11.4 | 12.8 | 13.1 |
| The state budget | 7.3 | 16.2 | 7.6 | 16.2 | 6.8 | 7.8 | 8.5 |
| - Corporate tax | 0.8 | 1.7 | 0.8 | 1.7 | 0.7 | 0.7 | 0.8 |
| - Income tax | 1.2 | 2.4 | 1.1 | 2.2 | 1.1 | 1.2 | 1.2 |
| - VAT | 2.8 | 6.3 | 3.0 | 6.3 | 2.4 | 3.1 | 3.3 |
| - Excise duty (including tax on vice) | 1.4 | 3.0 | 1.4 | 3.0 | 1.3 | 1.4 | 1.2 |
| - Customs duties | 0.1 | 0.1 | 0.1 | 0.1 | 0.1 | 0.1 | 0.1 |
| - Other incomes | 1.0 | 2.7 | 1.4 | 2.9 | 1.3 | 1.1 | 1.9 |
| The budget of the National Health Insurance Fund | 1.6 | 3.3 | 1.6 | 3.1 | 1.5 | 1.6 | 1.4 |
| State social insurance budget | 3.0 | 6.3 | 3.3 | 6.6 | 3.1 | 3.4 | 3.1 |
| Unemployment insurance budget | 0.1 | 0.2 | 0.1 | 0.2 | 0.1 | 0.1 | 0.1 |

Source: ANAF (2019, 2020, 2020b, 2021, 2022)
[a]Agenția Națională de Administrare Fiscală (ANAF)/National Agency for Fiscal Administration (NAFA)

Measures adopted in the area of taxation have various effects on the economy and society. The coronavirus crisis exerted considerable strain on public finances, significantly impacting the revenue generated for the budget, primarily due to a decrease in the tax base. This reduction was due to the increase in the period taxpayers could pay the due taxes. In the future, it is essential to identify ways to spur economic growth without putting even greater pressure on taxpayers, who are already in great difficulty.

Corporate and employee taxation should be revised, emphasising the tax burden and not just the tax rate because the tax is calculated on income or profit. Still, other taxes and contributions are related to the income/profit. Improving this situation would stimulate employment and investment, significantly impacting economic growth. In Romania, there is a reduction in total revenues (as share of GDP) in the 1st semester of 2020 compared to the 1st semester of 2019 (Table 6.4).

The budget deficit is a critical macroeconomic indicator, emphasising the situation in which expenditures exceed budget revenues, thus reflecting the financial health of a country. In 2020, budget deficits in the Euro area and EU significantly increased due to COVID-19 response measures. In the Euro area, the share of government deficit to GDP increased from 0.6% (2019) to 7.2% (2020) and then

**Table 6.5** Government deficit, expenditure and revenue in Romania, 2017–2022, % of GDP

| Indicator | 2017 | 2018 | 2019 | 2020 | 2021 | 2022 |
|---|---|---|---|---|---|---|
| Government deficit/surplus | −2.6 | −2.9 | −4.3 | −9.2 | −7.1 | −6.2 |
| Government expenditure | 33.5 | 34.9 | 36.0 | 41.5 | 39.8 | 39.7 |
| Government revenue | 30.8 | 32.0 | 31.6 | 32.3 | 32.7 | 33.5 |

Source: Eurostat (2021, 2023a, 2023b)

fell to 3.6% (2022). In the EU, it went from 0.5% to 6.9% (2020), dropping to 3.4% (2022).

All Member States reported deficits in 2020, with the largest in Spain (−11.0%) and Greece (−10.1%). Denmark (−0.2%) and Sweden (−2.8%) were the only EU countries with deficits below 3% of GDP (Eurostat, 2021, 2023a, 2023b).

Twenty Member States recorded a deficit in 2022. The countries with the most significant deficits were Malta (−5.8%), Hungary (−6.2%), Romania (−6.2%) and Italy (−8.0%). Eleven countries had deficits that exceeded 3% of GDP. The first three countries with the highest surpluses were Ireland (+1.6%), Cyprus (+2.1%) and Denmark (+3.3%).

The budget deficit in Romania saw a significant increase between 2019 and 2020 (Table 6.5). The government may adopt measures to reduce spending or increase taxation. Still, both solutions have adverse effects on taxpayers, with risks related to increased tax evasion or deteriorating the relationship between authorities and taxpayers.

## The Impact of Diseases on Budget Revenues: The Romanian Case

This section analyses the impact of diseases on indirect taxation, considering critical macroeconomic indicators for the Romanian case, using quarterly data from Q1 2009 to Q3 2021 (Table 6.6). The authors included the influenza A virus subtype H1N1 cases in the dummy variable for diseases. This dummy is also taking into consideration the COVID-19 cases, as well as cases of acute respiratory infections. This section also emphasises the need to verify hypotheses in the regression model to avoid inaccurate results. The categories of tests used to check the specification of the equation are residual diagnostics and stability diagnostics.

The independent variables considered in this analysis refer to the unemployment rate, inflation rate, foreign trade (imports) and a dummy for diseases. In the literature, various studies analyse the factors that have direct or indirect relationships with tax revenues.

Some authors identified a direct relationship between taxation and unemployment (Tagkalakis, 2013; Zirgulis & Šarapovas, 2017), an inverse relationship between taxation and inflation (Poterba & Rotemberg, 1990; Kalaš et al., 2018) and a direct

**Table 6.6** Variables used in the analysis

| Variables | Description | Source | Expected sign |
|---|---|---|---|
| INDTAX | Indirect taxes, %[a] | ANAF (2010–2021)<br>Institutul Național de Statistică (2022) | Dependent variable |
| UNEMPLR | Unemployment rate % | ANAF (2010–2021) | (+) |
| INFR | Inflation rate % | Institutul Național de Statistică (2022) | (−) |
| IMP | Imports, %[b] | ANAF (2010–2021) | (+) |
| DIS | Dummy variable for diseases[c] | Authors | (−) |

Source: authors' contribution

[a] The share of VAT and excise duties to gross domestic product (GDP); VAT and excise duties are sourced from ANAF (2010–2021); GDP is sourced from Institutul Național de Statistică (2022).

[b] Data are in millions of euros by quarters in ANAF (2010–2021), but in analysis, shares in the total of the year were used.

[c] Set to 1 for the periods when there were cases of influenza A virus subtype H1N1 and COVID-19 (the 2009 swine flu pandemic was during June 2009—August 2010, and the pandemic began in March 2020, according to the World Health Organization); also, the variable has the value of 1 for the periods when there were cases of acute respiratory infections (according to Ministerul Sănătății/Ministry of Health, Institutul Național de Sănătate Publică din România/Romanian National Institute of Public Health); the variable has the value of 0 when there are no registered cases.

**Table 6.7** The hypotheses of the study and the tests for the equation specification

| No. | Hypotheses |
|---|---|
| 1 | Direct relationship: indirect taxes and UNEMPLR (unemployment rate) |
| 2 | Inverse relationship: indirect taxes and INFR (inflation rate) |
| 3 | Direct relationship: indirect taxes and IMP (imports) |
| 4 | Inverse relationship: indirect taxes and DIS (disease dummy) |
| No. | Tests for the equation specification |
| 1 | Residual diagnostics |
| 2 | Stability diagnostics |

Source: authors' contribution

relationship between taxation and imports (Ahmed & Mohammed, 2010; Velaj & Prendi, 2014). The variables are shown in the following table.

The following table presents the study's hypotheses and the tests for the equation's specification (Table 6.7). The analysis aims to create an econometric model showing the relationships between indirect taxes, unemployment and inflation rates, imports and a disease dummy variable for the Romanian case (Table 6.8).

The model is defined using the least squares method as follows:

$$Y_t = \alpha + \beta X_t + u_t \tag{6.1}$$

**Table 6.8** Estimation of the parameters

| Dependent variable: INDTAX | | | | |
|---|---|---|---|---|
| Sample: 2009Q1 2021Q3 | | | | |
| Included observations: 51 | | | | |
| Variable | Coefficient | Std. error | t-statistic | Prob. |
| UNEMPLR | 0.003655 | 0.001645 | 2.222298 | 0.0312 |
| INFR | −0.006388 | 0.002428 | −2.630766 | 0.0116 |
| IMP | 0.005614 | 0.098919 | 0.056755 | 0.9550 |
| DIS | −0.011383 | 0.004637 | −2.455023 | 0.0179 |
| C | 0.099377 | 0.027833 | 3.570420 | 0.0008 |
| R-squared | 0.302657 | Mean dependent var. | | 0.105268 |
| Adjusted R-squared | 0.242019 | S.D. dependent var. | | 0.016927 |
| S.E. of regression | 0.014737 | Akaike info criterion | | −5.503998 |
| Sum squared resid | 0.009990 | Schwarz criterion | | −5.314604 |
| Log likelihood | 145.3520 | Hannan-Quinn criter. | | −5.431625 |
| F-statistic | 4.991169 | Durbin-Watson stat | | 1.470657 |
| Prob(F-statistic) | 0.001996 | | | |

Source: authors' contribution

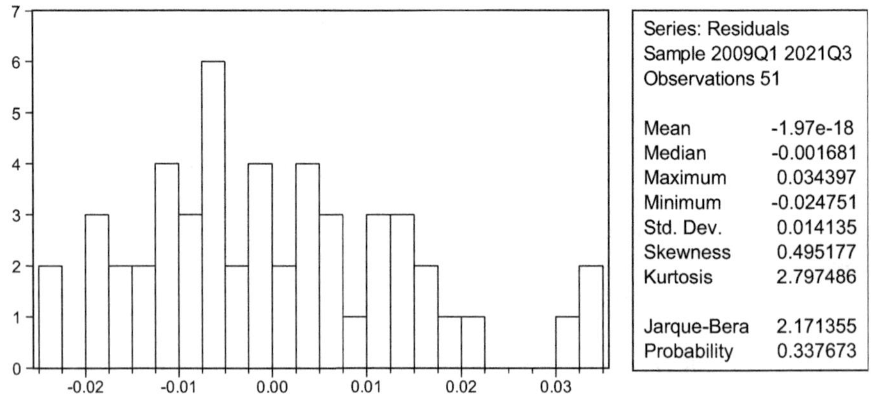


**Fig. 6.2** The histogram and descriptive statistics of the residuals (Source: authors' contribution)

The equation consists of $Y_t$ (INDTAX) as the dependent variable and $X_t$ (unemployment and inflation rates, imports and a disease dummy) as the independent variables. The least squares method is utilised to estimate the parameters.

There are categories of tests to check the specification of the equation, such as residual diagnostics and stability diagnostics. Regarding residual diagnostics, the Jarque-Bera test assesses whether the series is normally distributed. The residuals are normally distributed for this model, and the Jarque-Bera statistic is insignificant. The hypothesis of the normal distribution is accepted (Fig. 6.2).

**Table 6.9** Breusch-Pagan-Godfrey heteroscedasticity test

| | | | | |
|---|---|---|---|---|
| F-statistic | 0.641490 | Prob. F(4,46) | | 0.6356 |
| Obs*R-squared | 2.694560 | Prob. chi-square(4) | | 0.6102 |
| Scaled explained SS | 1.970146 | Prob. chi-square(4) | | 0.7412 |
| Test equation: | | | | |
| Dependent variable: RESID^2 | | | | |
| Method: least squares | | | | |
| Sample: 2009Q1 2021Q3 | | | | |
| Included observations: 51 | | | | |
| Variable | Coefficient | Std. error | t-statistic | Prob. |
| C | 0.000467 | 0.000508 | 0.918534 | 0.3631 |
| UNEMPLR | 1.78E-05 | 3.00E-05 | 0.591783 | 0.5569 |
| INFR | −7.21E-06 | 4.43E-05 | −0.162497 | 0.8716 |
| IMP | −0.001600 | 0.001806 | −0.885722 | 0.3804 |
| DIS | 8.16E-05 | 8.47E-05 | 0.963801 | 0.3402 |
| R-squared | 0.052835 | Mean dependent var. | | 0.000196 |
| Adjusted R-squared | −0.029528 | S.D. dependent var. | | 0.000265 |
| S.E. of regression | 0.000269 | Akaike info criterion | | −13.50984 |
| Sum squared resid | 3.33E-06 | Schwarz criterion | | −13.32045 |
| Log likelihood | 349.5010 | Hannan-Quinn criter. | | −13.43747 |
| F-statistic | 0.641490 | Durbin-Watson stat | | 2.307903 |
| Prob(F-statistic) | 0.635633 | | | |

Source: authors' contribution

The residual diagnostics necessitate some tests to identify the presence of homoscedasticity (constant variance of residuals with any value of the $x_i$ variable) (Tables 6.9 and 6.10).

Based on the obtained results, the data exhibit homoscedasticity, and the White test confirms the absence of heteroscedasticity.

The following graphs show the lack of a relationship between residuals and exogenous variables (Fig. 6.3).

The analysis of the residuals should take into consideration the testing of the following two hypotheses (Săvoiu, 2011):

(a) The mean of errors is zero (or tends to zero)—this is verified by examining the residuals' descriptive statistics and the mean value; our results indicate that the mean tends to zero ($-1.97 \times 10^{-18}$) (Fig. 6.4, Table 6.11).

(b) The Durbin-Watson test (Durbin & Watson, 1950, 1951) is used to check the hypothesis of independent residuals or uncorrelated errors; according to our

**Table 6.10** White heteroscedasticity test

| | | | | |
|---|---|---|---|---|
| F-statistic | 0.763144 | Prob. F(4,46) | | 0.5547 |
| Obs*R-squared | 3.173765 | Prob. chi-square(4) | | 0.5292 |
| Scaled explained SS | 2.320521 | Prob. chi-square(4) | | 0.6770 |
| Test equation: | | | | |
| Dependent variable: RESID^2 | | | | |
| Method: least squares | | | | |
| Sample: 2009Q1 2021Q3 | | | | |
| Included observations: 51 | | | | |
| Variable | Coefficient | Std. error | t-statistic | Prob. |
| C | 0.000204 | 0.000250 | 0.817446 | 0.4179 |
| UNEMPLR^2 | 2.29E-06 | 2.99E-06 | 0.764181 | 0.4487 |
| INFR^2 | −2.12E-05 | 2.33E-05 | −0.913524 | 0.3657 |
| IMP^2 | −0.001340 | 0.003452 | −0.388179 | 0.6997 |
| DIS^2 | 7.98E-05 | 8.34E-05 | 0.956021 | 0.3441 |
| R-squared | 0.062231 | Mean dependent var. | | 0.000196 |
| Adjusted R-squared | −0.019314 | S.D. dependent var. | | 0.000265 |
| S.E. of regression | 0.000268 | Akaike info criterion | | −13.51981 |
| Sum squared resid | 3.30E-06 | Schwarz criterion | | −13.33042 |
| Log likelihood | 349.7553 | Hannan-Quinn criter. | | −13.44744 |
| F-statistic | 0.763144 | Durbin-Watson stat | | 2.295851 |
| Prob(F-statistic) | 0.554687 | | | |

Source: authors' contribution

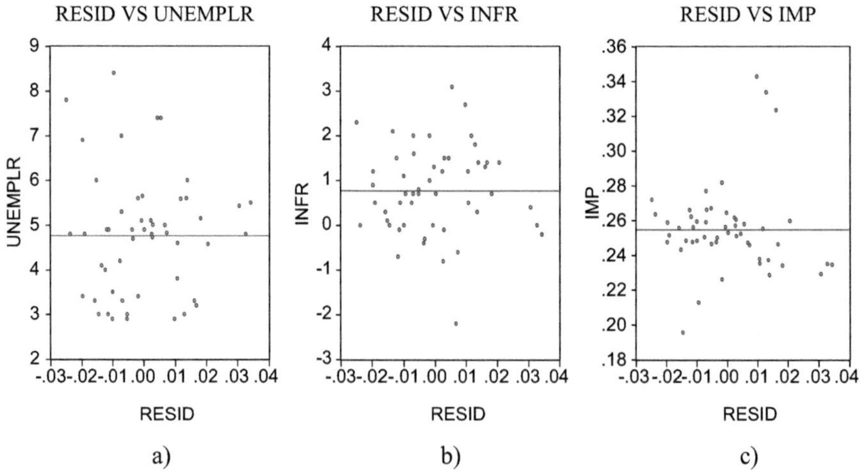


**Fig. 6.3** Residuals' relationships with exogenous variables: (**a**) RESID vs UNEMPLR; (**b**) RESID vs INFR; (**c**) RESID vs IMP (Source: authors' contribution)

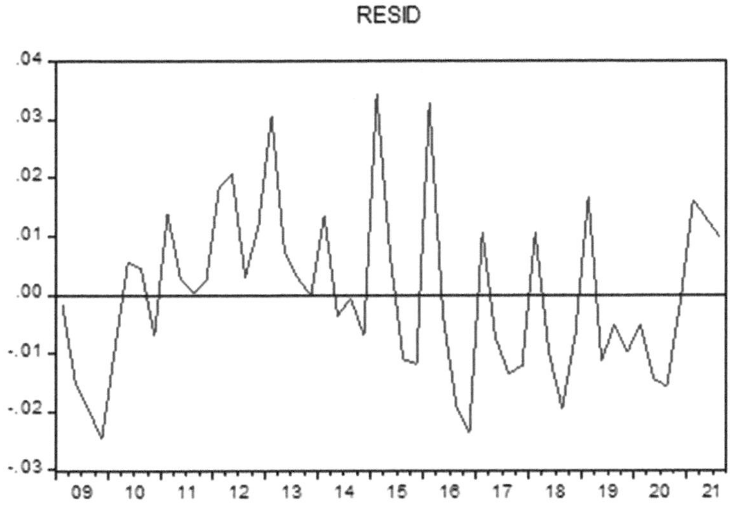


**Fig. 6.4** Residuals' variation around a zero mean (Source: authors' contribution)

results, the value of d is 1.470657, and the corresponding critical values, dL and dU, for $n = 50$, are 1.378 and 1.721, respectively. The result falls within dL ≤ d ≤ dU, leading to an inconclusive outcome at the 0.05 threshold.

Various tests in stability diagnostics assess model parameter stability across different data subsamples. According to the recursive least squares method, larger data subsets are repeatedly used to estimate the equation. The recursive residual is the one-step ahead forecast error obtained from the prediction. Some tests may be performed within this method, such as the CUSUM test and the CUSUM of squares test (Figs. 6.5 and 6.6).

The CUSUM test analyses the recursive residuals' cumulative sum (Brown et al., 1975). The method underlines that the parameter instability is present if the obtained values appear outside the area represented by the critical lines. In this case, this test does not indicate instability in the equation. Also, in the case of the CUSUM of squares test (Brown et al., 1975), if the values are found outside the critical lines, then the parameter instability may be present. The results are generally within the significance lines, meaning the model is somewhat stable.

**Table 6.11** Residuals' descriptive statistics

| Residuals | | | | | | | | Descriptive statistics for the residuals | |
|---|---|---|---|---|---|---|---|---|---|
| 2009Q1 | −0.00168 | 2012Q2 | 0.020677 | 2015Q3 | −0.01107 | 2018Q4 | −0.0067 | Mean | −1.97E-18 |
| 2009Q2 | −0.01511 | 2012Q3 | 0.003064 | 2015Q4 | −0.01175 | 2019Q1 | 0.016858 | Median | −0.00168 |
| 2009Q3 | −0.01956 | 2012Q4 | 0.011858 | 2016Q1 | 0.032828 | 2019Q2 | −0.01133 | Maximum | 0.034397 |
| 2009Q4 | −0.02475 | 2013Q1 | 0.030741 | 2016Q2 | −0.00328 | 2019Q3 | −0.00516 | Minimum | −0.02475 |
| 2010Q1 | −0.00936 | 2013Q2 | 0.007466 | 2016Q3 | −0.01896 | 2019Q4 | −0.00993 | Std. dev. | 0.014135 |
| 2010Q2 | 0.005633 | 2013Q3 | 0.00293 | 2016Q4 | −0.02359 | 2020Q1 | −0.00523 | Skewness | 0.495177 |
| 2010Q3 | 0.004552 | 2013Q4 | −0.00022 | 2017Q1 | 0.010871 | 2020Q2 | −0.01443 | Kurtosis | 2.797486 |
| 2010Q4 | −0.00688 | 2014Q1 | 0.013696 | 2017Q2 | −0.00743 | 2020Q3 | −0.01575 | Jarque-Bera | 2.171355 |
| 2011Q1 | 0.014035 | 2014Q2 | −0.00358 | 2017Q3 | −0.01344 | 2020Q4 | −0.0017 | Probability | 0.337673 |
| 2011Q2 | 0.002708 | 2014Q3 | −0.00056 | 2017Q4 | −0.01222 | 2021Q1 | 0.016215 | Sum | −5.55E-17 |
| 2011Q3 | 0.000333 | 2014Q4 | −0.00694 | 2018Q1 | 0.010764 | 2021Q2 | 0.013018 | Sum sq. dev. | 0.00999 |
| 2011Q4 | 0.002439 | 2015Q1 | 0.034397 | 2018Q2 | −0.00986 | 2021Q3 | 0.009877 | Observations | 51 |
| 2012Q1 | 0.018286 | 2015Q2 | 0.006865 | 2018Q3 | −0.01962 | | | | |

Source: authors' contribution

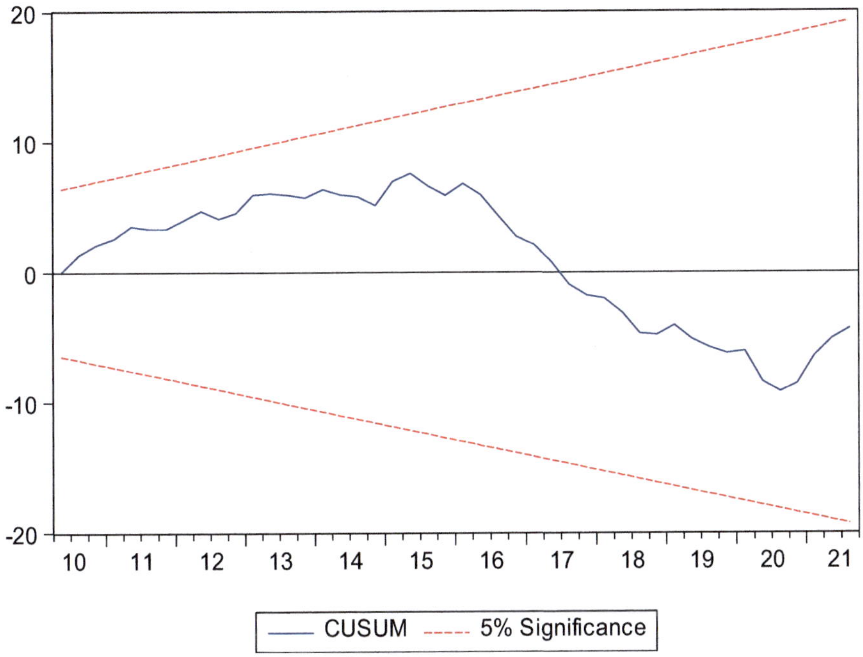


Fig. 6.5 Recursive residuals' cumulative sum (Source: authors' contribution)

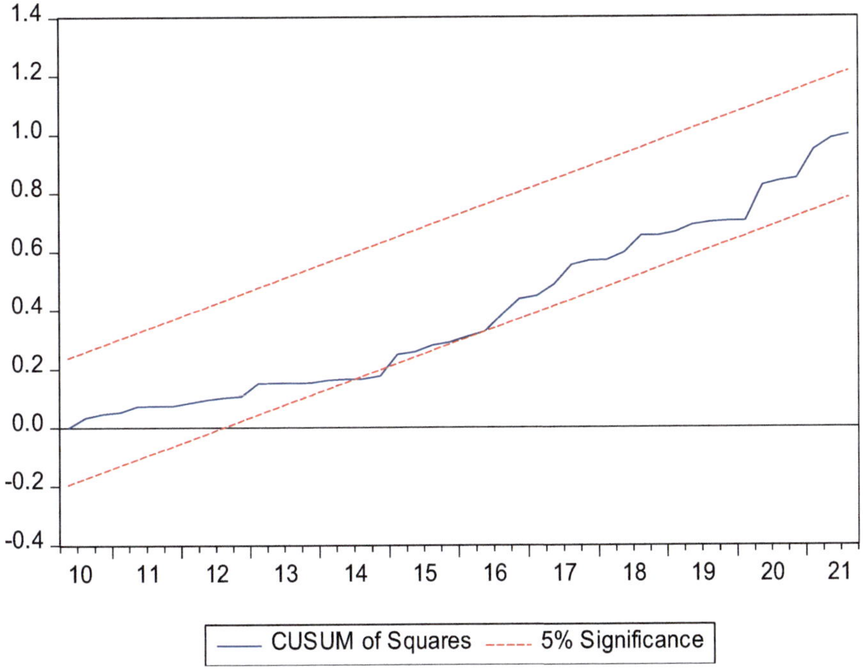


Fig. 6.6 Recursive residuals' cumulative sum of squares (Source: authors' contribution)

## Conclusions

The COVID-19 crisis has impacted countries' budgets, leading to substantial declines in tax revenues. Measures taken by governments to support specific activities have also contributed to this situation. The tax measures adopted have strongly impacted the economy and society. To maintain a relationship of trust with taxpayers, the policymaker can aim to provide tax services and support and develop digital solutions in this area. Also, adopting measures to prevent tax evasion can contribute to developing this relationship between the authorities and the taxpayer.

Some proposals of measures for the case of Romania may take into account the following aspects:

- Cutting tax rates to aid businesses adversely affected by the COVID-19 crisis—a measure targeting companies in severely affected sectors (e.g. tourism)
- Reducing the rates of taxes paid by employers for employees working from home
- Encouraging the adoption of remote work for seniors—encouraging retired workers to return to work, but working from home, ensuring that pension rights are not affected, with reduced tax rates on labour income

In various countries, the policymaker focused on adopting measures for vulnerable sectors, but those measures have contributed to increasing the budget deficit. In the long run, the tax measures may be aimed at reducing these deficits. These measures should strengthen budget revenues and take into account the principles of taxation, such as neutrality (equal conditions), certainty (clear rules), tax equity (tax burden based on contributory power), predictability of taxation (stability of taxes for some time when no changes can occur), etc.

The model examines the impact of unemployment, inflation, imports and diseases on Romania's indirect tax revenue, identifying statistically significant relationships. Three variables significantly impact indirect taxes (unemployment, inflation rates and disease dummy). Unemployment and imports are positively associated with indirect taxes, but the coefficient for variable IMP lacks statistical significance. Inflation rate and disease dummy are negatively related to indirect taxes. Further research with diverse methodologies is essential due to the topic's importance. The analysis underscores the significance of checking hypotheses for regression models, employing multiple tests to verify equation specifications.

The analysis is limited by the data set used. New data will be available for future research to develop the disease dummy variable. Extending the group of variables with influence on tax revenues is also essential. This might bring interesting new results.

Lessons learned from this period of pandemic in the area of public policy might refer to the following:

- Tax-related measures were very important in lessening COVID-19's impact on household and business incomes.
- Although measures to support sectors in difficulty have been economically and socially beneficial, they should be redesigned once the activities will return to normal to ensure the much-needed financial flows to the economy.

- The support of disadvantaged people is essential, as they are in a situation of losing their job due to closing or restricting the activities of businesses, and it is also necessary to create measures to return to the labour market.

  Challenges of tax policy following this period of pandemic might be related to the following:

- Identification of measures that can be adopted in the tax area which do not have adverse effects on economic development.
- Enhancing tax system design to encourage workers and enterprises to transition from the shadow economy.
- Tax increases/new taxes adoption should target those taxpayers who can bear them, sparing those for which even the current level of taxation is already a burden. Presently, the low-income population and small businesses have been significantly impacted by the pandemic, and they lack the resources to manage additional taxes.
- Using public revenues for investments can positively influence the economy in the post-pandemic period, being essential to prioritise investments that generate the most significant positive effects in areas such as health, innovative technologies and digitalisation.

## References


Ahmed, Q. M., & Mohammed, S. D. (2010). Determinant of Tax Buoyancy: Empirical Evidence from Developing Countries. *European Journal of Social Sciences, 13*(3), 408–414.

Almeida, V., Barrios, S., Christl, M., De Poli, S., Tumino, A., & van der Wielen, W. (2021). The impact of COVID-19 on households´ income in the EU. *The Journal of Economic Inequality, 19*, 413–431. https://doi.org/10.1007/s10888-021-09485-8

ANAF. (2010-2021). *Buletinul statistic fiscal/Tax statistical bulletin*. www.anaf.ro

ANAF. (2019). *Raport de activitate*. Semestrul I 2019. https://static.anaf.ro/static/10/Anaf/Informatii_R/Rap_activitate_semI_2019.pdf

ANAF. (2020). *Raport de performanță 2019*. https://static.anaf.ro/static/10/Anaf/Informatii_R/Raport_performanta_07072020.pdf

ANAF. (2020b). *Raport de activitate*. Semestrul I 2020. https://static.anaf.ro/static/10/Anaf/Informatii_R/Raport_activitateS1_11122020.pdf

ANAF. (2021). *Raport de activitate*. Semestrul I 2021. https://static.anaf.ro/static/10/Anaf/Informatii_R/Raport_activitate_S1_2021_261021.pdf

ANAF. (2022). *Raport de activitate*. Semestrul I 2022. https://static.anaf.ro/static/10/Anaf/Informatii_R/Raport_activitateANAF_2022_SI_V6.pdf

Anderson, J., Bergamini, E., Brekelmans, S., Cameron, A., Darvas, Z., & Domínguez Jíménez, M. (2020). *The fiscal response to the economic fallout from the coronavirus*. https://www.bruegel.org/publications/datasets/covid-national-dataset/

Brown, R. L., Durbin, J., & Evans, J. M. (1975). Techniques for Testing the Constancy of Regression Relationships Over Time. *Journal of the Royal Statistical Society, Series B, 37*, 149–192.

CIAT/IOTA/OECD. (2020). *Tax Administration Responses to COVID-19: Measures Taken to Support Taxpayers*. OECD.

Deloitte Luxembourg. (2020). *New tax measures implemented in response to COVID-19*. https://www.taxathand.com/article/13164/Luxembourg/2020/New-tax-measures-implemented-in-response-to-COVID-19

Deloitte Luxembourg. (2021). *European Commission proposes new and ambitious business tax policy agenda*. https://www.taxathand.com/article/17645/European-Union/2021/European-Commission-proposes-new-and-ambitious-business-tax-policy-agenda

Durbin, J., & Watson, G. S. (1950). Testing for serial correlation in least squares regression, I. *Biometrika, 37*(3–4), 409–428. https://doi.org/10.1093/biomet/37.3-4.409

Durbin, J., & Watson, G. S. (1951). Testing for serial correlation in least squares regression, II. *Biometrika, 38*(1–2), 159–179. https://doi.org/10.1093/biomet/38.1-2.159

Eurostat. (2021). *Provision of deficit and debt data for 2020–second notification*. Euro area government deficit at 7.2% and EU at 6.9% of GDP. Government debt at 97.3% and 90.1% respectively, 119/2021. https://ec.europa.eu/eurostat/documents/2995521/11563331/2-21102021-AP-EN.pdf/257365fa-8a66-cab8-f60c-06ca9c916a7a

Eurostat. (2023a). *Government deficit/surplus, debt and associated data*. https://ec.europa.eu/eurostat/databrowser/view/GOV_10DD_EDPT1__custom_7025285/default/table?lang=en

Eurostat. (2023b, April 21). *Provision of deficit and debt data for 2022–first notification*. Euro area government deficit at 3.6% and EU at 3.4% of GDP. Government debt at 91.6% and 84.0% respectively, 47/2023. https://ec.europa.eu/eurostat/documents/2995521/16349856/2-21042023-AP-EN.pdf/6c5d7d4d-1988-dd8b-ea8e-7af2f5049031

IMF. (2020). *Tax law design considerations when implementing responses to the COVID-19 crisis*.

Institutul Național de Statistică. (2022). *Tempo Online, GDP*. http://statistici.insse.ro:8077/tempo-online/

Kalaš, B., Mirović, V., & Andrašić, J. (2018). Empirical analysis of value added tax and inflation rate: Tuckey's HSD test in selected Western Balkan Countries. *Економика, 64*(2), 99–109. https://doi.org/10.5937/ekonomika1802099K

KPMG. (2020a, April 28). *Netherlands: Tax measures proposed to provide business tax relief (COVID-19)*. https://home.kpmg/us/en/home/insights/2020/04/tnf-netherlands-tax-measures-proposed-provide-business-tax-relief.html

KPMG. (2020b, April 27). *Hungary: Expedited refunds of VAT (COVID-19)*. https://home.kpmg/us/en/home/insights/2020/04/tnf-hungary-expedited-refunds-vat.html

KPMG. (2020c, April 27). *Portugal: Postponed deadline for transfer pricing documentation (COVID-19)*. https://home.kpmg/us/en/home/insights/2020/04/tnf-portugal-postponed-deadline-for-transfer-pricing-documentation-covid-19.html

KPMG. (2020d, April 24). *Czech Republic: Tax loss carryback, carryforward relief proposals (COVID-19)*. https://home.kpmg/us/en/home/insights/2020/04/tnf-czech-republic-tax-loss-carryback-carryforward-relief-proposals-covid-19.html.

KPMG. (2020e, April 21). *France: Update of tax relief, other relief measures (COVID-19)*. https://home.kpmg/us/en/home/insights/2020/04/tnf-france-update-of-tax-relief-other-relief-measures-covid-19.html#

KPMG. (2020f, April 20). *Denmark: New tax measures aim to increase corporate liquidity (COVID-19)*. https://home.kpmg/us/en/home/insights/2020/04/tnf-denmark-new-tax-measures-aim-to-increase-corporate-liquidity-covid-19.html

KPMG. (2020g, April 20). *Netherlands: Details of emergency tax measures (COVID-19)*. https://home.kpmg/us/en/home/insights/2020/04/tnf-netherlands-details-emergency-tax-measures.html.

KPMG. (2020h, April 16). *Greece: Summary of tax relief (COVID-19)*. https://home.kpmg/us/en/home/insights/2020/04/tnf-greece-summary-tax-relief.html.

KPMG. (2020i, April 15). *Italy: Tax relief, support for business in "liquidity decree" (COVID-19)*. https://home.kpmg/us/en/home/insights/2020/04/tnf-italy-tax-relief-support-business-liquidity-decree.html

KPMG. (2020j, April 7). *France: Overview of tax relief, other relief measures (COVID-19).* https://home.kpmg/us/en/home/insights/2020/04/tnf-france-overview-tax-relief-other-relief-measures.html

KPMG. (2020k, April 3). *Greece: Additional tax relief measures (COVID-19).* https://home.kpmg/us/en/home/insights/2020/04/tnf-greece-additional-tax-relief-measures.html

KPMG. (2020l, April 2). *Poland: Tax relief measures include extended filing, paying deadlines (COVID-19).* https://home.kpmg/us/en/home/insights/2020/04/tnf-poland-tax-relief-measures-include-extended-filing-paying-deadlines-covid-19.html

KPMG. (2020m, April 1). *Belgium: Tax relief includes extended tax return filing, tax payment deadlines (COVID-19).* https://home.kpmg/us/en/home/insights/2020/04/tnf-belgium-tax-relief-includes-extended-tax-return-filing-tax-payment-deadlines-covid-19.html

KPMG. (2020n, April 1). *Czech Republic: Tax relief measures (COVID-19).* https://home.kpmg/us/en/home/insights/2020/04/tnf-czech-republic-tax-relief-measures.html

KPMG. (2020o). *OUG 29/2020–Măsuri fiscale pentru perioada stării de urgență determinată de epidemia de COVID-19*, 23 martie 2020. https://home.kpmg/ro/ro/home/publicatii/2020/03/oug-29-2020-masuri-fiscale-pentru-perioada-starii-de-urgenta.html

KPMG. (2020p). *Romania–Government and institution measures in response to COVID-19.* https://home.kpmg/xx/en/home/insights/2020/04/romania-government-and-institution-measures-in-response-to-covid.html

Morosan-Danila, L., & Bordeianu, O. M. (2021). Tax facilities for Romanian companies in combating the crisis generated by COVID-19. "Ovidius" University Annals. *Economic Sciences Series, XXI*(1/2021), 369–376. https://stec.univ-ovidius.ro/html/anale/RO/2021/Section%203/28.pdf

Onofrei, M., Cigu, E., Gavriluta, A.-F., Bostan, I., & Oprea, F. (2021). Effects of the COVID-19 Pandemic on the Budgetary Mechanism Established to Cover Public Health Expenditure. A Case Study of Romania. *International Journal of Environmental Research and Public Health, 18*(3), 1134. https://doi.org/10.3390/ijerph18031134

Popa, C. E. (2021). The impact of the first year of Covid-19 pandemic on Romania's economic growth. *Revista Economica, 73*(4), 65–75. http://economice.ulbsibiu.ro/revista.economica/archive/73405popa.pdf

Poterba, J. M., & Rotemberg, J. J. (1990). Inflation and Taxation with Optimizing Governments. *Journal of Money, Credit and Banking, 22*(1), 1. https://doi.org/10.2307/1992124

Prelipcean, G., Boghean, C., & Lupan, M. (2021). The impact of the COVID-19 on entrepreneurship in the North East region–resilient growth solutions. In G. C. Pascariu, R. Crudu, L. M. Simionov, & C. Încălțărău (Eds.), *Assessing the EU's Actorness in the Eastern Neighbourhood–EURINT 2021*. Editura Universității "Alexandru Iona Cuza" din Iași. https://eurint.uaic.ro/proceedings/articles/EURINT2021.pdf

Săvoiu, Gh. (2011). *Econometrie*. Ed. Universitară.

Saint-Amans, P. (2020). *Tax in the time of COVID-19.* https://www.oecd-forum.org/users/369395-pascal-saint-amans/posts/63721-tax-in-the-time-of-covid-19

Sobolevschi David, M. I., Petcu, M. A., Țâțu, L., Cataramă, D., Ciobanu, R., Jinga, G., Gavril (Moldovan), I. A., Balaban, G., & Avram (Zamfir), M. (2021). The Impact of COVID-19 Crisis on Fiscal Environment in Romania, 189-206. In A. M. Dima, I. Anghel, & R. C. Dobrea (Eds.), *Economic Recovery After COVID-19. Springer Proceedings in Business and Economics.* Springer. https://doi.org/10.1007/978-3-030-86641-9_10

Strupczewski, J., & Abnett K. (2021). *EU proposes 3 new taxes to repay COVID-19 recovery fund borrowing.* https://www.reuters.com/business/eu-commission-proposes-three-new-eu-taxes-repay-recovery-fund-borrowing-2021-12-22/

Tagkalakis, A. O. (2013). The unemployment effects of fiscal policy: recent evidence from Greece. *IZA Journal of European Labor Studies, 2*, 11. https://doi.org/10.1186/2193-9012-2-11

Taxation and Customs Union. (2020a). *Guidance on Customs issues related to the COVID-19 emergency.* https://ec.europa.eu/taxation_customs/covid-19-taxud-response/guidance-customs-issues-related-covid-19-emergency_en

Taxation and Customs Union. (2020b). *COVID-19: Waiving VAT and customs duties on vital medical equipment*. https://ec.europa.eu/taxation_customs/covid-19-taxud-response/covid-19-waiving-vat-and-customs-duties-vital-medical-equipment_en

Taxation and Customs Union. (2020c). *Import duties and VAT exemptions on importation*. https://ec.europa.eu/taxation_customs/sites/taxation/files/03-04-2020-import-duties-vat-exemptions-on-importation-covid-19-list-of-goods.pdf

Ţibulcă, I. L. (2021). The impact of the COVID-19 pandemic on tax revenues in the EU. *Economic Research–Ekonomska Istraživanja, 35*(1), 2442–2459. https://doi.org/10.1080/1331677X.2021.1954967

Velaj, E., & Prendi, L. (2014). Tax revenue–the determinant factors–the case of Albania. *European Scientific Journal, 1*, 526–531. https://eujournal.org/index.php/esj/article/download/4121/3955/0

Zirgulis, A., & Šarapovas, T. (2017). Impact of Corporate Taxation on Unemployment. *Journal of Business Economics and Management, 18*(3), 412–426. https://doi.org/10.3846/16111699.2016.1278400

***, Commission Decision (EU) 2020/491 of 3 April 2020 on relief from import duties and VAT exemption on importation granted for goods needed to combat the effects of the COVID-19 outbreak during 2020 (notified under document C(2020) 2146).

***, GEO no. 30 of March 18, 2020 for the modification and completion of certain normative acts / OUG nr. 30 din 18 martie 2020 pentru modificarea şi completarea unor acte normative.

***, GEO no. 48 of April 9, 2020 regarding certain financial and fiscal measures / OUG nr. 48 din 9 aprilie 2020 privind unele măsuri financiar-fiscale.

***, GEO no. 69 of May 14, 2020 for the amendment and completion of Law no. 227/2015 on the Tax Code, as well as for the establishment of certain tax measures / OUG nr. 69 din 14 mai 2020 pentru modificarea şi completarea Legii nr. 227/2015 privind Codul fiscal, precum şi pentru instituirea unor măsuri fiscale.

***, GEO no. 92 of May 28, 2020 for the establishment of active support measures for employees and employers in the context of the epidemiological situation determined by the spread of the SARS-CoV-2 coronavirus, as well as for the modification of certain normative acts / OUG nr. 92 din 28 mai 2020 pentru instituirea unor măsuri active de sprijin destinate angajaţilor şi angajatorilor în contextul situaţiei epidemiologice determinate de răspândirea coronavirusului SARS-CoV-2, precum şi pentru modificarea unor acte normative.

***, GEO no. 99 of June 25, 2020 regarding certain tax measures, the modification of certain normative acts and the extension of certain deadlines / OUG nr. 99 din 25 iunie 2020 privind unele măsuri fiscale, modificarea unor acte normative şi prorogarea unor termene.

***, GEO no. 153 of September 3, 2020 for the establishment of tax measures to stimulate the maintenance/increase of own capital, as well as for the completion of certain normative acts / OUG nr. 153 din 3 septembrie 2020 pentru instituirea unor măsuri fiscale de stimulare a menţinerii/creşterii capitalurilor proprii, precum şi pentru completarea unor acte normative.

# Part II
# Constraints on Labor Market Participation. Changing the Employment Paradigm

# Chapter 7
# The (Post)Pandemic Employment Model

**Ana-Maria Ciuhu**

**Abstract** The year 2020 was a historic turning point, shaped by the COVID-19 pandemic and the digital revolution. This chapter explores how these forces have reshaped the employment landscape, with a focus on Romania.

Before the pandemic, work was often rigid, with an 8-h workday in physical offices. However, the pandemic brought swift changes, introducing flexibility in where and when work takes place. Teleworking became the norm, challenging the traditional 5-day workweek, with the 4-day workweek gaining traction.

Global companies like Unilever and Microsoft had already experimented with the 4-day workweek, proving its potential to boost productivity and employee satisfaction. Its wider adoption could drive post-pandemic recovery, offering benefits for both companies and employees.

The pandemic also accelerated automation in Romania, streamlining tasks and optimising resource allocation. Artificial intelligence and artificial general intelligence are reshaping employment.

This chapter concludes by examining job transformation due to automation, highlighting both opportunities for upskilling and concerns about job displacement. Insights from an OECD survey shed light on AI's impact in finance and manufacturing sectors.

In summary, this chapter navigates a changing employment landscape influenced by the pandemic and digitalisation, emphasising the need for proactive measures to ensure a fair and productive future of work.

A.-M. Ciuhu (✉)
Institute of National Economy - Romanian Academy; National Institute of Statistics, Bucharest, Romania

 
V. Vasile, E. Bunduchi (eds.), *The Economic and Social Impact of the COVID-19 Pandemic*, Contributions to Economics,
https://doi.org/10.1007/978-3-031-47780-5_7

## General Framework

Revolutions involve radical crossroads and occur throughout history when social and economic systems are influenced by new technologies or ways of perceiving the world (Schwab, 2016, p. 11). The year 2020 will certainly be seen in history as a turning point. Related to the COVID-19 pandemic and its implications on human capital, the digital revolution produces externalities and, implicitly, positive and negative adjustments, which change the profile of professions.

Until the onset of the COVID-19 pandemic, the work standard was rigid: it hardly supported any changes, in most economic activities being clearly set at 8 h a day, 5 days a week, spent in the workspace provided by the employer. The situation changed radically following the pandemic, both spatially and temporally. Many economic activities are carried out today by teleworking. The 5 working days are contested by the 4-day system, and work is directly associated with personal or family life, as a result of online preschool and school education.

Globally, the 4-day working week has already been tested even before the pandemic in large corporations, such as Unilever and Microsoft (Kelly, 2019), with proven effects in increasing productivity and employee satisfaction. This measure, implemented on a large scale and not only on an experimental level, could be the drive for recovery and post-pandemic resilience, through the results it may imply: increased productivity and decreased general expenses for companies, but also the possibility for employees to take care of their personal life one extra day a week without sacrificing their income or professional career.

Last, but not least, the COVID-19 pandemic has forced the implementation of automated technologies in most economic sectors at a faster pace than ever before. This will substantially contribute to the remodelling of employees' working time, because those repetitive daily or monthly tasks will be automated, which will lead to more efficient allocation of time and resources. The most recent developments are focused on artificial intelligence (AI) and on its newest form, artificial general intelligence (AGI), and they will involve new emerging forms of employment.

## Coordinates of Working Time During the Pandemic: The Case of Romania

The main data source regarding the labour market and working time is the Labour Force Survey, carried out annually by the National Institute of Statistics and harmonised at European level (National Institute of Statistics, 2023a, 2023b). There is a difference between the two indicators that outline the working time, i.e. the usual duration and the effective duration of the working week. The usual duration represents the duration of the typical working week, which also includes extra time, if these are systematically performed. The effective duration is the duration regulated in industrial relations, being provided by the collective labour contract or other types of labour agreement.

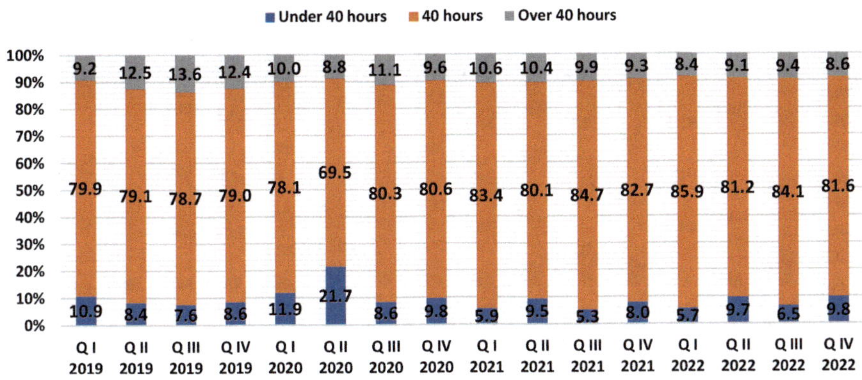


**Fig. 7.1** Distribution of the full-time employed population by the effective weekly working schedule, 2019–2022, quarterly data (%) (Source: Author's calculation based on Romanian National Institute of Statistics, Tempo online, AMG116E, http://statistici.insse.ro:8077/tempo-online/#/pages/tables/insse-table)

In Romania, the distribution of the employed population with a full working schedule by effective duration of the working week proves very clearly the reality of the reduction of the working schedule at the beginning of the pandemic. In the second quarter of 2020, only 69.5% of the employed population had a normal work schedule of 40 h, while in the first quarter, their share was 78.1%. Annual data show that in 2020, the share of people employed under 40 h increased by 4.1 percentage points compared to the previous year. In the ongoing 2 years, the share decreased by 5.8 (in 2021) and 5.0 (in 2022) percentage points (Fig. 7.1).

Regarding the part-time employed population, a possibility to increase the number of hours worked could be observed during the pandemic. In 2020, for 46.1% of employees with a temporary work regime, the effective duration of the workweek was 40 h, compared to 48.1% in 2019 (Pisică & Moldoveanu, 2022). Data from the next figure shows that in 2021 and 2022, more and more people worked between 25 and 30 h per week; meanwhile, the share of the ones who worked between 11 and 20 h decreased from 40.5% in 2019 to 26.5% in 2022 (Fig. 7.2).

Significant differences are noticed within the economic activities and economic status (Pisică & Moldoveanu, 2022). The usual average duration of the working week in the main activity for employed persons was, in 2020, 39.8 h per week, with variations from 35.8 h per week in agriculture, forestry and fishing to 41.1 h per week in construction, without significant differences compared to the previous year. In the main activity, 38.5 h was actually worked on average per week, this duration being longer for employers (40.9 h, 1.3 h less than in 2019) and for employees (40.1 h, respectively, 0.5 h less than in 2019).

In 2020, a percentage of 9.6% of the employed population worked below the usual duration of the working week. The main causes for the reduction of their working time were represented by technical unemployment, strike or labour conflict (21.6%), unfavourable weather conditions (18.2%), rest leave (17.5%), days off and holidays (11.3%), maternity or child rearing leave (8.4%) and variable hours (8.1%).

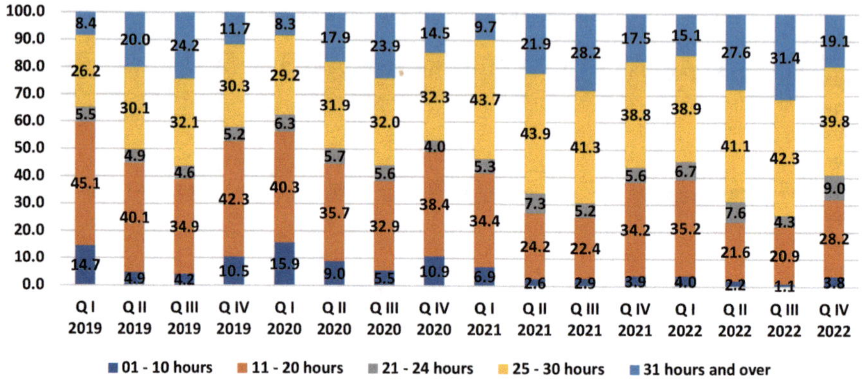


**Fig. 7.2** Distribution of the part-time employed population by the usual duration of the working week, 2019–2022, quarterly data (%) (Source: Author's calculation based on Romanian National Institute of Statistics, Tempo online, AMG115E, http://statistici.insse.ro:8077/tempo-online/#/pages/tables/insse-table)

In terms of causes for the reduction of the working time, the COVID-19 pandemic forced unemployment and strikes or labour conflict to outrank unfavourable weather conditions, which, in 2019, represented 34% of total underemployment. In 2020, 2.1% of the employed population worked over the usual duration of the working week, compared to 2.6% in 2019, because they mainly had variable hours or worked overtime. The annual decrease in this share could be explained by the fact that part of the time allocated to the regular work schedule was replaced by other activities that occurred as a result of the pandemic: online education, medical care activities, etc.

In the first year of the COVID-19 pandemic, full-time employed people represented 93.2% of the total (with 0.3 percentage points less than in 2019), and for 90.2% of them, the usual duration of the working week was at least 40 h. Of the total employed population, 10.1% could not indicate a usual duration of the working week; this category of employed people represented 6.4% of people with a full work schedule and 60.4% of people with a partial schedule (Pisică & Moldoveanu, 2022).

We will further describe some measures for the redefinition of the working time, and that will help employees to cope with unforeseen personal situations, such as those generated by the restrictions of the pandemic, for Romania:

(a) Sharing the decision to start and end the work schedule between the employer and the employee

In Romania, in the second quarter of 2019, only 22.6% of employed people could completely decide on the beginning and end of the working hours, while 11.8% could only decide with certain restrictions, depending on certain legal regulations or customer programmes (National Institute of Statistics, 2020).

(b) The possibility for employees to benefit from one or two free days spontaneously, without planning, in an interval of 1 week

In the second quarter of 2019, approximately one third/ (34.1) of the employed people could benefit very easily or quite easily from 1 or 2 days off without planning, in an interval of three working days (idem).

(c) Recording of hours worked, as a measure to protect employees against situations in which they might frequently work more than agreed upon by contract, or as an indicator of constant availability outside of working hours

At the national level, automatic registration, by the time attendance system or connecting to the computer, was achieved in the second quarter of 2019 for 34.5% of employed people (idem).

(d) The employees' possibility to influence the order and content of professional tasks

In Romania, in the second quarter of 2019, only 19.8% of employed people declared that they had a great influence in deciding how they carried out their professional tasks, namely, the approach, working methods or tools (idem).

(e) Organisation of teleworking

In Romania, in the second quarter of 2019, only 6.2% of employed persons carried out their activity in non-fixed places (e.g. vehicles), and 0.6% at home (idem). In 2020, the share of employed persons aged 15–64 who teleworked has risen to 2.5%, far below the European average of 12% (Eurostat, 2021).

(f) Financial support for teleworkers

It is already regulated in Romania by Law 296/2020, which allows companies to pay up to 400 RON monthly to cover the costs related to telework—heating, electricity, Internet fee, data subscription, etc.

## European Measures Transposed at National Level

Digitalisation is supported in the resilience plan of the European Union at three levels (European Union, 2021):

- The use of technology to improve everyday life, care and medical security, through the following measures: acceleration of Internet speed, promotion of technology in the health sector, development of individuals' digital skills and competences and increased protection in the online environment
- Online services and activities, through the following measures: supporting green digital solutions of innovative start-ups and increasing the availability and use of digital services
- The sustainability of the digital society – with the goal of a carbon-neutral Europe by 2050

The Recovery and Resilience Facility launched by the European Commission (2021) was transposed at the national level in the National Recovery and Resilience

Plan (NRRP) (Romanian Government, 2021). It is based on six main pillars: (1) transition to green economy; (2) digital transformation; (3) smart, sustainable and inclusive economic growth; (4) social and territorial cohesion; (5) health and institutional resilience; and (6) children, youth, education and skills. Among other things, the NRRP also foresees investments for digitalisation in the sector of work and social protection, aimed at the digitalisation of enterprises and the public sector and the development of digital data services in the public and private sectors in order to enhance teleworking, online learning and homeschooling. In addition to the effect of increasing resilience and productivity, this transition can also contribute to the green transformation of the economy and the integration of vulnerable groups into economic and social life. Another category of investments provided in the NRRP is for digital transformation and RPA-type automation in public administration to counter bureaucratic work processes, the use of mainly paper documents and fragmented IT systems.

A McKinsey report (2021) shows that the post-pandemic recovery will propel the rapid adoption of automation to redesign work processes and cope with increased demand to provide services or perform tasks, as automation has proven its effectiveness during the pandemic in addressing cost control and reducing human interaction to allow operations to continue without exposing employees to the virus. The three trends accelerated by the pandemic will remain: remote work/e-work/telework (expected to be 20–25% in advanced economies in the long term), digitalisation and automation using RPA processes and artificial intelligence (McKinsey Global Institute, 2021).

## Jobs' Transformation

Even if worker displacement due to automation has historically been offset by the creation of new jobs (Hatzius et al., 2023), the rapid advancements in automation technologies have raised concerns about job displacement and its implications for the labour force, while AI is seen as harmful (Acemoglu, 2021). This section explores the phenomenon of job displacement resulting from AI and delves into the challenges and opportunities it presents. Understanding the dynamics of job displacement is essential for individuals, organisations and policymakers to navigate this transformative era effectively.

Firstly, it is important to underline the difference between AI and AGI, in order to understand how fast the digital revolution evolves. AI refers to the broader field of computer science and technology that aims to create intelligent systems capable of performing tasks that typically require human intelligence. AI encompasses a wide range of techniques, algorithms and applications designed to enable machines to perceive, reason, learn and make decisions. AI systems can be specialised and focused on specific tasks, such as image recognition, natural language processing and playing chess. They excel in performing specific tasks but may lack in broader generalisation and adaptability. AGI, on the other hand, represents a hypothetical form of AI that is capable of exhibiting intelligence and cognitive abilities at a level comparable to human beings across a wide range of tasks. AGI systems would possess the ability to understand, learn and apply knowledge across various domains, similar to how humans can adapt their intelligence to perform a diverse set of tasks. Moreover, it is proved that AGI achieves a level of versatility and generality that goes beyond specialised AI systems and 'can solve novel and difficult tasks that span mathematics, coding, vision, medicine, law, psychology and more' (Bubeck et al., 2023).

Jobs' transformation can occur in different ways due to AI and automation. The displacement of work by AI is twofold: task-based displacement (Brynjolfsson & McAfee, 2014; Autor & Salomons, 2018) and occupation-based displacement (Arntz et al., 2016; Acemoglu & Restrepo, 2020).

Task-based displacement refers to the automation or elimination of specific tasks within a job role, often facilitated by AI and automation technologies. The following are some examples of automated work tasks:

- Data entry: AI-powered systems can automate data entry tasks by extracting information from documents, forms or databases, reducing the need for manual data entry by humans (Bunduchi et al., 2022).
- Customer support: Virtual assistants equipped with natural language processing capabilities can handle customer inquiries and provide automated support, reducing the need for human customer service representatives for routine queries.
- Online assistance: For example, in virtual health care, chatbots are able to provide answers to patient questions 'that are of comparable quality and empathy to those written by physicians' (Ayers et al., 2023).
- Manufacturing and assembly: Robotic systems and automation technologies can perform repetitive and standardised tasks on assembly lines, such as packaging, sorting and product assembly, leading to reduced reliance on manual labour.
- Financial analysis: AI algorithms can analyse vast amounts of financial data, generate reports and provide insights for investment decisions, potentially reducing the need for human financial analysts for certain tasks.
- Document processing: Document automation and optical character recognition (OCR) technologies have the potential to significantly impact occupations that involve manual document processing, such as data entry clerks or document review professionals.

Occupation-based displacement occurs when entire job roles or occupations are significantly impacted or rendered obsolete due to automation and AI technologies. Some examples are given below:

- Cashiers: The rise of self-checkout systems and automated payment technologies in retail environments has reduced the need for human cashiers.
- Drivers: Autonomous vehicles and advanced logistics systems have the potential to disrupt transportation and delivery industries, potentially displacing truck drivers, delivery drivers and taxi-/ride-hailing service providers.
- Stock traders: AI-powered algorithms and high-frequency trading systems have transformed the landscape of financial markets, reducing the need for human stock traders in certain aspects of trading operations.

As Romania is currently in an ongoing process of OECD accession (OECD, 2022), we will present some insights of their statistics regarding AI in the context of jobs' transformation in order to gain an overview of the currently AI impact among employers and workers. According to data collected by the 2022 OECD employer survey on the impact of AI on the workplace (Lane et al., 2023) for two industries—finance and manufacturing—larger employers are more likely to admit they use AI, i.e. 42% in finance and insurance services and 29% in manufacturing, and they adopted AI in order to improve worker performance (48%) and reduce staff costs (44%). The most common uses for AI in finance are in data analytics (52%), fraud detection (50%) and customer service and administration (30%). For the manufacturing industry, the most AI uses are in production processes (60%), quality control (35%) and robotics (31%). About a third of workers whose companies use AI say that they have some interaction with AI in both industries (OECD, 2023). Another interesting finding of the survey (idem) is that AI users are more likely to be younger (26% for aged 25–34 and 43% for aged 35–49), male (59%) and more educated (university degree 64%) than non-users.

## Policy Implications and Future Outlook

Considering the unpredictability of the health crisis caused by the COVID-19 pandemic, a series of measures are required worldwide to make the employees' working schedule more flexible, to give them the opportunity to balance their personal and professional lives, in safe health conditions. A sustainable tool in this regard is technology, i.e. digitalisation of the working process. In the medium term, this will involve the upskilling of employees, i.e. the ability of workers to use AI in order to improve their efficiency and productivity.

The rapid advancement of digitalisation has transformed the traditional concept of working time, and the COVID-19 pandemic has also forced the implementation of automated technologies in most economic sectors at a faster pace than ever before. A 2021 study (International Data Corporation) shows that in the short term, almost half of the companies are considering the implementation of robotic process automation (RPA). This approach will substantially contribute to the remodelling of employees' working time, because those repetitive daily or monthly tasks will be automated, which leads to more efficient allocation of time and resources.

Currently, even in Romania, types of robots that can perform a series of tasks specific to humans are being developed (UiPath, 2021): authenticating in applications, connecting to Application Programming Interfaces (API), copying data, moving files, extracting and processing structured information and unstructured documents and emails, reading and writing databases and opening emails and attached files. These tasks are performed repetitively, automatically and without mistakes, based on artificial intelligence. The main advantages are the reduction of routine activities and improvement of consumption of human resources and time, implicitly of costs, i.e. a redefinition of costs with the human factor and of the overall cost of the activity, but also the increase of productivity and the development of new products and services. This new trend of intelligent automation is twofold: on the one hand, it will cause a complete restructuring of the labour market, with a large number of job categories possibly being replaced by intelligent robots, and on the other hand, it will bring new opportunities for employment that will require the upskilling of the current labour force and the emphasis on certain skills that will be developed by the education system in the future.

Given this framework, a comprehensive set of measures and solutions for redefining working time are being proposed below. Most of them are not new concepts, but they are in the spotlight in the (post)pandemic context:

1. Flexible schedules with the following solutions:

   - Flextime: Allowing employees to set their own start and end times within certain parameters. It provides individuals with the freedom to adapt their work hours to accommodate personal commitments or optimise productivity during their most productive hours (Berkery et al., 2020).
   - Compressed workweek: Condensing the standard workweek into fewer days while maintaining the same total hours, such as working four 10-h days instead of five 8-h days. This allows employees to have additional days off while maintaining the same total number of working hours. One common practical implementation of this measure is the 4-day duration of the workweek. A 4-day workweek involves that instead of the traditional 5-day workweek, employees work for longer hours on each of the four work days but have an additional day off.

     The exact schedule may vary depending on the organisation and industry (Barnes & Jones, 2020):
   - Job sharing: Splitting a full-time position between two or more employees, each working part-time. This arrangement enables individuals to share responsibilities, maintain work continuity and achieve a better work-life balance (Arkin & Dobrofsky, 2022).
   - Results-only work environment (ROWE) as business model: Emphasising productivity and outcomes rather than specific working hours. ROWE is an approach that focuses on measuring employees' performance based on outcomes rather than traditional notions of working hours. It empowers individuals to work when and where they are most productive, as long as they meet their goals and deliverables (Ressler & Thompson, 2008).

2. Remote work with the following solutions:

   - Telecommuting: Enabling employees to work from locations other than the traditional office, typically from their homes or other remote locations. It relies on technology and digital connectivity to facilitate communication and collaboration (Golden & Veiga, 2008).
   - Virtual teams: Leveraging technology to facilitate collaboration among geographically dispersed employees. Virtual teams are groups of employees who collaborate and work together on projects or tasks despite being

geographically dispersed. They leverage digital communication tools and platforms to maintain effective teamwork and coordination (Bell & Kozlowski, 2002).

- Work-from-home policies: Establishing guidelines and infrastructure to support remote work arrangements. Work-from-home policies establish guidelines and frameworks for remote work arrangements. These policies define expectations, requirements and support mechanisms to ensure successful remote work experiences for employees (Choudhury & Foroughi, 2020).
- Digital communication tools: Using platforms for seamless virtual interactions, meetings and project management. Digital communication tools encompass a variety of software and platforms, such as videoconferencing, instant messaging and project management tools. These tools enable seamless virtual interactions, meetings and collaboration among remote team members.

3. Work-life integration with the following solutions:

- Boundaries and flexibility: Encouraging employees to define boundaries between work and personal life while allowing flexibility in managing responsibilities. It encourages individuals to blend work and personal commitments in a way that suits their needs, allowing for greater work-life harmony.
- Employee well-being programmes: Promoting physical and mental well-being through initiatives like wellness benefits, mindfulness training and stress management (Aryanti et al., 2020).
- Supportive company culture: Fostering a culture that values work-life balance, prioritises family needs and encourages open communication. A supportive company culture prioritises work-life balance and recognises the importance of personal commitments outside of work. It fosters an environment that encourages open communication, understanding and empathy towards employees' personal lives.

4. Leveraging technology by using:

- Time-tracking tools: Implementing digital tools to monitor and manage working hours, tasks and productivity. Time-tracking tools are digital solutions that allow employees to monitor and manage their working hours, tasks and productivity. These tools provide insights into how time is allocated, helping individuals optimise their work schedules and identify areas for improvement.
- Automation and AI: Utilising technology to automate repetitive tasks, optimise workflows and enhance efficiency. Automation and artificial intelligence technologies are utilised to streamline workflows, automate repetitive tasks and improve efficiency. By reducing manual workloads, employees can allocate their time more effectively and focus on higher-value work.
- Collaboration platforms: Adopting digital platforms that facilitate real-time collaboration, file sharing and project coordination. Collaboration platforms are digital tools that facilitate real-time collaboration, file sharing and project coordination among team members. These platforms provide a centralised

space for communication, ensuring seamless teamwork and enabling effective remote collaboration.

A SWOT analysis of the implementation of the above solutions is proposed in order to emphasise some overall challenges and vulnerabilities.

Strengths:

- Increased productivity of employees and companies
- Decreased overall expenses for companies
- The possibility for employees to take care of their personal life one extra day a week, without sacrificing their income or professional career
- Supporting gender equality by encouraging men to get involved in household activities
- Lower carbon emissions, very important especially in the context of the new UN 'red code for humanity' warnings (Intergovernmental Panel on Climate Change, 2021)

Weaknesses:

- If the measure comes together with a wage reduction, the situations of economically and socially disadvantaged groups will worsen.

Opportunities:

- Reduction of unemployment and inactivity
- Upskilling of employees
- Expanded talent pool and access to a diverse labour force

Threats:

- In some economic sectors on the front line of the fight against the pandemic, such as the health sector, it was difficult or even impossible to implement some of the measures.

## Conclusions and Remarks

A joint US-European Union report (White House, 2022) states that AI may have a substantial impact on the economy 'with respect to productivity, growth, inequality, market power, innovation, and employment'.

The jobs' transformation due to AI implementations is a large-scale and permanently open debate. Even so, it is clear enough that the new AGI could raise global GDP by 7% and lift productivity growth by 1.5 percentage points over a 10-year period (Goldman Sachs, 2023); therefore, we could conclude that the benefits are quantifiable.

The COVID-19 pandemic is definitely a turning point in history. It has shifted societal priorities and highlighted the importance of digitalisation. Redefining working time in the context of digitalisation offers significant opportunities for organisations to optimise productivity, enhance employee well-being and foster work-life balance. By implementing flexible schedules, embracing remote work, promoting work-life integration and leveraging technology, organisations can create a conducive work environment that meets the needs of a changing labour force. However, it is crucial to address challenges and considerations to ensure fairness, avoid burnout and maintain effective communication. Through proactive measures, organisations can successfully navigate the digital landscape and redefine working time for the benefit of both employees and the organisation as a whole.

## References


Acemoglu, D., & Restrepo, P. (2020). Robots and jobs: Evidence from US labor markets. *Journal of Political Economy, 128*(6), 2188–2244.

Acemoglu, D. (2021). Harms of AI. In *NBER working paper 29247*. National Bureau of Economic Research. https://www.nber.org/papers/w29247

Arkin, W., & Dobrofsky, L. R. (2022). Job sharing. In *Working couples* (pp. 122–137). Routledge.

Arntz, M., Gregory, T., & Zierahn, U. (2016). *The risk of automation for jobs in OECD countries: A comparative analysis. OECD social, employment and migration working papers, no. 189*. OECD Publishing.

Aryanti, R., Diah S., & Widiana H. (2020). *A literature review of workplace well-being*. https://doi.org/10.2991/assehr.k.201017.134.

Autor, D. H., & Salomons, A. (2018). Is automation labor-displacing? Productivity growth, employment, and the labor share. *Brookings Papers on Economic Activity, 49*(1), 1–87.

Ayers, J. W., Poliak, A., Dredze, M., Leas, E. C., Zhu, Z., Kelley, J. B., Faix, D. J., Goodman, A. M., Longhurst, C. A., Hogarth, M., & Smith, D. M. (2023). Comparing physician and artificial intelligence Chatbot responses to patient questions posted to a public social media forum. *JAMA Internal Medicine, 183*(6), 589–596. https://doi.org/10.1001/jamainternmed.2023.1838

Barnes, A., & Jones, S. (2020). *The 4 day week: How the flexible work revolution can increase productivity, profitability and Well-being, and create a sustainable future*. Piatkus.

Bell, B. S., & Kozlowski, S. W. (2002). A typology of virtual teams: Implications for effective leadership. *Group & Organization Management, 27*(1), 14–49.

Berkery, E., Morley, M. J., Tiernan, S., & Peretz, H. (2020). From start to finish: Flexi-time as a social exchange and its impact on organizational outcomes. *European Management Journal, 38*(4), 591–601. https://doi.org/10.1016/j.emj.2020.02.003. https://www.sciencedirect.com/science/article/pii/S0263237320300244.

Brynjolfsson, E., & McAfee, A. (2014). *The second machine age: Work, progress, and prosperity in a time of brilliant technologies*. W.W. Norton & Company.

Bubeck, S., Chandrasekaran, V., Eldan, R., Gehrke, J., Horvitz, E., Kamar, E., Lee, P., Lee, Y. T., Li, Y., Lundberg, S., Nori, H., Palangi, H., Ribeiro, M. T., & Zhang, Y. (2023). *Sparks of artificial general intelligence: Early experiments with GPT-4*, https://arxiv.org/abs/2303.12712v5. https://doi.org/10.48550/arXiv.2303.12712

Bunduchi, E., Vasile, V., Stefan, D., & Comes, C. A. (2022). Reshaping jobs in healthcare sector based on digital transformation. *Romanian Statistical Review, 1*, 84.

Choudhury, R., & Foroughi, C. (2020). Working from home in the COVID-19 lockdown: Changing preferences and experiences across demographic groups. *Journal of Vocational Behavior, 119*, 103436.

European Commission. (2021). *Recovery and resilience facility*. Available at: https://ec.europa.eu/info/business-economy-euro/recovery-coronavirus/recovery-and-resilience-facility_en#the-facility-and-nextgenerationeu

European Union. (2021). *Conference on the future of Europe*. [Interactive] Available at: https://futureu.europa.eu/pages/digitalinfo

Eurostat. (2021). *Eurostat database–Employment and unemployment*. [Interactive] Available at: https://ec.europa.eu/eurostat/web/lfs/data/database

Golden, T. D., & Veiga, J. F. (2008). The impact of extent of telecommuting on job satisfaction: Resolving inconsistent findings. *Journal of Management, 34*(2), 317–337.

Goldman Sachs. (2023). https://www.goldmansachs.com/intelligence/pages/generative-ai-could-raise-global-gdp-by-7-percent.html

Government of Romania. (2021). *National recovery and resilience plan*. [Interactive] Available at: https://mfe.gov.ro/pnrr/

Hatzius J., Briggs J., Kodnani D., & Pierdomenico G. (2023). *The potentially large effects of artificial intelligence on economic growth, in Goldman Sachs economics research series*. https://www.gspublishing.com/content/research/en/reports/2023/03/27/d64e052b-0f6e-45d7-967b-d7be35fabd16.html

Intergovernmental Panel on Climate Change. (2021). *Climate change 2021: The physical science basis*. Cambridge University Press.

International Data Corporation. (2021). *Automation as a force for Good–6 steps to transform theory into practice*. UiPath.

Kelly, J. (2019). *Microsoft Japan launched a four-day workweek to much success: Is this the key to attracting talent in the tight US job market?* Available at: https://www.forbes.com/sites/jackkelly/2019/11/05/microsoft-japan-launched-a-four-day-week-work-to-much-success-is-this-the-answer-to-attract-talent-in-the-tight-us-job-market/?sh=2befb88b59ff

Lane, M., Williams, M., & Broecke, S. (2023). The impact of AI on the workplace: Main findings from the OECD AI surveys of employers and workers. In *OECD Social, Employment and Migration Working Papers, No. 288*. OECD Publishing. https://doi.org/10.1787/ea0a0fe1-en

McKinsey Global Institute. (2021). *The future of work after COVID-19*. https://www.mckinsey.com/featured-insights/future-of-work/the-future-of-work-after-covid-19#/download/%2F~%2Fmedia%2Fmckinsey%2Ffeatured%20insights%2Ffuture%20of%20organizations%2Fthe%20future%20of%20work%20after%20covid%2019%2Fthe-future-of-work-after-covid-19-report-vf.pdf.

National Institute of Statistics. (2023a). *Tempo online database*. http://statistici.insse.ro:8077/tempo-online/#/pages/tables/insse-table.

National Institute of Statistics. (2023b). *Labour force survey*. National Institute of Statistics.

National Institute of Statistics. (2020). *Work organization and typology of the work schedule in the second quarter of 2019*. National Institute of Statistics.

OECD. (2022). *Meeting of the council at ministerial level, 9–10 June 2022, roadmap for the OECD accession process of Romania*. https://www.oecd.org/mcm/Roadmap-OECD-Accession-Process-Romania-EN.pdf

OECD. (2023). *OECD 2022 AI surveys of employers and workers Data*. https://www.oecd.org/future-of-work/reports-and-data/AI_Report_Main_findings__employers_and_workers_surveys_graphs%20.xlsx

Pisică, S., & Moldoveanu, R. (2022). *Labor force in Romania: Employment and unemployment in* .... National Institute of Statistics (yearly publication).

Ressler, C., & Thompson, J. (2008). *Why work sucks and how to fix it: The results-only revolution*. Penguin.

Schwab, K. (2016). *The fourth industrial revolution*. World Economic Forum.

UiPath. (2021). *Robotic process automation*. Available at: https://www.uipath.com/automate/robotic-process-automation

White House. (2022). The Impact of Artificial Intelligence on the Future of Workforces in the European Union and the United States of America, https://www.whitehouse.gov/wp-content/uploads/2022/12/TTC-EC-CEA-AI-Report-12052022-1.pdf

# Chapter 8
# The Impact of the Pandemic on the Participation in the Labour Market of Vulnerable Groups: Women, Young People, the Elderly and Self-Employed Workers

**Cristina Boboc and Simona Ghita**

**Abstract** This chapter aims to highlight and analyse the changes in the Romanian labour market situation of four vulnerable categories (women, young people, the elderly and self-employed workers), as a result of the pandemic crisis generated by COVID-19, compared to the pre-pandemic period. The analysis was carried out under two main aspects: the first aspect covers the period 2019–2020, in order to identify the initial changes in the situation of vulnerable groups on the labour market, as an immediate effect of the outbreak of the pandemic, as well as an estimate of the evolution of labour indicators for the next 2 years. The second aspect aims to compare the estimates made with the real evolution of the same indicators for the years 2021 and 2022, in order to highlight the final impact of the pandemic crisis on the labour market situation of the four vulnerable groups. The changes in the labour market were captured by using absolute and relative indicators of employment and unemployment, structured by socio-demographic characteristics (age, education, gender), but also by a series of variables related to the type of employment and work regime (work schedule, type of ownership, activity sector, work type, major occupational groups, employment status).

The European labour market has undergone significant changes in recent decades. Increasing participation of women in the labour market, the development of technology, digitalisation and the emergence of online platforms have all led to significant changes in occupations, demand and supply in the labour market, as well as to

C. Boboc (✉) · S. Ghita
Department of Statistics and Econometrics, Bucharest University of Economic Studies: Institute of National Economy- Romanian Academy, Bucharest, Romania



V. Vasile, E. Bunduchi (eds.), *The Economic and Social Impact of the COVID-19 Pandemic*, Contributions to Economics,
https://doi.org/10.1007/978-3-031-47780-5_8

greater flexibility in the labour market and outsourcing[1] work for independent contractors (Nikos Koutsimpogiorgos, 2020).

The main purpose of this chapter is to highlight the impact of the COVID-19 pandemic on the main vulnerable categories in the labour market, in order to draft and develop macroeconomic policies to mitigate its negative effects. The evolution of the main indicators of the labour market in the case of four categories considered vulnerable, women, young people, elderly and self-employed workers, is analysed under two aspects. On the one hand, the 2019–2020 period is analysed in order to identify the initial changes in the labour market situation for vulnerable groups, changes which occurred immediately after the outbreak of the COVID-19 pandemic, compared to the year before it; thus, the first impact of the pandemic on these groups is identified, and estimates are made regarding the evolution during the next 2 years. On the other hand, the estimates made are compared to the real evolution of the labour market indicators in the years 2021 and 2022, in order to see the final impact, but also the challenges that this crisis brought to the most vulnerable groups on the labour market, in the next period. This chapter uses a series of absolute and relative labour market indicators focused mainly on employment and unemployment, structured according to a series of demographic characteristics (gender, age, education) and to a series of variables related to the type of employment (major occupational groups, sectors of activity, employment status, work schedule, work type, ownership type of the workplace, etc.), in order to characterise the employment of women, young people and the elderly, but also the characterisation of self-employed workers, as well as the level and structure changes that occurred in the pandemic year (2020) compared to the previous year (2019), and in the next 2 years, 2021 and 2022. The values of the indicators for the 2 years are applicable to Romania and were taken from the databases of the National Institute of Statistics, Eurostat and the European Institute for Gender Equality (EIGE).

Based on the analysis of the main indicators regarding the employment and unemployment of vulnerable categories for the period 2019–2020, a SWOT analysis of the Romanian labour market was performed and is presented at the end of this chapter. Next, the most important changes that took place regarding the situation of vulnerable groups are identified in 2021, the year in which the pandemic was still ongoing, as well as in the following year 2022, the year in which the pandemic was coming to an end. At the same time, a comparison is made between the vulnerabilities reported and caused by the first shock of the pandemic with what really happened to these groups during 2021–2022. Labour market policies can be drafted based on this SWOT analysis, policies meant to leverage the opportunities of the current pandemic context and to mitigate shocks for vulnerable groups in the labour market.

[1]In economics, outsourcing is defined as the delegation of tasks, objectives, non-strategic (non-essential) business sections to organisational segments that belong to external parties, which offer a better value for money or have greater expertise (produce better) in specialised fields.

In just 1 month of manifestation, the pandemic cancelled the progress made from an economic perspective, following the recovery of the economy after the financial crisis of 2008–2009 (OECD, 2021). At the OECD level, unemployment registered a 3% increase, reaching a level of 8.8% in April 2020; the time worked by employees decreased, and the number of people outside the labour force, who were no longer available for work, increased (OECD, 2021). Women, in particular, responded to the growing need for work within the households and the care of the sick or children, after the schools closed. After the initial shock of the pandemic, women—whose working time was reduced to a greater extent than in the case of men—recovered from this loss at a higher rate than men. These changes are valid for the entire OECD, but there is a large degree of variation in the territorial profile between countries. At the OECD level, young people were more influenced by the pandemic crisis, especially those who worked in sectors that greatly reduced their activity during the crisis, those who worked with short-term employment contracts or those who had finished their studies and wanted to enter the labour market (OECD, 2021). The unemployment rate among young people has increased to a greater extent than that of the elderly (OECD, 2021; Eurofound, 2022). All this led to an increase in the number of people not in employment, nor in education or training (NEET), to a greater extent than in the pre-crisis time period. Self-employed workers were also disproportionately affected by the crisis, their incomes suffering changes. Gros and Ounnas (2021) notice a difference between the evolution of the unemployment rate in European countries compared to the USA during the pandemic crisis. Thus, if in the USA the level of the indicator had a more pronounced increase in March and April 2020, with a faster recovery, in Europe its increase was of a smaller amplitude, although it also experienced a longer recovery. These developments were explained by the authors through the shock received by the economy of these countries as a result of the outbreak of the pandemic, something that affected the demand and supply of labour. The pandemic has practically interrupted some progress made in reducing gender discrepancies on the labour market. Thus, a report by the International Labour Organization shows that the gender gap in terms of working time had an unfavourable evolution during the pandemic crisis, reaching approximately 4 percentage points in the second quarter of 2020. Due to the lifting of restrictions during the pandemic and the resuming of economic activities, at the end of 2021 the time worked by women increased more, favouring the reduction of the difference compared to men. In 2021, the partial recovery of jobs which had been lost by women during the pandemic was done, to a certain extent, on the basis of informal work. Also, the job recovery was stronger in the case of occupations that require tertiary education, compared to those that require secondary or primary education (ILO, 2022). Regarding the elderly employed population, it was less prone to teleworking during the pandemic compared to the other age groups, especially since even before the pandemic they had experienced less this type of work. Although employment among the elderly was less affected by the pandemic, some groups of people belonging to the elderly had difficulties in finding a new job and retired earlier than they had anticipated. This led governments to take certain measures to support the employment of the elderly, financially stimulating companies that employed the elderly (Eurofound, 2022). Spasova et al. (2021) draw attention to the need to adopt social protection measures for non-standard workers, including the self-employed, categories that were greatly affected by the crisis generated by the pandemic, but also to the need of reducing the existing gap between self-employed and other groups of workers, considering the access to various support schemes or benefits.

For these reasons, our work focuses on vulnerable groups on the labour market in Romania, analysing their progress during the pandemic and the chances of recovery after it ends. It is structured in five sections, four sections corresponding to each vulnerable category, women, youth, elderly and self-employed and one section corresponding to the changes on the labour market corresponding to these vulnerable categories after the COVID-19 pandemic.

## The Impact of COVID-19 on Women's Situation on the Romanian Labour Market

Even if significant improvement was made in recent years, the situation of women in the business environment is still marked by vulnerability, and the current pandemic crisis we are experiencing threatens to slow down or even reverse this progress (PwC UK, 2021). Globally, women have not yet achieved the desired economic independence, the quality of employment is still lower than that of men, and equal access to economic resources is still a goal that has not been achieved (Săseanu et al., 2019). In this chapter we will analyse the coordinates of women's situation in the labour market in Romania, and how they have changed in the context of the current pandemic crisis.

### *Employment by Gender and Age Groups*

In the first year of the pandemic, 2020, the employment rate among women decreased with 0.8% compared to the previous year, reaching 43.2%, still well below the one for men (by about 20%). The indicator registered the lowest value among young people (15–24 years), of only 19.7%, which means that less than 1 in 5 young people were employed in the labour market. The highest value of the indicator (of 73.2%) can be found in the age group 35–54. Just over a third of older women (aged 55–64) were employed this year (37.5%). Compared to 2019, there have been some changes in the employment rate among women, the level of the indicator registering the largest decrease in the age group 25–34 years (−2.3%), but also slight increases in the extreme age groups (+0.4% for the 15–24 age group and +1% for the 55–64 age group) (Fig. 8.1).

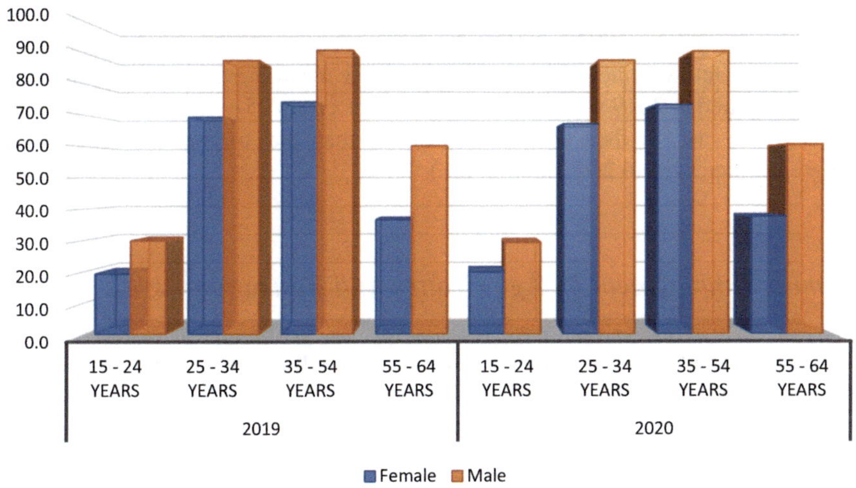


**Fig. 8.1** Employment rate by gender and age groups in Romania, in 2019 and 2020 (%)

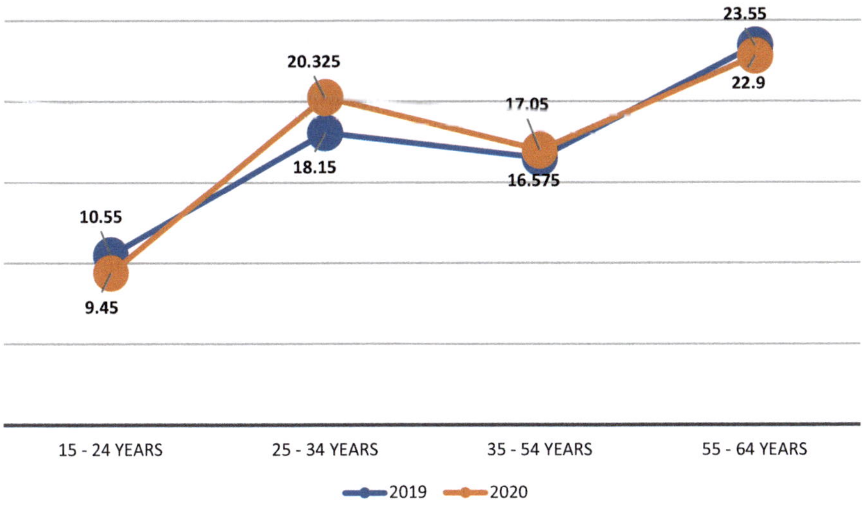


**Fig. 8.2** Gender gap in employment rate, by age groups in Romania, in 2019 and 2020 (%)

In comparison, the overall male employment rate varied by a smaller margin (the range of the male employment rate variation was smaller) in 2020 compared to 2019, but the evolution was negative in the first three age groups. However, it can also be noted that the gender difference in the employment rate has always been in favour of the male population, as it has been increasing with age (Fig. 8.2).

Thus, it can be noticed that, in 2020, the employment rate among young men (15–24 years old) is 9.45 percentage points higher than that of young women in the same age group—down from 10.55% in 2019. The greatest difference between the rate of employment for male and that for women is in the 55–64 age group, of almost 23 percentage points in 2020, slightly decreasing compared to the previous year. The most significant dynamics of the gender difference regarding the employment rate in 2020 compared to 2019 was registered in \the age group 25–34 years. If in 2019 the employment rate for men was 18.15% higher than that for women, in 2020 the difference increased to 20.32% (Fig. 8.2).

## *Female Employment by Age Groups and Education Levels*

The most important relative time changes—although in opposite directions—that were registered in 2020 compared to 2019 characterise the employed female persons with a low education level (with no education, with primary or secondary school), but also the female employees with a high educational level (university education). Thus, it is noted that the female employed population with low levels of education experienced the largest relative decrease in the pandemic year, compared to the previous year, especially in the age group of 25–34 years (−17.36%) and in the age group of 55 years and over (−13.95%). On the other hand, the dynamics was favourable among the female employed persons with higher education, as in this category there were even increases in the female employment compared to the pre-pandemic year. The highest increase could be observed among young people aged 15–24 (+6.56%) and adults aged 35–54 (+3.33%) with tertiary education, but there was also a negatively affected age group—the 25–34 years group (decrease by 9.32%). It seems that the sensitivity of female employment to the manifestations of the health pandemic was lower among people with secondary education (vocational education, complementary, high school, post-secondary education), as the time rate was low in all age groups, compared to 2019 (Fig. 8.3).

## *Female Employment by Major Occupation Groups*

In the pandemic year 2020, the employed female population of Romania registered a total decrease of over 93,000 people, respectively a 2.5% decrease compared to the previous year. By major occupational groups, the most significant decreases in female employment were registered for occupations that involve a lower qualification or that are found in primary branches of the economy. On the contrary, the occupations characterised by a higher level of qualification and training either registered increases or smaller decreases in absolute values. Thus, the most significant reductions in 2020 compared to 2019 (between 7.35 and 7.5 percentage points) occurred among the skilled and assimilated workers and the unskilled ones. There was also a significant reduction among skilled workers in agriculture, forestry and fishing (6%). A change in the opposite direction was noticed among legislators, senior officials and managers in public administration, a group in which the female

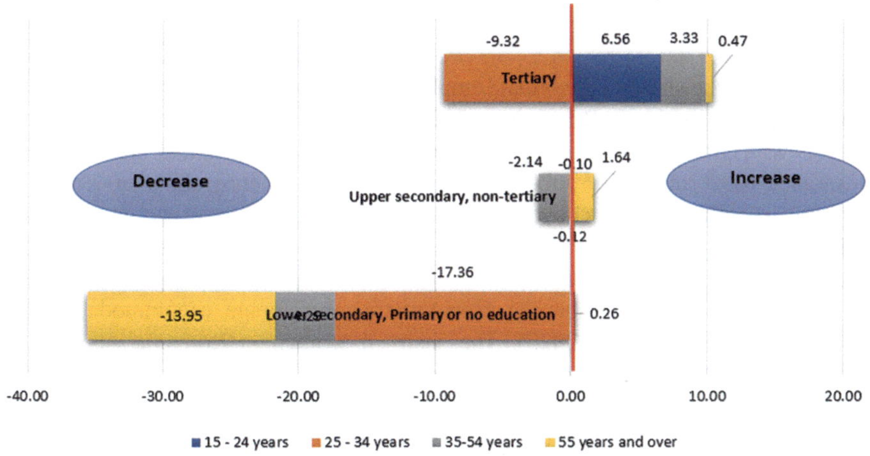


**Fig. 8.3** Relative change in female employment in 2020 compared to 2019, by age group and education level (%)

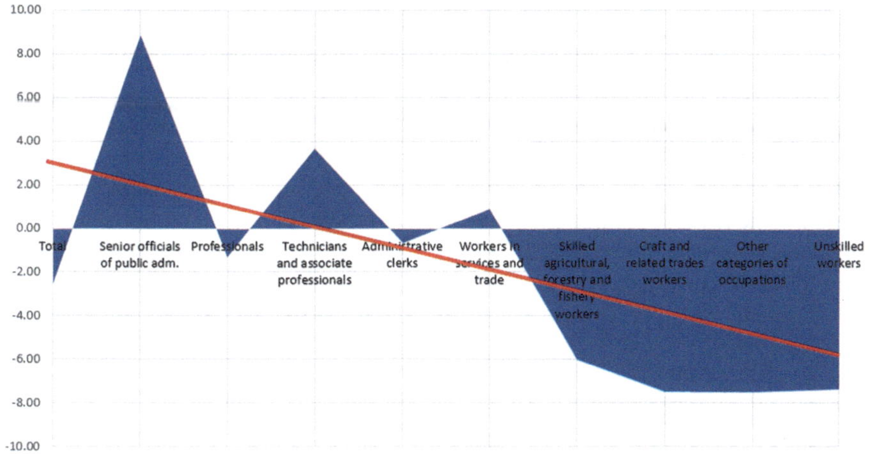


**Fig. 8.4** Relative change of female employment by major occupation groups, in Romania, in 2020 compared to 2019 (%)

employed population increased by almost 9% in 2020 compared to 2019. Meanwhile, the group of technicians and other specialists in the technical domain registered a more modest increase (of 3.7%) in the same period (Fig. 8.4).

Across all major occupational groups, the decrease of the female employed population in 2020 compared to 2019 is statistically significant, for a maximum probability of 97%.

### *Women's Employment by the Main NACE Activities*

If we analyse the share of the female employment from the total employment by the main NACE activities in Romania in 2019 and 2020, we will notice that there are sectors with (traditional) female predominance, such as financial intermediation and insurance (68% in 2020), public administration and defence (63% in 2020), or cultural, recreational and entertainment activities, repair of household goods and other services (56.68% in 2020). Women also represent a significant share (almost half of the employed population in the sector) of real estate transactions (almost 50% in 2020) or in retail and wholesale, transportation and storage, accommodation and food services (45.31% in 2020). The share of women in Romania's employed population in 2020 had only a minor, insignificant decrease, as the sectors with a greater female predominance were those services of vital importance to society, such as education, health and social assistance or trade. Some of these sectors did not significantly reduce their activities during the pandemic, nor did they show significant changes in the share of women's participation in economic activities, or the share of the female employed population (Fig. 8.5). However, on the other hand, there were also sectors dramatically affected by COVID-19, in which a significant share of the employed population are women (trade, hospitality industry).

Analysing the change of the female employment in 2020 in comparison with the previous year by main activity sectors, we can notice that the year 2020 was characterised by reductions in the level of the indicator in most sectors. Thus, in absolute terms, the largest reduction was recorded in agriculture, forestry and fishing (of over 58,000 people), followed by the manufacturing industry, electricity, gas, water, waste (over 35.4 thousand people) and entertainment and cultural-recreational activities (with over 17.6 thousand people). In relative terms, the largest reductions took place in construction (by over 16%, a branch in which, however, the female employment has the lowest share, of only 4.75% in 2020), followed by

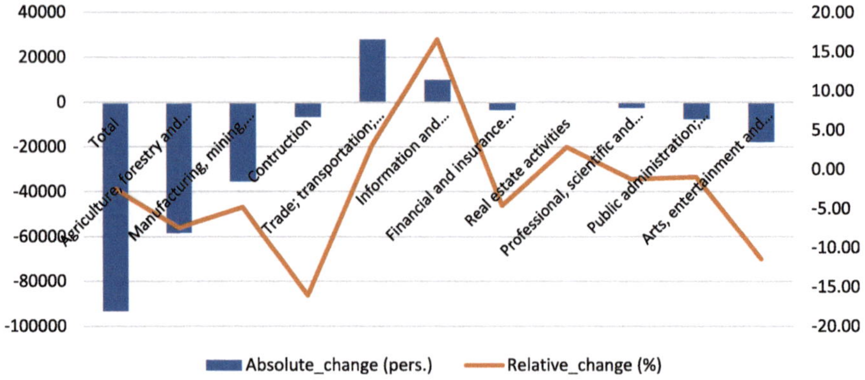


**Fig. 8.5** Absolute and relative change of female employment in Romania, activity sectors, in 2020 compared 2019 (persons, %)

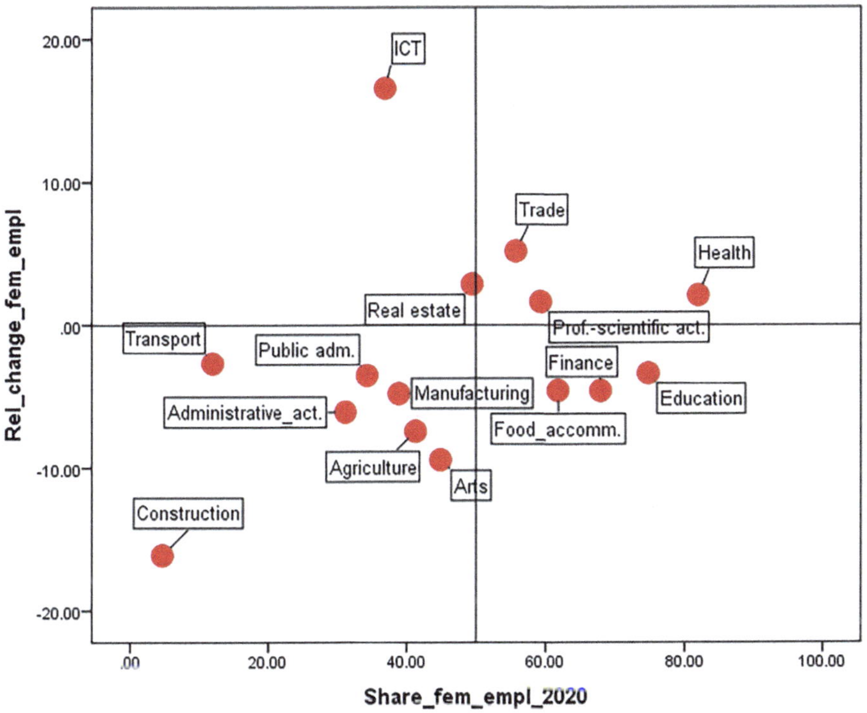


**Fig. 8.6** Scatter plot between the share of female employment (2020) and relative change of female employment in 2020 compared to 2019, by activity sectors (%)

entertainment and cultural-recreational activities (with 11.46%, a branch in which women represent 45% of the employed population of the sector). On the other hand, there are also sectors of activity that have been developing during the pandemic crisis, such as information and communications (ICT) (increase by over 10,000 people, representing 16.57%, in a branch in which women represent only 37% of the employed population of the sector) or trade (increase of over 35,800 people, representing 5.15%, in a domain in which women hold over 55.86% of the employed population of the sector) (Fig. 8.6).

The previous scatter plot shows that out of the six activity sectors in which women are predominant in the total employment of the sector, three sectors recorded increases in female employment, as the pandemic favoured an expansion of activity (trade, health and social assistance and professional, scientific and technical activities), while three other sectors—in which the activities were restricted during the pandemic—suffered reductions in the female employment (hotels and restaurants, financial intermediation and education). With the exception of the information and communications field—which boomed during the pandemic and where 10,000 more women were employed than the previous year—all other sectors of activity, in which

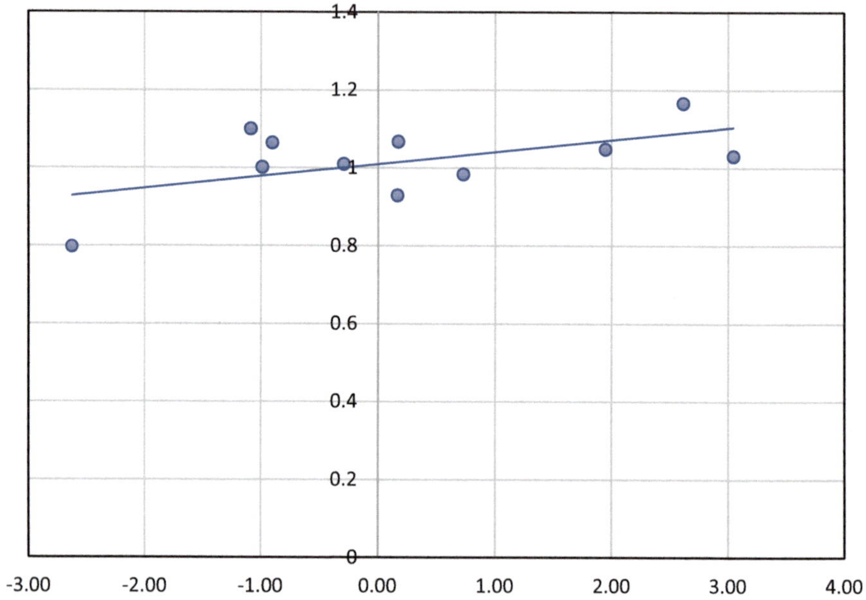


**Fig. 8.7** Correlation between changes in women's share in total employment (%) and dynamics index of Gross Value Added, by activity sectors

women own less than 50% of the total employment, registered activity reductions to a certain extent, resulting in a decrease of female employees.

Studying the correlation between the changes in the proportion of female employment in 2020 compared to 2019 and the dynamics of economic activities in the main NACE sectors (quantified by the *Gross Value Added* Index in 2020 compared to 2019), a positive correlation of medium intensity is highlighted, which is statistically significant at 5% level of significance. This result indicates that in the sectors where there was a more significant decrease in the share of women in the total employment, the economic activity in 2020 did not show any significant dynamics. On the contrary, in the sectors characterised by an expansion of economic activity in the pandemic and an increase in economic results compared to the pre-pandemic period, the share of women in total employment of the sector also increased during the same period (Figs. 8.7 and 8.8, Table 8.1).

The share of women in the total employment of the main NACE activities in 2020 is negatively correlated with the dynamics of the results obtained in these sectors in 2020 compared to 2019. This can be explained by the higher degree of precarious employment of women, by the fact that they are mainly active in sectors with less important results, which are less productive, and which had a negative dynamic in the pandemic context.

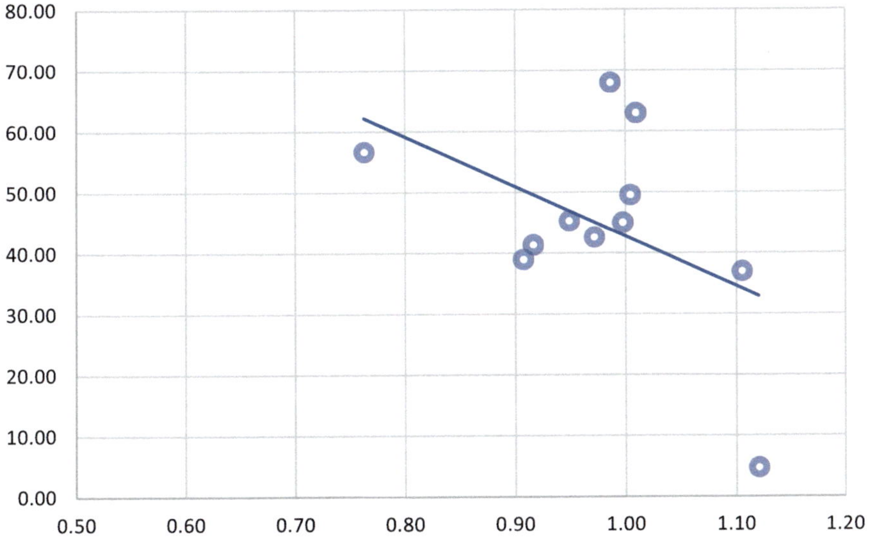


**Fig. 8.8** Correlation between women's share in total employment (%) and dynamics index of Gross Value Added, by activity sectors (2020/2019)

## *Employment by Gender and Professional Status*

If we analyse the dynamics of the employed population in Romania by professional status in 2020 compared to 2019, regardless of gender, it can be seen that there have been reductions in all employment categories. However, the most significant decrease in absolute numbers took place among employees (by 81,394 people), followed by self-employed workers (by 41,437 people) and unpaid family workers (by 33,347 people). In relative terms, in women's case, the dynamics of the employment was negative in the pandemic year compared to the previous year for all categories of employment by professional status (decreases between 1.58% for employees and 7.58% for unpaid family workers), except for the "Employer" category, for which there was an increase of almost 2%. With the exception of this category, the relative reductions were more pronounced for women than for men. These developments can be explained by a greater sensitivity of the number of male employees to employment adjustment schemes, as a result of the restriction of many economic activities in the pandemic year 2020. Thus, in the first part of 2020, over 1.2 million employment contracts were suspended or terminated; many employees became technically unemployed, especially in some sectors of activity in which men held significant or fairly significant shares (manufacturing, wholesale and retail trade as well as hotels and restaurants and construction). On the other hand, the favourable evolution of the "female employers" category may be due to the fact that female employees whose labour contracts have been suspended or terminated as a result of

**Table 8.1** Descriptive and correlation analysis for the variables: changes in women's share in total employment and dynamics index of Gross Value Added, by main activity sectors

| Descriptive statistics | | | | Correlations | | | |
|---|---|---|---|---|---|---|---|
| | Mean | Standard deviation | *N* | | | Fem_share_change | Gross_Value_Added_Index |
| Fem_share_change | 0.2527 | 1.72582 | 11 | Fem_share_change | Pearson Correlation | 1 | 0.557* |
| | | | | | *p*-value | | 0.038 |
| | | | | | N | 11 | 11 |
| Gross_Value_Added_Index | 1.0181 | 0.09607 | 11 | Gross_Value_Added_Index | Pearson Correlation | 0.557* | 1 |
| | | | | | *p*-value | 0.038 | |
| | | | | | N | 11 | 11 |

* Correlation is significant at the 0.05 level (1-tailed)

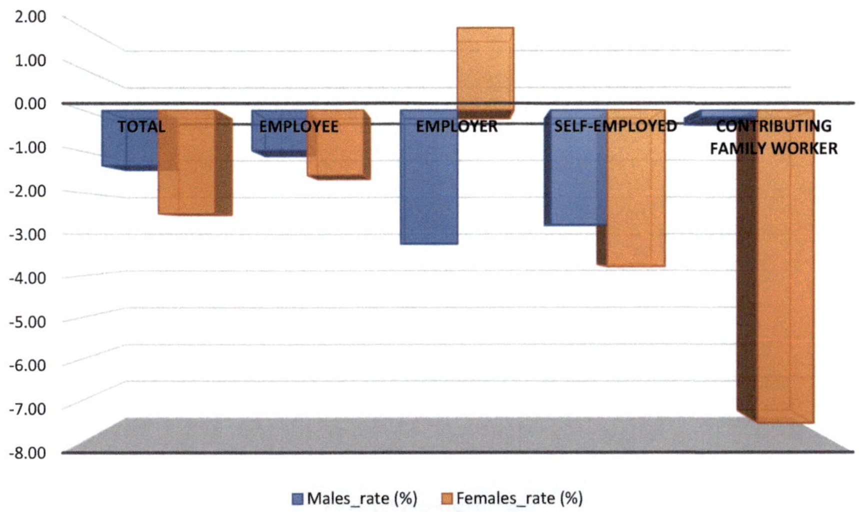


**Fig. 8.9** Employment change in Romania, by gender and professional status, in 2020/2019 (%)

the pandemic have reoriented themselves towards starting their own business, especially online, in order to survive and have an income (Fig. 8.9).

Women in Romania are not very well represented in decision-making positions in large companies, compared to other European Union countries. In 2020, only 6.7% of the "president" positions and almost 13% of the companies' board members were women, while they accounted for almost a third of the "executive director" positions in the same year (higher than the EU average, although in time the difference has been decreasing). In most decision-making positions, the share of women decreased slightly in the pandemic year 2020, so that the first half of 2021 will bring slight returns to previous situations (Fig. 8.10).

## *Employment by Gender, by Work Schedule (Full-Time/Part-Time, Permanent/Temporary) or by Having a Second Job*

Almost all female employees work full-time, with no significant changes in the structure during the pandemic year. Regarding the dynamics of the number of employees working full-time in 2020 compared to 2019, this was negative for both genders, the decrease being more pronounced among women (−40,326 female employees, compared to −29,731 male employees; −1.41% for women, compared to −0.82% for men). By the actual length of the working week, the sharpest decrease in absolute numbers was recorded among female employees who work 40 hours a week (with 14,9180 people, representing a decrease of almost 6%); instead, the

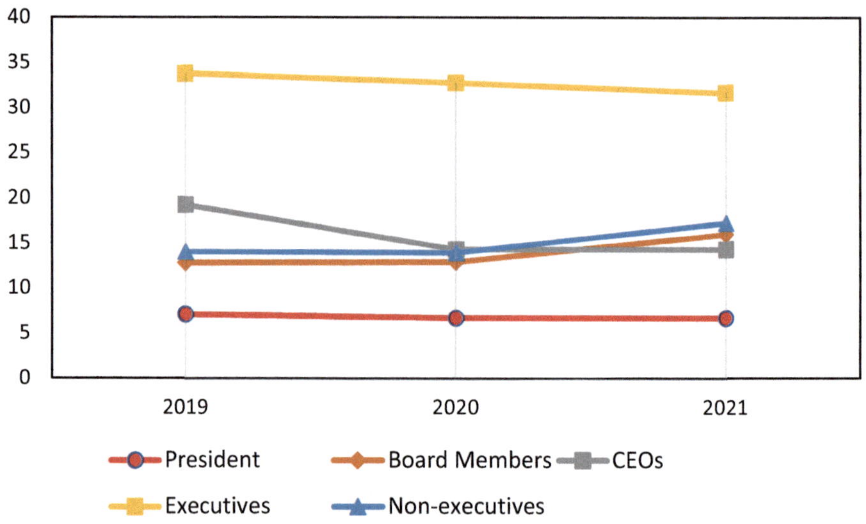


**Fig. 8.10** Share of women with top-management positions in large companies in Romania, 2019–2021 (%)

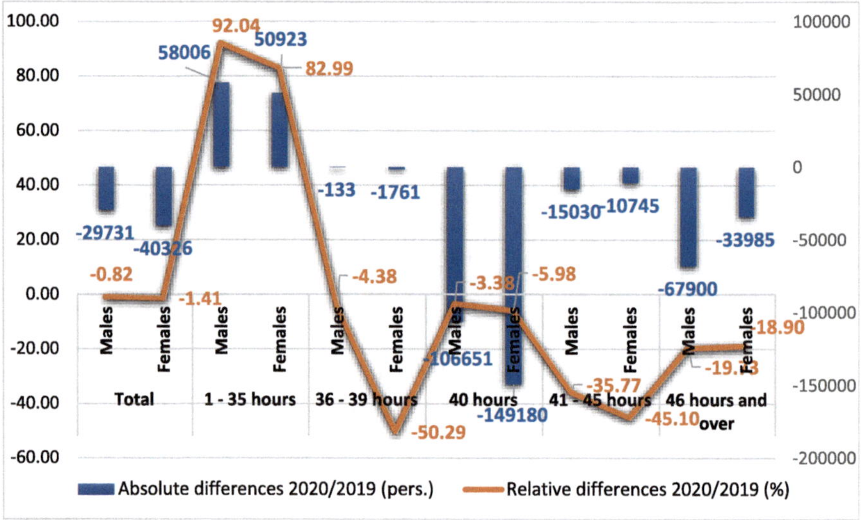


**Fig. 8.11** Absolute (pers.) and relative (%) change in the number of full-time employees, by actual duration of working week and gender, in 2020/2019

number of women employees who worked a maximum of 35 h (between 1 and 35 h) increased, the increase being almost double in 2020 compared to 2019. Therefore, the pandemic has led to a decrease in the actual working time for more employees (Fig. 8.11).

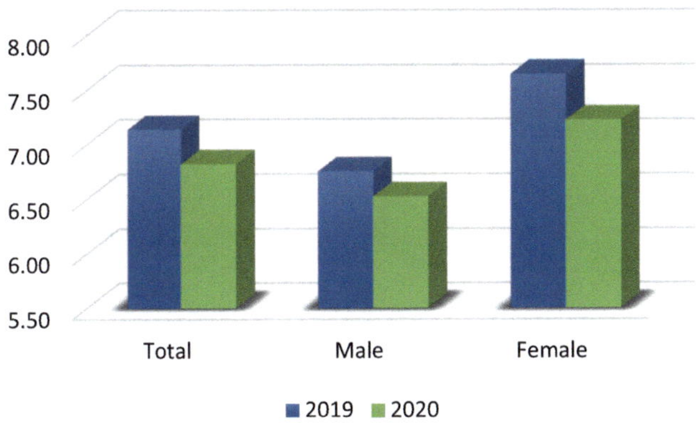


**Fig. 8.12** Share of part-time employment in Romania, 2019 and 2020 (%)

A similar evolution was seen in the number of employees with temporary work, with the observation that the share of these employees is only 1.25% in 2020, decreasing from 1.40% in 2019. The share of male employees with such a work regime is lower than that of female employees, and in the pandemic year, it was even lower than in the previous year.

Only a small share of the employed population in Romania works part-time, 7.14% in 2019 and 6.82% in 2020, but the proportions are slightly higher for women than for men, both in 2019 and in 2020 (women, 7.22%; men, 6.52% in 2020—slightly lower than the previous year).

In Romania, in 2020 there were almost 130,000 people who had a second job, out of which 2 times more men than women (Fig. 8.12). Due to the impact of the pandemic, which has led to restrictions for many businesses and to health measures, this number has decreased by over 18,000 people compared to 2019 (the decrease in absolute numbers being slightly more impactful in the case of the female population), but in relative terms, the reduction has been more than twice as high for women (22% for women, compared to 10.4% for men). Most women with a second job in 2020 have an average level of education (70.86%), being almost 10% less than men. Almost 16% of women with a second job have university degrees, a percentage that is more than twice as high as that of men. This may suggest that the satisfaction in terms of income from work among women with higher education is lower than in the case of men with the same level of education and that women feel the need to supplement their income by occupying more jobs. Only 13.33% of women who have multiple jobs have a low level of education (Fig. 8.13). The pandemic did not cause any significant structural changes in people with multiple occupations in terms of education, compared to the pre-pandemic year 2019.

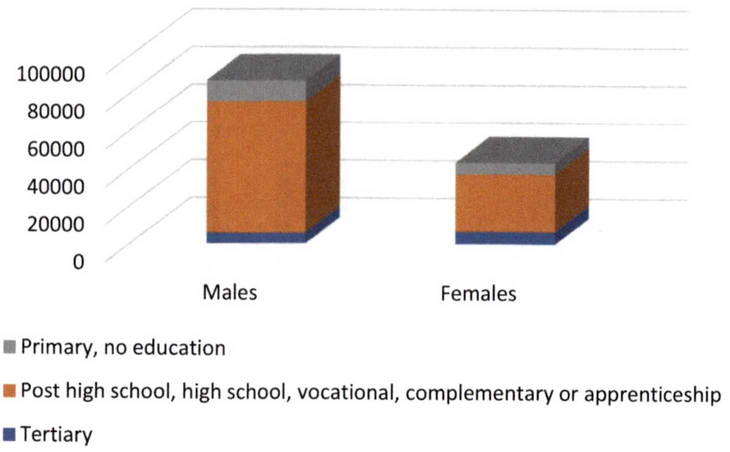


**Fig. 8.13** Employment with a second job, by gender and education level, 2020 (pers.)

## *Female Unemployment by Age Groups and Education Level*

The ILO unemployment rate among women increased from 3.4% in 2019 to 4.7% in 2020, the increase being higher than in the case of men (1.3 percentage points, in comparison with 1.0 percentage point). Similar dynamics were registered in the case of the 25–54 and 55–74 age groups. The evolution of the indicator was somehow more atypical in the case of the young female population (15–24 years old), as its level was less affected by the pandemic in 2020 (the rate decreased by 1 percentage point, from 17.5% in 2019 to 16.5% in 2020). However, the young people have the highest unemployment rate, while the elderly (55–74 years) have the lowest unemployment rate (1.7% in 2019, 2.7% in 2020) (Fig. 8.14). These developments can be explained by a greater flexibility/mobility of the young female workforce compared to other age groups, which has helped them to adapt better to maintaining a job or finding a new job in areas less affected by the pandemic.

As in the case of the male population, the highest value of the unemployment rate was registered among the female population with a lower education level at most, a category of population that was most affected by the pandemic, as it is characterised by the sharpest increase in unemployment rate (by 2.3 percentage points in 2020 compared to 2019). At all levels of education, the increase in the value of the indicator was higher for the female population than for the male population, which means that from this point of view women were more negatively affected by the pandemic crisis than men, and their situation on the labour market has become more precarious. Comparing the three levels of education, it is noted that in the case of women, as well as in the case of men, women with a higher level of education (tertiary education) had the lowest unemployment rates, both in the pandemic year and in pre-pandemic year, the increase in the unemployment rate for this category of women being the most insignificant (in 2020 compared to 2019, the increase was under 1%) (Fig. 8.15).

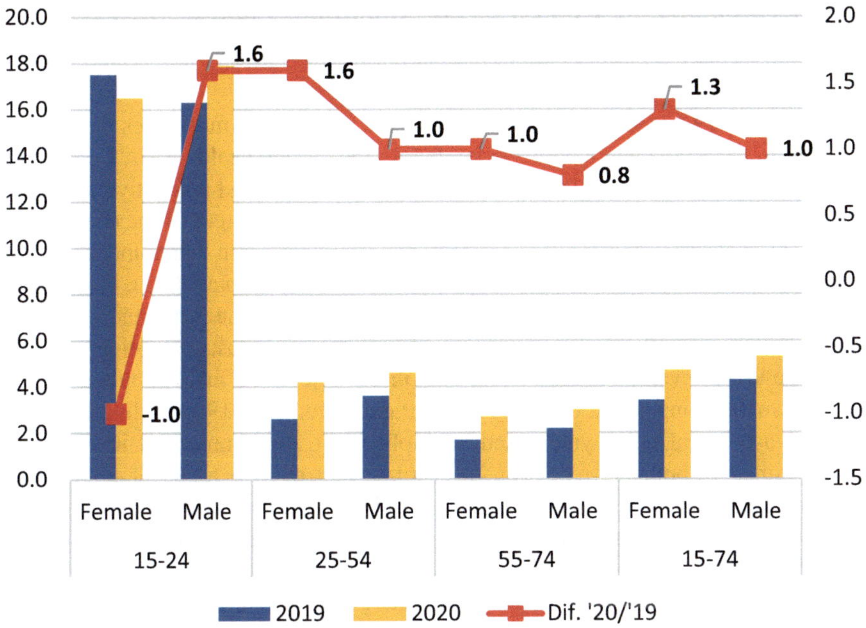


**Fig. 8.14** ILO unemployment rate, by gender and age groups, 2019 and 2020 (%)

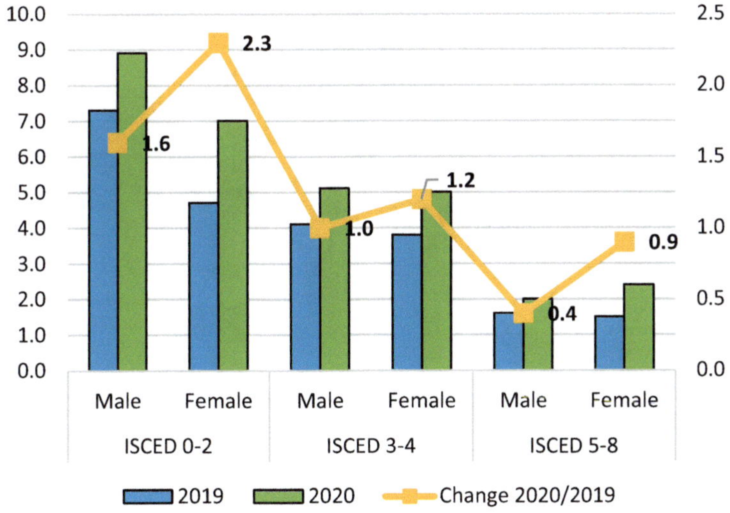


**Fig. 8.15** ILO unemployment rate, by gender and education level, 2019 and 2020 (%)

## *What Happened to Women in the Romanian Labour Market in the COVID-19 Pandemic Context?*

The COVID-19 pandemic further accentuated some gender imbalances that already existed in the Romanian labour market before the current health crisis, aggravating the precariousness of female employment. The pandemic had a negative impact on employment for both genders, but it appeared in different stages of the crisis and in different measures, due to the existing gender segregation phenomenon which characterises many economic activities (Zarrilli & Luomaranta, 2021).

However, we can say that in the case of women, during the pandemic year 2020, the main labour market indicators had a progress that was mostly negative, and their magnitude was even more significant than in the case of the male population.

The main changes that occurred in 2020 compared to 2019 regarding the quantitative aspects of employment and unemployment are summarised in Fig. 8.16. They aimed at both the reduction in absolute and relative terms of total female employment and its categories (in most activity sectors, for people with lower education, for adult age groups, in the private sector, for occupational groups with a lower level of professional training, etc.). Female unemployment was on the rise, more pronounced than male unemployment, targeting primarily women in the 25–54 age group and those with lower education.

Equally important are the issues related to the quality of employment. The share of temporarily employed women has decreased, not due to the increase in those

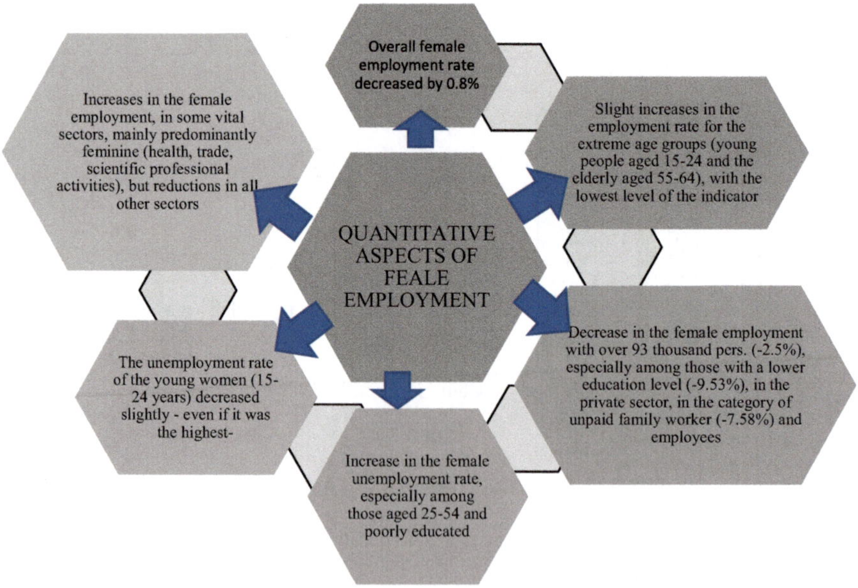


**Fig. 8.16** Dynamics of labour market indicators, targeting quantitative aspects of female employment and unemployment, in 2020 compared to 2019

permanently employed but as a result of the restriction of activities due to the pandemic crisis. The negative effect of the pandemic was felt less by the employed female population with higher education, although the gender pay gap is important, the share of highly educated women with a second job being twice as high as that of men in the same education category in 2020. Occupations characterised by a higher level of qualification and training registered either increase or lower decrease in absolute value of the female employment. The actual working time has decreased, with the number of salaried women working no more than 35 h per week almost doubling in comparison with the previous year. As a result of the reduction in female employment, especially in the employees' category, in 2020 the number of women with the "employer" status increased by almost 2%. Female leadership has not been significantly affected by the pandemic, with the share of women in top-management positions in business declining slightly in 2020 compared to 2019. However, the level of indicators remains well below that of male leadership. The main developments regarding the qualitative aspects of female employment on the labour market are summarised in Fig. 8.17.

## The Impact of the Pandemic on Young People's Participation in the Labour Market

During the COVID-19 pandemic, youth unemployment increased more than for other categories (an increase of almost 9% for youth unemployment compared with 3.7% for total unemployment). The economic consequences of the pandemic have been more severe for the younger generation from several perspectives:

- Disruptions in the education system, vocational training and on-the-job learning
- Difficulties in finding jobs, especially for new entrants to the labour market
- Deteriorating employment quality: many losses of jobs and income

Young people are overrepresented in certain activity sectors like tourism, culture, sports, etc., which were strongly affected during the pandemic period. Therefore, the vulnerability of young people increased, as they were more exposed to the reduction of working hours, income and number of jobs.

At national level, in the pre-pandemic year (2019), there were about 2052 million young people (age 15–24). Out of these, about 1454 million young people were inactive and 509,590 were employed, while 102,639 were unemployed in 2019. The analysis of the situation of the employed young people shows that their total number decreased by only 1.5% in 2020 compared to 2019, but for the category 15–19 years, the decrease was higher, of 13%, a decrease which was lessened by an increase in the number of employed young people in the 20–24 age categories. This is a first proof that the shocks related to COVID-19 in the labour market were felt differently for the various categories of young people, which could also have an impact on the quality

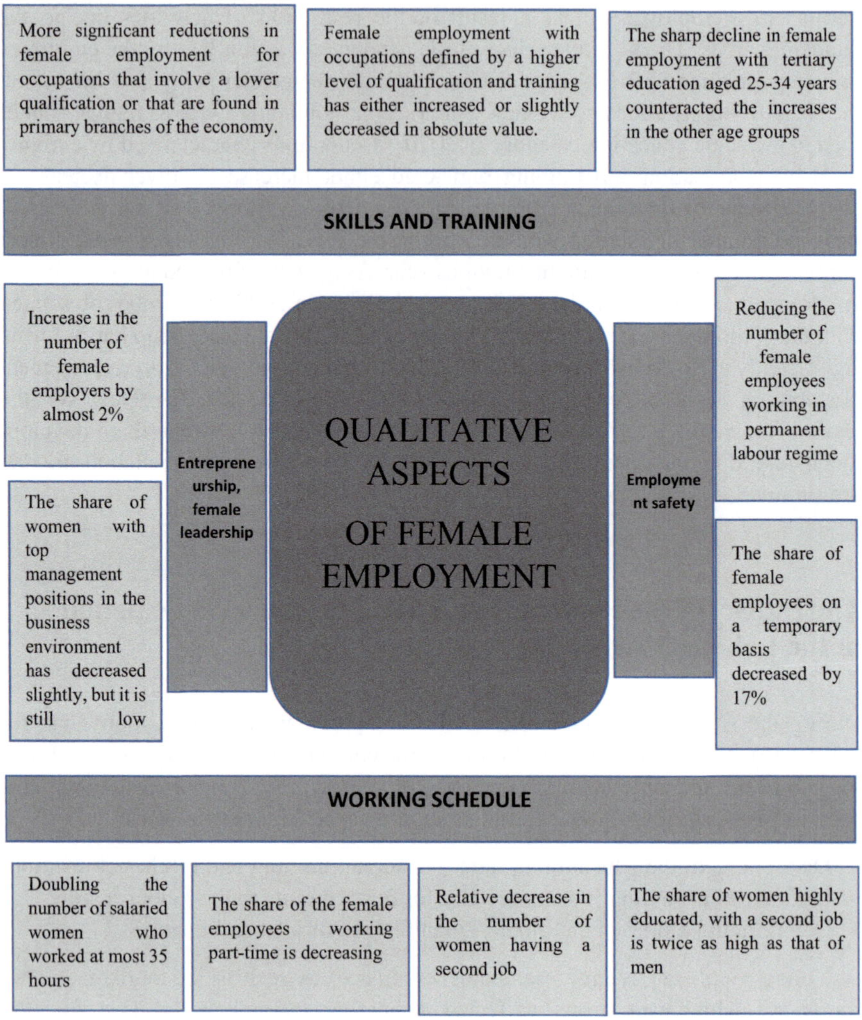


**Fig. 8.17** Dynamics of labour market indicators, aiming at qualitative aspects of female employment, in 2020 compared to 2019

of jobs addressed to them, either in the form of a "zero-hours" type contract or part-time or informal employment.

Next, in order to define the categories of young people most affected by the COVID-19 pandemic, we carried out analyses on young people employment by gender, socio-professional status, working time, activity sectors and major occupational groups.

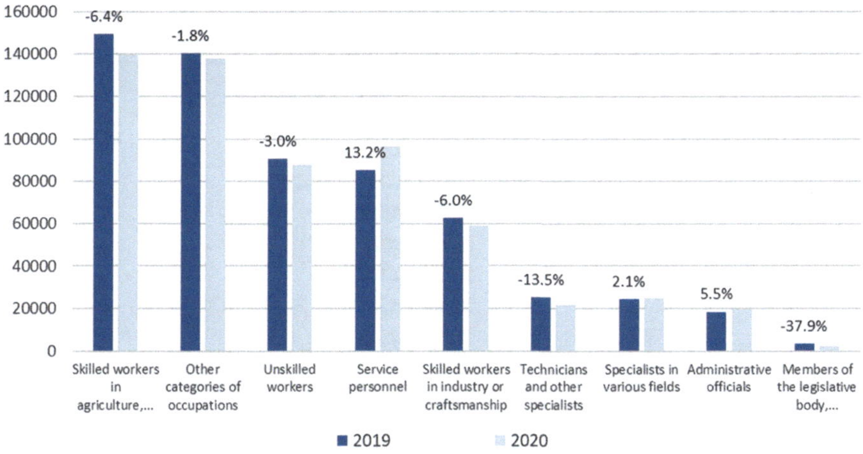


**Fig. 8.18** Youth employment by major occupational groups in 2019 and 2020 (pers.). Note: The graph also shows the relative differences between employment for 2020 compared to 2019 (%)

## *Youth Employment by Major Occupational Groups*

In the pandemic year 2020, the most significant reductions in the number of young people employed were in the case of occupations defined by a higher level of qualification and training, such as legislator, senior officials and managers (−37.9%) or in the group of technicians (−13.5%). In other groups—such as skilled and assimilated workers; skilled workers in agriculture, forestry and fishing; unskilled workers; and other occupations—the decrease in the number of employed young people was much more modest (up to 6.5%). Opposite changes were seen in the case of young service workers where the increase was significant (of 13.2%), but also in the case of administrative officials or specialists in various fields, with more modest increases (of up to 6%) (Fig. 8.18).

### Youth Employment by the Main NACE Activities

From the analysis of the share of the young, employed population (15–24 years) in the total employment on the main NACE activities in Romania in 2019 and 2020, we could find that there are sectors where the share of young people is higher than the average employment of young people in the total employed population (which is 5.9%) in the two reference years. Such sectors are hotels and restaurants (14.4% in 2020); agriculture, forestry and fishing (9.7% in 2020); other activities (7% in 2020); trade and car repair (6.9% in 2020); and construction (6.7%), whose share increased by up to 1.4% in 2020 compared to 2019, or entertainment, cultural and recreational activities (6.8% in 2020) where the share decreased by 2.4% in 2020 compared to 2019 (Fig. 8.19).

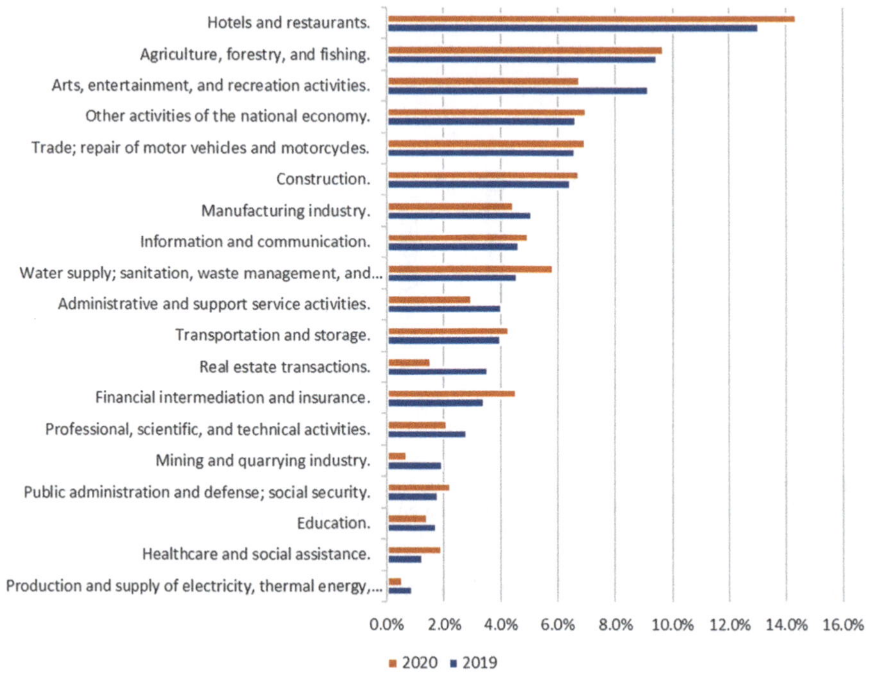


**Fig. 8.19** The share of young, employed population (15–24 years old) in the total employment, by the main NACE activities in 2019 and 2020

If we analyse the changes in the volume of the young, employed population (15–24) by the main NACE activities, we can notice that there are activities such as mining and quarrying, real estate transactions and production and supply of electricity, where there were very significant decreases (over 35%) of the number of young people employed in those activities. At the other end of the spectrum, there are activities such as health and social welfare, public administration and defence, water and sanitation distribution and financial intermediation and insurance, where there has been a substantial increase in the number of young people employed, by over 20%. Overall, the number of employed young people (15–24 years old) in Romania has experienced in 2020 only a minor, insignificant decrease, by 1.5%, lower than the one registered in the total employed population (1.8%). Nevertheless, young people went to sectors where the activity either continued during the pandemic, being vital sectors for society (such as health, trade, public administration and defence, water distribution and sanitation, etc.), or recorded a special extension of activity (information and communications). However, on the other hand, there were also sectors affected dramatically by the COVID-19 pandemic, in which young people had a significant share in the total employment (such as entertainment activities, manufacturing, etc.) (Fig. 8.20).

From the previous Fig. 8.21, one can note that in sectors with a high share of young, employed population, the changes in 2020 compared to 2019 are small,

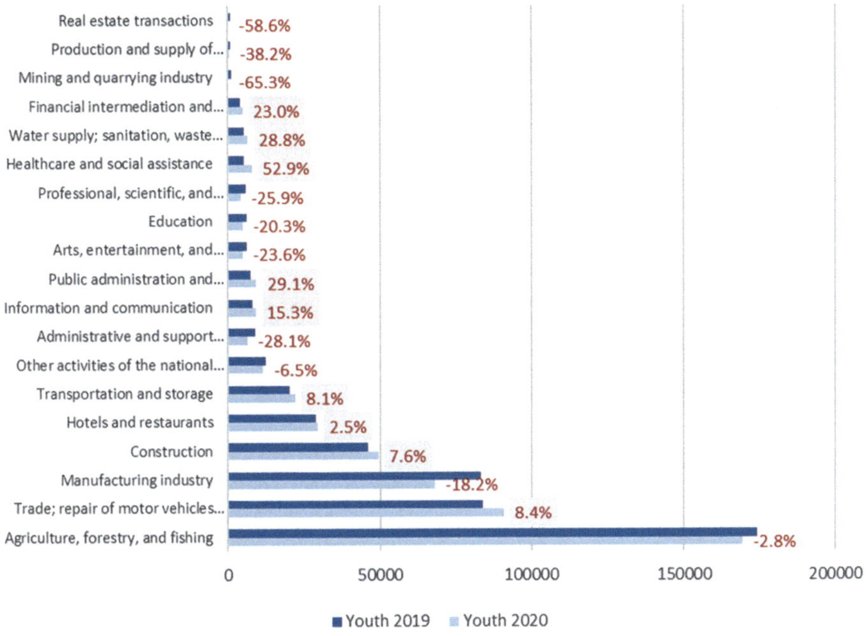


**Fig. 8.20** Youth employment (15–24-year-old) by the main NACE activities, in 2019 and 2020. Note: The graph also reveals the relative differences between employment for 2020 compared to 2019 (%)

regardless of their sign (positive or negative). The lower the share, the higher the changes, as the biggest changes were the decreases in the young, employed population.

## *Employment of Young People by Gender and Professional Status*

The analysis of young people's employment by professional status shows that most of them are employees or unpaid family workers. There was a gender difference in terms of the dynamics of the employed young population in Romania according to their professional status in 2020 compared to 2019. For example, in 2020 the largest decrease in the number of employed young people was registered among young male employees (−4.1%), as the number of young female employees grew (2.6%). For all other categories of young, employed persons, there were decreases in 2020 compared to 2019 for females, the most affected category being that of young female employers. For young men, however, the increases were registered in two categories: unpaid family workers and employers. Young self-employed workers dropped by 8.2% for both genders. These changes can be explained by a greater sensitivity of

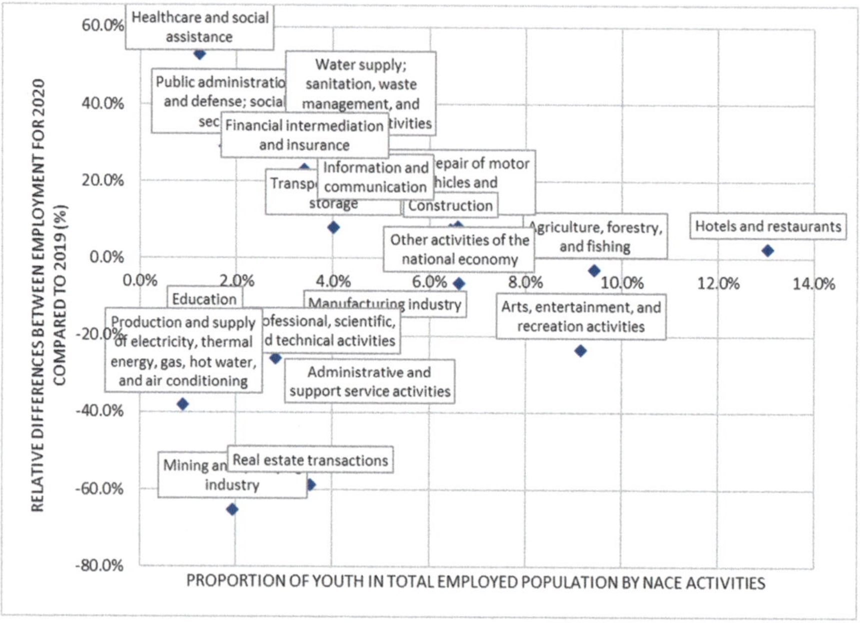


**Fig. 8.21** Scatter between the share of young, employed population (2020) and the relative dynamics of the young, employed population in 2020 compared to 2019, by the main activity sectors (%)

the number of young employees to employment adjustment schemes, as a result of the reduction of many economic activities in the pandemic year (Fig. 8.22).

Thus, in the first part of 2020, more than 1.2 million employment contracts were suspended or terminated, many employees became technically unemployed, and self-employed workers or limited-term contracts were suspended. On the other hand, the positive evolution of the employed male population with the professional status of "employer" may be due to the fact that young men whose employment contracts have been suspended or terminated as a result of the pandemic or who have not been able to perform liberal activities in the context of the pandemic have shifted towards starting their own businesses, especially in the online environment, in order to survive and earn an income.

## *Youth Unemployment by Gender, Age Group and Education Level*

Due to the pandemic, the number of ILO unemployed increased, reaching 105,268 young people. If we analyse the case of young people who have had a job, we can see that the number of unemployed young people has doubled in 2020 compared to

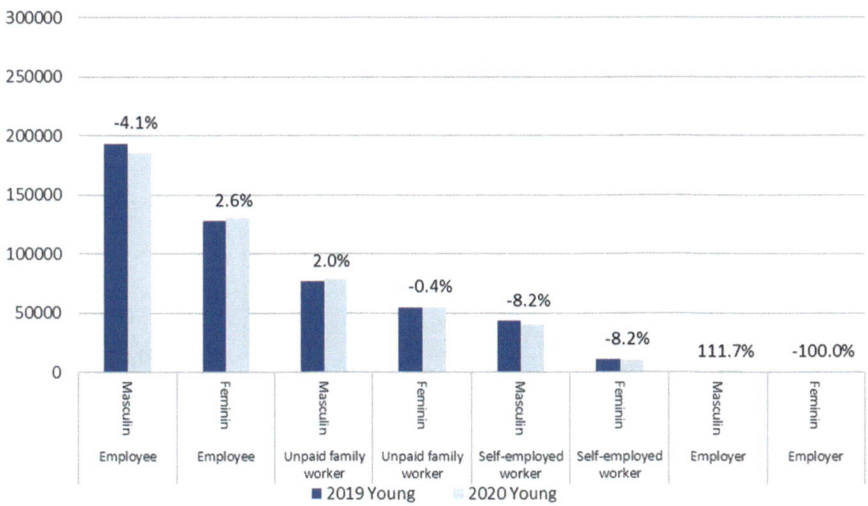


**Fig. 8.22** Employment by professional status and gender, in 2019 and 2020, for young age groups. Note: The graph also reveals the relative differences between employment for 2020 compared to 2019 (%)

2019, while for adults this increase is 0.67 times. Therefore, in 2020, the COVID-19 pandemic had a harsher impact for young people rather than for adults in terms of unemployment. This is also based on the fact that the unemployment rate for young people (age 15–24) is already three times higher than the unemployment rate for adults.

The number of registered unemployed beneficiaries of financial aid was higher among the young population with a high level of education (university studies), reaching an increase of 62.6%. But if we take a look at the number of ILO unemployed, it declined in 2020 compared to 2019. An explanation for this phenomenon could be the fact that they were recently hired, possibly on probation or on a fixed-term contract, and in crisis conditions this category was the first to be laid off. However, the increase in the number of young unemployed people who benefit from financial support was lower compared to the total number, regardless of the level of education. In terms of the number of ILO unemployed, it was much higher among young people without a high school diploma or among those with post-secondary or vocational education, which means that from this point of view young people without a high level of education were more negatively affected by the pandemic crisis, as their situation on the labour market became more precarious. Highly educated young people have refocused on areas and sectors of activity that developed during the pandemic, such as online commerce, health and social assistance, etc. (Figs. 8.23 and 8.24).

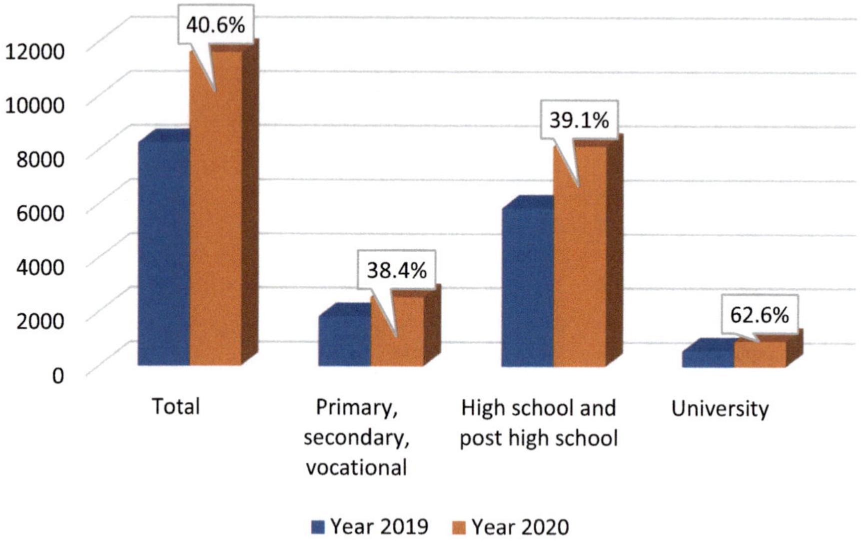


**Fig. 8.23** Number of registered unemployed, beneficiaries of financial aid, in 2019 and 2020 for young people, by level of education (pers.) Note: The graph also reveals the relative differences between unemployment for 2020 compared to 2019 (%)

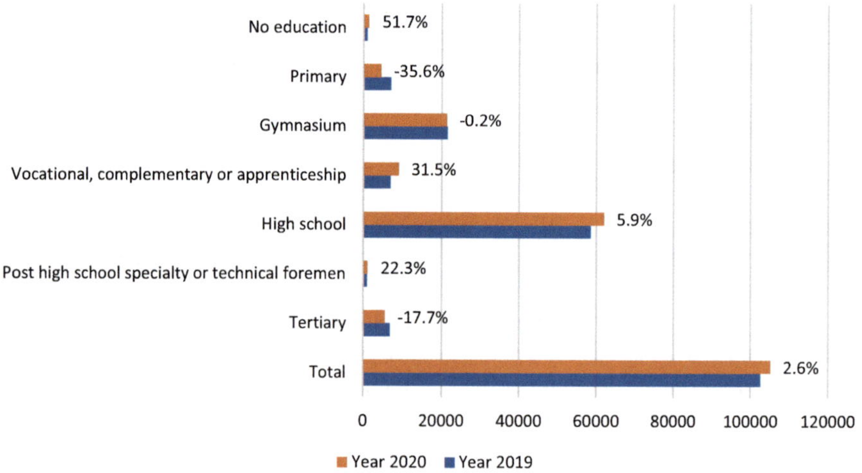


**Fig. 8.24** Number of ILO unemployed, in 2019 and 2020 for young people, by level of education (pers.). Note: The graph also reveals the relative differences between unemployment for 2020 compared to 2019 (%)

### *How Have Young People in the Labour Market Been Affected by the COVID-19 Pandemic?*

The COVID-19 pandemic has accentuated some existing disparities on the labour market in Romania before the current health crisis, aggravating the precarious employment of young people. Their income has decreased, and social protection has become limited, as prices for essential goods and services have risen.

The number of NEETs highly increased in Romania in the first quarter of 2021, according to Eurostat estimates, from 16.4 in Q1 2020 to 21.6 in Q1 2021. The needs of young people were not totally covered by social protection measures, their vulnerability increasing during COVID-19 and being pushed into extreme poverty (ECOSOC Youth Forum 2021).

In the pandemic year 2020, the developments of the main indicators of the labour market were mostly negative, and their magnitude was more pronounced for the young population. The main changes that occurred in 2020 compared to 2019 regarding the quantitative aspects of youth employment and unemployment are summarised in the following diagram (Fig. 8.25). Their aim was reducing the unemployment of young people in absolute and relative terms, which was more significant for young people aged 15–19, male or those with a higher level of education. Young self-employed workers have also been more affected by this crisis compared to other socio-professional categories. Regarding the sectors of activity, it can be noted that in the sectors with a high share of young, employed population, the changes produced in 2020 compared to 2019 are small, regardless of their being positive or negative, for the sectors hotels and restaurants, entertainment activities and agriculture.

In terms of youth unemployment, it has been rising, much more than in the case of total unemployment. Also, unemployment among young people with a low level of education has increased more than in the case of those with higher levels of education, the latter having the ability to reorient themselves to areas and sectors of activity that have developed during the pandemic, such as online commerce, health and social assistance, etc.

## Active Ageing in Romania During COVID-19

The demographic ageing process is a reality for Europe as a whole, of which Romania is no stranger, with long-term demographic, economic and social consequences. The demographic ageing index in Romania has increased in the last 10 years by over 16 percentage points, reaching 118.8 people aged 65 and over per 100 children (0–14 years) in 2019. The phenomenon is mainly explained by a decline in the birth rate, the rise of life expectancy, but also by the increased emigration of the young population, especially in recent years (INS—Tendințe sociale, 2019). Changes are needed in both society and the economy to meet these

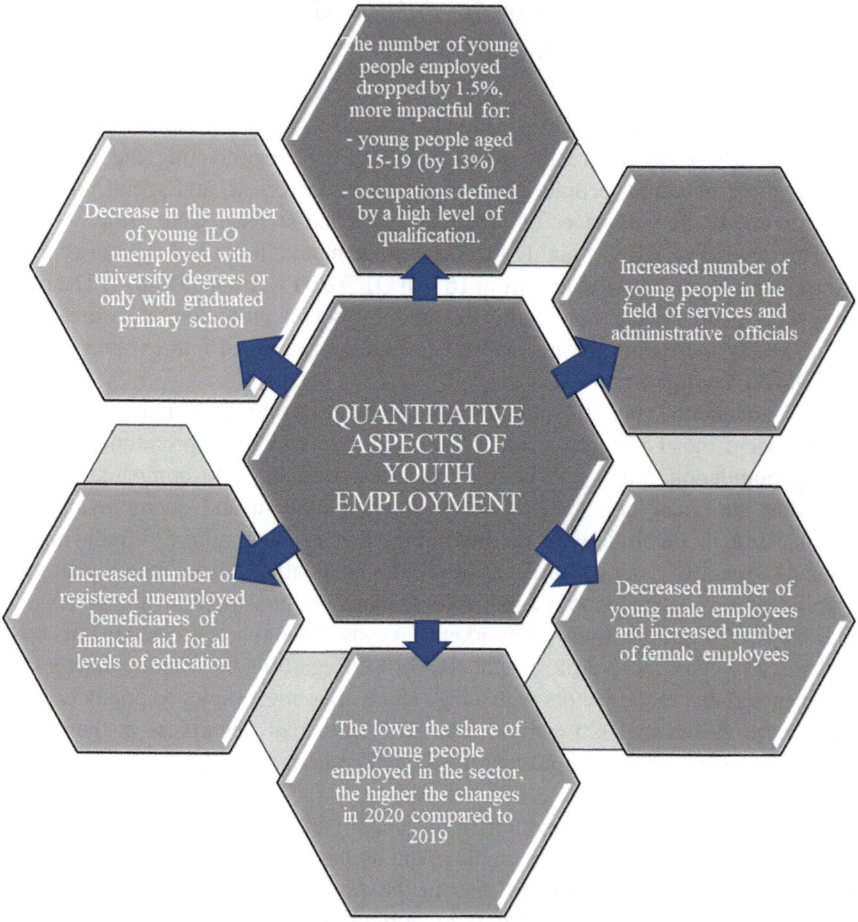


**Fig. 8.25** Quantitative aspects of youth employment and unemployment in 2019 and 2020

challenges, to ensure the health and a decent living for the elderly, beyond the risk of poverty. In addition, the current pandemic has negatively affected both the physical and mental health of the elderly population and their quality of life, aggravating the phenomenon of social isolation (Council of the European Union, 2021—*Integrarea problematicii îmbătrânirii în politicile publice*). According to a survey organised by IRES in February 2021 (IRES: *Impactul COVID-19 asupra calității vieții românilor*, 2021), only 7% of respondents aged 51–65 and only 3% of those over 65 believe that things changed for the better in their lives under the impact of the pandemic—the lowest percentage of all age groups—while those aged 51 and over were more likely to experience social isolation than younger groups (IRES—*1 AN DE COVID-19 ÎN ROMÂNIA: Impactul COVID-19 asupra calității vieții românilor*, 2021). In these conditions, the analysis of the situation of the elderly on the labour market in

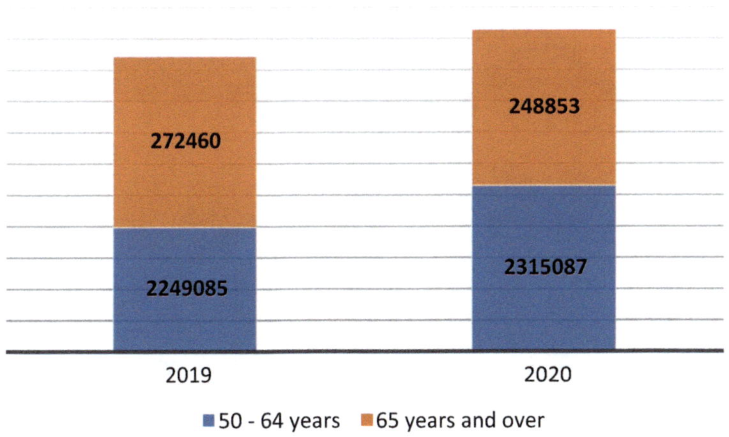


**Fig. 8.26** Employment aged 50+ in Romania, by age subgroups, in 2019 and 2020 (persons)

Romania is of particular interest, as well as the impact of the COVID-19 pandemic on it.

The broadly defined group of older people (aged 50 and over) is characterised by heterogeneity, hiding some inequalities between age subgroups from different points of view, which is why we will refer—where possible—distinctly to the subgroup 50–64 years and 65 years and over, respectively, in order to identify differences in behaviour on the labour market in the context of the current health pandemic.

Almost a third of the employed population of Romania is aged 50 and over (respectively 30% in 2020). By age subgroups, people aged 50–64 represented 90% of the total employment aged 50+ in 2020 (about 1% more than in 2019) (Fig. 8.26). Analysing the dynamics of the employed elderly population (50+), we need to mention that it increased in 2020 by 1.68% compared to 2019. As there are different behaviours and dynamics in terms of the employed population aged 50–64 compared to those aged 65 and over, we will perform the analysis by age subgroups in 2019 and 2020. Thus, the employed population aged 50–64 increased by almost 3% in 2020 in comparison with the previous year, while the number of elderly people aged 65+ decreased by 8.66% compared to the pre-pandemic year.

## *Employed Population and Employment Rate for the 50+ Age Group by Gender and by Education Level*

The distributions of the elderly in the age groups 50–64 and 65 and over, by the level of education, have opposite skewness, both in 2019 and 2020. Thus, the employed population aged 50–64 with a high school level of education holds the largest share in the total employed population in this age group (40.16% in 2020). Over a quarter

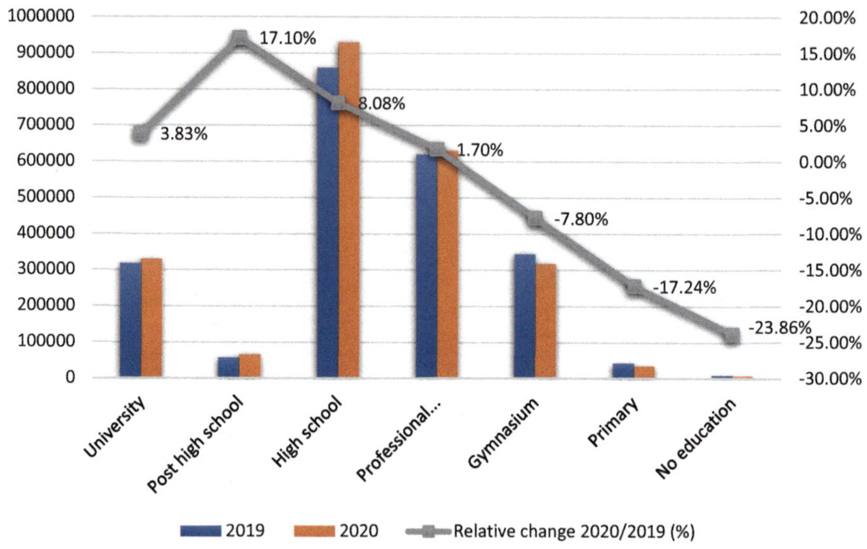


**Fig. 8.27** Employment for the population aged 50–64, by education level, 2019 and 2020 (pers.). Relative change 2020/2019 (%)

of the total employed population aged 50–64 graduated from vocational, complementary or apprenticeship education (27.24% in 2020), and only 14.26% were graduates of higher education in the same year. The most positive dynamics of the employed population aged 50–64 was registered in 2020 among post-secondary graduates (+17.1% compared to 2019), while the most important relative decrease is found among graduates with a low level of education (−17.24% for those with primary education and −23.86% for those with no school) in the same period. Among the employed elderly population in this age group, the highly educated were less affected by the pandemic (Fig. 8.27).

Regarding the population aged 65 and over, the highest share is held by graduates of lower secondary education (44.53% of the total employed in the corresponding age group in 2020), while those with higher education represent only 5.24%. The employed population aged 65 and over experienced a positive dynamic in the pandemic year 2020 for those with higher education (+ 5.82%) and a negative one for those with a lower level of education (−14.52% for people without school), compared to the previous year (Fig. 8.28).

In 2020, the male employed population represented 58.09% of the total employment in the age group 50–64 and only 49.72% in the age group 65 and over. The dynamics of the indicator in 2020 compared to 2019 was different for the two age subgroups. Thus, if among the employed persons in the 50–64 age group there was an increase for both genders (without significant gender differences, respectively an increase of 2%–4%), for those aged 65+, the number of employed persons has decreased for both genders, but the absolute decrease was twice as high for women (female, 15,174 people; male, 8434 people) (Fig. 8.29).

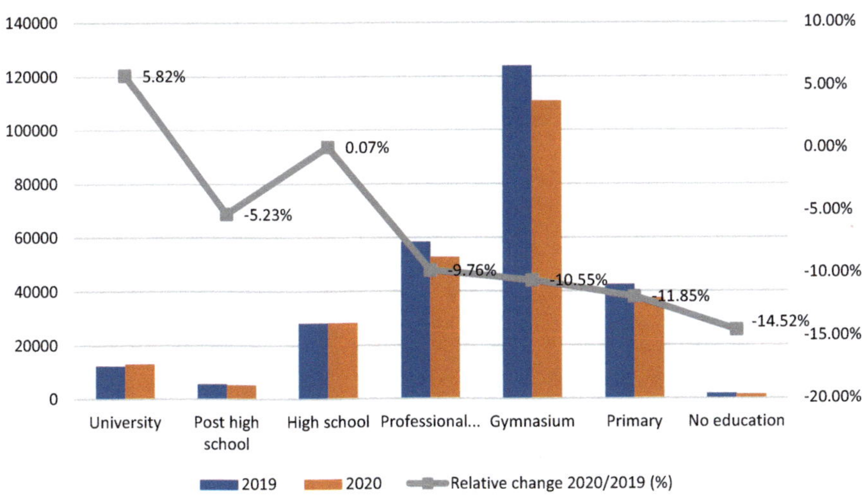


**Fig. 8.28** Employment for the population aged 65 and over, by education level, 2019 and 2020 (pers.). Relative change 2020/2019 (%)

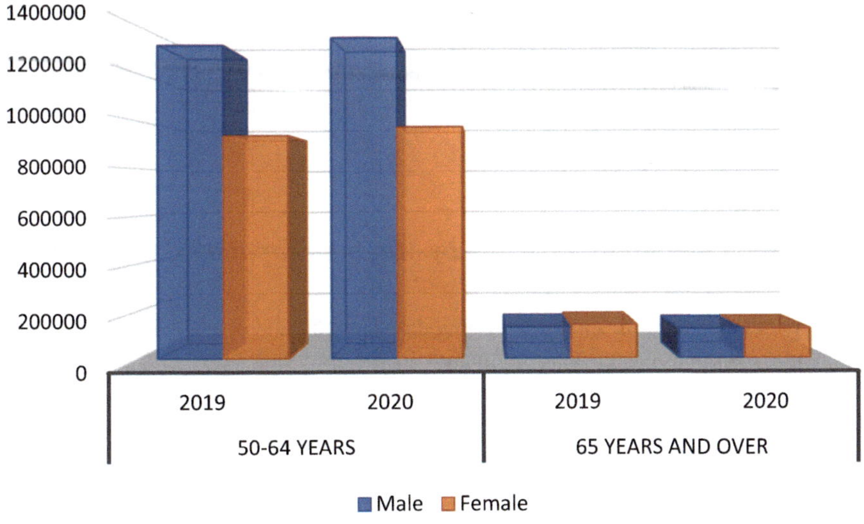


**Fig. 8.29** Employment for the population aged 50 years and over, by age subgroups and gender, 2019 and 2020 (pers.)

The employment rate for the 55–64 age group was 48.5% in 2020, slightly lower than the total level (52.3% in the same year). The level of the indicator is lower than that of the population aged 25–54, but higher than that corresponding to young people (15–24 years). From a dynamic perspective, if both the national employment rate and that of 15–24 and 25–54 age groups registered a slight decrease in the

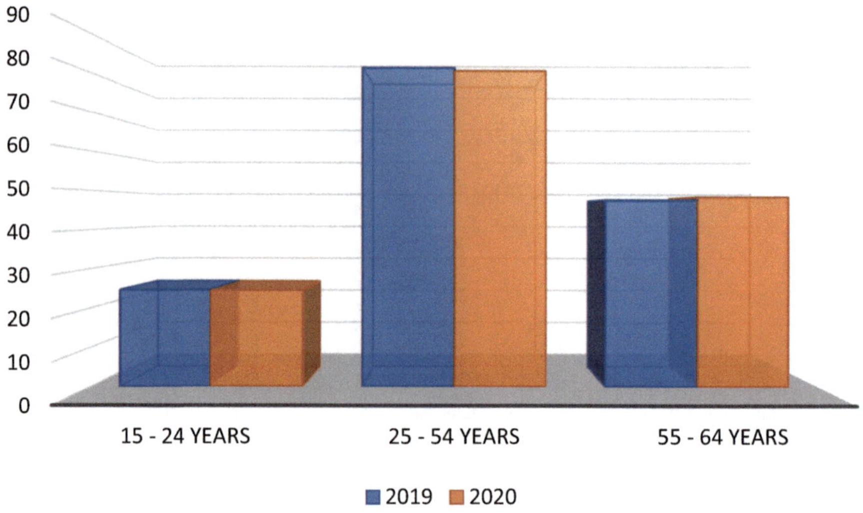


**Fig. 8.30** Employment rate by age groups in 2019 and 2020 (%)

pandemic year compared to the previous one, for the elderly population (55–64 years), the employment rate recorded an opposite dynamic, increasing by 0.7 percentage points. It can be stated, therefore, that from the point of view of this indicator and for this segment of the population, the negative impact of the pandemic was less significant (Fig. 8.30).

## *Employed Population Aged 50+ by Major Occupational Groups*

In the pandemic year, the employed population aged 50 and over evolved differently by major occupational groups, compared to the previous year. Thus, there were groups of occupations for which the employed population increased (the highest increases, between 9.1% and 9.5%, were among technicians, administrative officials and service workers), but there were also other groups which experienced reductions in the elderly employed population (by 6–8%, among legislators, senior officials and managers as well as unskilled workers) (Fig. 8.31).

Within most major occupational groups, the dynamics were significantly differentiated across the two age subgroups, although the absolute level of the employed population aged 50–64 is obviously much higher than in the 65+ group. Thus, in the occupation-group legislators, senior officials and managers, the employed population aged 65+ increased by 18.43%, while the employed population aged 50–64 decreased by 9.12%. In the occupation-group technicians, specialists in the technical field, the employed population aged 65+ decreased by 28.26%, whereas the employed population aged 50–64 increased by 10.34%. The relative increase in the number of administrative staff aged 65+ was much higher than in the 50–64 age

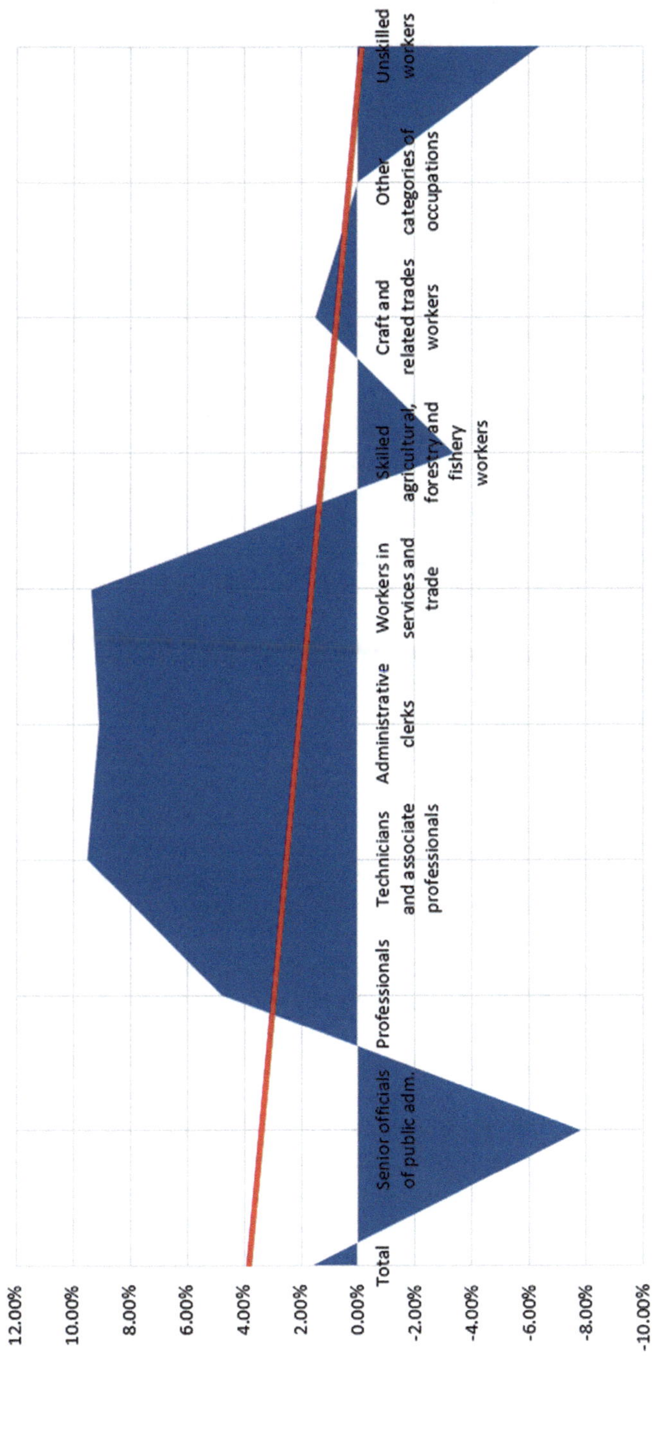


**Fig. 8.31** Relative change of employment aged 50 years and over, by major occupation groups, in Romania, in 2020 compared to 2019 (%)

group (104.77% compared to 8.58%), with a similar trend for service workers (+36.15% for the employed population aged 65+, vs. 8.97% for the 50–64 age group). On the other hand, in the group of unskilled workers, the number of employed people aged 65+ halved in 2020 compared to 2019, compared to those aged 50–64, who faced only a slight decrease (−2.25%) (Fig. 8.32).

## *Employed Population Aged 50+ by NACE Activities*

If we take into account the employed population aged 50 and over, by age subgroups and activities of the national economy in 2019 and 2020, we find that in agriculture there is an ageing workforce, the share of people employed in this sector aged 65 and over being the largest out of all activities (13.1% in 2019, 12.28% in 2020). In 2020, the number of employed elderly population (50 years and over) decreased by more than 40,000 people compared to the previous year, the decrease being more impactful in the age group 65 and over (−11.18%), compared to the group 50–64 (−2.51%). The financial intermediation and real estate transactions sector also faced a sharp relative reduction in the elderly aged 65 and over, a reduction of 72.54% in 2020 compared to 2019, although in terms of absolute numbers, the decrease is not as significant. There was a positive dynamic in trade, transport, accommodation and food activities, on one hand, and in health and education, public administration or social security, on the other hand. In these sectors, where activity was not restricted during the pandemic, as they are essential, the employed population in the 50–64 age group recorded significant absolute increases (by 25,799, respectively by 26,338 people in 2020 compared to 2019), representing 5.69% and 8.67%, respectively. A significant absolute increase, of over 13,000 people, was also registered in constructions, in the age group 50–64, representing 7.63%, with constructions being one of the activities that developed and even expanded during the pandemic, due to the increase in the demand for houses, especially new houses and those located outside large cities (Fig. 8.33).

The activity sectors can be divided into four categories: there are activity sectors in which people aged 50 and over have shares of over 35% in total employment of the respective sector, but which also registered significant increases in 2020 (of 11–12%) of the employed elderly compared to 2019: *production and supply of electricity and heat* and *extractive industry*. In education, health, construction and public administration, the elderly hold between 25 and 30% of the total employed population of the sector, registering also increases (although smaller ones) of the elderly employed population in 2020 in comparison with the previous year (between 7 and 10%). The explanation for these developments is that, as these activities are essential, they were less affected by the COVID-19 pandemic and operated in normal parameters even during the state of alert or emergency. The labour shortage was even covered with "old-generation" specialists. The information and communications sector has the lowest share of the elderly (12% in 2020), but even in these conditions, due to the expansion that such activities have experienced in the

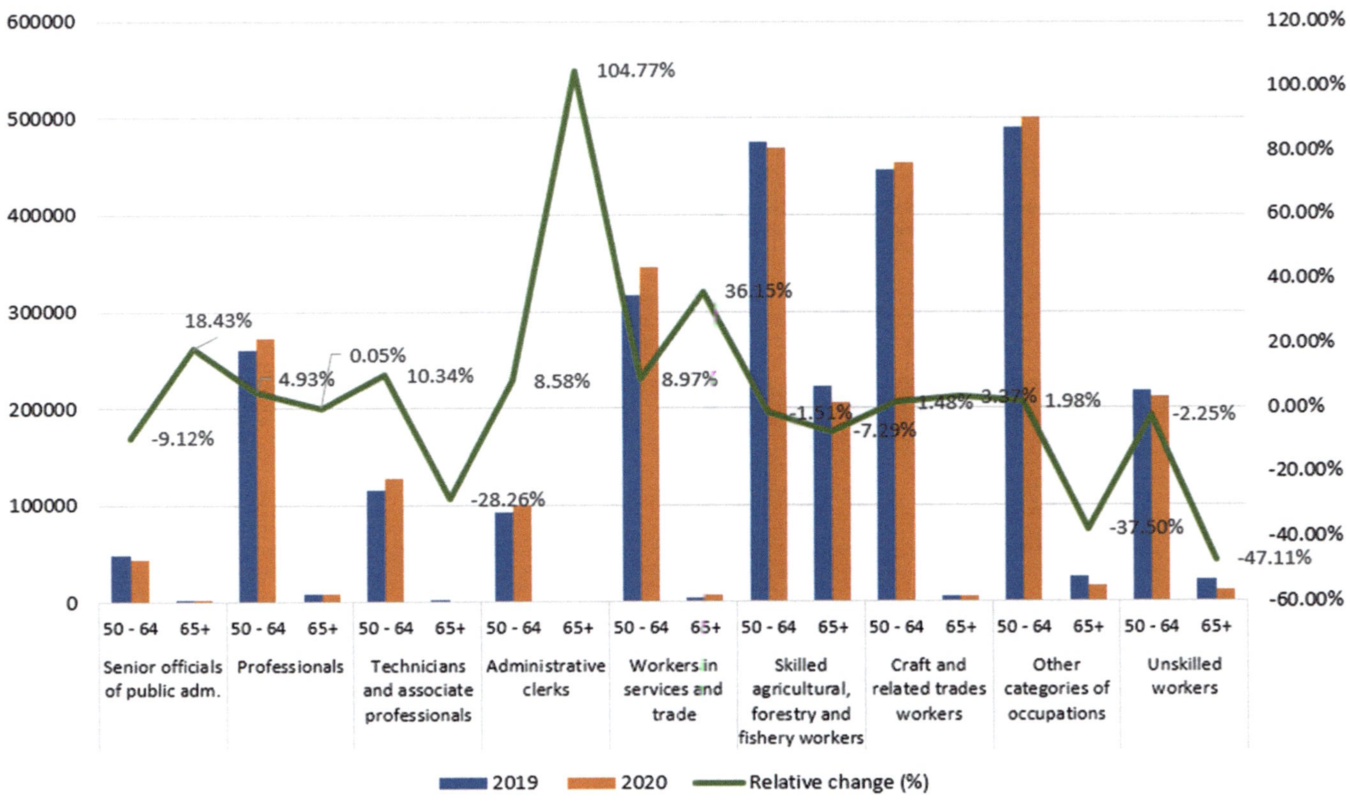


**Fig. 8.32** Employment aged 50+, by major occupation groups in Romania, in 2019 and 2020 (persons). Relative change 2020/2019 (%)

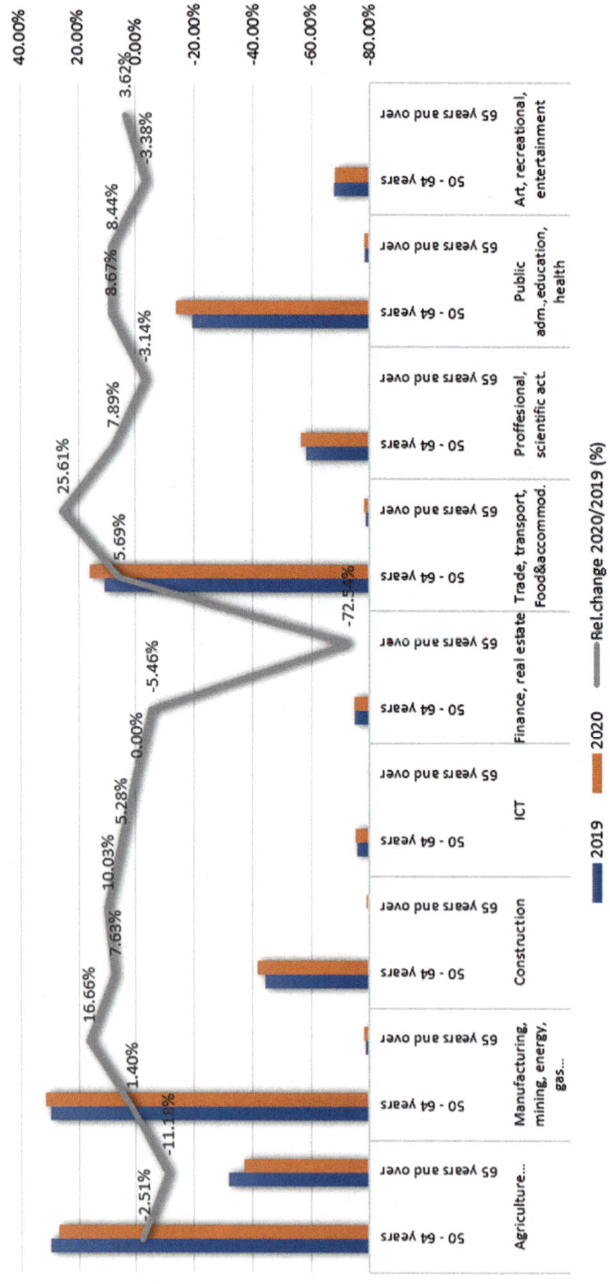


**Fig. 8.33** Employment aged 50 years and over in 2019 and 2020, by NACE activity (persons). Relative change 2020/2019 (%)

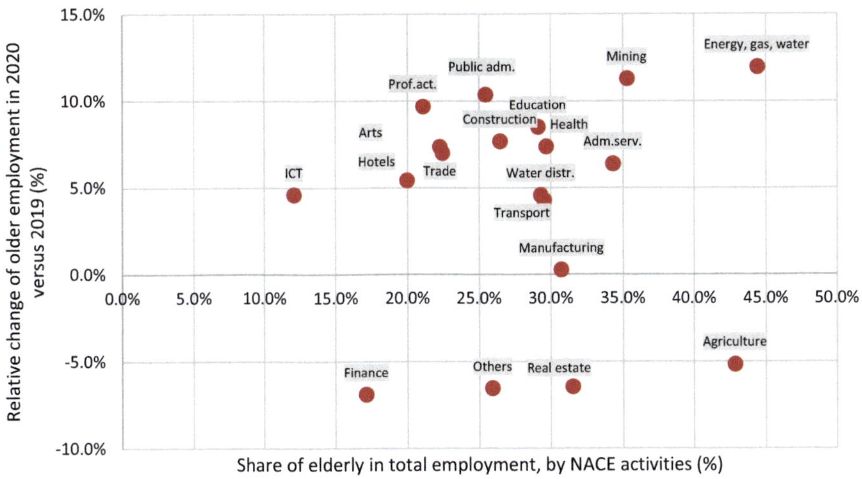


**Fig. 8.34** Scatter plot between the share of elderly in total employment and the relative change of older employment in 2020 compared to 2019, by NACE activity (%)

pandemic and given the labour shortage in this sector, the elderly employed population increased by about 5% in 2020 compared to the previous year (Fig. 8.34).

On the other hand, agriculture, forestry and fishing as well as real estate transactions are characterised by a fairly high share of the elderly in the employed population of the sector (42.84%, respectively, 31.52% in 2020), but also by a reduction of 5–7% of the number of 50+ people employed in 2020 compared to 2019. These are, moreover, sectors whose activity has been restricted to a certain extent due to the pandemic. Another sector with similar dynamics is financial intermediation (a decrease of about 7%), in which the elderly hold only 17.11% of its total employed population (Fig. 8.34).

## *Elderly Employed Population by Professional Status*

In 2020, people aged 50 and over accounted for more than a quarter of employees in Romania (a slightly higher share than in the previous year) and almost a third of employers and unpaid family workers (a slightly lower share than in 2019). At the same time, 45% of self-employed workers existing in 2020 in Romania were aged 50 and over (Fig. 8.35).

According to their professional status, the only category of elderly people with an increase in 2020 compared to 2019 was that of employees (an increase of over 82,000 people, representing almost 5%). The category of elderly unpaid family workers registered the sharpest decrease in absolute and relative terms in the same period (over 21,000 people, representing 10.13%). Approximately 1000 employers aged 50 and over and 18,000 self-employed workers in the same age group ceased

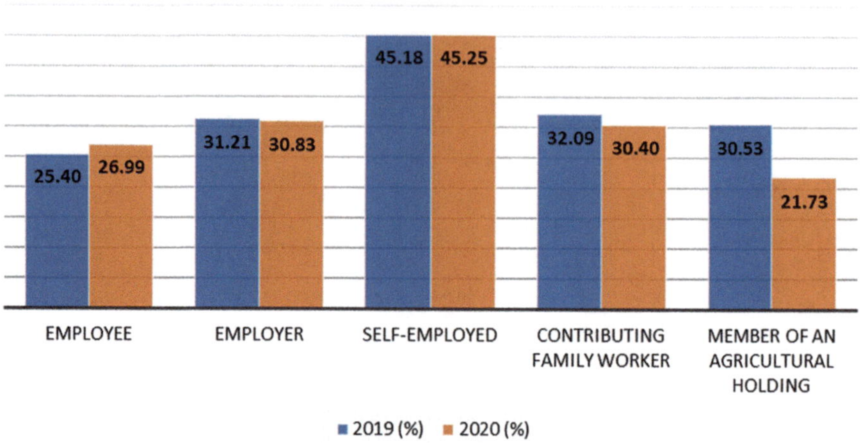


**Fig. 8.35** Share of employment aged 50 and over in total employment, by professional status, in 2019 and 2020 (%)

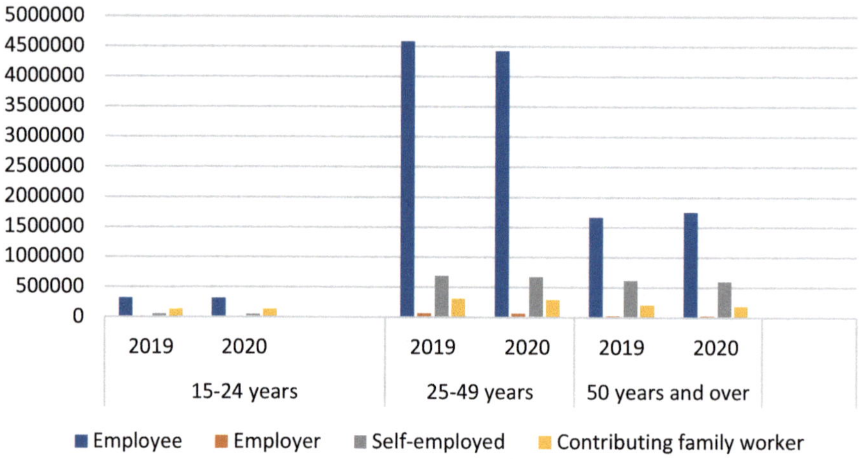


**Fig. 8.36** Employment by age and professional status in Romania, in 2019 and 2020 (pers.)

their activity in the year of the pandemic compared to the previous year (relative decreases of around 3%) (Fig. 8.36).

## *Unemployment Among the Elderly Population*

In 2020, the number of ILO unemployed aged 50 and over increased by almost 22,000 people compared to 2019, exceeding 79,000 people (relative increase of over 38%). Of these, 56.69% are men and almost all belong to the 50–64 age group. The

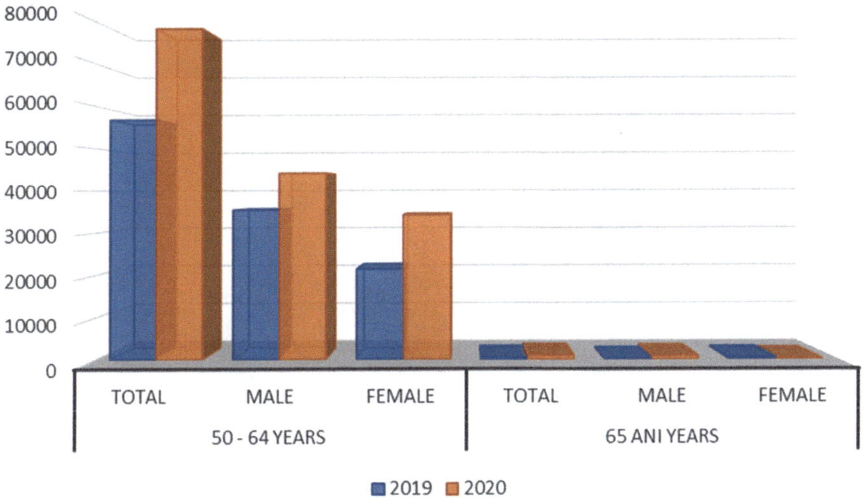


**Fig. 8.37** ILO unemployment (50 and over) by gender and age, in 2019 and 2020 (%)

ILO unemployed people aged 50 and over account for 17.53% of all ILO unemployed registered in 2020 (Fig. 8.37).

Analysing the unemployment among the elderly in relative figures, it can be seen that both in 2019 and in 2020 the ILO unemployment rate of people aged 55–64 was at the lowest level compared to other age groups (15–24 years and respectively 25–54 years). The level of the indicator increased slightly by one percentage point (from 2.4% to 3.4%) in the first year of the pandemic, due to the new coronavirus, in comparison with the year before the pandemic (2019). The gender gap in the ILO unemployment rate for the population aged 55–64 has narrowed in 2020; whereas the rate was slightly larger in men's case than in women's case (2.6% compared to 2.1%) in 2019, its level was equalised for the two genders in 2020 (Fig. 8.38).

## *What Was the General Impact of the COVID-19 Crisis on the Elderly in the Labour Market?*

The elderly population is known as one of the groups in the labour market characterised by several vulnerabilities, and the current health pandemic, overlapping with the demographic ageing phenomenon, could lead to their chronicity, affecting the conditions and life quality of the elderly. The higher risk of deteriorating the economic situation of older workers under the impact of the pandemic may have negative effects on labour productivity (Vasile, 2020). Even if in the first part of 2020 there was a lack of interest on the part of some people to look for a new job and to get involved in the labour market after losing their old job or accentuating the phenomenon of early retirement due to the risk of exposure to the

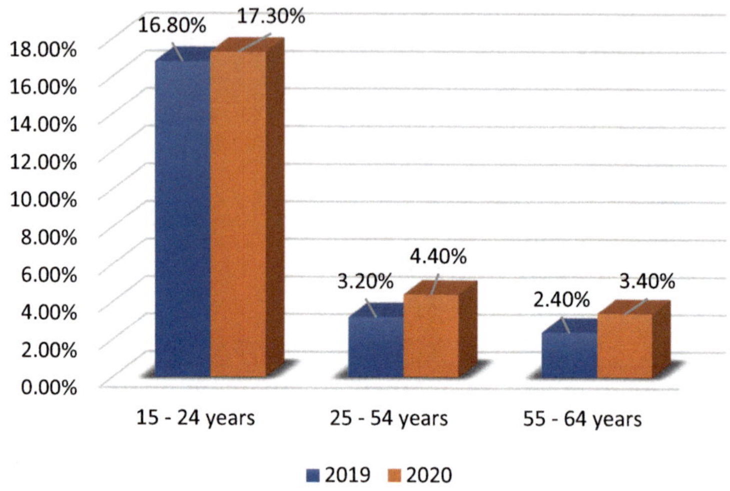


**Fig. 8.38** ILO unemployment rate by age subgroups, in 2019 and 2020 (%)

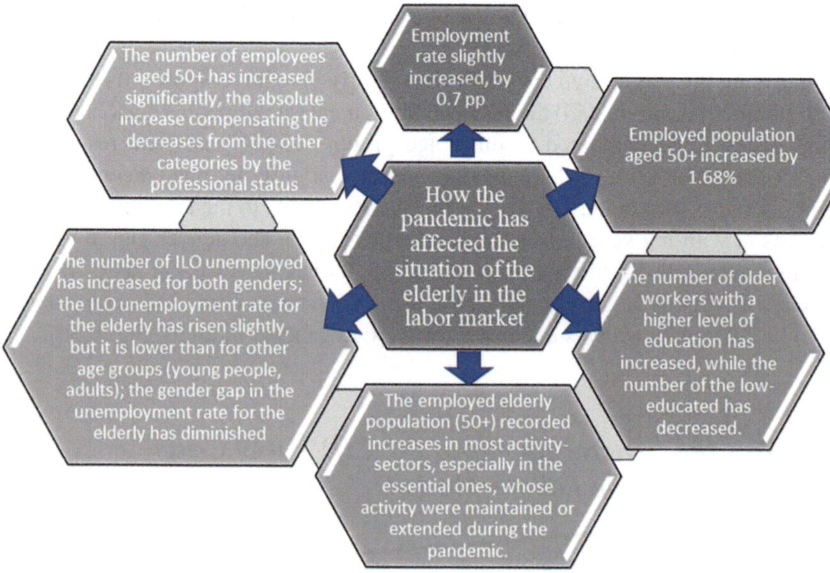


**Fig. 8.39** Ways the pandemic affected the situation of the elderly in the labour market

new coronavirus infection, in the second half of 2020, the situation improved even for the elderly (Vasile, 2020).

Figure 8.39 summarises the main changes in the situation of the elderly involved in the labour market, in the context of the current health pandemic.

Although the pandemic has exacerbated some existing imbalances in the labour market, not all developments related to the situation of the elderly have been negative in 2020 compared to the pre-pandemic period. Thus, the employment rate of the population aged 55–64 increased slightly in 2020, by 0.7 percentage points compared to the previous year. Similarly, the employed population aged 50 and over increased by 1.68% in 2020 compared to 2019, with different trends by age subgroups: slight increase in the 50–64 age group, both for male and female population and decrease in the group aged 65 and over, more pronounced in women's case. The pandemic negatively affected older workers with lower levels of education, with their numbers declining during the analysed period, while the number of those with higher levels of education increased. The employed elderly population (50+) recorded increases in most sectors of activity, especially in the essential ones that were maintained or expanded during the pandemic (industry, construction, education, health, trade, public administration, IT). The number of employees aged 50 and over has risen significantly, their absolute increase compensating for the decreases in the other categories of workers by professional status (employers, unpaid family workers, self-employed). In both men's and women's cases, the number of ILO unemployed has risen, the ILO unemployment rate for the elderly has also increased slightly, but it is lower than the rate for other age groups (young people, adults); in addition to this, the gender gap in the unemployment rate of the elderly decreased in 2020, in comparison with 2019 (Fig. 8.39).

The contribution of older people should be valued in terms of life experience, skills and knowledge acquired and updated, in order to achieve economic performance in the workplace, to improve the entrepreneurial environment and to strengthen social cohesion (Council of the European Union, 2021—*Integrarea problematicii îmbătrânirii în politicile publice*). Therefore, it is necessary for economic policy measures to take into account the needs and preferences of the elderly population, to create opportunities for their involvement in the life of society, to stimulate participation in economic activity, as a support for the active ageing process.

## How Was Labour Market Flexibility Impacted by the Pandemic?: The Case of Self-Employed Workers

The ability of any group to respond to and recover from the crisis will depend on a number of factors at several levels. Many self-employed people are sole traders or small entrepreneurs. In such cases, the circumstances and personal characteristics of the self-employed persons will have a significant effect on their survival in times of crises (Ratten, 2020a, 2020b).

Under the circumstances of the COVID-19 pandemic, the restrictions that governments have placed on economic activity as a result of this crisis have had a major impact with unequal effects on self-employed workers. Those who operate larger

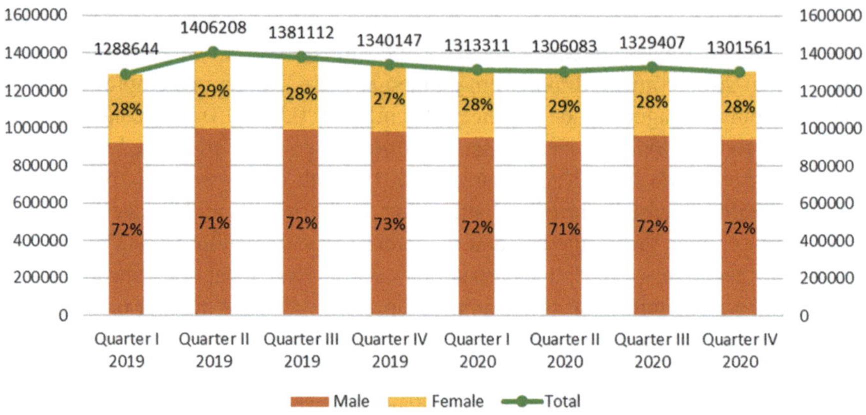


**Fig. 8.40** Quarterly self-employed workers by gender, 2019–2020

businesses and use digital technologies or those who have managed to quickly transform their businesses have had better results, tending to further increase any existing inequalities.

At national level, at the beginning of the pandemic, in the first quarter of 2020, there were approximately 1.313 million self-employed persons, 72% male and 28% female. The largest decrease is observed in the second quarter of 2020 compared to the same time period of 2019, with a difference of almost 100,000 self-employed (Fig. 8.40).

The analysis of the age distribution of self-employed workers shows that around 70% of self-employed workers are between 35 and 64 years old; hence, they are experienced people who sought greater flexibility at maturity (Fig. 8.40).

Next, in order to define the categories of self-employed workers most affected by the COVID-19 pandemic, analyses were carried out on the number of self-employed workers according to age, socio-professional status, working time, sectors of activity and major occupational groups.

The most affected category at the beginning of the pandemic was that of young self-employed workers. Compared to 2019, female self-employed workers up to the age of 24 recorded a 27% decrease in both the second and the third quarters of 2020, and those aged 25–34 recorded decreases of 18.3% and 14.3%, respectively, in 2020 compared to 2019 in the second and third quarters, respectively. However, due to their quick adaptability, female self-employed workers are starting to move towards new job opportunities generated by the COVID crisis, reaching an increase in the number of young self-employed workers aged 15–24 by 12% in the fourth quarter of 2020, and for those aged 25–34—an increase of 1.6%. Male self-employed workers had a different behaviour. Young self-employed workers aged 15–24 and the elderly over the age of 65 were the most affected by the COVID-19 pandemic, with their numbers declining by up to 26.8% in the second quarter of 2020, compared to the

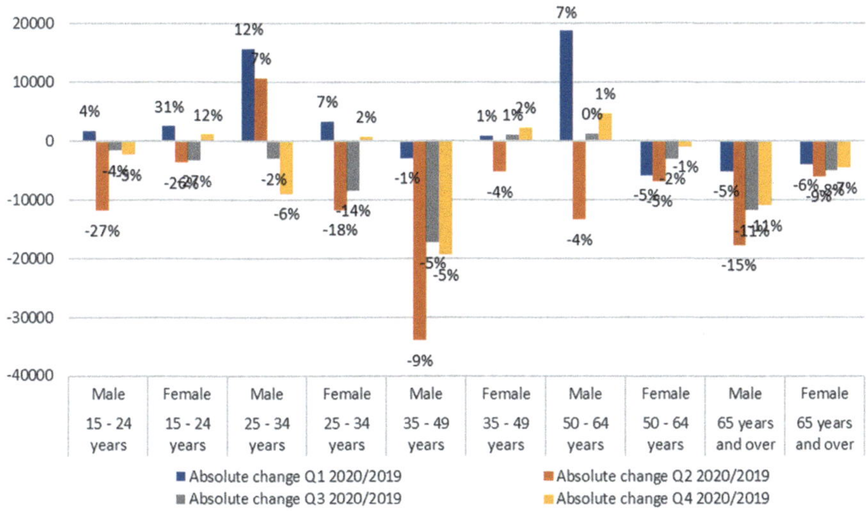


**Fig. 8.41** Self-employed workers by gender and age

corresponding time period of the previous year. In the next quarters, the decreases were slower, but still significant as absolute or relative value (Fig. 8.41).

As for the elderly self-employed (over 65), they decreased by more than 10% in the second and the third quarters of 2020, in comparison with the corresponding quarters of 2019, decreases that continued in the fourth quarter of 2020, more pronounced for men than for women.

This is further evidence that the COVID-19 shocks on the labour market have been felt differently for the various categories of people employed, referring in this case to self-employed by gender and age.

## *Self-Employed by the Number of Hours Worked Full-Time*

In terms of working hours or schedule, over 70% of self-employed worked full-time, and less than 30% worked part-time, regardless of the quarter of the analysed year.

During the lockdown period that took place between April and June 2020, the share of people working full-time over 40 h decreased by over 15% compared to the second quarter of 2019, and in the next two quarters, their percentages returned to the values recorded in the corresponding quarters of previous years. The largest decreases occurred in the second quarter for the self-employed working full-time, 40 h or more than 45 h, both in relative and absolute terms. Self-employed people with a working time between 31 and 39 h recorded the largest relative declines in all three quarters since the start of the pandemic. These results prove that—during the COVID-19 pandemic—those who carried out full-time activities were the most affected (Figs. 8.42 and 8.43).

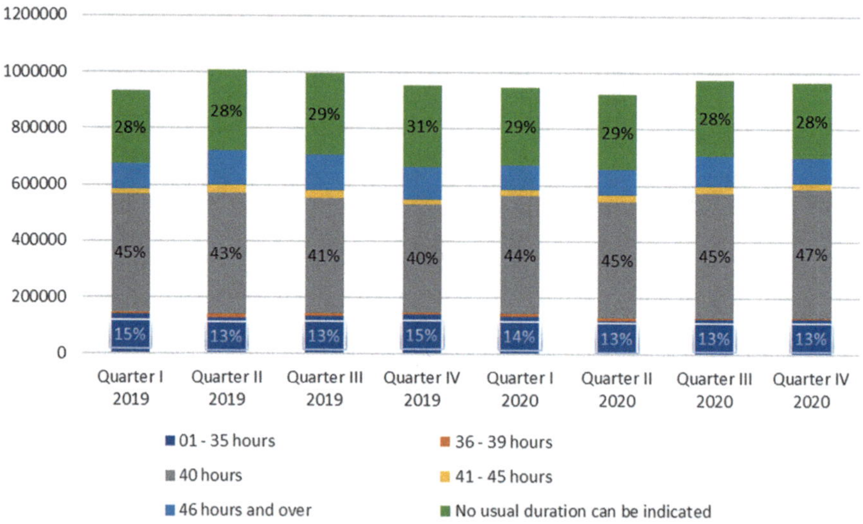


**Fig. 8.42** Self-employed who work full-time by the number of hours worked

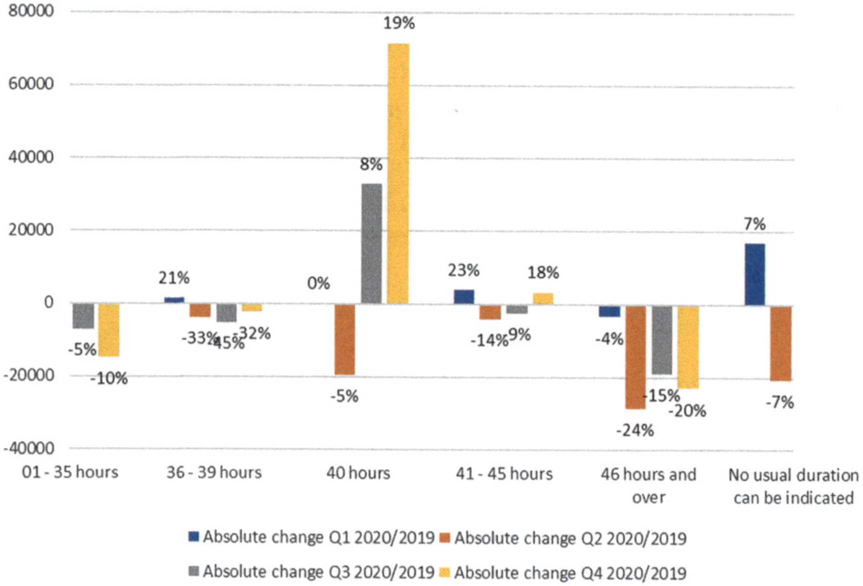


**Fig. 8.43** Absolute and relative dynamics of the number of self-employed with permanent work regime, by the actual duration of the working week, in 2020/2019, by quarters (persons, %)

## *Employment of Self-Employed Workers by the Main NACE Activities*

In Romania, the sector of activity in which the employed population mainly consists of self-employed workers (60% of the total employed population in 2020) is the agriculture, forestry and fishing sector. This sector of activity lost 55,637 self-employed workers in 2020 compared to 2019, representing a 5.6% decrease.

The next three important sectors in terms of the share of self-employed are the construction and other activities sectors of the national economy (with shares of about 25%) and entertainment, cultural and recreational activities (with a share of 13.6%). In 2020, two of these sectors of activity experienced increases in the number of self-employed workers: 1.6% increase in construction and 18.6% increase in entertainment, cultural and recreational activities. Despite this, these increases are not very important in absolute value (2590 self-employed for construction and 1615 self-employed for entertainment, cultural and recreational activities). Another particularly important category in terms of qualifications is that of self-employed workers in the professional, scientific and technical activities sector, with a share of 9.2%, a sector in which the number of self-employed workers increased by 22.1% in 2020 compared to 2019, meaning an increase in absolute value of 4236 workers (Fig. 8.44).

In comparison with 2019, the largest relative growth in the number of self-employed workers in 2020 was registered by the water distribution and sanitation sector, by 162.7% (with 6632 self-employed workers in absolute value). The next two sectors of activity that benefited substantially during the pandemic were information and communications, with an increase of 88.2% in 2020 compared to 2019

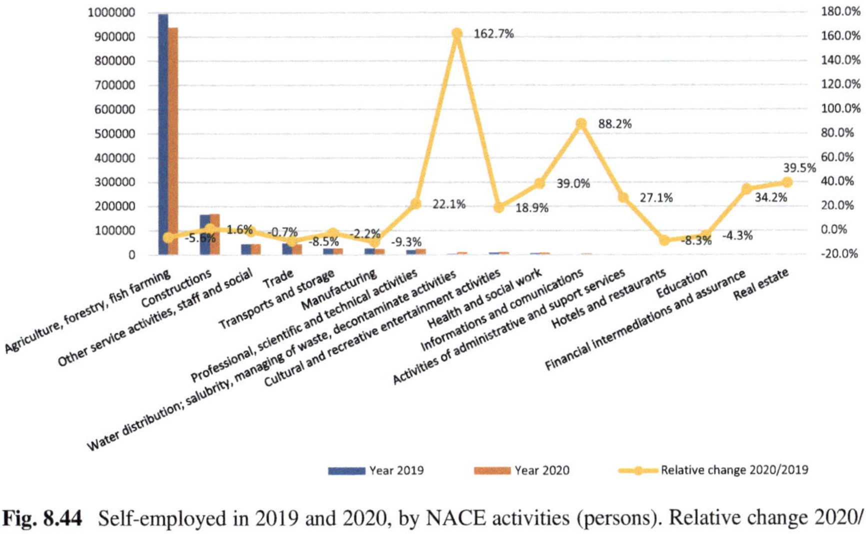


**Fig. 8.44** Self-employed in 2019 and 2020, by NACE activities (persons). Relative change 2020/2019 (%)

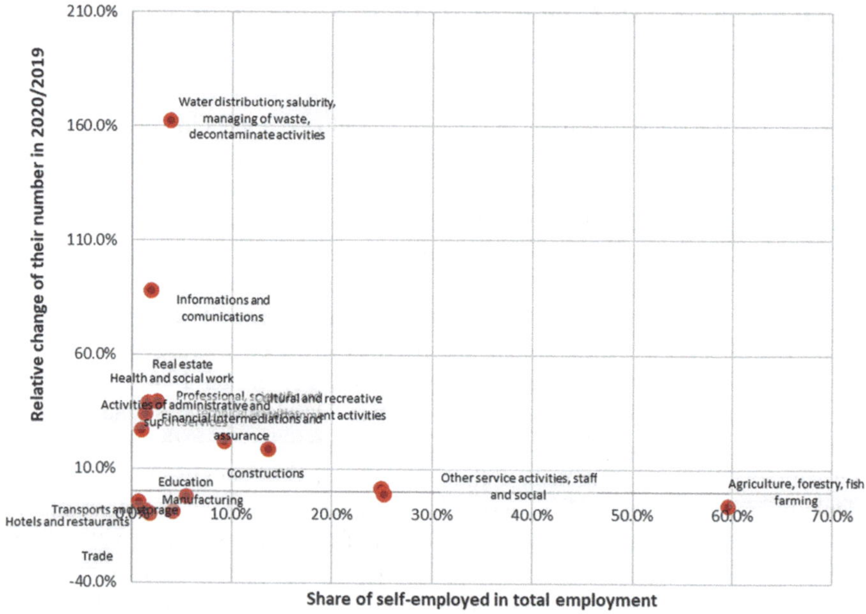


**Fig. 8.45** Scatter between the share of self-employed in total employment and the relative change of their number in 2020/2019, by NACE activities (%)

(i.e. an increase of 2713 self-employed), and health and social assistance with 39% in 2020 compared to 2019 (i.e. an increase of 2534 self-employed) (Fig. 8.44).

From the analysis of the correlation between the share of self-employed workers and the relative change in their number in 2020 compared to 2019, by NACE activities it can be seen that the activities that recorded the largest increases in self-employment were generally activities that do not have large shares of self-employed workers in Romania. The explanation for these developments is that these activities require a high level of qualification (professional, scientific and technical activities) or activities that were developed during the pandemic due to the increasing needs of people employed in those areas of activity, the deficit being covered by self-employed workers who may have reoriented themselves from non-vital areas and whose activity was substantially reduced during the pandemic (waste management, water distribution, sanitation, information and telecommunications, health and social assistance) (Fig. 8.45).

## *What Was the Overall Impact of the COVID-19 Crisis on Self-Employed Workers?*

Job losses have been more significant among self-employed workers than among employees, as they often face great difficulties in maintaining their business or projects. The inequalities between the various categories of self-employed are huge, there are categories that have suffered very high losses from the interruption of activities in the field in which they worked and from their lack of ability for professional conversion, but there are also other categories of self-employed who had good or even very good results, namely, those who used digital technologies to continue their activities or those who quickly transformed their business to areas where labour was needed.

In crisis situations, the circumstances and personal characteristics of the individual will have a significant effect on the survival and recovery of a business or on the reorientation in the labour market. Thus, many of the young adult males who are self-employed (25–34 years old) managed to safeguard their activities at the beginning of the pandemic (quarter II 2020), but then they also began to feel its effects. Due to the increasing needs of households in the early period of the pandemic crisis (second quarter 2020), women recorded rapid declines in their professional activity. However, starting with the third quarter of 2020, some of them have chosen to work as self-employed workers, including part-time and remote (at-home, teleworking) arrangements, as flexible means of working and of spending more time caring for children. Thus, female self-employed workers aged 15–24 recorded the greatest relative increases, starting with the third quarter of 2020.

## Labour Market Vulnerabilities in Romania in the Context of the COVID-19 Pandemic and Post-Pandemic Period

### *SWOT Analysis of Labour Market Vulnerabilities in Romania in the Context of the COVID-19 Pandemic*

The COVID-19 pandemic, in general, and the obstacles due to lockdowns and increased demand for remote work, in particular, have all forced companies and employees to rethink the existing ways of working. Advances in information and communication technology have enabled many skilled workers to transition to telework or other forms of remote work. In Europe, their percentage has increased from 5% in 2019 to 40% in 2020 (Milasi et al., 2020). The COVID-19 pandemic has also worsened gender and social inequalities.

Technological development, especially digitalisation, has major implications for labour markets and the nature of labour itself, as there is an increase in alternative types of work. The transformation of the way we work will accelerate. Even though there are still uncertainties about the long-term economic implications of the pandemic, we already know that digitalisation and the labour market will have to interact and work together. Based on the previous analysis of the labour market vulnerabilities in Romania during the COVID-19 pandemic, we could identify certain development opportunities of the Romanian labour market model, but also weaknesses

**Table 8.2** SWOT analysis of labour market vulnerabilities in Romania

| *Strengths* | *Weaknesses* |
|---|---|
| • The high level of digital education among young people gives them the opportunity to quickly adopt and adapt to the new changes that will occur in the labour market model<br>• Women, employees, the self-employed, the young or the elderly were less affected by the COVID-19 pandemic than other categories, which indicates their greater adaptability and resilience in times of crisis compared to other categories<br>• Employees from vulnerable groups with higher levels of education have been less affected by the current pandemic (women, the elderly)<br>• Some employees from vulnerable groups (e.g. women) who have lost their jobs have refocused their efforts to start small businesses<br>• Female leadership has not been affected significantly by the health pandemic | • Low level of digital education among the elderly<br>• Difficulties for women to ensure a proper balance between work and personal life in the context of the pandemic (due to changes in the education system, work from home, etc.)<br>• Harsher negative effects of the pandemic on the self-employed and on small business owners<br>• Reducing the actual working time<br>• Increased risk of poverty/reduced income among people from vulnerable groups |
| *Opportunities* | *Threats* |
| • Increasing the employment of women through part-time employment and self-employment<br>• Professional conversion for people in vulnerable groups who lost their job during the pandemic, or who want to change it, emphasis on areas/specialisations that are frequently required in the post-pandemic period and for which there is a labour shortage<br>• Training in the information and communication field in order to acquire digital skills and increase work efficiency at the workplace<br>• Reduce the risk of poverty and income distribution inequality by transitioning workers from vulnerable groups to high-income fields (IT)<br>• The flexibility of the working schedule, of the types of employment, the option of choosing to work from home (constantly or occasionally) can lead to an increase in the employment of people from certain vulnerable groups | • Demographic ageing<br>• Lack of digital education among the elderly<br>• Reduced ability among the elderly to adapt to new professions and modern/teleworking, which also have an important digital component<br>• External migration for work opportunities, especially among young people<br>• The persistence of the pandemic, the risks of exposure to the new coronavirus, the adoption of distance measures/restrictions may further affect business in some areas (HoReCa, tourism, transport) |

that can be improved to meet the new labour market requirements. A brief summary of those findings is presented as a SWOT analysis whose results can be used in formulating policies for adapting the labour market to the new national and international context (Table 8.2).

## *The Post-Pandemic Period*

While the country has made progress in recovering from the pandemic, there are still challenges and uncertainties that may continue to affect the labour market in the coming years. The pandemic had significant impacts on the Romanian labour market in 2021 and 2022 too.

The pandemic has increased existing gender inequalities in the Romanian labour market. Women are overrepresented in sectors that have been most affected by the pandemic, such as tourism and hospitality. Women are also more likely to have caregiving responsibilities, which can make it difficult to maintain a balance between work and family responsibilities.

Female employment—both in absolute and relative terms—has continued to drop in 2021, more dramatically in the first quarter of this year (when the female employment rate fell below 38%). However, in 2022 there are signs of a return to normality, and—although the level of the indicator for quarters I–IV is still lower than in the corresponding period in 2019–2020—it is still higher than in 2021. At the same time, unemployment among women continued to increase in 2021, reaching a maximum value in the first quarter of this year (5.6%). After this quarter, the unemployment rate among women follows a slightly downward evolution, which continues in 2022 (Fig. 8.46). We consider that this reversal of the evolution of the two indicators in 2021–2022 compared to 2019–2020 represents the effect of the relaunch of economic activities, of the economic, social and political measures adopted to return to normality, and these signs have been visible since 2021, when the pandemic was not over.

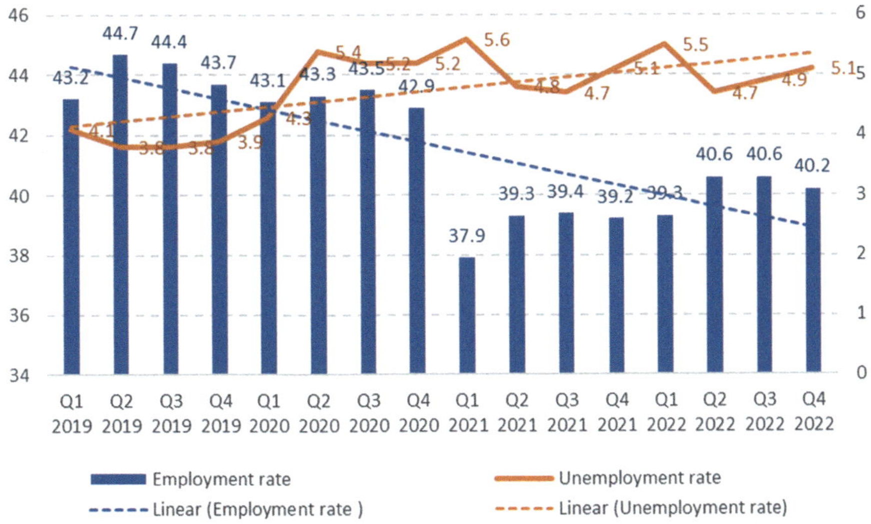


**Fig. 8.46** Quarterly female employment and unemployment rate in Romania, 2019–2022 (%)

As far as the younger generation is concerned, the economic consequences of the health crisis have been more serious for them, for a few reasons, such as disturbances in the education system; difficulties in finding jobs; loss of jobs and income; as well as a deterioration in the quality of employment. The post-pandemic period has brought some specific challenges and multiple opportunities for youth employment, accelerating the adoption of remote work and digitalisation, creating new opportunities in fields such as IT and e-commerce. Moreover, the pandemic inspired many young people to start their own businesses. The Romanian government has implemented various initiatives to support entrepreneurship, including funding and mentorship programmes. Young people with entrepreneurial ambitions may find support in these programmes. The growing interest in sustainable industries such as renewable energy, green transportation and eco-tourism create new opportunities for young people with skills and experience in these areas.

In 2021, the drop in the total number of young people (aged 15–24) in employment is higher by 14.8% compared to the pandemic period. This comes from the decrease in the number of young skilled workers in agriculture and related domains (fishing, forestry), the profession with the youngest workers, from 139,888 in 2020 to 49,845 in 2021. Numbers of young workers in professions such as specialists in various fields, administrative officials, service personnel or workers in skilled trades in industry or crafts have increased during the pandemic periods and those that follow them, in the context of the changing preferences of consumers, distribution channels, service needs, etc. In 2022, the downward trend of youth employment continues, although more attenuated than in 2021, the number of young people employed in the fourth quarter of 2022 being 8851 persons higher than in the third quarter of the same year (Fig. 8.47).

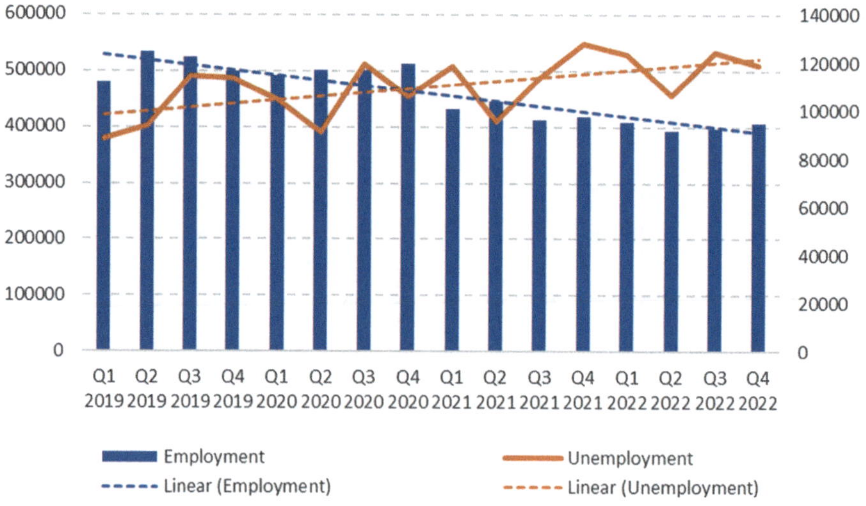


**Fig. 8.47** Quarterly youth employment and unemployment (15–24 years) in Romania, 2019–2022 (number of persons)

As for youth unemployment, it has increased, much more than in the case of total unemployment. Also, the unemployment of low-educated young people has increased more than that of highly educated young people, the latter having the ability to reorient themselves towards fields and sectors of activity that have developed during the pandemic, such as e-commerce, health and social assistance, etc. In the 2021–2022 period, the number of young unemployed people continued its upward movement from the previous period, recording an increase of almost 22,000 people in the last quarter of 2021, compared to the similar period of 2020—the largest increase in the analysed period (Fig. 8.47).

Although the pandemic has exacerbated some existing imbalances in the labour market, not all developments in the post-pandemic period have been negative. Thus, the employment rate of the population aged 55–64 increased slightly in 2020, by 0.7 percentage points compared to the previous year. In the first quarter of 2021, the number of elderly people in employment fell sharply and then recovered during the year 2021. In the period 2021–2022, the employment rate of the elderly (55–64 years old) has an upward evolution, with a more pronounced increase than in the period 2019–2020. Thus, in the third quarter of 2022, the employment rate of people aged 55–64 reached the highest level for the analysed period, of 47.5%, 3.3% higher than in the same period of the previous year (Fig. 8.48).

The health crisis had negative effects on older workers with a low level of education, their number decreasing during the pandemic and post-pandemic period, while the number of those with a higher level of education increased. The employed older population (50+) has recorded increases in most sectors of activity, particularly in essential sectors which have been maintained or developed during the pandemic

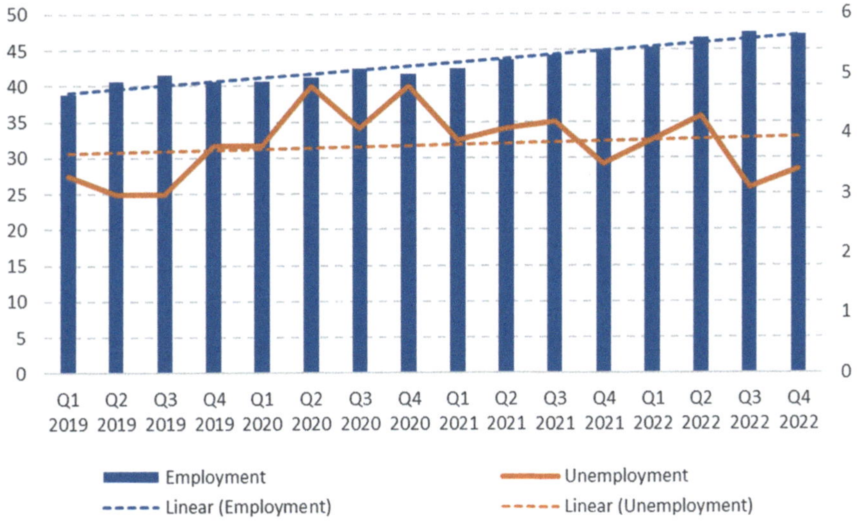


**Fig. 8.48** Quarterly employment and unemployment rate of the population aged 55–64 in Romania, 2019–2022 (%)

(industry, construction, education, health, commerce, public administration, computer science).

The elderly unemployment rate (55–64 years old) has increased slightly, but with a lower intensity than for other categories of vulnerable people. The elderly unemployment rate reverses its evolution in the period 2021–2022, compared to the period 2019–2020. Thus, if until the end of 2020 the level of the indicator increased, starting from 2021 and until the end of 2022, the unemployment rate decreases, the level of the third quarter of 2022 (of 3.1%) being close to the level of the same quarter of 2019 and one of the lowest levels of the entire time period. The degree of participation in the labour market of the elderly fluctuated less than other age groups during the pandemic crisis (Fig. 8.48).

The restrictions that governments have imposed on economic activity during the health crisis had a major impact with unequal effects on the self-employed. Those who have used digital technologies or have managed to transform their businesses quickly achieved better results. Nationally, in the first quarter of 2020, there were approximately 1.313 million self-employed workers, 72% men and 28% women. The largest drop is seen in the first quarter of 2021 compared to the previous quarter and compared to the first quarter of 2020, with a difference of more than 500,000 self-employed. Although in the second quarter of 2021 the level of the indicator registered an increase of almost 170,000 people compared to the previous quarter, the number of self-employed still remains low compared to the period 2019 (the relative increase was more pronounced in the case of women compared to that of men). In the fourth quarter of 2022, there were nearly 870,000 self-employed workers in Romania, of whom over 76% were men (Fig. 8.49).

Vulnerable groups of people will continue to require special attention in the post-pandemic period for their integration on the labour market. The government and

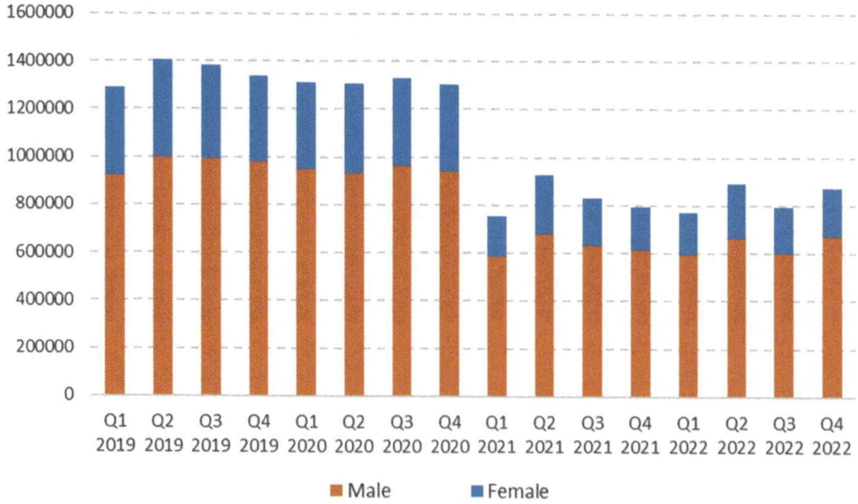


**Fig. 8.49** Quarterly number of self-employed in Romania, by gender, 2019–2022 (persons)

other organisations will need to focus on providing support for training and upskilling programmes, as well as ensuring that there are sufficient job opportunities available. This may involve promoting sectors that are expected to grow in the post-pandemic economy, such as healthcare, green jobs and digital technology. Additionally, measures such as flexible work arrangements and improved access to digital technology can help vulnerable groups participate more fully in the labour market.

## References


Eurofound. (2022). *COVID-19 and older people: Impact on their lives, support and care*. Publications Office of the European Union.

Gros, D., & Ounnas, A. (2021). Labour market responses to the Covid-19 crisis in the United States and Europe, CEPS Working Document No. 2021-01, April 2021.

ILO. (2022). ILO Monitor on the world of work. Tenth edition Multiple crises threaten the global labour market recovery, October 2022.

Koutsimpogiorgos, N., van Slageren, J., Herrmann, A., & Frenken, K. (2020). Conceptualizing the Gig Economy and Its Regulatory Problems. *Policy & Internet, 12*, 525–545. https://doi.org/10.1002/poi3.237

OECD. (2021). Labour market developments: The unfolding COVID-19 crisis, in OECD employment Outlook 2021: Navigating the COVID-19 crisis and recovery, OECD Publishing, Paris. https://doi.org/10.1787/7e1e1ad3-en

PwC UK. (2021). Women in work 2021, The impact of COVID-19 on women in work, Strategy&. Available on: https://www.pwc.co.uk/economic services/WIWI/women-in-work-2021-executive-summary.pdf

Ratten, V. (2020a). Coronavirus and international business: an entrepreneurial ecosystem perspective. *Thunderbird International Business Review, 6*(25), 629–634.

Ratten, V. (2020b). Coronavirus (covid-19) and the entrepreneurship education community. *Journal of Enterprising Communities: People and Places in the Global Economy, 1*(13), 4760.

Săseanu, A. S., Ghiță, S. I., & Gogonea, R. M. (2019). Perspective of feminine leadership in the socio-political field. Comparative analysis of the European countries. *Transformations in Business & Economics, 18*(3), 137–154. ISSN: 1648-4460. http://www.transformations.knf.vu.lt/48/article/pers

Spasova, S., Ghailani, D., Sabato, S., Coster, S., Fronteddu, B., & Vanhercke, B. (2021). *Non-standard workers and the self-employed in the EU: social protection during the Covid-19 pandemic* (p. 51). ETUI.

Vasile, V. (coord.), Boboc, C., Ghiță, S., Apostu, S., Pavelescu, F. M., & Mazilescu, R. (2020). Efectele pandemiei SARS COV 2 asupra ocupării. Rolul politicilor publice și reziliența pieței muncii în contextul adaptării mediului de afaceri, Romanian Academy, Bucharest. Available at: https://acad.ro/SARS-CoV-2/doc/d19-Efectele_pandemiei_asupra_ocuparii.pdf

Zarrilli, S., & Luomaranta, H. (2021). UNCTAD - Gender and unemployment: Lessons from the COVID-19 pandemic. Available at: https://unctad.org/news/gender-and-unemployment-lessons-covid-19-pandemic

# Chapter 9
# Propensity for Migration of Healthcare Professionals: Push-Pull Factors Analysis

**Elena Bunduchi, Valentina Vasile, Daniel Stefan, and Calin-Adrian Comes**

**Abstract** The migration of healthcare professionals from less developed countries is a significant phenomenon, and it has adverse consequences for the source country. Examining the healthcare labour market over the past two decades reveals a growing appeal of migration, not only for medical specialists but also for students and recent graduates. This chapter aims to identify the push-pull factors that encourage medical students to pursue education and employment abroad. The results of logistic regression analysis based on the questionnaire data highlight a concerning situation with far-reaching implications for the Romanian healthcare system. Young professionals display a strong propensity towards migration, whether it involves studying or seeking employment opportunities abroad. This fact is largely due to poor working conditions and lack of career perspectives in the home country. Within this framework, it becomes imperative for Romanian authorities and healthcare institutions to proactively develop strategies for retaining medical specialists and enhancing working conditions within the healthcare sector.

## Introduction

The challenges of mobility and migration, especially labour migration of health professionals, are not new and have been studied and analysed internationally (Mejia, 1978). Migration patterns and the extent of health professionals' migration from developing to developed countries have been a constant focus for research (Karan et al., 2016; Boros et al., 2022). The main migration flow of health workers is from less developed countries to more developed countries, a fact known as the

E. Bunduchi (✉) · D. Stefan · C.-A. Comes
Institute of National Economy - Romanian Academy, Bucharest, Romania

Faculty of Economics and Law, George Emil Palade University of Medicine, Pharmacy, Science, and Technology of Targu Mures, Targu Mures, Romania

V. Vasile
Institute of National Economy - Romanian Academy, Bucharest, Romania

 
V. Vasile, E. Bunduchi (eds.), *The Economic and Social Impact of the COVID-19 Pandemic*, Contributions to Economics,
https://doi.org/10.1007/978-3-031-47780-5_9

'brain drain' phenomenon (Ifanti et al., 2014; Bertoni et al., 2023). Worldwide, the demand for medical specialists is constantly increasing, especially in certain countries/areas (Gupta et al., 2003) and for certain epidemiological situations, as was the case of the COVID-19 pandemic outbreak (Vasile et al., 2023a).

In Europe, the creation of a borderless labour market and its expansion with the 2004, 2007 and 2013 EU enlargements gave health professionals the right to provide services and move to another EU member state (Boboc et al., 2015; Becker & Teney, 2020; Buhaljoti & Abazi, 2022).

After the experience of health services during the pandemic, a significant change in the employment pattern and requirements for healthcare jobs is clearly emerging. This change is radical for professionals in the field, offering them better opportunities and increased income compared to similar positions in their home countries, as well as the possibility of greater flexibility in job choice and future mobility in OECD countries (OECD, 2020; Socha-Dietrich & Dumont, 2021; OECD/ILO, 2022).

In addition, adapting to the skill needs of the health workforce becomes a priority, focusing on meeting the needs of users, in contrast with chronic funding problems, insufficient inter-institutional coordination and low stakeholder engagement. This new approach aims to reduce the discrepancy between the required smart skills and the desired policy goals in less developed countries, emphasising external mobility for better training and specialisation (Kangasniemi et al., 2007; Li & Sun, 2019).

This redefinition of the motivation for work mobility in the field of health is driven by the increasingly radical expectations of the new medical professionals. They want an employment model in the future that offers optimal technological and logistical conditions, the availability of information through databases based on artificial intelligence and opportunities for professional specialisation in an interdisciplinary approach to ensure efficiency and quality in the provision of medical services (Timus et al., 2020; Baydas & Serhat, 2021; Vasile et al., 2023).

During the COVID-19 pandemic, developed countries in the EU and other regions presented attractive opportunities for young immigrant professionals, facilitating their access by recognising professional qualifications in the field of health, eliminating additional exams and granting/extending residence permits, among other specific requirements (European Commission, 2020). These measures have stimulated the interest of students to continue their studies abroad or to engage in labour migration, given the better career prospects and more efficient medical services offered in these countries.

## Data Analysis

A cross-sectional study was carried out in medical universities in Romania, which involved the participation of final-year students. The purpose of this study was to explore the migration intention for studies and for work of these students. In this

**Table 9.1** Demographic characteristics of respondents, persons

| | Gender | | | | Area | |
|---|---|---|---|---|---|---|
| | | | Total | | | |
| Specialisation | Female | Male | Persons | % | Rural | Urban |
| Pharmacy | 50 | 11 | 61 | 15.5 | 10 | 51 |
| Medicine | 171 | 66 | 237 | 60.5 | 36 | 201 |
| Dental medicine | 59 | 8 | 67 | 17.1 | 6 | 61 |
| Healthcare (nurse) | 23 | 4 | 27 | 6.9 | 5 | 22 |
| Total | 303 (77.3%) | 89 (22.7%) | 392 | 100 | 57 (14.5%) | 335 (85.5%) |

Source: questionnaire respondents' answers

regard, a questionnaire was developed and distributed on the official information channels for healthcare students between September and December 2022. To ensure the confidentiality and anonymity of the participants, the questionnaire was built using the Google Forms platform and did not request personal information.

In order to validate and adapt the questionnaire to the specific needs in Romania, a preliminary test was carried out on a group of 30 students, who were later not included in the final analysis. The questionnaire was designed considering the research directions from the specialised literature on migration for studies and work and was adapted according to the particularities identified in the specific context of Romania.

In this study, the questionnaire was applied to students from medical faculties, and received 456 responses in the initial stage. In order to ensure the quality of the collected data, invalid questionnaires were removed, that is, those answers received from respondents who did not successfully pass the control questions.

Following the data validation process, 392 valid responses were retained and included in the final analysis of the study. The elimination of invalid questionnaires was aimed at ensuring the accuracy and reliability of the results, thus allowing to obtain more relevant and consistent conclusions in the research. The final number of valid responses represented an appropriate sample to carry out a comprehensive and representative analysis of the attitudes and opinions of students from medical faculties regarding study and labour migration.

The need to apply this questionnaire derives from the identification of the socio-economic profile of students in the medical field and the reasons underlying the intention to migrate in order to continue their studies or for work (Table 9.1).

For a better analysis and centralisation of the study results, we grouped the respondents according to the specialisation they follow: Pharmacy (61 respondents), Medicine (237 respondents), Dental medicine (57 respondents) and Healthcare (27 respondents). The significant difference in the number of students and the registration of a majority of over 60% of those from the Faculty of Medicine is determined by the general trend of preferences at the national level (National Institute of Statistics, 2022).

At the same time, there is a discrepancy between the number of women respondents (77.3%) and that of men (22.7%). This difference in answers by gender can be explained by the fact that, in the field of health, the number of female students is at least twice that of male students (Annex 9.1). Women have also been found to be more open to participating in questionnaires, surveys and other qualitative data analysis tools (Nistor, 2013; Slauson-Blevins & Johnson, 2016).

A significant discrepancy was also observed in terms of area: 85.5% of the participants live in urban areas and only 14.5% in rural areas. The residential environment of young people, mainly in urban areas, is influenced by the fact that most young people from rural areas do not continue their studies, but choose to work in the country or, unfortunately, abroad (Constantin, 2023). Another determining factor derives from the fact that in Romania the population aged 18–25 years is continuously decreasing in rural areas, there are entire localities without inhabitants or with no more than ten elderly inhabitants (Zaharia, 2007; Paun, 2018).

## The Socio-Economic Profile of Healthcare Professionals

Due to the acute shortage of medical personnel, especially in rural areas, it is very important to follow the tendency of students to migrate for studies or work, by creating a socio-demographic profile and identifying their specific characteristics associated with migration propensity.

From the 392 final-year students received answers, we find that in general the propensity to migrate for work (46.9% of all respondents) is much higher than that for studies (28.8% of all students included in the study).

Analysing the socio-economic characteristics of the respondents, we have the following situation (Table 9.2).

***Gender*** From the perspective of gender, it is noticed that male students want to migrate more than female students, but the tendency, in both cases, is migration for work, more than migration for studies. Thus, over 50% of male students and over 44% of female students tend to migrate for work upon completing their studies in Romania, a huge percentage considering the acute shortage of medical personnel that Romania is facing. This may be one of the reasons why the number of graduates of medical faculties is increasing, but the shortage of doctors is not considerably reduced (Vasile et al., 2021).

Another aspect highlighted by the results of the questionnaire is that of predominantly increased migration among male students, regardless of its nature, a conclusion supported by other similar studies, according to which male students and doctors tend to migrate more compared to female students and doctors (Domagała & Dubas-Jakóbczyk, 2019; Clarke et al., 2017).

***Area*** The proportion of those who want to migrate for work is higher in the urban area (48.1%) than in the rural area (40.3%), while the propensity to migrate for

**Table 9.2** Students' characteristics and the propensity to migrate

| Characteristics | | Propensity to migrate for studies | | Propensity to migrate for work | |
|---|---|---|---|---|---|
| | | Persons | % of total respondents by demographic characteristics | Persons | % of total respondents by demographic characteristics |
| *Gender* | | | | | |
| | Female | 83 | 27.4 | 136 | 44.9 |
| | Male | 30 | 33.7 | 48 | 53.9 |
| *Area* | | | | | |
| | Rural | 17 | 29.8 | 23 | 40.3 |
| | Urban | 96 | 28.6 | 161 | 48.1 |
| *Specialisation* | | | | | |
| | Pharmacy | 10 | 16.4 | 26 | 42.6 |
| | Medicine | 75 | 31.6 | 108 | 45.5 |
| | Dental medicine | 24 | 35.8 | 40 | 59.7 |
| | Healthcare (nurse) | 4 | 14.8 | 10 | 37.0 |
| Grades position in class | | | | | |
| | Very good | 51 | 31.1 | 76 | 46.3 |
| | Good | 57 | 26.6 | 102 | 47.7 |
| | Sufficient | 5 | 35.7 | 6 | 42.8 |
| Economic status | | | | | |
| | Very good | 7 | 25.0 | 11 | 39.3 |
| | Good | 51 | 25.9 | 77 | 39.1 |
| | Neutral | 41 | 30.8 | 75 | 56.4 |
| | Poor | 13 | 46.4 | 16 | 57.1 |
| | Very poor | 1 | 16.7 | 5 | 83.3 |
| Total | | 113 | 28.8 | 184 | 46.9 |

Source: questionnaire respondents' answers

studies does not show a significant difference between the two areas, recording an average of approximately 29%.

***Specialisation*** Analysing students by specialisation, the greatest propensity to migrate for work (59.7%) and for studies (35.8%) is observed among Dental medicine students, followed by Medicine students with a migration intention of 45.5% and 31.6%, respectively. Pharmacy and Healthcare students show a lower propensity to migrate for both studies and work.

Future pharmacists do not have the same tendency to migrate. In countries with lower levels of development, like Romania, there tends to be a higher prevalence of pharmacies in the market and a greater number of pharmacists per 100,000 inhabitants compared to other European countries (Eurostat, 2022). A study conducted by the Federal Union of German Associations of Pharmacists revealed that Romania holds the ninth position among EU member states, with more than 40 pharmacies per

100,000 inhabitants (ABDA, 2022). This phenomenon can be largely attributed to the relatively poor state of public health due to inadequate investments in the healthcare system and the prevalence of self-medication practices. In less developed countries, especially those with lower income levels, higher numbers of dependents and limited access to proper healthcare (Torres et al., 2019), individuals often opt for the services of pharmacists (Ha et al., 2019), which are usually free, instead of seeking paid medical consultations, particularly when they lack insurance coverage. Consequently, this scenario has led to the expansion of significant pharmaceutical chains, and graduates from pharmacy faculties find ample job opportunities and more satisfactory remuneration compared to some other sectors. This contrasts with instances where graduates often face job shortages and low pay. The inclination of these graduates to pursue studies abroad, with the possibility of remaining in the destination country's labour market, becomes less reasonable, especially if the allure of the pharmaceutical sector is not as strong in more developed countries.

***Grades Position in Class*** Students with very good results have the highest propensity to migrate, whether for studies (31.1%) or work (46.3%). As for the students in the good category, a very high tendency is observed for migration for work, but a slight restraint regarding migration for studies. This may be due to the need for equivalence and all the procedures for the recognition of the previous studies, respectively potential exams that need to be taken again.

***Economic Status*** Students with a weaker economic status (poor and very poor) show a greater propensity to migrate for work, followed by those whose family income level is in the neutral category. If the economic motivation is of significant importance in making the decision to migrate for work, migrants may aim to send remittances to help raise the living standards of their families back home. In the case of study migration, however, a new perspective on the economic factor opens up. Thus, the higher income students included in the study are more likely to migrate for studies, compared to those with low and very low income, as the latter will face difficulties in the migration process for studies. Usually, the studying and living costs in destination countries far exceed those in the country of origin, and these expenses play an important role in making the decision to migrate (Boros et al., 2022). For this reason, previous studies (Xiang & Shen 2009; Xiang, 2016) have shown that students with greater financial resources are more likely to choose migration as an option to continue their studies. However, the propensity to migrate for work is present among those with low incomes, being motivated by the economic factor—higher wages (Hervey, 2017; Biagi et al., 2023)—which would allow them to ensure a high standard of living not only for themselves in the country of destination but also for the family remaining in the country of origin.

Among the countries preferred by medical final-year students are France, Germany and the UK, both as a destination for studies and for work (Table 9.3). In addition to the well-developed educational and medical system, which is very attractive for Romanian students, the linguistic component plays a major role. Romanians are among the people with a high percentage of knowledge of English and French (Ivan, 2013), and foreign language programmes conducted by some university centres facilitate access to these markets. In addition to the states of

**Table 9.3** Medical students preferred destination countries for study and work

| Destination countries for studies | Persons | Destination countries for work | Persons |
|---|---|---|---|
| France | 40 | France | 60 |
| Germany | 36 | Germany | 56 |
| UK | 17 | UK | 28 |
| Switzerland | 13 | Switzerland | 23 |
| Hungary | 6 | Belgium | 9 |
| USA | 5 | Spain | 7 |
| Belgium | 4 | | |
| Netherlands | 4 | | |
| Canada | 3 | | |
| Italy | 3 | | |

Source: questionnaire respondents' answers

Western Europe, we also find Hungary among the students' preferences for further studies, also due to the linguistic element. In Romania, some universities are located in areas where there are large Hungarian communities, which tend to maintain close ties with Hungary. Moreover, there are universities supported by the Hungarian authorities that operate in Romania with various profiles, and some Romanian faculties have study programmes with teaching not only in Romanian, English or French but also in Hungarian, thus facilitating access to the educational system in Hungary. However, it seems that the employment preferences do not include Hungary, medical final-year students focusing on other markets.

In general, migration for studies or work should not generate only negative effects on the country of origin, because return migration comes with a gain of human, technological and financial capital (Vasile et al., 2023b). However, the trend recorded among final-year students is not one of returning but rather of leaving Romania permanently (Table 9.4).

Therefore, we find that regardless of the criterion by which we analysed the intention to migrate according to the duration, the result is the same; the young graduates tend in the largest proportion towards permanent migration, without the probability of returning to the country of origin. This phenomenon is all the more alarming as those whose initial intention was to migrate for studies tend to remain in another destination country after completing their studies abroad. Thus, almost half of those who expressed their interest in migration for studies (49 respondents out of 113) do not consider returning to Romania. A comparable scenario (75 respondents out of 184) is also observed among those who express the intention to finalise their studies in Romania and subsequently relocate to another country to engage in the labour market there. In this instance, the repercussions for Romania will be even more significant, given that the education of these specialists leads to the utilisation of resources that will not be harnessed to their fullest potential, failing to contribute added value to both the healthcare system and at the national level.

Another more gratifying trend is the intention of a part of the respondents to return after a maximum period of 5 years, recorded both among those with the

**Table 9.4** Graduates by specialisation and by duration of migration for studies and for work

| | Return immediately after studies | <1 year work abroad before return migration | >5 years before return migration | | 5–10 years before return migration | | >10 years before return migration | | Never return in Romania | |
|---|---|---|---|---|---|---|---|---|---|---|
| | | | Study | Work | Study | Work | Study | Work | Study | Work |
| *Specialisation* | | | | | | | | | | |
| Pharmacy | – | – | 2<br>*20%* | 6<br>*23%* | – | 6<br>*23%* | 3<br>*30%* | 3<br>*12%* | 5<br>*50%* | 11<br>*42%* |
| Medicine | 5<br>*7%* | 6<br>*5%* | 19<br>*25%* | 31<br>*29%* | 12<br>*16%* | 17<br>*16%* | 9<br>*12%* | 12<br>*11%* | 30<br>*40%* | 42<br>*39%* |
| Dental medicine | 1<br>*4%* | – | 5<br>*21%* | 9<br>*23%* | 4<br>*17%* | 9<br>*23%* | 1<br>*4%* | 4<br>*10%* | 13<br>*54%* | 18<br>*44%* |
| Healthcare | – | 2<br>*20%* | 1<br>*25%* | 3<br>*30%* | 1<br>*25%* | 1<br>*10%* | – | – | 2<br>*50%* | 4<br>*40%* |
| Total | 6<br>*5%* | 8<br>*4%* | 27<br>*24%* | 49<br>*27%* | 17<br>*15%* | 33<br>*18%* | 13<br>*12%* | 19<br>*10%* | 50<br>*44%* | 75<br>*41%* |
| *Economic status* | | | | | | | | | | |
| Very good | 1<br>*14%* | 1<br>*9%* | 1<br>*14%* | 2<br>*18%* | 1<br>*14%* | 1<br>*9%* | 2<br>*28%* | 3<br>*27%* | 2<br>*28%* | 4<br>*36%* |
| Good | 4<br>*8%* | 5<br>*6%* | 14<br>*27%* | 22<br>*29%* | 7<br>*14%* | 14<br>*18%* | 4<br>*8%* | 6<br>*8%* | 22<br>*43%* | 30<br>*39%* |
| Neutral | 1<br>*2%* | 2<br>*3%* | 9<br>*22%* | 21<br>*28%* | 9<br>*22%* | 16<br>*21%* | 6<br>*15%* | 8<br>*11%* | 16<br>*39%* | 28<br>*37%* |
| Poor | – | – | 3<br>*23%* | 3<br>*19%* | – | 1<br>*6%* | 1<br>*8%* | 2<br>*12%* | 9<br>*69%* | 10<br>*63%* |
| Very poor | – | – | – | 1<br>*20%* | – | 1<br>*20%* | – | – | 1<br>*100%* | 3<br>*60%* |
| Total | 6<br>*5%* | 8<br>*4%* | 27<br>*24%* | 49<br>*27%* | 17<br>*15%* | 33<br>*18%* | 13<br>*12%* | 19<br>*10%* | 50<br>*44%* | 75<br>*41%* |

Note: The values in italic represent the share of respondents in total respondents by each category, who intend to migrate for studies, respectively, for work.
Source: questionnaire respondents' answers

intention of migrating for studies and for work. This intention is found especially among future doctors and people with a good or neutral economic level. Therefore, approximately 40% of the respondents with a good or neutral income level do not intend to return to Romania, and over 28% of them aim to migrate in the medium term of 5 years. Paradoxically, those with low incomes have no qualms about migrating (more than 60% of them tend to migrate for education or work), even if it involves considerable initial costs.

If this tendency to return will be kept at least at the same value, return migration may contribute to the creation of added value and to the transfer of knowledge, techniques and skills from medical specialists working abroad to those in medical units in Romania.

## Determinants of Healthcare Students' Propensity to Migrate

According to Table 9.5, the reasons behind the decision to migrate for studies or for work can be divided into two broad categories: social and economic.

### *Social Factors*

Contrary to expectations, the main determinants of migration are not economic, but rather social or related to personal and professional development. Hence, within the aspiring healthcare specialists who see migration as a career move, a substantial majority (66.9%) consider that Romania's potential for supporting their professional growth is severely limited. This perspective emerges as a result of the prevailing unfavourable working conditions within the public hospital institutions, which have

**Table 9.5** Push-pull factors of students' propensity to migrate for education and work

| | Education migration | Labour migration |
|---|---|---|
| *Push factors* | | |
| Lack of career perspective | 77 (22.1%) | 123 (66.9%) |
| Poor educational systems | 62 (17.8%) | |
| Poor working condition | | 116 (63.5%) |
| Corruption | | 116 (63%) |
| Political instability | | 79 (42.9%) |
| Poverty | | 15 (8.2%) |
| *Pull factors* | | |
| Career opportunities | 128 (36.7%) | 137 (74.5%) |
| Better living standards | – | 127 (69%) |
| Wage differential | 72 (20.6%) | 100 (54.3%) |

Source: questionnaire respondents' answers

become emblematic of the challenges facing the healthcare sector in the country. These conditions encompass a range of issues including insufficient resources, outdated equipment and limited access to cutting-edge medical technologies. Within the context of healthcare funding, Romania stands out as one of the countries allocating the least resources towards the enhancement of medical institutions. As of 2020, it has the lowest average expenditure per inhabitant, merely 713 €, as reported by Eurostat (2023b) latest available data. These statistics align with previous research (Humphries et al., 2019) that highlight the fact that even if medical personnel were to receive substantial salaries, this financial incentive alone would prove inadequate in compelling specialists to remain within the domestic labour market. Such deficiencies often hinder the specialists' ability to provide the highest standard of care, thereby diminishing their job satisfaction and hampering their personal and career development.

Furthermore, the sentiment of disillusionment is exacerbated by the perceived reluctance of certain segments of the health personnel to embrace positive change and innovation. This perceived resistance to progress can manifest in a variety of ways, such as a resistance to adopting new medical practices, reluctance to collaborate with specialists from other fields or an aversion to engaging with modern approaches to patient care (Reßing et al., 2020).

Moreover, according to the respondents, the spectre of corruption within certain circles of the medical profession casts a shadow on the overall integrity of the healthcare sector. Instances or even just rumours of unethical behaviour or underhanded dealings can erode trust and confidence in the medical field, leading potential specialists to question whether their career aspirations can be realised in an environment where integrity and fairness are compromised. As a result, 116 respondents view the presence of corruption in Romanian healthcare sector as a compelling enough rationale to pursue career opportunities abroad. This underscores deep-seated concerns regarding the integrity of the medical system and professional ethics in Romania. Furthermore, an investigation conducted by the European Commission (2017) positions Romania within the top of the EU's most corrupt medical systems. This ranking pertains not only to the prevalence of bribery involving patients but also encompasses the practice of offering bribes for securing positions within public medical institutions.

Yet another determinant for migration lies in the perceived political instability reported by the surveyed individuals. A striking 79% of final-year medical students consider the prevailing political uncertainty in Romania significant enough to warrant their departure from the country. This sentiment can be attributed to the substantial political intrusion into the selection and administration of medical establishments. Consequently, the process of appointing individuals to specific positions is frequently influenced by political considerations (Vulcan, 2021), a scenario that dissuades young specialists and erodes their faith in the potential for establishing a fulfilling career trajectory.

Push factors are linked with the pull factors of migration, according with the final-year students.137 out of 184 respondents resonate strongly with the opportunity of a fulfilling and rewarding professional career abroad, backed by medical facilities and technological endowment. This concept aligns seamlessly with existing studies (Boros et al., 2022), which highlights that the prospects for professional advancement, coupled with the availability of well-equipped medical establishments, are central determinants that heavily influence individuals' job choices.

## *Economic Factors*

Economic factors undeniably play a role in driving future medical specialists to migrate for studies or work. These factors include the desire of better living conditions and the prospect of wage differentials that may be more favourable in destination countries. It is worth noting that these considerations operate within a broader spectrum of motivations that guide these important life decisions.

For instance, when analysing final-year students who tend to migrate for studies, the aspiration for improved living conditions doesn't emerge as a primary determinant. Instead, the focus tends to centre around the allure of higher wages, a factor considered significant for only 20.6% of them. Conversely, among those who are inclined to migrate for work, better living standards surface as a more pronounced reason. This includes not only personal well-being but also extends to family members. The desire for better living standards, both individually and collectively, emerges as a key reason. However, no matter how much the future medical specialists consider this aspect important, studies show that the tendency to remit to family members tends to decline as the duration of mobility increases (Sechet & Vasilcu, 2015). This insight poses a significant consideration for origin countries that consider remittances as a spur for economic development (Vasile et al., 2020). Especially within fields like healthcare, where the expertise and contributions of specialists are crucial, a recalibration of policies that encourage migration might be warranted.

An equally critical determinant driving future healthcare specialists to seek employment in foreign countries is the presence of high poverty level within their country of origin. This factor stands as an illustration of the interconnection between economic circumstances and migration decisions. It's important to recognise that this dynamic operates within a larger context where wage disparities play a key role.

The connection between poverty in the home country and the aspiration for higher wages in destination countries is deeply connected. Previous studies (Kopetsch, 2009; Brugha et al., 2016) have demonstrated the close correlation between the low standard of living in the country of origin and the desire for comparatively higher wages in the destination countries.

The allure of better financial prospects, often synonymous with enhanced living standards, becomes an attractive reason for healthcare specialists who are driven by aspirations to alleviate themselves and their families from poverty.

Economic stability, coupled with the aspiration for professional development and a better quality of life, forms a powerful blend of motivations that collectively guide the decision to seek opportunities abroad.

## Long-Term Implications for the Country of Origin

The situation presented following the analysis of the questionnaire is an alarming one, as a result of the fact that more and more young healthcare specialists tend to move to other destination countries after completing their studies in Romania. This phenomenon creates a series of consequences for Romania, as a medical education hub for developed countries, through which we find:

- Lost financial investment: The authorities bear significant costs for the teaching of future healthcare personnel in the Romanian education system. If these students choose to migrate to another country of destination to start their career, Romania loses the financial investment made in their education, especially if we refer to those who complete the residency studies, which involve enormous costs at the national level along with the increase in the salary received by a resident doctor (Boghicevici, 2023).
- Shortage of healthcare personnel: The migration of healthcare students aggravates the shortage of healthcare personnel in Romania. Countries like Romania, which have limited financial resources, may have difficulties in offering a competitive salary and attractive working conditions to keep doctors in the home country's medical institutions. Consequently, the health system can become vulnerable and overburdened, which can affect the quality of medical care, the success rate of surgical interventions, the response time of doctors to patients' needs and the satisfaction felt by patients, among others.
- Brain drain: The migration of medical students represents a form of "brain drain" for Romania. When the country invests resources in the professional training of students and they go abroad to practise, the country loses the expertise and potential of these specialists.

This phenomenon is noted when we analyse the origin of doctors who practise in the developed countries of the EU or OECD (OECD, 2019), Romania being one of the countries with the largest number of exported health personnel.

In the long term, the phenomenon begins to show its negative consequences. The brain drain together with the ageing of the healthcare personnel in the Romanian medical system will lead to serious effects. The average age of Romania doctors already exceeds 55 years (Dzhambazova, & Ciobanu, 2018), and the brain drain phenomenon does nothing but aggravate even more the medical deficit that Romania is facing:

– The reputation of the education system: In the last decade, medical faculties in Romania have adopted an internationalisation trend, with the aim to expand and develop. By developing programmes in English and French, many of these institutions have managed to attract a growing number of international students and be attractive to Romanian students who intend to migrate for work after completing their studies, especially due to the fact that they graduate from a faculty with studies done in an international language. With the maintenance of relatively low study costs for foreigners and scholarships for national students and the possibility of obtaining a medical degree recognised at the European level, they have become attractive destinations not only for their own students but also for students from various countries.

However, it is important to emphasise that the internationalisation of medical education takes place in parallel with the traditional role of medical schools to train new doctors to meet the needs of the Romanian healthcare sector. This internationalisation approach does not directly contribute to the achievement of the health systems' objectives, particularly in terms of ensuring adequate levels of health staff:

- Romania offers national students the opportunity to complete their studies, most of the time without incurring costs (as they are covered by the national scholarship programmes) and to continue their studies, by enrolling in residency studies, which implies an attractive salary. However, the tendency among students is to migrate after graduation in more developed countries, which offer them better opportunities, Romania thus becoming a launching pad.
- For international students, Romania is an attractive option for obtaining a quality medical degree, especially if they cannot pursue their studies in their home countries due to higher costs, the numerus clausus policy or other capacity constraints (OECD, 2019). However, the country is not a very attractive destination for completing specialist postgraduate training and pursuing a career in the medical field.

## Brief Final Considerations

The changes generated by the pandemic have significantly influenced the healthcare sector and employment patterns. Professionals in this field face increased opportunities for professional development, higher wages and more flexible access to jobs, while new technologies and interdisciplinary specialisations become the key to a successful future in the healthcare industry. At the same time, young people aspire to the opportunities offered by developed countries, which increases the interest in international mobility in search of higher academic training and more promising prospects on the labour market.

This qualitative data analysis brings a clearer and more grounded perspective on the intention to migrate for studies and work among final-year healthcare students. Moreover, they can serve as a basis for formulating decisions and developing appropriate policies in the medical and educational fields.

Following the analysis of the questionnaire, an alarming situation with long-term implications for the Romanian medical system becomes evident: young specialists show a considerable inclination towards migration, regardless of whether it involves studies or work abroad. With increased gravity, it is noted that many of the respondents will complete their studies (mostly financed from public resources) and then go to another country in search of employment opportunities. A worrying finding is represented by the general tendency (approximately 50% of respondents) do not want to return to Romania, regardless of the initial reason for migration (studies or work). This trend is due to a combination of push-pull factors, present both in the country of origin and in the country of destination. So, the complex relationship between poverty and wage gaps and the desire to improve living standards are the fundamental factors that stimulate future health professionals to seek employment opportunities abroad.

At the same time, there is a tendency to internationalise the Romanian educational system, which, although it has brought significant benefits to medical schools in the country, can have negative consequences, such as the exodus of talented graduates in search of more favourable conditions for professional development. In this context, it becomes essential that Romanian authorities and health institutions explore ways to retain medical human resources and improve working conditions in the healthcare field.

## Annexes

### *Annex 9.1 Number of students enrolled in tertiary education in health programmes, by gender, persons*

| | 2013 | 2014 | 2015 | 2016 | 2017 | 2018 | 2019 | 2020 |
|---|---|---|---|---|---|---|---|---|
| *UE-27* | | | | | | | | |
| Female | 1,480,633 | 1,577,691 | 1,486,832 | 1,494,802 | 1,625,338 | 1,672,133 | 1,691,707 | 1,757,499 |
| Males | 588,388 | 634,037 | 617,661 | 630,191 | 674,804 | 662,336 | 669,498 | 686,250 |
| *Romania* | | | | | | | | |
| Female | 52,294 | 49,925 | 45,871 | 46,876 | 49,070 | 50,477 | 50,895 | 52,432 |
| Males | 24,780 | 24,955 | 22,359 | 22,057 | 23,420 | 23,588 | 22,535 | 23,219 |

Source: Eurostat database (2023a)

## References


ABDA. (2022). *German pharmacies—Figures, data, facts*. ABDA. Retrieved June 10, 2023 from https://www.abda.de/fileadmin/user_upload/assets/ZDF/ZDF22/ABDA_ZDF_2022_Brosch_english.pdf

Baydas, A., & Serhat, A. (2021). Sağlik kurumlarinda ilişkisel pazarlama. In *Sağlık Sektöründe Uygulanan Güncel Pazarlama Yaklaşımlar*. Kriter Yayıncılık Publishing. https://www.kriteryayinevi.com/urun/saglik-sektorunde-uygulanan-guncel-pazarlama-yaklasimlari/

Becker, R., & Teney, C. (2020). Understanding high-skilled intra-European migration patterns: The case of European physicians in Germany. *Journal of Ethnic and Migration Studies, 46*(9), 1737–1755. https://doi.org/10.1080/1369183X.2018.1561249

Bertoni, M., Chattopadhyay, D., & Gu, Y. (2023). *Medical brain drain – Assessing the role of job attributes and individual traits*. IZA Discussion Paper No. 16243. https://doi.org/10.2139/ssrn.4488740

Biagi, B., Detotto, C., & Faggian, A. (2023). Evidence of self-selection and spatial mismatch in interregional migration: the case of Italy. *Oxford Economic Papers, 75*(3), 858–872. https://doi.org/10.1093/oep/gpac043

Boboc, C., Boncea, I., & Manea, D. (2015). The international migration of Romanian physicians. *Economic Computation & Economic Cybernetics Studies & Research, 49*(4).

Boghicevici, C. (2023). The impact of healthcare wage increases on the quality of health services in Romania. In *Proceedings of the International Conference on Business Excellence* (Vol. 17, No. 1, pp. 997–1008). https://doi.org/10.2478/picbe-2023-0091

Boros, L., Dudás, G., Ilcsikné Makra, Z., Morar, C., & Pál, V. (2022). The migration of health care professionals from Hungary–global flows and local responses. *The Central European Journal of Regional Development and Tourism, 14*(1), 164–188.

Brugha, R., McAleese, S., Dicker, P., Tyrrell, E., Thomas, S., Normand, C., & Humphries, N. (2016). Passing through–reasons why migrant doctors in Ireland plan to stay, return home or migrate onwards to new destination countries. *Human Resources for Health, 14*, 45–54. https://doi.org/10.1186/s12960-016-0121-z

Buhaljoti, A., & Abazi, A. (2022). Opportunities and challenges in transitioning to circular economy in Albanian construction industry. *Circular Economy*, 130. https://eprints.uklo.edu.mk/id/eprint/7727/1/cei%20proceedings.pdf#page=122

Clarke, N., Crowe, S., Humphries, N., Conroy, R., O'Hare, S., Kavanagh, P., & Brugha, R. (2017). Factors influencing trainee doctor emigration in a high income country: a mixed methods study. *Human Resources for Health, 15*(1), 1–12. https://doi.org/10.1186/s12960-017-0239-7

Constantin, C. (2023). România este abandonată! Tinerii nu se mai gândesc la facultate şi părăsesc ţara în număr tot mai mare! Unde este reacţia autorităţilor? *Daily Business*. Retrieved June 05, 2023 from https://www.dailybusiness.ro/stiri-interne/romania-este-abandonata-tinerii-nu-se-mai-gandesc-la-facultate-si-parasesc-tara-in-numar-tot-mai-mare-unde-este-reactia-autoritatilor-356368/

Domagała, A., & Dubas-Jakóbczyk, K. (2019). Migration intentions among physicians working in Polish hospitals–Insights from survey research. *Health Policy, 123*(8), 782–789. https://doi.org/10.1016/j.healthpol.2019.06.008

Dzhambazova, B., & Ciobanu, C. (2018). Health care on the brink in Romania, Bulgaria. *Deutsche Welle*. Retrieved June 05, 2023 from https://www.dw.com/en/medical-exodus-leaves-romania-bulgaria-in-pain/a-44487178

European Commission. (2017). *Updated study on corruption in the healthcare sector*. Final Report. Publications Office of the European Union. ISBN: 978-92-79-73245-4. https://doi.org/10.2837/68580

European Commission. (2020). Guidelines on EU Emergency Assistance on Cross-Border Cooperation in Healthcare Related to the COVID-19 Crisis, Communication from the Commission (2020/C 111 I/01). Retrieved June 15, 2023 from https://eur-lex.europa.eu/legal-content/EN/TXT/PDF/?uri=CELEX:52020XC0403(02)&from=EN

Eurostat. (2022). Health personnel (excluding nursing and caring professionals) - historical data (1980–2021). HLTH_RS_PRS1__custom_4911175. Retrieved June 10, 2023 from https://ec.europa.eu/eurostat/databrowser/view/HLTH_RS_PRS1__custom_4911175/default/table

Eurostat. (2023a). *Students enrolled in tertiary education by education level, programme orientation, sex and field of education*. EDUC_UOE_ENRT03. Retrieved June 30, 2023 from https://ec.europa.eu/eurostat/databrowser/view/EDUC_UOE_ENRT03__custom_4955446/default/table?lang=en

Eurostat. (2023b). *Total health care expenditure. Population and social conditions*. Online data code TPS00207. Retrieved June 15, 2023 from https://ec.europa.eu/eurostat/databrowser/product/view/HLTH_SHA11_HC

Gupta, N., Diallo, K., Zurn, P., & Dal Poz, M. R. (2003). Assessing human resources for health: What can be learned from labour force surveys? *Human Resources for Health, 1*(1), 1–16. https://doi.org/10.1093/ije/7.3.207

Ha, T. V., Nguyen, A. M. T., & Nguyen, H. S. T. (2019). Self-medication practices among Vietnamese residents in highland provinces. *Journal of Multidisciplinary Healthcare, 493–502*. https://doi.org/10.2147/JMDH.S211420

Hervey, G. (2017). The EU exodus: When doctors and nurses follow the money. *Politico*. Retrieved April 30, 2023 from https://www.politico.eu/article/doctors-nurses-migration-health-care-crisis-workers-follow-the-money-european-commission-data/

Humphries, N., Connell, J., Negin, J., & Buchan, J. (2019). Tracking the leavers: towards a better understanding of doctor migration from Ireland to Australia 2008–2018. *Human Resources for Health, 17*, 1–10. https://doi.org/10.1186/s12960-019-0365-5

Ifanti, A. A., Argyriou, A. A., Kalofonou, F. H., & Kalofonos, H. P. (2014). Physicians' brain drain in Greece: A perspective on the reasons why and how to address it. *Health Policy, 117*(2), 210–215. https://doi.org/10.1016/j.healthpol.2014.03.014

Ivan, O. R. (2013). Why do Romanians speak foreign languages so well? *Quaestus Multidisciplinary Research Journal, 1*(2), 119–123.

Kangasniemi, M., Winters, L. A., & Commander, S. (2007). Is the medical brain drain beneficial? Evidence from overseas doctors in the UK. *Social Science & Medicine, 65*(5), 915–923. https://doi.org/10.1016/j.socscimed.2007.04.021

Karan, A., DeUgarte, D., & Barry, M. (2016). Medical "brain drain" and health care worker shortages: how should international training programs respond? *AMA Journal of Ethics, 18*(7), 665–675. https://doi.org/10.1001/journalofethics.2016.18.7.ecas1-1607

Kopetsch, T. (2009). The migration of doctors to and from Germany. *Journal of Public Health, 17*, 33–39. https://doi.org/10.1007/s10389-008-0208-7

Li, W., & Sun, H. (2019). Migration intentions of Asian and African medical students educated in China: A cross-sectional study. *Human Resources for Health, 17*, 1–7. https://doi.org/10.1186/s12960-019-0431-z

Mejia, A. (1978). Migration of physicians and nurses: A world wide picture. *International Journal of Epidemiology, 7*(3), 207–215. https://doi.org/10.1093/ije/7.3.207

National Institute of Statistics. (2022). *Activity of the Sanitary and Health Protection Network in 2021*. Press Release No. 167, July 1 2022. https://insse.ro/cms/sites/default/files/com_presa/com_pdf/activ_unit_sanitare21r.pdf

Nistor, N. (2013). Stability of attitudes and participation in online university courses: Gender and location effects. *Computers & Education, 68*, 284–292. https://doi.org/10.1016/j.compedu.2013.05.016

OECD. (2019). *Recent trends in international migration of doctors, nurses and medical students*. OECD. https://doi.org/10.1787/5571ef48-en

OECD. (2020). *Contribution of migrant doctors and nurses to tackling COVID-19 crisis in OECD countries*; OECD Policy Responses to Coronavirus (COVID-19). OECD. Retrieved June 30, 2023 from https://www.oecd.org/coronavirus/policy-responses/contribution-of-migrant-doctors-and-nurses-to-tackling-covid-19-crisis-in-oecd-countries-2f7bace2/

OECD/ILO. (2022). *Equipping health workers with the right skills: Skills anticipation in the health workforce, getting skills right*. OECD Publishing. https://doi.org/10.1787/9b83282e-en

Paun, C. (2018). A Romanian village feels the country's emigration pain. *Politico*. Retrieved June 07, 2023 from https://www.politico.eu/article/intorsura-romania-village-migration-feels-the-countrys-emigration-pain/

Reßing, C., Mueller, M., Knop, M., Freude, H., & Niehaves, B. (2020). Building digital bridges: Exploring the digitized collaboration of general practitioners and mobile care in rural areas. In *AMCIS (HEALTHCARE INFORMATICS & HEALTH INFORMATION TECH (SIGHEALTH))*. https://aisel.aisnet.org/amcis2020/healthcare_it/healthcare_it/21/

Séchet, R., & Vasilcu, D. (2015). Physicians' migration from Romania to France: a brain drain into Europe? *Cybergeo: European Journal of Geography, 743*. https://doi.org/10.4000/cybergeo.27249

Slauson-Blevins, K., & Johnson, K. M. (2016). Doing gender, doing surveys? Women's gatekeeping and men's non-participation in multi-actor reproductive surveys. *Sociological Inquiry, 86*(3), 427–449. https://doi.org/10.1111/soin.12122

Socha-Dietrich, K., & Dumont, J. (2021). *International migration and movement of nursing personnel to and within OECD countries - 2000 to 2018: Developments in countries of destination and impact on countries of origin*. OECD Health Working Papers, No. 125, OECD Publishing. https://doi.org/10.1787/b286a957-en

Timus, M., Ciucan-Rusu, L., Stefan, D., & Popa, M. A. (2020). Student relationship management optimization using organizational process automation tools. *Acta Marisiensis, Seria Oeconomica, 14*(1), 31. https://doi.org/10.2478/amso-2020-0004

Torres, N. F., Chibi, B., Middleton, L. E., Solomon, V. P., & Mashamba-Thompson, T. P. (2019). Evidence of factors influencing self-medication with antibiotics in low and middle-income countries: A systematic scoping review. *Public Health, 168*, 92–101. https://doi.org/10.1016/j.puhe.2018.11.018

Vasile, V., Bunduchi, E., Boboc, C., & Vasile, R. (2021). Graduates and the labor market deficit. In *The Romanian health sector. CKS 2021-challenges of the knowledge society* (pp. 919–924).

Vasile, V., Bunduchi, E., Stefan, D., & Comes, C. A. (2023a). Migrant critical workers during and after COVID-19 pandemic. In *International labour mobility: How remittances shape the labour migration model* (pp. 197–214). Springer International Publishing. https://doi.org/10.1007/978-3-031-18683-7_10

Vasile, V., Bunduchi, E., Stefan, D., & Comes, C. A. (2023b). Social effects of migration and of remittances from the perspective of the home country and of the host country. In *International labour mobility: How remittances shape the labour migration model* (pp. 139–159). Springer International Publishing. https://doi.org/10.1007/978-3-031-18683-7_7

Vasile, V., Bunduchi, E., Stefan, D., Comes, C. A., Vasile, R., & Stefan, A. B. (2023). Are we facing a radical change in the migration behavior of medical graduates from less developed countries? Demographic profile vs. social push factors. *International Journal of Environmental Research and Public Health, 20*(6), 4894. https://doi.org/10.3390/ijerph20064894

Vasile, V., Ştefan, D., Comes, C. A., Bunduchi, E., & Ştefan, A. B. (2020). FDI or remittances for sustainable external financial inflows. Theoretical delimitations and practical evidence using granger causality. *Romanian Journal of Economic Forecasting, 23*(4), 131.

Vulcan, D. (2021). Interimatul şefilor sau cum se controlează politic un spital de stat. Europa Liberă România. https://romania.europalibera.org/a/interimate-conduceri-politice-spitale/31178469.html

Xiang, B. (2016). Emigration trends and policies in China. In *Spotlight on China*. Brill. Retrieved June 12, 2023 from https://brill.com/view/book/edcoll/9789463006699/BP000016.xml

Xiang, B., & Shen, W. (2009). International student migration and social stratification in China. *International Journal of Educational Development, 29*(5), 513–522. https://doi.org/10.1016/j.ijedudev.2009.04.006

Zaharia, M. (2007). Villagers home alone as Romania speeds up. *Reuters*. Retrieved June 07, 2023 from https://jp.reuters.com/article/us-romania-farming-idUSL3191393420070904

# Chapter 10
# Features of the Policies Adopted for the Mitigation of the Pandemic Recession Impact on the Labour Market Operation

**Florin Marius Pavelescu**

**Abstract** Considering the European Union experience, firstly, the chapter reveals the informational technologies role in activating the labour supply and maintaining the jobs and also the high degree of vulnerability of the jobs generated by the traditional consumption services under the conditions of a pandemic shock. During the first semester of 2020 year, the block out measure implementation caused an impressive jobs loss and significant increases in the rate of unemployment. In this context, the member states implemented labour market policies representing combination of best practices, used during previous recessions and innovative solutions, adequate to the pandemic context. Even there were some differences caused by the level of development and the variants of economic and social model established in each member state, the labour market policies implemented in the pandemic context remained in the area of European social model. In fact, the pandemic shock contributed to the broading of the European Commission prerogatives and to the design and implementation of innovative solutions related to financial assistance granted to member states. As a result of the implementation of the above-mentioned policies, practically in all member states, in December 2022, the rate of unemployment came back to the levels registered in January 2020.

F. M. Pavelescu (✉)
Institute of National Economy - Romanian Academy, Bucharest, Romania



V. Vasile, E. Bunduchi (eds.), *The Economic and Social Impact of the COVID-19 Pandemic*, Contributions to Economics,
https://doi.org/10.1007/978-3-031-47780-5_10

## Introduction

The COVID-19 pandemic forced the adoption of a series of measures for sanitary protection, which hurt the labour market operation. This was not, however, a new situation. During the centuries, we can identify many pandemics of influenza or coronavirus types with a high degree of aggressivity.[1]

The COVID-19 pandemic was the first to occur in the context of a high degree of globalisation of the economic activity, a considerable extension of the use of informational-communicational technologies in almost all the economic and social activities and of the implementation of deep supranational economic integration processes.

The outbreak of the COVID-19 pandemic in February 2020 and its persistence for more than 2 years have caused a far-reaching negative impact on economic and social activities. Many bottlenecks occurred in the goods and services markets, and in the labour market as well. Under these conditions, the public authorities had to adopt measures designed to decrease the negative consequences of a recession of a particular kind. As such, we deal with a significant experience concerning the role of the population's health condition in reaching sustainable economic growth, and the types of policy measures implemented for ensuring social protection and job retention in a recessionist context.

## Features of Pandemic Recession

The COVID-19 pandemic shocked both the labour supply and the demand side. Sudden deterioration of the active population's health condition had damaging effects on the human capital (Beland et al., 2020). Poor health conditions and increased risk of death caused a diminishing in both the number of hours worked by the active persons and the level of labour productivity. Because at the start of the pandemic crisis no medical technologies that could maintain the population's health conditions at acceptable levels were available, the only ways to avoid increased mortality were the lockdown of economic activities and the limitation of social contacts. This way, the public authorities have deliberately induced a recessionary situation. The depth of the recession depended on the extension degree and length of the lockdown.

[1]During the last seven centuries, four pandemics caused more than two million deaths, namely: (1) the Black Death (1347–1352), 75 million deaths; (2) the Great Plague of Seville (1647–1652), two million deaths; (3) the Spanish Influenza Pandemic (1918–1920), 100 million deaths; and (4) the Asian Flu Pandemic (1957–1958), two million deaths (cf. O. Jordas et al., 2020). By the beginning of May 2023, the COVID-19 pandemic caused more than 6.92 million deaths. We note that on 5 May 2023, the WHO announced the end of the above-mentioned pandemic as a public emergency.

Another effect on the labour supply caused by the pandemic crisis were the disturbances of the various educational and training activities. Therefore, in the long run, it was possible that the labour supply qualification level would decrease, as well as the innovation rate.

The diminished level of economic and social activities has generated a notable impact on the different employed population categories. In fact, we deal with a segmentation of the employed population into essential and non-essential workers and employees (Beland et al., 2020).

The essential workers are the persons employed in activities ensuring the operation of the public institutions, maintaining the population's health conditions within acceptable limits and avoiding the chronic shortages of essential goods and services.[2] In a pandemic context, the respective category of the employed population is fully active. Also, in the case of some critical workers, the number of working hours sensibly increased to maintain the operation of the base functions of a modern state. In the case of non-essential workers, we deal with considerable differentiation of the opportunities to continue their activities, depending on the possibilities of connection and use of the informational and communicational technologies.

Fana et al. (2020) proposed a classification of economic branches by considering three criteria, namely: (a) essential feature of the analysed economic branch, (b) teleworking exposure and (c) opportunities for the activity to be maintained during restrictions. This way, we can define five categories of economic branches, namely:

(A) Essential and fully active economic branches in the context of a pandemic situation (health care, agriculture, foods industry, public utilities (energy, gas, water).
(B) Active economic branches via teleworking (education, main components of public administration, financial and insurance activities, information and telecommunications). The respective activities play a crucial role in an information society. For these reasons, we may consider these economic branches as essential activities of second degree. Within this category of economic branches, we can also include the scientific, technical and professional services. The respective services are not defined as essential activities in all the European Union member states.
(C) Mostly essential, partial active and non-teleworkable economic branches (wholesale and retail trade, chemical industry, pulp and paper industry).
(D) Mostly non-essential and inactive, not teleworkable economic branches (most of the manufacturing industry and construction).

---

[2]In the USA, the essential workers are associated with employed persons ensuring the critical infrastructure operations. For these reasons, they include the employed persons from health care, law enforcement, armed forces, public authorities' management, agriculture, foods industry, the manufacturing industry sub-branches involved in the maintenance and development of the critical infrastructure and financial services. The other categories of the employed population are considered non-essential workers (Dingel & Neiman, 2020).

(E) Blocked economic branches (most activities contribute to the development of the consumption—hotels, restaurants, catering, event organising, cultural and leisure services—and real estate activities). [3]

If we consider the classification mentioned above, we notice that the implementation of measures designed to reduce the initial negative consequences of the COVID-19 pandemic created the premises for asymmetric shocks in the labour force employment. At the level of the whole European Union, in 2018, the weight of the essential economic branches in the employed population was higher than 25%. Romania, Poland and Denmark registered the highest values, while Estonia, Austria, Portugal and Slovakia represented the exceptions to the rule (Table 10.1). The respective weights cover a considerable heterogeneity of the economic activities seen as essential. Thus, the higher weight of agriculture in the employed population, like in the case of Romania, implicitly leads to a higher relative importance of the essential activities. For these reasons, the analysis has to consider the situation of the medical staff and the particular features of the labour force employed in agriculture in the member states, determined by the property structure, the level of the technical endowment of labour or the appeal to the seasonal workers from abroad.

---

[3] The grouping of the economic activities proposed by Fana et al. (2020) for studying the impact of the COVID-19 pandemic on the employment of labour force has both advantages and disadvantages. The main advantage includes highlighting the opportunities to continue the activity in the context of serious threats to the health conditions of the whole population. The main disadvantage is that the respective segmentation is dependent on the public authorities' views concerning the essential or non-essential features of the various economic and social activities. Thus, the analysis of the legislative changes adopted during the March–April 2020 period in the European Union member states shows that in Spain and Italy, the weight of the non-essential economic branches in the total employed population was higher in comparison with Northern or Western member-states.

The above-mentioned classification is not the only one used for the evaluation of the consequences of the COVID-19 pandemic on the utilisation of human potential. Considering the standard classification of the economic branches, ILO (2020b) estimated the size of the respective impact on the output level worldwide. Thus, a low negative impact was seen in education, health care and social assistance, public administration and public utilities. The low-medium negative impact was found in agriculture, forestry and fishing, but with some differentiation between component activities depending on the epidemic persistence in rural areas, while the medium negative impact was registered in construction, financial and insurance activities and mining and quarrying. The medium-high negative impact was observed in transportation, storage and communication and cultural and entertainment services but with significant differentiation within the mentioned activities depending on the exposure to information technologies or teleworking. A high negative impact was identified in the manufacturing industry, accommodation services, real estate, business and administration services and wholesale and retail trade.

We note that a low influence was registered in services, which are essential for the existence of a modern state and are decisively dependent on the allocation of the financial resources from the state budget. The greatest demand decrease was registered by the economic branches essentially depending on the level of the population's incomes or the existence of complex supply chains. This assessment of the impact of the pandemic shock on the level of the output has the advantage of using the economic branches' standard classification and reveals one of the essential premises of the labour demand.

**Table 10.1** The structure of the employed labour force from the point of view of the resilience to the pandemic shock in the European Union member countries in 2018 year, %

| Country | Essential economic branches (%) | Active via telework and partial active economic branches (%) | Non-essential economic branches (%) | Blocked economic branches (%) |
|---|---|---|---|---|
| Malta | >25 | >50 | >25 | 15.68 |
| Spain | >25 | >50 | >25 | 14.19 |
| Cyprus | >25 | >50 | >25 | 14.16 |
| Greece | >25 | >50 | >25 | 13.03 |
| Ireland | >25 | >50 | 25 | 12.67 |
| Italy | >25 | >50 | >25 | 11.58 |
| Croatia | >25 | >50 | >25 | 11.42 |
| Estonia | <25 | <50 | >25 | 10.86 |
| Austria | <25 | 50 | >25 | 10.77 |
| Latvia | >25 | >50 | >25 | 10.76 |
| Portugal | <25 | <50 | >25 | 10.70 |
| Netherlands | >25 | >50 | 25 | 9.91 |
| France | >25 | >50 | >25 | 9.54 |
| Sweden | 25 | >50 | >25 | 9.43 |
| Finland | >25 | >50 | >25 | 8.84 |
| Bulgaria | 25 | >50 | >25 | 8.78 |
| Czech Republic | <25 | >50 | >25 | 8.75 |
| Hungary | >25 | >50 | >25 | 8.74 |
| Denmark | >25 | >50 | >25 | 8.54 |
| Germany | 25 | >50 | >25 | 8.34 |
| Slovenia | >25 | 50 | >25 | 8.33 |
| Luxemburg | >25 | >50 | >25 | 7.91 |
| Slovakia | <25 | >50 | >25 | 7.81 |
| Belgium | >25 | >50 | >25 | 7.78 |
| Lithuania | >25 | >50 | >25 | 7.61 |
| Poland | >25 | >50 | >25 | 6.33 |
| Romania | >25 | >50 | >25 | 4.71 |
| UK | <25 | >50 | >25 | 11.67 |
| UE 28 | >25 | >50 | >25 | 9.88 |

Estimations based on data from Fana et al. (2020)

The active, via telework and partial active economic branches' weight in the employed population was of at least 50% in each European Union member state, except Estonia. The relative importance of the non-essential economic activities was higher in all the member states. The weight of the blocked economic branches was 9.88% at the level of the whole European Union, higher proportions than the community average for Southern European member states, Estonia, Latvia, Austria, Ireland, the Netherlands and the UK. Hence, the countries where the consumption services play a significant role have a lower resilience for labour force employment in front of the pandemic shock.

The lower weight of the blocked economic branches in the employed population does not mean the existence of favourable premises for sustainable labour force employment. The group of countries where the respective weight was lower than 8% is heterogeneous. Here, we find Luxembourg, where the proportion of the financial services in labour force employment is sensibly higher than the average registered throughout the European Union, and Romania, where we deal with an overestimation of the population employed in agriculture.[4]

Throughout the European Union, the five categories of economic activities show sensible differences in terms of the socio-demographic features of the employed population. Compared to the European average, the women's proportion in the employed population is lower only in the case of the non-essential economic branches (Table 10.2). This fact reveals the lower proportion of the respective segment of the labour supply in the manufacturing industry and construction. We note that the female labour force employment is conditioned by multiple factors. During the last decades, the changes in the institutional framework and the implementation of new technologies have favoured an increase in the number of jobs held by women, especially in the service sector. However, we may not ignore the growing differentiation of the qualification requirements between the traditional and the knowledge-intensive services.

We also observe a differentiation of the age structure of the employed population within the five categories of economic branches. Young people appear to be over-represented in the blocked economic branches, as well as in the mostly active ones. The weight of the persons over 50 is higher in economic branches which remain active in the case of a pandemic context. The persons employed in the active economic branches via telework have a high qualification level and low exposure to various forms of employment flexibilisation, such as temporary labour contracts and self-employment. As a rule, the persons employed in the blocked economic branches are lower qualified and more exposed to non-standard employment forms, which could become precarious in a recessionist climate. The sudden decrease of the labour demand caused an increase in the unemployment rate. During the January–June 2020 period, the seasonally adjusted unemployment rate grew from 6.6% to 7.2% at the level of the whole European Union and from 7.4% to 7.8% in the case of the Eurozone (Table 10.3).

The number of unemployed persons seasonally adjusted grew in 21 member states. The indicator decreased in Bulgaria, France, Ireland, Italy and Portugal, and increased by more than 40% in Croatia, Cyprus, Latvia, Lithuania, Luxemburg and the Netherlands. Throughout the European Union, the unemployment rate tended to

[4]In 2020, Romanian official statistics amended the definition of the population employed in agriculture. Thus, the number of employed persons in agriculture has decreased by about 700,000. By default, the structure of the employed population from the point of view of resilience to the pandemic shock has changed.

**Table 10.2** The weight of some socio-demographic groups in the employed population on categories of economic branches in the European Union, %

| Indicator | Whole economy | Essential economic branches | Active economic branches via telework | Partial active economic branches | Non-essential economic branches | Blocked economic branches |
|---|---|---|---|---|---|---|
| Weight of women | 46.00 | 51.05 | 52.90 | 48.45 | 24.44 | 56.29 |
| Weight of persons aged between 15 and 29 | 18.24 | 16.02 | 14.93 | 21.61 | 17.30 | 28.34 |
| Weight of persons over 50 years old | 32.57 | 36.27 | 33.48 | 29.99 | 32.00 | 26.48 |
| Weight of persons with temporary labour contracts | 14.05 | 14.07 | 12.09 | 14.02 | 13.29 | 21.58 |
| Weight of self-employed persons | 14.34 | 15.19 | 11.07 | 14.51 | 13.64 | 21.66 |
| Weight of high-qualified persons | 35.05 | 31.71 | 60.56 | 24.21 | 21.73 | 26.17 |
| Weight of low-skilled persons | 17.34 | 19.12 | 6.42 | 21.51 | 22.40 | 21.46 |
| Weight of persons with teleworking | 10.23 | 8.36 | 17.49 | 7.40 | 6.40 | 9.48 |

Source: Fana et al. (2020)

grow from 6.5% to 7.1%. Also, the gap between the minimum and the maximum level of unemployment in the member states has narrowed.

The increased number of unemployed persons was a consequence of the decrease in the number of the employed population. The estimations made by Conte et al. (2020) have considered a decrease in the number of employed persons by about 12% in 2020, in the context of a contraction of the gross domestic product by about 13.9%, of consumption by about 14.9% and of investments by about 16.7% throughout the European Union.

The decrease in the number of employed persons caused by the pandemic recession occurred both in the European Union and worldwide. ILO Monitor (2020a) estimated that, compared to the last quarter of 2019, the number of working hours decreased by 5.4%, equivalent to 185 million lost jobs in the context of a working week of 40 h, during the first quarter of 2020 and by 14% during the second quarter, equivalent to 480 million lost jobs.

**Table 10.3** Unemployment rate and the dynamics of the seasonally adjusted number of unemployed persons in European Union member states during the first semester of 2020, %

| | January 2020 | February 2020 | March 2020 | April 2020 | May 2020 | June 2020 | Index number of unemployed persons June 2020/January 2020 |
|---|---|---|---|---|---|---|---|
| European Union | 6.5 | 6.5 | 6.5 | 6.7 | 7.0 | 7.1 | 106.8 |
| Eurozone | 7.4 | 7.2 | 7.2 | 7.5 | 7.7 | 7.8 | 104.6 |
| Belgium | 5.1 | 5.0 | 5.1 | 5.3 | 5.4 | 5.5 | 109.7 |
| Bulgaria | 4.5 | 4.2 | 4.1 | 4.8 | 4.6 | 4.4 | 98.7 |
| Czech Republic | 2.0 | 2.0 | 2.1 | 2.2 | 2.4 | 2.6 | 127.5 |
| Denmark | 4.9 | 4.9 | 4.8 | 5.0 | 5.5 | 5.8 | 117.4 |
| Germany | 3.4 | 3.6 | 3.8 | 3.9 | 4.1 | 4.2 | 123.8 |
| Estonia | 4.7 | 4.7 | 4.8 | 6.0 | 7.0 | ... | ... |
| Ireland | 4.9 | 4.8 | 5.2 | 5.0 | 5.0 | 4.6 | 87.6 |
| Greece | 16.2 | 15.9 | 14.5 | 15.7 | 17.0 | ... | ... |
| Spain | 13.8 | 13.6 | 14.5 | 15.4 | 15.4 | 15.6 | 105.4 |
| France | 7.9 | 7.6 | 7.6 | 8.8 | 8.2 | 7.7 | 97.5 |
| Croatia | 6.3 | 6.2 | 6.8 | 8.1 | 8.9 | 8.8 | 143.8 |
| Italy | 9.5 | 9.2 | 8.4 | 6.8 | 8.3 | 8.8 | 90.1 |
| Cyprus | 6.1 | 6.0 | 6.7 | 8.9 | 10.2 | 9.8 | 160.7 |
| Latvia | 6.9 | 6.9 | 7.4 | 9.0 | 9.8 | 10.1 | 146.3 |
| Lithuania | 6.1 | 6.3 | 6.6 | 8.6 | 9.3 | 9.4 | 154.4 |
| Luxemburg | 5.7 | 5.8 | 6.6 | 7.5 | 7.7 | 7.7 | 133.3 |
| Hungary | 3.4 | 3.6 | 3.7 | 4.1 | 4.8 | ... | ... |
| Malta | 3.4 | 3.4 | 3.5 | 4.1 | 4.3 | 4.2 | 122.2 |
| Netherlands | 3.0 | 2.9 | 2.9 | 3.4 | 3.6 | 4.3 | 142.3 |
| Austria | 4.4 | 4.5 | 4.7 | 5.0 | 5.9 | 5.7 | 128.1 |
| Poland | 3.0 | 3.0 | 2.9 | 2.9 | 2.9 | 3.0 | 100.6 |
| Portugal | 6.8 | 6.4 | 6.2 | 6.3 | 5.9 | 7.0 | 99.7 |
| Romania | 3.7 | 4.3 | 4.6 | 4.8 | 5.2 | 5.2 | 138.2 |
| Slovenia | 4.2 | 4.2 | 4.3 | 4.7 | 4.8 | 4.8 | 114.0 |
| Slovakia | 6.1 | 6.1 | 5.8 | 6.4 | 6.5 | 6.6 | 109.7 |
| Finland | 6.8 | 6.9 | 7.0 | 7.2 | 7.4 | 7.6 | 111.7 |
| Sweden | 7.2 | 7.6 | 6.8 | 7.9 | 8.5 | 9.2 | 128.0 |

Source: EUROSTAT database

In Northern Europe, during the first quarter of 2020, the relative decrease in the working hours was lower than the global trend. During the second quarter of 2020, in most European countries, the proportion of the working hour decrease was higher than the trend observed worldwide (Table 10.4). In a European context, the strongest negative impact was felt in the Southern part of the Old Continent.

**Table 10.4** Estimation of the number of lost jobs caused by the pandemic crisis during the first semester of 2020

| | Relative modification (%) | | Number of lost jobs, equivalent 40 working hours per week (millions) | |
|---|---|---|---|---|
| Area | First quarter | Second quarter | First quarter | Second quarter |
| World economy | 5.4 | 14.0 | 185 | 480 |
| Northern Europe | 3.1 | 15.3 | 1 | 7 |
| Western Europe | 4.0 | 14.3 | 3 | 12 |
| Southern Europe | 5.3 | 18.0 | 3 | 12 |
| Eastern Europe | 2.6 | 11.6 | 3 | 15 |

Source: ILO Monitor (2020b)

For the last quarter of 2020, the estimations considered a decrease by 4.9% (140 million lost jobs) compared to the similar period of 2019.

During the second half of 2020, throughout the European Union, the unemployment rate continued to grow, but at a slower pace, namely, from 7.2%, in June, to 7.9%, in December (Table 10.5). In the case of the Eurozone, the indicator increased from 7.8% to 8.6%. In December 2020, the unemployment rate was higher than in Greece and Spain and lower than 5% in the Czech Republic, Germany, Malta and Poland. As an exception from the rule, the analysed indicator has decreased in Estonia, Greece, Latvia, Lithuania, Luxemburg, Hungary, Malta, the Netherlands and Romania.

During 2021 year, the unemployment rate decreased in all member states. The sharpest reductions were recorded in the Czech Republic, Germany and Ireland, and the lowest in France, Latvia, Romania and Slovakia. In December 2021, the weight of the unemployed persons in the active population was higher than 12.5% in Greece and Spain, and lower than 5% in the Czech Republic, Poland, Germany, Malta, Hungary, the Netherlands, Austria, Slovenia and Ireland. The above-mentioned indicator dynamics were modelled by the structure and, implicitly, by the economy resilience, the quality of the labour market institutions and the features of the politics implemented at the level of the whole European Union and each member state. The external mobility of the workers between member states influenced the unemployment rate. In the context of a free circulation of the labour force, we deal with migration flows from the lower developed to the most developed member states. A paradoxical situation occurs. The Eurozone unemployment rate is constantly higher compared to that recorded throughout the European Union. Thus, the analysis of the labour market operation and resilience to various types of external shocks within the European Union has to consider the role of territorial mobility between member states.

During 2022, the unemployment rate at the level of the whole European Union has decreased from 6.3% in December 2021 to 6.1% in December 2021 (Table 10.6).

The respective indicators recorded in the Eurozone were 6.9% in December 2021 and 6.7% in December 2022, and continued to be higher compared to the whole European Union.

**Table 10.5** Unemployment rate in European Union member states during the June 2020–December 2021 period, %

| | June 2020 | Sept. 2020 | Dec. 2020 | March 2021 | June 2021 | Sept. 2021 | Dec. 2021 | Index December 2020/ June 2020 | Index December 2021/ December 2020 |
|---|---|---|---|---|---|---|---|---|---|
| European Union | 7.2 | 7.7 | 7.9 | 7.7 | 6.9 | 6.6 | 6.3 | 109.7 | 79.7 |
| Eurozone | 7.8 | 8.6 | 8.6 | 8.3 | 7.6 | 7.3 | 6.9 | 110.3 | 80.2 |
| Belgium | 5.1 | 6.4 | 6.8 | 6.7 | 6.0 | 6.4 | 5.6 | 133.3 | 82.4 |
| Bulgaria | 5.5 | 4.9 | 6.4 | 6.3 | 5.1 | 4.5 | 5.0 | 116.4 | 78.1 |
| Czech Republic | 2.6 | 2.8 | 3.3 | 3.4 | 2.7 | 2.5 | 2.1 | 126.9 | 63.6 |
| Denmark | 5.9 | 6.2 | 6.4 | 5.8 | 4.5 | 5.3 | 5.1 | 108.5 | 79.7 |
| Germany | 4.0 | 4.0 | 4.2 | 4.0 | 3.5 | 3.2 | 2.9 | 105.0 | 69.0 |
| Estonia | 8.0 | 7.8 | 7.1 | 6.7 | 6.7 | 5.5 | 5.1 | 88.8 | 71.8 |
| Ireland | 6.2 | 7.1 | 7.2 | 7.6 | 6.9 | 5.0 | 4.9 | 116.1 | 68.1 |
| Greece | 17.3 | 16.1 | 16.9 | 17.6 | 14.4 | 12.3 | 13.1 | 97.7 | 77.5 |
| Spain | 15.5 | 16.4 | 16.1 | 15.8 | 15.0 | 14.3 | 12.8 | 103.9 | 79.5 |
| France | 6.8 | 9.1 | 8.4 | 8.1 | 7.4 | 7.9 | 7.7 | 123.5 | 91.7 |
| Croatia | 7.5 | 7.7 | 9.4 | 9.0 | 7.1 | 6.7 | 7.2 | 125.3 | 76.6 |
| Italy | 9.4 | 10.4 | 10.7 | 10.4 | 9.2 | 9.0 | 8.6 | 113.8 | 80.4 |
| Cyprus | 7.1 | 8.0 | 8.8 | 8.7 | 8.7 | 5.5 | 6.6 | 123.9 | 75.0 |
| Latvia | 8.6 | 8.0 | 8.1 | 8.1 | 7.8 | 6.7 | 7.6 | 94.2 | 93.8 |
| Lithuania | 9.0 | 9.9 | 7.5 | 6.9 | 7.5 | 6.3 | 5.8 | 83.3 | 77.3 |
| Luxemburg | 7.2 | 6.4 | 6.5 | 6.3 | 5.3 | 5.1 | 5.2 | 90.3 | 80.0 |
| Hungary | 5.0 | 4.6 | 4.5 | 4.0 | 4.0 | 3.3 | 3.5 | 90.0 | 77.8 |
| Malta | 4.8 | 4.8 | 4.0 | 3.7 | 3.5 | 3.5 | 3.4 | 83.3 | 85.0 |
| Netherlands | 5.3 | 5.4 | 4.9 | 4.7 | 4.2 | 4.2 | 3.6 | 92.5 | 73.5 |
| Austria | 7.4 | 6.0 | 8.2 | 7.3 | 5.8 | 4.6 | 4.7 | 110.8 | 57.3 |
| Poland | 3.2 | 3.2 | 4.1 | 4.1 | 3.3 | 3.0 | 2.8 | 128.1 | 68.3 |

| | | | | | | | | | |
|---|---|---|---|---|---|---|---|---|---|
| Portugal | 7.0 | 8.0 | 7.2 | 6.8 | 6.4 | 6.4 | 6.1 | 102.9 | 84.7 |
| Romania | 6.6 | 6.1 | 6.2 | 6.1 | 4.8 | 5.3 | 5.5 | 93.9 | 88.7 |
| Slovenia | 5.2 | 4.9 | 5.8 | 5.2 | 4.2 | 4.5 | 4.6 | 111.5 | 79.3 |
| Slovakia | 6.8 | 7.2 | 7.1 | 7.0 | 6.9 | 6.6 | 6.3 | 104.4 | 88.7 |
| Finland | 7.7 | 7.5 | 8.3 | 8.2 | 7.6 | 7.0 | 6.7 | 107.8 | 80.7 |
| Sweden | 9.8 | 8.3 | 9.7 | 10.0 | 10.3 | 8.2 | 7.3 | 99.0 | 75.3 |

Source: EUROSTAT database

**Table 10.6** Unemployment rate in European Union member states during the December 2021–December 2022 period, %

| | Dec. 2021 | March 2022 | June 2022 | Sept. 2022 | Dec. 2022 | Index December 2022/December 2021 | Index December 2022/December 2020 |
|---|---|---|---|---|---|---|---|
| European Union | 6.3 | 6.2 | 6.1 | 6.1 | 6.1 | 96.83 | 77.17 |
| Eurozone | 6.9 | 6.8 | 6.7 | 6.7 | 6.7 | 97.10 | 77.88 |
| Belgium | 5.6 | 5.2 | 5.8 | 5.4 | 5.8 | 103.57 | 85.34 |
| Bulgaria | 5.0 | 4.5 | 4.4 | 4.0 | 4.0 | 80.00 | 62.48 |
| Czech Republic | 2.1 | 2.3 | 2.4 | 2.3 | 2.3 | 109.52 | 69.66 |
| Denmark | 5.1 | 4.5 | 4.3 | 4.6 | 4.8 | 94.12 | 75.01 |
| Germany | 2.9 | 2.9 | 3.0 | 3.1 | 3.0 | 103.45 | 71.38 |
| Estonia | 5.1 | 5.5 | 5.8 | 5.4 | 5.3 | 103.92 | 74.62 |
| Ireland | 4.9 | 5.1 | 4.2 | 4.4 | 4.4 | 89.80 | 61.15 |
| Greece | 13.1 | 12.2 | 12.5 | 11.9 | 11.8 | 90.08 | 69.81 |
| Spain | 12.8 | 13.4 | 12.6 | 12.9 | 13.0 | 101.56 | 80.74 |
| France | 7.7 | 7.3 | 7.5 | 7.1 | 7.2 | 93.51 | 85.75 |
| Croatia | 7.2 | 6.3 | 6.9 | 6.8 | 6.6 | 91.67 | 70.22 |
| Italy | 8.6 | 8.3 | 8.0 | 8.0 | 7.9 | 91.86 | 73.86 |
| Cyprus | 6.6 | 5.1 | 7.0 | 6.9 | 7.4 | 112.12 | 84.09 |
| Latvia | 7.6 | 6.7 | 6.6 | 7.0 | 6.8 | 89.47 | 83.93 |
| Lithuania | 5.8 | 6.1 | 5.7 | 6.1 | 6.1 | 105.17 | 81.30 |
| Luxemburg | 5.2 | 4.3 | 4.4 | 4.6 | 4.7 | 90.38 | 72.31 |
| Hungary | 3.5 | 3.2 | 3.5 | 3.7 | 3.8 | 108.57 | 84.47 |
| Malta | 3.4 | 3.2 | 3.0 | 2.9 | 2.9 | 85.29 | 72.50 |
| Netherlands | 3.6 | 3.3 | 3.4 | 3.8 | 3.5 | 97.22 | 71.46 |
| Austria | 4.7 | 4.3 | 4.2 | 5.2 | 4.9 | 104.26 | 59.74 |
| Poland | 2.8 | 2.7 | 2.9 | 3.0 | 2.9 | 103.57 | 70.74 |
| Portugal | 6.1 | 5.9 | 6.0 | 6.2 | 6.7 | 109.84 | 93.03 |
| Romania | 5.5 | 5.5 | 5.5 | 5.5 | 5.6 | 101.82 | 90.31 |
| Slovenia | 4.6 | 4.0 | 4.3 | 3.8 | 3.4 | 73.91 | 58.61 |
| Slovakia | 6.3 | 6.3 | 6.2 | 6.0 | 6.1 | 96.83 | 85.88 |
| Finland | 6.7 | 5.4 | 6.9 | 7.3 | 7.2 | 107.46 | 86.72 |
| Sweden | 7.3 | 7.7 | 7.6 | 7.1 | 7.5 | 102.74 | 77.36 |

Source: EUROSTAT database

The unemployment rate was lower in December 2022 in comparison with December 2021 in 14 member states and higher in 13 member states. Spain and Greece were the only two countries where the analysed indicator was higher than 11%. The number of member states where the unemployed persons represented less than 5% of the active population has increased from 10 in December 2021 to 12 in December 2022 by including Denmark and Luxembourg. We note that in December 2022, compared to December 2020, the level of the respective indicator was lower.

This way, we can conclude that the impact of COVID-19 on the unemployment rate tended to disappear.

## External Mobility of Critical and Seasonal Workers: Measures Adopted in the Framework of the European Union Under the Conditions of the COVID-19 Pandemic

On 30 March 2020, the European Commission adopted a series of guidelines for the workers' free movement during the COVID-19 pandemic. These guidelines set out a series of measures to facilitate the free movement of workers throughout the European Union and to avoid bottlenecks that may arise as a result of labour shortages in countries with a high level of development. In this context, the categories of workers whose mobility contributes to the minimisation of the negative impact of the pandemic and maintains the flexibility of labour market operations have been defined.

The following categories of workers were considered: (a) workers in critical operations, (b) cross-border and posted workers and (c) seasonal workers (Comisia Europeană, 2020a). We note that the qualification level of the above-mentioned categories of workers is very diverse. This fact reveals the high degree of complexity of the employment model within the European Union (Pavelescu & Platon, 2002) and the fragile equilibrium established in the labour market of the most developed member states. The respective classification also represents a recognition of the role played by the labour migration from new member states, like Romania, in ensuring the economic and social stability for the most developed member states.

The resumption of labour migration, especially for agricultural workers from the new member states, starting in May 2020, has not been followed by strict enforcement of medical checks and the granting of appropriate legal status to seasonal workers. Examples in this regard, in which Romanian citizens were involved, were numerous from May to July 2020. Failure to meet the conditions for ensuring the health security of seasonal workers and their accommodation in locations where social distance was not observed caused new outbreaks of COVID-19. As a result, the intervention of public authorities, both in Romania and those in the host countries, was necessary in order to identify the causes of infections, as well as to monitor the mechanisms of recruitment, transport, accommodation and work organisation for seasonal work.

On 16 July 2020, the European Commission published new guidelines for cross-border seasonal workers, which complemented the guidelines issued on 30 March 2020. This reaffirmed the role played by seasonal workers in supporting agri-food tourism activities in the host countries and the fact that they are more exposed to precarious employment, living conditions and health. To reduce the economic and social vulnerability of seasonal workers, it was recommended that the principle of equal treatment be firmly applied to the nationals of the host state, as well as a legal status as evidenced by the granting of a residence visa or a work permit for non-EU nationals. Member states were called upon to take firm action against undeclared work and to increase the effectiveness of inspections carried out on companies employing seasonal workers (Comisia Europeană, 2020b).

Special attention was paid to ensuring adequate working conditions and maintaining health. In this context, it was necessary to create favourable conditions for the real functioning of the mechanisms for consultation and participation of seasonal workers in the implementation of solutions to improve occupational safety and health. It emphasised the importance of initiating actions aimed to strengthen the capacity of small businesses to ensure that measures were taken to reduce the risk of infection with infectious diseases. Small businesses employ a significant portion of seasonal workers, but in many cases, they lack financial strength. For these reasons, greater involvement of public authorities was recommended, both by conducting rigorous workplace inspections and by providing support for the purchase of protective equipment and the appropriate accommodation of those workers.

The European Commission encouraged the adoption of codes of conduct for the recruitment of seasonal workers and the amendment of national legislation in favour of imposing clear clauses on the rights of persons recruited to work abroad and their correct information on working conditions in the host countries. At the same time, the obligation of employers to ensure easy access, both formally and linguistically, to information on health and occupational risks, as well as procedures and how to access health care, was reiterated.

The Guidelines recommended to maintain the contacts between line ministries of source and host countries for seasonal workers on labour migration flows, and that data be collected on conducting a study on seasonal work in the European Union, especially in the pandemic conditions. It was also intended to increase cooperation between community bodies responsible for seasonal workers and the implementation of the directive and other programmatic documents related to that issue.

## Measures Implemented at International Level for the Mitigation of the Negative Consequences of the COVID-19 Pandemic on the Labour Market

The lockdown of some economic and social activities considered non-essential by the public authorities created the conditions for an economic recession, due to the demobilisation of labour supply, on the one hand, and the creation of a state of uncertainty, which leads to compressing aggregate demand for goods and services and, thus, labour demand, on the other hand. Therefore, an epidemic curve (the evolution of the number of infections and deaths) and a recession curve have emerged (Gourinchas, 2020). We note that the measures implemented to flatten one of the curves could cause a significant inflammation of the other one.

In this context, the economic policy measures had to solve a problem of dynamic optimisation, related to the development of economy and population both in the short and medium run (Robalino, 2020). The introduction by the public authorities of measures meant to drastically decrease economic activity and social contacts created favourable premises for the epidemiological curve flattening, but induced a state of severe recession, causing appreciable economic and social costs (Baldwin &Weder di Mauro, 2020b).

Internationally, the lockdown measures began to be adopted by public authorities, except in China, at the end of February 2020 and were extended during March 2020 (ILO Monitor, 2020a).

As of April 2020, some of the restrictions imposed on activities considered non-essential have been relaxed, depending on the evolution of the epidemiological situation, as well as the pressure exerted by public opinion to waive those restrictions. The trend intensified in May and June, in the context of reducing the incidence of infections. In July and August 2020, in many European countries, most of the restrictions were lifted amid pressure from business representatives, who were subject to restrictions, but also from consumers.

Under these conditions, because in the northern hemisphere it was the holiday season, the infection rate increased significantly. A paradox occurred, namely, in the first phase of the epidemic (during the spring), severe measures were taken to restrict the conduct of activities considered non-essential or with an increased risk of contamination of the population, but during the holiday season, there was a relaxation of the restrictions, even with the risk of deterioration of the epidemiological situation.

We note that the economic and social pressures led to secondary concerns about limiting the spread of the pandemic. An example of this are not only some European countries whose economies are highly dependent on tourism but also India. The Indian government took measures to ease restrictions, even in the context of a record number of daily infections, in order to reduce the pressures exerted by the substantial growth of the number of unemployed persons.

The severe limitation of economic and social activities was accompanied by the design and implementation of social protection and job retention programmes (schemes). The number of states and territories that have adopted such measures increased from 45 on 20 March to 106 on 3 April, to 151 on 23 April, to 181 on 15 May and to 195 on 12 June 2020 (U Gentilini et al., 2020a). Almost all states adopted social protection and employment measures to limit the COVID-19 pandemic consequences, except for states (territories) with autarkic tendencies, such as Laos and Turkmenistan, or marked by internal conflicts, such as Syria, Yemen and Western Sahara.

The measures can be classified as social assistance, social security and labour market activation. On 12 June 2020, the total number of measures adopted was 1024, which were distributed as follows: 621 in the field of social assistance in 173 states,[5] 263 in the field of social insurance in 125 states[6] and 140 in the field of labour market activation and labour market stimulation in 85 states.[7]

During July–December 2020, the number of states and territories that adopted social protection or labour market activation measures continued to grow and reached 215, while the number of measures implemented was 1414 (Gentilini et al., 2020b). The number of social protection measures was 870, introduced in 193 countries. It was estimated that in December 2020, social protection measures to diminish the impact of the above-mentioned pandemic were applied to 1.28 billion people representing 16% of the world's population. The number of social security measures increased to 346, implemented in 136 states and territories. The number of labour market activation measures rose sharply to 198 in 107 countries.

In 2021, we note a further increase in the number of measures to diminish the negative consequences of COVID-19 worldwide, but with significantly different dynamics during the year under review. Thus, Gentilini (2021) reveals that the total number of new measures was 1919 between January 2021 and May 2021 and 523 between May 2021 and January 2022. Under these conditions, in January 2022, 223 countries and territories implemented 3856 measures to decrease the negative effects of the pandemic on the labour market. Also, 2349 social protection measures were introduced in 218 countries, while the number of social security measures was 719, implemented in 179 countries and territories. Also, 188 countries and territories have implemented 788 measures to activate the labour market.

The adoption by public authorities of certain types of social protection and labour market activation measures depended on multiple factors, such as the phases of the pandemic crisis, local traditions and the level of economic development. Each type of social protection or labour market activation measure entailed considerable costs for state budgets and is a major challenge in the face of drastic declines in income amid a recessionary climate.

Thus, social assistance and social security measures included increasing the amounts of payment, broadening the social categories to which they are addressed and reducing the bureaucratic procedures required for granting them. The stringency of granting such aid, combined with the requirement to limit social contacts, has led to the use of information technology for transfer to beneficiaries, as was the case in Romania. These types of measures were taken by all countries but had a higher share

[5]The measures of social protection include conditional and unconditional money transfers, universal one-off cash, childcare support, cash for work, social pensions granting, in-kind food/voucher schemes, subsidy for school feeding and utility and financial obligation support (postponement) (cf. U. Gentilini et al., 2020a).

[6]The measures of social insurance refer to paid sick support, health-care insurance support, contributory pensions support, social security contribution waiver/subsidy and unemployment benefits (cf. U. Gentilini et al., 2020a).

[7]The measures for labour market activation consist in wage subsidies, training measures, labour market regulation and shorter work time benefits (cf. U. Gentilini et al., 2020a).

in the first phase of the pandemic as well as in countries with lower per capita incomes.

Theoretically, the implementation of social protection or social security measures had several advantages, the most important being (a) reducing social tensions and avoiding the spread of poverty among broad social groups; (b) slowing down the decrease of solvent demand, as a result of declining incomes; and (c) limiting the transmission of the virus, because implementing some forms of assistance or social insurance stimulated the isolation of potentially infected people at home. It also removed the threat of losing revenues.

Labour market activation measures were adopted especially since the second phase of the fight against the pandemic, especially in the countries with a consolidated market economy, after the effects of the economic downturn began to manifest.

## Measures for the Activation of Labour Market Adopted by EU and OECD Member Countries

The higher propensity for labour market activation measures in developed countries has been favoured by the higher level of social labour productivity, the greater possibilities for public authorities to intervene in the labour market and the existence of extended social protection systems. Short-term working schemes (Kurzarbeit),[8] successfully tested by Germany during the 2007–2008 recession, were promoted especially in the European Union. The European Parliament has also expressed support for extending the implementation of the respective schemes (Muller, 2020).[9]

At the same time, in the USA, in the context of the limitations imposed on the economic activity starting from the last week of March 2020, there were significant extensions of the equivalent of that form of employment (Griswold, 2020).

Among the advantages of using short-time working schemes is avoiding not negligible costs incurred by employers in connection with dismissal and subsequent re-employment of employees. Also, maintaining staff, even with reduced working

[8] S. Aiyar and M.C. Dao (2021) show that the concept of Kurzarbeit is much older. Its origins can be found in the Weimar Republic period. The essential components of the respective concept are (a) eligibility (only the employed persons who contribute to social security systems), (b) replacement rate obtained by the wage earners for the time they did not work, (c) the decrease of the cost paid by employers for the social security contributions, (d) creation of 'working time balances' in the framework of the forms depending on the changes of the labour demand and (e) duration of the implementation of the respective measure. In Germany, before the COVID-19 pandemic, the usual duration of Kurzarbeit was 6 months. In the new context, the duration was extended to 24 months.

[9] Short-time working schemes during the recessions existed not only in Germany but also in other European Union developed member states, namely, France (*Activite Partielle-Partial Activity*), Belgium, Luxembourg, Italy (*Casa Integrazione Guadagni-Home Earnings Integration*) and Spain (*Expedientes de Regulación Temporal de Empleo-Temporary Work Regulation Files*).

hours, has beneficial effects on hourly labour productivity, and promotes technological change, avoiding a sharp drop in aggregate domestic demand. A disadvantage is the generation of overcrowding and thus a reduction in apparent labour productivity.

Given the potential benefits of short-time working schemes, the institutional framework of the labour market has been changed not only in the European Union but also in other OECD member countries. Thus, conditions for the extended use of short-term employment schemes, wage subsidies and other social protection measures have occurred.

Throughout the OECD, the large-scale implementation of the short-time working and wage-subsidy schemes has contributed to the retention of about 50 million jobs, 10 times higher compared to the 2007–2008 recession. In the context of the pandemic recession, the respective schemes were practically used in all the economic branches, unlike during the 2007–2008 recession, when they were concentrated in the manufacturing industry (OECD, 2020b). The two forms of job retention are an emergency solution to a recession of medium duration and intensity or temporary difficulties for companies. Expanding the use of various short-time working schemes did not preclude the granting of aid to companies by public authorities and the implementation of programmes designed to stimulate the emergence and consolidation of entrepreneurship and the digitalisation extension.

Even if the Kurzarbeit and wage-subsidy schemes were most widely used, we have not overlooked that the respective schemes were not the only ones implemented within the European Union. Thus, in the case of Denmark and other Scandinavian countries, the measures adopted to decrease the negative effects of the pandemic situation on the operation of the labour market were inspired by the concept of flexicurity (Greve et al., 2020). Social protection has been strengthened by increasing the level of unemployment and other social benefits and the mention of their universality. At the same time, the flexibility of the labour market was ensured, by maintaining the provisions regarding the employment protection and dismissal of staff. Active job search behaviour was stimulated, as well as various forms of lifelong learning. Public authorities have also supported the extension of social dialogue.

The use of different methods for the limitation of the negative impact of COVID-19 was caused by the existence in the framework of the European Union of several variants of the consolidated market economy. Thus, the design and implementation of Kurzarbeit-type measures were linked with the continental variant of social market economy, which exists in Germany, France, Austria and Belgium. The use of the flexicurity principles was strongly correlated with the northern (Scandinavian) type of social market economy.

Ohman (2021) defines the measures of Kurzarbeit type as one of the forms of dualising liberalisation and the measures adopted by some of the Scandinavian countries and the Netherlands as embedded flexibilisation. In the case of the other two variants of the social market economy, which have a lower level of GDP per capita compared to the EU average, namely, the Mediterranean type and the Central and Eastern European type, the measures implemented in the pandemic context were mainly correlated to the creation of the legislative framework to allow for the existence and implementation of short-term working or wage-subsidy schemes. This development has been stimulated by open support from the European Commission and from the European Parliament for the respective scheme implementation.

However, putting into practice the two main types of measures mentioned above had a quite high cost for the public authorities, especially in the context of the aggravation of the budget deficit. It has been estimated that between March and September 2020, the implementation of short-time working schemes and other job retention schemes generated expenditures of around 100 billion euros across the European Union (European Commission, 2021). As a result, in the context of easing measures to block economic activity, there is a need to make changes in the time length and way of implementation of job retention schemes. We have to keep in mind that these schemes have a positive economic and social impact only in the short run. Excessive recourse to job retention schemes has potential negative effects, resulting in blocking the reallocation of labour supply to activities with higher labour productivity or in reducing incentives for entrepreneurs to improve the company's financial situation and ensure the long-term viability of jobs.

For these reasons, it is important to analyse both the short-term prospects of the activities of companies receiving aid from public authorities and the possible medium- and long-term developments. Public authorities and entrepreneurs have to be convinced of the prominence of ensuring the jobs viability in the medium and long run. Under these conditions, in France, Greece, the Netherlands and the UK, from June to July 2020, a series of changes have been made to the implementation of job retention schemes (OECD, 2020b). Thus, the coverage by public authorities of wages paid to workers with short-term working schemes has been reduced. At the same time, it was stipulated that companies in which job retention schemes were implemented were not allowed to distribute dividends and/or award prizes and bonuses. In some cases, the short-time working schemes might be maintained, from the employee's point of view, but the employer's contribution to the insurance fund was increased.

Another direction of action was the introduction of incentives for active job-seeking behaviour by persons covered by job retention schemes, by:

(a) Imposing the condition of participation in professional training courses for the receipt of the income supplement, which results from the application of the job retention schemes
(b) Reduction of the difference between the income resulting from the implementation of the job retention schemes and the unemployment benefits
(c) Providing incentives for the transfer of workers from implicitly or explicitly subsidised jobs to unsubsidised (viable) jobs
(d) Strengthening the authority and effectiveness of the Labour Inspection activity

In the case of the European Union, the design and implementation of the measures aimed to diminish the impact of the above-mentioned pandemics imposed significant changes in the way of operating various institutions and mechanisms of the above-mentioned organisation. The pandemic context gave impulse for important innovations in the institutional framework. Dellhomme & Harvey (2023) noted that the crisis situations caused by the COVID-19 led to the initiation of important legal changes concerning the health protection of the entire population, the internal market definition and operation, consumer protection and the redistributive powers of the European Commission.

During 2020, the European Commission has used its past experiences related to the Great Recession from the late 2000s and the available financial resources from the 2014 to 2020 programming period. Drella et al. (2021) showed that during 2020, the main instruments were the flexibility of the EU Funds for the above-mentioned programming period and the European Stability Mechanism. Also, new instruments were created, such as SURE (temporary instrument for support to mitigate unemployment risks in emergency), established on 2 April 2020. Andor (2020) showed that SURE represented an institutional innovation, because the new instrument, inspired by the good practices of the European Commission during the previous economic recessions, also brought new methods. Therefore, the above-mentioned instrument was projected to be financed from loans obtained under favourable conditions. Previously, in a recessionist situation, the instruments used by the European Commission to reduce the negative impact of the higher rate of unemployment represented grants to the member states. The assessments made by the European Court of Auditors (2022) revealed that in August 2022, the value of the loans approved in the framework of this instrument was 93.3 billion euros for 19 member states. The auditors estimated that these loans prevented about 1.5 million persons from becoming unemployed over the course of 2020.

In the context of a new programming period which started in 2021, the European Commission designed new instruments dedicated to ensuring the relaunch of economic activity and improving the resistance to the various external shocks of the member states' economies. One of the most important new instruments was the Recovery and Resilience Facility. Also, it is worth mentioning that the European Union Budget destined to resolve structural problems concerning the 2021–2027 period increased (Drella et al., 2021).

In 2021, the intensity of measures meant to limit economic activity to reduce the morbidity and mortality produced by the pandemic situation decreased. This orientation was determined by the imperative to avoid maintaining a state of deep economic recession. Labour market policies have been marked by a remarkable diversity. The European Commission (2021) points out that each member state implemented measures to create new jobs for vulnerable social groups. The minimum wage increased in most of the member states, except Greece, Estonia and Belgium. In parallel, some emergency support measures were withdrawn in the Czech Republic, Hungary, Poland and the Baltic countries until August 2021, in the Netherlands and Sweden in September 2021 and in Cyprus in October 2021.

In the near future, the implementation of the National Recovery and Resilience Plans will significantly influence the policies aimed to reduce the negative impact of the COVID-19 pandemic on the labour market operation. The extended use of components of active labour market policies, such as (a) lifelong learning and professional retraining of the unemployed, (b) facilitating access to digital education, (c) improving the functioning of public employment services, (d) supporting the development of entrepreneurship and the creation of new small and medium enterprises, (e) reforming vocational and dual education, (f) integration into the labour market of vulnerable groups and (g) expanding and strengthening social dialogue, will be stimulated.

## Particularities of the Measures Adopted by Romania to Reduce the COVID-19 Pandemic Impact on the Labour Market Operation

In Romania, the measures adopted by the public authorities to reduce the negative consequences of the COVID-19 pandemic on the labour market operation had certain peculiarities determined by the pandemic waves (Pavelescu, 2020), the national tradition regarding social protection and activation of labour supply, but also by the accumulated experience at national and European level in the 2020–2021 period. It needs to be mentioned that the government instituted a state of emergency between 16 March and 15 May 2020, and a state of alert between 16 May 2020 and 8 March 2022.

Under these conditions, by Emergency Government Ordinance (EGO) no. 30/21 March 2020, several measures were implemented to reduce the COVID-19 pandemic shock. Social assistance measures included the electronic transmission of social assistance and the introduction of technical unemployment for persons employed in blocked economic and social activities. Paid parental leave has been granted to parents of children under the age of 12 whose schools or kindergartens have been closed. The allowances granted represented 75% of the previous gross salary, but not more than 75% of the average salary per economy. The application period was about 2 months, respectively March 21–May 31, 2020. Gentilini et al. (2022) show that 1,175,462 persons benefited from the respective measures, according to official estimations.

The measures for activating the labour market consisted of facilitating the development of online professional training activities, recognised by the Ministry of Labour and Social Protection. To recognise those activities, it was necessary to demonstrate that the participants had the digital infrastructure to access online courses.[10] Teleworking in public institutions has been allowed. Extended use of this form of employment in private enterprises has been encouraged.

EGO no. 70/15 May 2020 extended the provisions regarding the social protection measures adopted previously in the new context of the state of alert. The provisions

[10]The social protection measures adopted by EGO no. 30/2020 were not the only interventions of the Romanian public authorities to decrease the COVID-19 pandemic negative consequences. Thus, OECD (2020a) notes that on 18 March 2020, the government announced an economic stimulus package that represented a budgetary effort of about 2% of GDP. Romania's National Bank has reduced interest rates and relaxed other components of monetary and credit policy. State guarantees have been extended and access to subsidised interest loans has been allowed for micro- and small enterprises.

of EGO no. 30/2020 regarding the professional training courses were extended for a period of another 30 days.

EGO no. 92/28 May 2020 introduced new provisions regarding the protection of jobs and employees' incomes. The unemployment benefit budget paid part of the salary costs for people whose employment contracts were suspended due to the COVID-19 pandemic. Entrepreneurs were also given some facilities to boost the employment of older people and young people during 2020.

EGO no. 132/7 August 2020 allowed the implementation of Kurzarbeit-type methods in labour market disequilibria alleviation. Thus, employers had the right to reduce their working time by up to 50% due to the decrease in demand for the products and services offered, due to the COVID-19 pandemic. The public authorities covered 75% of the decrease in the employees' salary caused by the working time reduction. At the same time, the daily workers were considered. Compensation was granted representing 35% of the daily earnings for a period of 3 months, but only until the end of 2020.

EGO no. 211/4 December 2020 amended some provisions of EGO no. 132/2020, by taking into account the evolution of the health status of the population, as well as the labour market policies within the European Union. Working time could be reduced by up to 80%, provided that the managers inform the trade unions or employees' representatives at least 5 days before the actual application. Provisions of the respective normative act applied until 30 June 2021.

EGO no. 220/30 December 2020 extended until 30 June 2021, the provisions of EGO 132/2020 regarding daily workers, and until 30 September 2021, the provisions of EGO 92/2020 regarding the employment of the elderly and young people.

Law no. 58/2021 for the approval of EGO no. 211/2020 and the amendment of EGO no. 132/2020 included new provisions on the implementation of Kurzarbeit methods. Thus, in companies where the method was implemented, collective lay-offs and the granting of bonuses and other additional earnings to managers were prohibited. It was also stipulated that the application period was both in the context of the state of alert and during the next 3 months after the lifting of that status.

EGO no. 111/2 October 2021 established that, during the last quarter of 2021, workers whose employment contracts have been temporarily suspended by the employer are entitled to an allowance representing 75% of the monthly salary of those persons, but not more than 75% of the national average salary.

The implementation of the above-mentioned changes of the labour legislation was made in the context of the use of the opportunities created by the instruments of intervention provided by the European Union. The European Court of Auditors Report (2023) mentioned that Romania had the right to receive loans of about 3 billion euros within the SURE instrument, but its public authorities did not demand the whole projected sum. The above-mentioned report mentioned that about 50% of the SURE loans were allocated for health-related measures. The auditors also remarked that, in the case of Romania, the use of SURE determined important savings of interest in expenditures concerning the measures dedicated to job protection during the COVID-19 pandemic.

During 2022 and the first part of 2023, we can speak about a stability of the labour legislation in the context of discussions about new laws concerning the pensions for older persons and the wages in the public sector as a part of the implementation of the provisions of the National Plan for Relaunch and Resilience.

## Conclusions and Lessons Learned on the Design and Implementation of Labour Market Policies Under Pandemic Conditions

The COVID-19 pandemic had asymmetric results on the human resources use, depending on the structure of the economy, as well as the characteristics of the institutional framework of the labour market in different national economies. Thus, the emergence of the pandemic recession required the intervention of public authorities, both to stop or limit the spread of SARS-COV-2 virus and to maintain the level of activities related to the functioning of social services, vital for the existence of a modern state.

The important role that information and communication technologies play in the context of a pandemic has also been highlighted. States with a high level of development and implementation of information and communication technologies have proven to be more resilient in the context of the worsening of the epidemiological situation.

In the first part of 2020, the vast majority of countries in the world adopted measures to block economic activity to limit the spread of the pandemic and, thus, the alarming increase in morbidity and mortality. The experience gained during that period shows that the public authorities' intervention to overcome the negative consequences of a pandemic shock is, above all, necessary. Thus, the importance of the functionality of essential social services, such as health care, education, administration and national defence, was highlighted.

The extent and effectiveness of public authorities' interventions to overcome the pandemic shock depended, to a large extent, on the dynamics of the economy, in the short term, but also on the employment model, the characteristics of the internal and external budgetary balance and the opportunities for international economic and health cooperation. There was a certain correlation between the level of development of the economy and the extent of the support provided to people who were affected by the reduction in labour demand.

Starting in the second half of 2020, we can notice not only pandemic waves but also waves of measures to relaunch and increase the resilience to shocks in the economies of different states. In the design and implementation of these measures, the level of economic development played an important role, as well as the national traditions regarding the mechanisms for mitigating the effects of crises on the functioning of the labour market and ensuring the premises for relaunching post-crisis growth. Within the European Union, the initial member states with a consolidated market economy have allocated impressive amounts for social protection from the social security budget. Public authorities have also designed and implemented labour market activation measures inspired by experiences of previous recessions and the particularities of the social model of the respective countries (Păuna et al. 2007).

In the new member states, measures to reduce the impact of the COVID-19 pandemic on the labour market operation have taken over some of the experiences of the older member states. For these reasons, labour legislation has been substantially amended so that public authorities can implement mitigation measures regarding the reduction of the number of jobs. Special attention was paid to ensuring the conditions for the implementation of Kurzarbeit-type schemes and the extension of telework. In the short run, those measures have mitigated the negative social effects of the economic downturn but have created the premise for strong medium-term inflationary pressures.

In the case of Romania, the extent of the intervention of the public authorities for social protection was lower compared to the developed countries of the European Union in terms of the share in the gross domestic product of the expenditures made. The number of measures and programmes implemented was lower compared to both the new and old member states. The adoption of the necessary legislation for the implementation of Kurzarbeit, the promotion of teleworking and the expansion of digitalisation in public administration were based, to a large extent, on the experiences of developed countries. We can thus speak of a demonstration effect in the case of labour market policies and, implicitly, of a certain homogenisation of that policy within the European Union.

## References

Aiyar, S., & Dao, M. C. (2021). *The effectiveness of job-retention schemes: COVID-19 evidence from the German States* (IMF Working Paper, 21/242, October 2021).

Andor, L. (2020). SURE-EU capacity for stabilizing employment and income during pandemics. *Intereconomics, 55*(3).

Baldwin, R., & Weder di Mauro, B. (Eds.). (2020a). *Economics in time of COVID- 19*. A VOX Eu.org, CEPR Press.

Baldwin, R., & Weder di Mauro, B. (Eds.). (2020b). *Mitigating the COVID economic crisis. Act fast and do whatever it takes*. A VOX Eu.org, CEPR Press.

Beland, L.-Ph., Brodeur, A., & Wright T. (2020). *The short-term economic consequences of COVID-19: Exposure to disease, remote work and government response* (IZA Discussion Paper no. 13159)

Comisia Europeană. (2020a). *Comunicare referitoare la Orientări privind exercitarea liberei circulației a lucrătorilor pe perioada epidemiei de COVID-19*, Jurnalul Oficial al Uniunii Europene, 30 martie 2020.

Comisia Europeană. (2020b). *Comunicare referitoare la Orientări privind lucrătorii sezonieri din UE în contextul pandemiei de COVID-19*, Jurnalul Oficial al Uniunii Europene, 16 iulie 2020.

Conte, A., Lecca, P., Saakas, S., & Salloti, S. (2020). *The territorial economic impact of COVID-19 in the EU. A rhomolo analysis*. European Commission, Territorial development insights series.

Delhomme, V., & Harvey, T. (2023). *The European Union's response to the COVID-19 crisis and (the legitimacy of) the Union's legal order.* Yearbook of European Law (pp. 1–35).

Dingel, J., & Neiman, B. (2020). *How many jobs can be made at home.* COVID Economics, Vetted and real time papers, Issue 1, CEPR Press.

Drella, K., Malkowska, A., Bera, A., & Tokarz-Kocik, A. (2021). Instruments for managing the EU labour market in the face of the COVID-19 crisis. *European Research Studies Journal, XXIV*(1).

European Commission. (2021). *Proposal for a Joint Employment Report 2022.* From Commission to Council, Brussels 2021.

European Court of Auditors. (2022). *Special Report. SURE (Support to mitigate the Unemployment Risks in an Emergency) financing contributed to preserving jobs during the COVID - 19 crisis, but its full impact is not known.* Luxembourg.

Fana, M., Tolan, S., Torrejón, S., Urzi Brancati, C., & Fernández-Macías, E. (2020). *The COVID confinement measures and EU labour markets.* EUR 30190 EN. Publications Office of the European Union, Luxembourg. ISBN 978-92-79-18812-4.

Gentilini, U., et al. (2020a). *Social protection and job responses to COVID -19. A real-time review of countries measures.* A living paper version 11 (12-th June 2020), World Bank Document.

Gentilini, U., et al. (2020b). *Social protection and job responses to COVID -19. A real-time review of countries measures.* A living paper version 14 (11-th December 2020), World Bank Document.

Gentilini, U., et al. (2022). *Social protection and job responses to COVID - 19. A real-time review of countries measures.* A living paper version 16 (2-nd February 2022), World Bank Document.

Gourinchas, P.-O. (2020). Flattening the pandemic and recession curves. In R. Baldwin & B. Weder di Mauro (Ed.) 2020a.

Greve, B., Blomqvist, P., Hvinsen, B., & Gerven, M. (2020). Nordic welfare states—still standing or changed by the COVID-19 crisis? *Social Policy Administration* Special Issue, November 2020, Wiley.

Griswold, A. (2020). *Europe is turning to an age-old German work scheme to protect jobs from COVID-19.* Quartz, 30 April 2020.

Jordas, O., Singh, S. R., & Taylor, A. M. (2020). Long-run consequences of the pandemics. *COVID Economics, Vetted and real time papers, Issue 1.* CEPR Press.

Muller, K. (2020). *EU support for national short-time work schemes.* European Parliamentary Research Service.

Ohman, L. (2021). *Liberalization in time of crisis? A comparative study of labour market policy responses to COVID-19 pandemic.* Master Thesis, Uppsala Universitat, Department of Gouverment Political Science.

Pavelescu, F. M. (coord.)& Platon, V. (2002). Costuri și beneficii ale restructurării modelului de funcționare a pieței forței de muncă. *Colecția "Biblioteca Economică", Seria Probleme Economice, Vol. 15-16/2002.* CIDE.

Pavelescu, F. M. (2020)- Challenges of COVID - 19 pandemics on employment model. Implications for Romania. *Romanian Journal of Economics, 51*(2).

Păuna, C. B. (coord.), Albu, L. L., Vasile, V., Stănescu, M., & Pavelescu, F. M. (2007). *Modelul Social European. Implicații pentru România, Studiul de strategie și Politici nr.4.* Institutul European din România.

Robalino, D. (2020). *The COVID - 19 conundrum in the developing world. Protecting lives or protecting jobs?* IZA Disscution Paper no. 13136, April 2020

OECD – *COVID crisis responses in South East European economies*, OECD, 15th April 2020a

OECD-*Job retention schemes during COVID - 19 lockdown and beyond,* oecd.org/coronavirus, OECD, 12 August 2020b

xxx – EUROSTAT database Statistics | Eurostat (europa.eu)

xxx - *ILO Monitor: COVID -19 and the world of work. Second edition. Updated estimations and analysis,* ILO, 7 April 2020a

xxx - *ILO Monitor: COVID -19 and the world of work. Fifth edition. Updated estimations and analysis,* ILO, 30 June 2020b

# Part III
# Health Sector! New Identity, Old Challenges

# Chapter 11
# The Impact of COVID-19 on the Healthcare Labour Market in European Countries and Romania in Particular

**Simona Andreea Apostu**

**Abstract** The health crisis that started in 2020 affected the entire world in all areas. Things have changed, with work experiencing another level, with domains where it was not possible to work online or companies that could not resist the changes in the economy; thus, many unemployed persons were registered, with the unemployment rate increasing a lot. The healthcare market has also suffered, having to face the pandemic with fewer doctors and personnel. In addition to this deficit, the entire healthcare system has proved less efficient in case of a health crisis, with countries experiencing low resilience. In this context, the paper analyses employment and unemployment in general and in the healthcare system, both in the EU and in Romania in particular, until and after the health crisis began.

## Introduction

The coronavirus crisis triggered in 2020 has produced undesirable effects worldwide, from health to socio-economic ones. Several measures have been implemented in order to prevent the spread of this virus, affecting the living status of the population. A World Labor Organization study (2021) indicated that the current crisis has proved to be unprecedented.

Many activities have stopped; some have changed their schedule and work programme, affecting the labour market. The changes in the work programmes led to a loss of about 8.8% of the total working hours in 2020, meaning 1 year of working hours of 255 million full-time workers (World Labor Organization Report). This shortfall regarding the working hours is the result of those who lost their jobs and, implicitly, their incomes, both those who retired and those who, being employed, worked less or not at all.

S. A. Apostu (✉)
Bucharest University of Economic Studies; Institute of National Economy - Romanian Academy, Bucharest, Romania

 
V. Vasile, E. Bunduchi (eds.), *The Economic and Social Impact of the COVID-19 Pandemic*, Contributions to Economics,
https://doi.org/10.1007/978-3-031-47780-5_11

This situation does not show that the crisis will end soon, continuing to have an effect on employees and businesses, the most disadvantaged being those who had problems before the coronavirus crisis, which is exacerbating the existing social and economic inequalities.

In this context, the pressure on the health system is enormous, the coronavirus crisis highlighting the fragility of this system, which has proved unprepared to face such a crisis.

In the case of Romania, the precarious situation and working conditions in the health sector highlighted the low efficiency in facing a crisis, the main resilience factor of the health sector being the human resources, fully involved, making extraordinary efforts, but having reached a high level of exhaustion; thus, the fight against the crisis has become more and more difficult for them.

The health services have been significantly impacted by the pandemic, the effects still being immeasurable. Entities in the field were forced to quickly set up and reorganise their offer, to train the personnel, to motivate employees without affecting safe patient care, in the absence of appropriate treatments and under the conditions of a high risk of infection.

Thus, the main purpose of this paper is to highlight the impact of the coronavirus crisis on the workforce, respectively on the health workforce in Europe and in the case of Romania in particular. As a result, the paper is structured as follows: the first part is a synthesis of the most important studies in the field of labour considering the health crisis. The second part reflects the analysis of the labour force at European and Romanian level, followed by the analysis of the labour force in the health system in the context of the health crisis at European and Romanian level, and the last part represents the study's conclusions and implications.

## Literature Review

2020 is the year when COVID-19 spread around the globe and caused the worst pandemic of the last centuries, changing the entire world. The main priorities have been to protect health and save lives, disrupting daily life and normality (Kuhlmann et al., 2020).

The health crisis generated by COVID-19 was reflected through sharp falls regarding the demand on the labour market, imposing the closure of many sectors of the economy, such as large sections of retail, hospitality and air travel, which stopped as a response to travel restrictions (Costa Dias et al., 2020).

Due to the strong restrictive measures imposed by the COVID-19 pandemic, the effects on the global economy were substantial, including the increasing unemployment rate worldwide (Kawohl & Nordt, 2020). The management during the pandemic comprised specific initiatives, both planned and calculated (Rega & Fink, 2014), the health services being forced to use special substances and HR actions (Gómez-Ibáñez et al., 2020).

In order to reinforce staffing levels, medical students in their final year of studies were hired in hospitals (Hayter & Jackson, 2020), representing a necessary human resource in the crisis context (Yonge et al., 2010).

Due to the fact that planning early action measures regarding healthcare delivery was impossible (Corley et al., 2010), the focus was on developing specific skills, such as resilience, new training in nursing (Cleary et al., 2018), improving the competences in order to handle infection eruptions (Lam et al., 2018) and measures considering immersive assumption (Rega & Fink, 2014).

During the coronavirus pandemic, studies suggested that workers in healthcare were facing high levels of stress (Tsamakis et al., 2020), experienced anxiety and uncertainty, expressed worry towards crucial health conditions and highlighted concern regarding becoming infected (Collado-Boira et al., 2020).

Romania, in line with all the European countries, also faced COVID-19: the first case was reported on 26 February 2020; until March, outbreaks were reported in the South region, West region and North region of Romania (Crețan & Light, 2020).

Romanians working abroad reflect an important transnational workforce (Duval, 2003), maintaining significant relations with the country of origin (Marcu, 2011, 2014). In March and April 2020, the COVID-19 pandemic exploded; thus, Romanian migrants had to return home. In March, it was estimated that 250,000 Romanians returned to Romania (Anon, 2020), while in April, 1.3 million Romanians were travelling home to celebrate Easter (Gherasim, 2020). This phenomenon brought together many people, increasing the infection rate.

In Romania, the health crisis affected labour significantly, in the number of jobs, quality of work and impact on specific groups more vulnerable to poor labour market results. The measures undertaken in order to contract the economic action and social connections generated a decrease of labour demand, and an increase of the unemployment rate (Davidescu et al., 2021).

Regarding the Romanian health system, most services are provided by the public institutions of healthcare (Vladescu et al., 2016). Furthermore, Romania registers low health expenditure, the lowest level from all EU countries (World Health Organization). In this context, issues arouse when facing the epidemic and crisis, due to the absence of equipment, deficient medical facilities and insufficient supplies (Dascalu, 2019).

As Romania faced sustained migration in case of medical personnel, the Romanian healthcare system is confronted with insufficient staff (Apostu et al., 2020a, b). Thus, these issues increased the challenges brought by the health crisis, especially in the situation where there are people who manifest a reluctant attitude towards vaccination (Dimian et al., 2022).

## Data and Methodology

To characterise the workforce, we used bibliometric analysis and descriptive analysis, especially graphs. The analyses were performed using the programmes VOSviewer and Excel Microsoft, the data sources being the Eurostat database and TEMPO-Online (database of the Romanian National Institute of Statistics). The variables analysed are:

- Labour and employment, unemployment, health graduates, health workforce migration, medical technology and hospital beds—for European countries
- Doctors, employment rate, medical personnel, unemployment rate and number of hospital beds—for Romania

The variables used and their description are reflected in Table 11.1.

## Results

In order to identify the associations between the coronavirus crisis and the labour force, respectively, the labour force in the health system, we performed a bibliometric analysis. To analyse the most relevant studies, we used the scientific articles encountered on the academic platform Web of Science. According to the

**Table 11.1** Variables' description

| Variables | Description | Unit of measure |
|---|---|---|
| Employment and activity | Total employment (resident population—20–64 years | Percentage of total population |
| Unemployment | Percentage of unemployed population in the labour force—15–74 years | Percentage in the labour force |
| Health personnel employed in hospitals | Health personnel working in hospitals, except physicians | Full-time equivalent (FTE) |
| Nursing and caring professionals | Nursing and caring professionals working in hospitals | Number of persons |
| Health graduates | Graduates in the heath domain | Number of persons |
| Health workforce migration | Migrants' medical doctors | Number of persons |
| Medical technology | Computed tomography scanners | Number |
| | Magnetic resonance imaging units | Number |
| Hospital beds | All hospital beds available for the care of admitted patients | Number |
| Employment rate | The share of the employed population in the total labour resources | Percentage |
| Physicians | Number of doctors working in hospitals | Number |
| Medical personnel | Medical staff, except doctors (nurses and auxiliary medical staff) | Number |

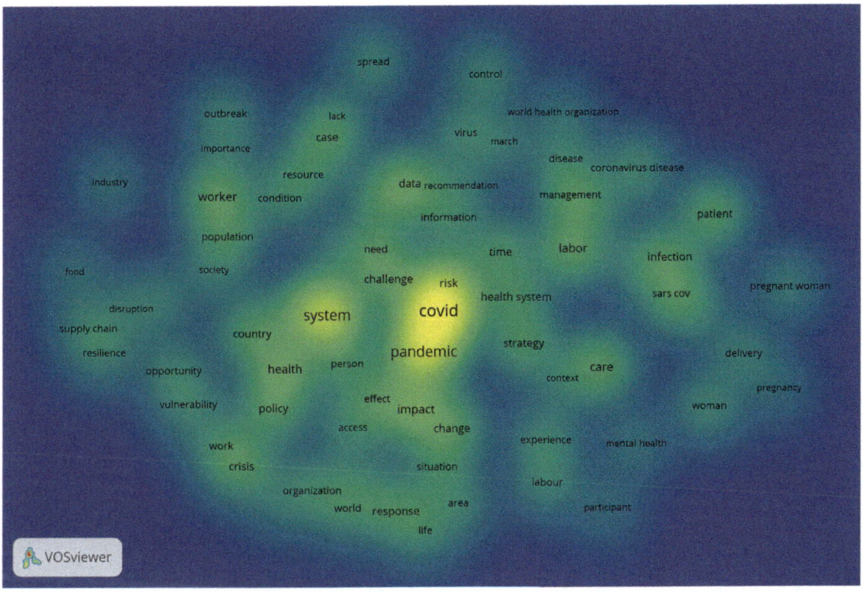


**Fig. 11.1** The most encountered words regarding labour, the health system and coronavirus (Source: WoS database, author's extraction based on selected words)

'labor health system covid' filter, we have analysed the content of 292 research articles. For the analysis, we considered a frequency of at least 20 times, and a correlation degree greater than 0.5, using VOS.

Based on content analysis, we identified the most common words on labour, health system and COVID. The results indicated that, apart from the keywords used, the most common words used are 'pandemic', 'risk', 'challenge', 'disruption', 'resilience', 'impact', 'society', 'mental health' and 'Worker' (Fig. 11.1).

The most common identified combinations are coronavirus disease-health system-strategy-infection-World Health Organization-labor-mental health-risk-care-control; need-recommendation-information-challenge-situation-access-change-experience-response; and covid-pandemic-impact-effect-crisis-vulnerability-resilience-outbreak-population-worker-health-opportunity-work (Fig. 11.2). So, there are three directions when we associate the labour force and the health system: one related to health, one related to needs and the other related to the labour market; therefore, the workforce is immediately and directly affected by the coronavirus crisis.

To highlight the most encountered combinations, the value of 0.5 was used as threshold. Considering the existent literature and theory, the following research hypotheses were created:

H1: The number of physicians increased with the onset of the health crisis.
H2: The unemployment rate has risen with the onset of the health crisis.
H3: Occupancy rate decreased with coronavirus pandemic.

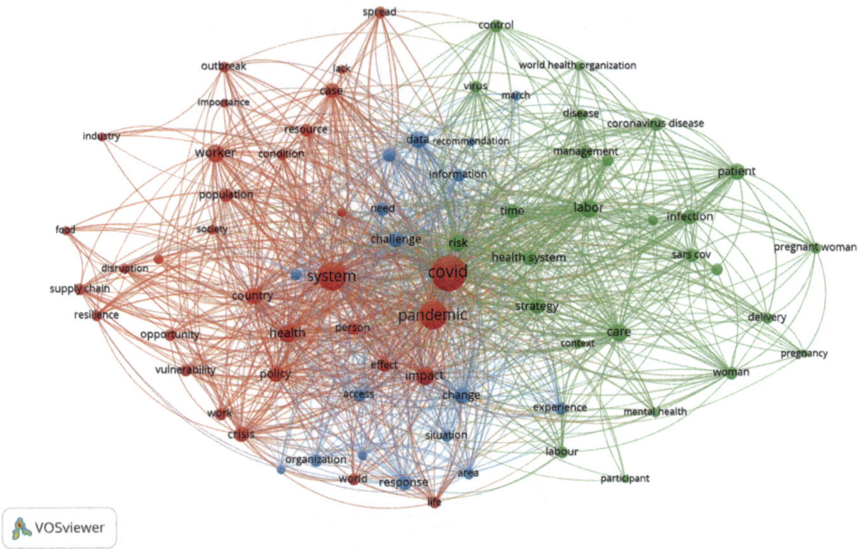


**Fig. 11.2** Word network regarding labour, the health system and coronavirus (Source: WoS database, author's extraction based on selected words)

## Labour and Employment in the COVID Pandemic Context: Europe and Romania

### *Labour and Employment in the Context of the COVID-19 Pandemic in Europe*

Although by 2019 the activity rate had increased in European countries, with the onset of the pandemic caused by coronavirus, it began to decline (Fig. 11.3), with slightly higher rates for men than for women. The territorial impact of the virus has been uneven, widening the existent inequalities between regions. Exceptions to the activity rate have been recorded for jobs that can be done from home, requiring less social interaction. All the other jobs registered a decrease regarding employment. This decline was not encountered in the case of frontline jobs, such as doctors, nurses and personal care and childcare workers.

Since the activity rate has decreased, the unemployment rate has risen in European countries to 8% (Fig. 11.4). Immediately after the pandemic broke out, measures were taken to prevent the spread of this virus, mainly through social distance. Thus, people resorted to working from home where it was possible, but this also increased the unemployment rate.

The unemployment rate rose sharply in the second quarter of 2020, and with the advent of the holidays, it then began to decline slightly, due to seasonal jobs. Thus, the unemployment rate was approximately constant between September and December 2020, but it increased from 6.5% to 7.5% over the year. The Eurostat

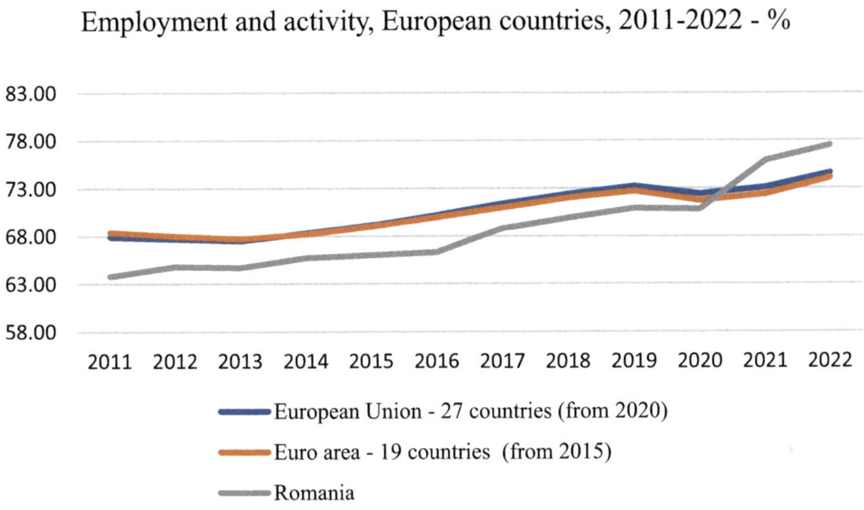


**Fig. 11.3** Employment and activity, EU 27, EU19 and Romania (Source: author's own projection)

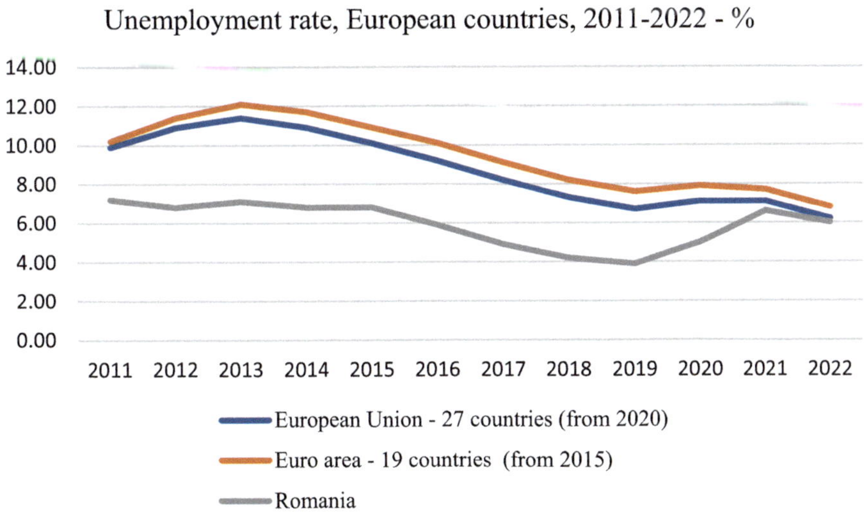


**Fig. 11.4** Unemployment rate, EU27, EU19 and Romania (Source: author's own projection)

estimations indicated 16 million unemployed in December 2020, 2 million more than those reported in the previous year. Approximately 3 million are aged under 25, and 2.6 million are encountered in the Euro area. The measures adopted to limit the spread of the virus impacted the number of people seen as unemployed. Some unemployed were not available for work, taking care of their children, this report reflecting the 'tip of the iceberg' (Etui, 2021).

## *Labour and Employment in the Context of the COVID-19 Pandemic in Romania*

In Romania, the EGO of March 2020 focused on impeding the spread of the COVID-19 virus led to dramatic results on the labour market. All regions in Romania, including Bucharest-Ilfov, were affected by these measures, the activity rate decreasing compared to previous years (Fig. 11.5), in Q2/2020 compared to Q2/2019 increasing by 3.5%, the number of hours worked in a week decreasing by 1.4%; 8.6% of employees had a job, but did not work, being in technical unemployment (European Foundation for the Improvement of Working and Living Conditions).

In 2020, the employment rate was 65.6%, down from 0.2% reported in 2019. In line with 2019, a higher employment rate for men was registered (74.4%, compared to 56.5% for women). Considering the areas of residence, a higher occupancy rate was registered in urban areas (67.1%, compared to 63.8% in rural areas).

The employment rate in case of young people was 24.6%, and that of the elderly was 48.5%. The highest employment for the elderly was encountered in case of graduates of higher education (88.8%). 68.1% of people with secondary education were employed, and 43.4% of people with low levels of education were engaged in work.

Compared to the previous year, employees are less than 81,000 people, registering the largest share (76.2%) in the total employed population. In 2020, the self-employed and unpaid family workers accounted for 22.6% of the employed population.

Skilled workers in agriculture, forestry and fishing accounted for 17.6% of the total employed population. Significant shares in the total employed population were

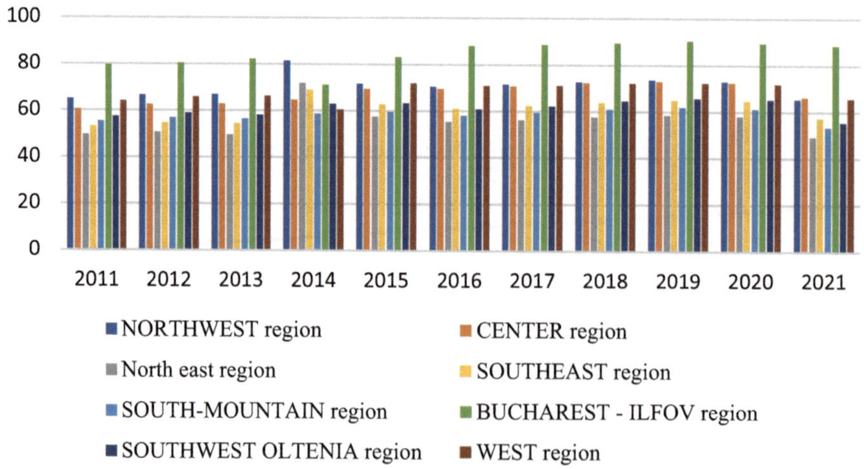


**Fig. 11.5** Employment rate, Romanian regions, 2011–2021 (Source: author's own projection)

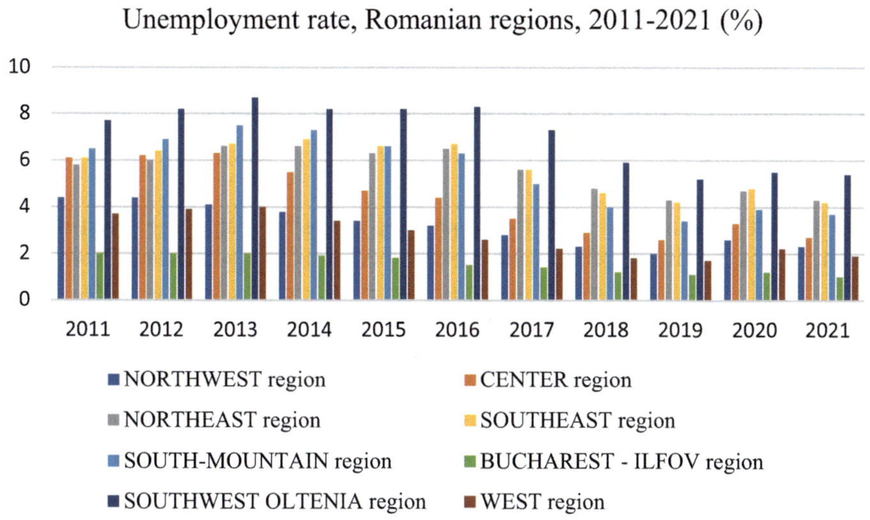


**Fig. 11.6** Unemployment rate, Romania, 2011–2021 (Source: author's own projection)

also held by skilled workers (15.8%), service workers (15.7%) and specialists in various fields of activity (15.5%).

Of the total employed, 20.5% worked in the sector of agriculture, 29.7% in industry or construction and 49.8% in services. 6774,000 people were employed in non-agricultural activities, significant shares of which were held by those who worked in the manufacturing industry (22.7%), trade (19.3%) and construction (10.9%).

One of the most serious consequences of this pandemic is the increase of the unemployment rate (Fig. 11.6), reaching thresholds of 5.0% in 2020, and registering higher values compared to 2019 (3.9% in 2019).

According to gender, the gap between the unemployment rate in case of women and the unemployment rate in case of men was 0.6% (5.3% for men compared to 4.7% for women), and the gap between area of residence was 1.4% (5.8% in rural areas compared to 4.4% in urban areas).

The unemployment rate registered the highest level (17.3%) in the case of young people. Unemployment affected graduates of primary and secondary education to a greater extent; the unemployment rate was 8.1% and 5.1%, respectively. The unemployment rate was only 2.2% for people with higher education.

The unemployment rate on long term was 1.5% and on short term was 29.9%. For young people, the rate of unemployment on long term was 8.2% and on short term was 47.2%.

## Healthcare Labour and Employment in the COVID-19 Pandemic Context: Europe and Romania

### *Healthcare Labour and Employment in the Context of the COVID-19 Pandemic in Europe*

The COVID-19 outbreak exerted great pressure on the National Health System and on the people serving therein. Healthcare workers were declared soldiers on the front lines. As physicians, nurses and other employees were ill, the burdens increased on the healthcare system, the staff in healthcare and the hospitals increasingly being recognised as vectors for spreading the virus.

The number of health personnel employed in hospitals increased in 2020 in European countries (Fig. 11.7), resorting in some situations to students in their final years and to an exceptional bonus given to healthcare workers, with a specific attention to those who have been employed in the departments most affected by the health crisis.

Nurses are crucial in ensuring care, both in hospitals and care institutions, and during the COVID-19 pandemic, their role was even more critical. The deficit of nurses was aggravated during the pandemic because many of them became infected. However, the number of nursing and caring professionals increased in 2020 in the European countries due to the large number of patients (Fig. 11.8).

Thousands of medical students in European countries are being fast-tracked into early service in an attempt to boost the health system. Thus, it is very important to register an important number of health graduates. However, probably due to the online system and student recruitment, in 2020 fewer students compared to the

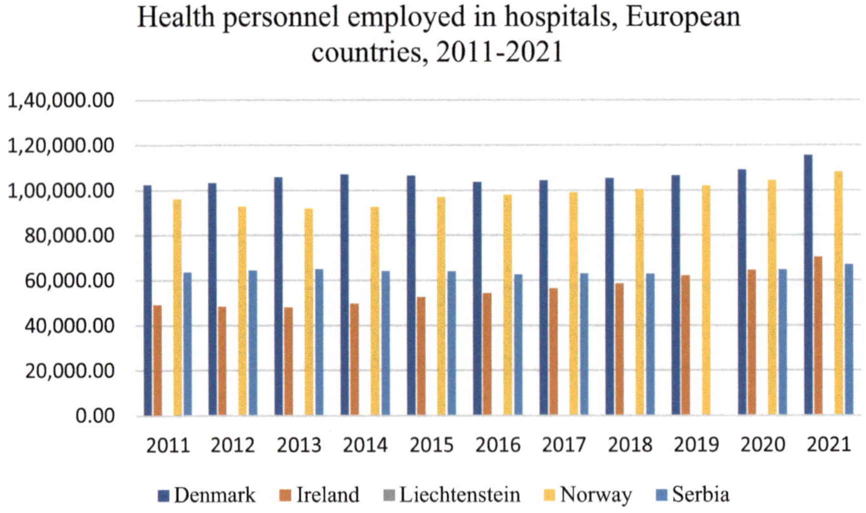


**Fig. 11.7** Health personnel, European countries, 2011–2021 (Source: author's own projection)

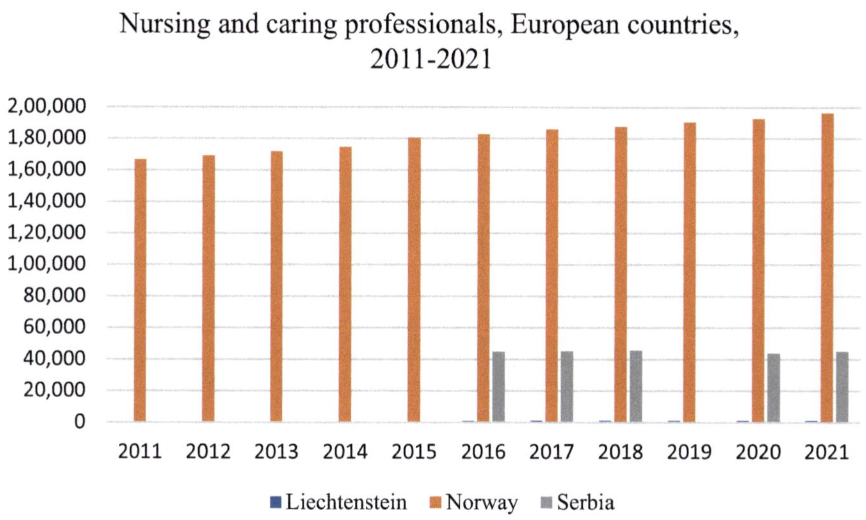


**Fig. 11.8** Nursing and caring professionals (Source: author's own projection)

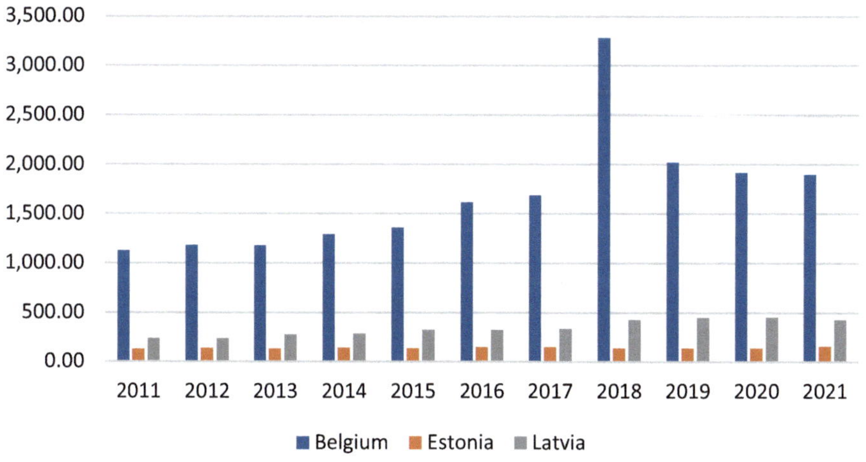


**Fig. 11.9** Health graduates, European countries, 2011–2021 (Source: author's own projection)

previous 2 years graduated in the health domain in Belgium, but in the other countries, the number remained the same (Fig. 11.9).

Another fact that leads to a shortage of medical staff is the physicians' migration. They migrate in order to find better working conditions and better wages (Apostu et al., 2020a, b). In 2020, in European countries, health workforce migration, especially the migration of physicians, has increased in some countries, but in other countries it has stagnated due to the imposed restrictions (Fig. 11.10). The increase of migrant physicians has taken place in countries where the damage caused

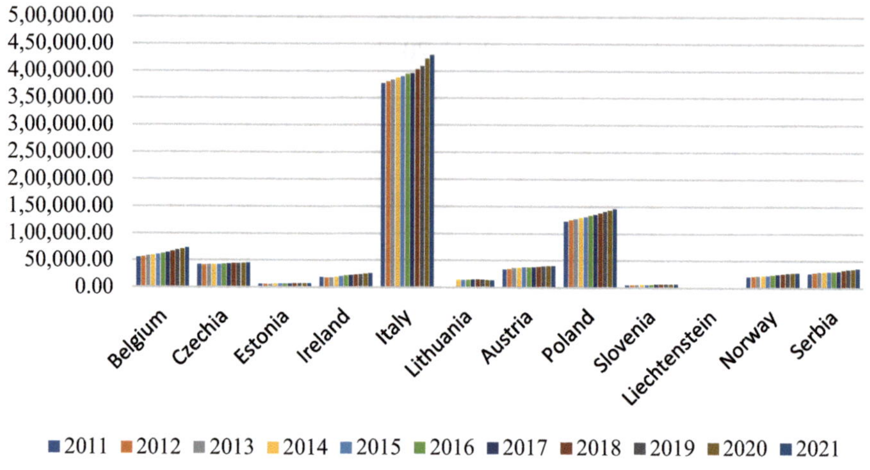


**Fig. 11.10** Medical migration, European countries, 2011–2021 (Source: author's own projection)

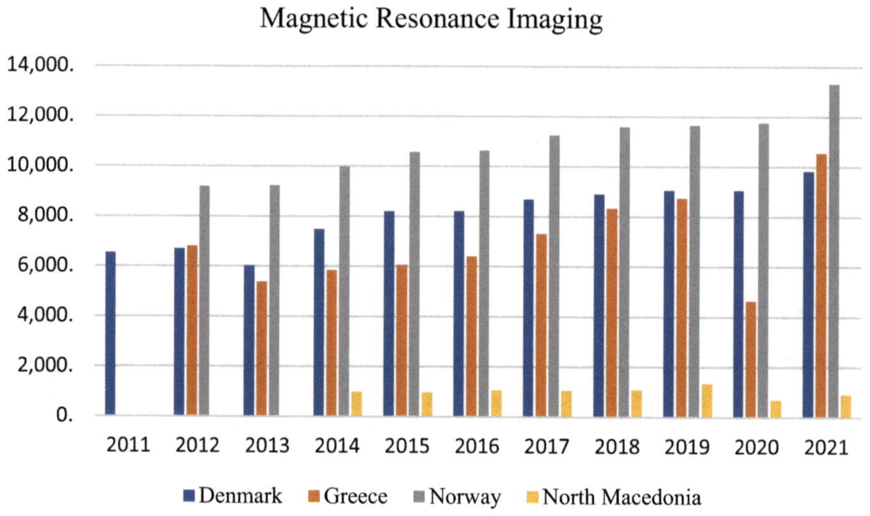


**Fig. 11.11** Magnetic resonance imaging units, European countries, 2011–2021 (Source: author's own projection)

by coronavirus has been significant, with very high numbers of registered illnesses and deaths.

In order to cope with the coronavirus crisis and to be resilient, a country, in addition to the medical staff, also needs medical equipment. Regarding medical technology, the number of magnetic resonance scanners increased in 2020 (Fig. 11.11), as did the number of computed tomography scanners (Fig. 11.12),

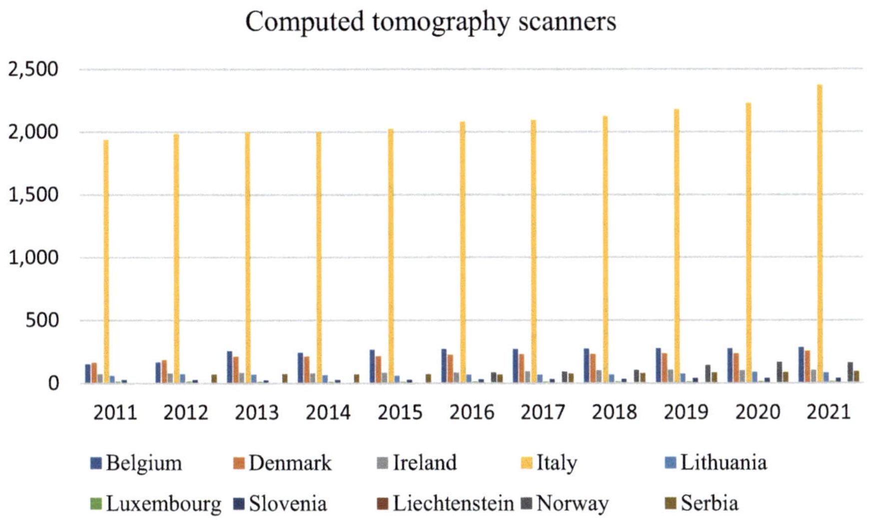


**Fig. 11.12** Computed tomography scanners, European countries, 2011–2021 (Source: author's own projection)

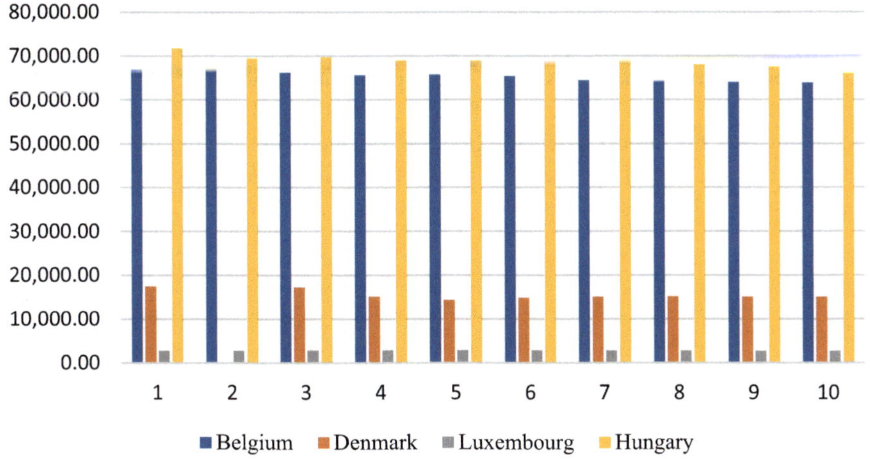


**Fig. 11.13** Hospital beds, European countries, 2011–2020 (Source: author's own projection)

reflecting awareness of the importance of healthcare efficiency and related investments.

The equipment of the sanitary system is also reflected by the number of hospital beds. The number of hospital beds in European countries has increased in 2020 (Fig. 11.13), due to an increased number of patients. The health crisis highlighted that the hospitals and the available hospital beds influence the health system's efficiency.

The healthcare resources' availability affects the health system efficiency, such as care accessibility, services cost and catastrophe preparedness, examining how healthcare resources vary in European countries.

## *Healthcare Labour and Employment in the Context of the COVID-19 Pandemic in Romania*

In this pandemic, the medical staff saw the most dramas, the most deaths. Sometimes it was even a personal drama, because almost 17,000 of them became infected with SARS-CoV-2. Physically and mentally, physicians and nurses began to give in. The staff was insufficient and was getting thinner from day to day, through resignations or medical leave. Romania had faced a shortage of physicians even before the pandemic, generated by low wages and precarious working conditions. A large part of Romanian physicians, generally young people and women, migrated to European countries, for a better life and decent working conditions (Apostu et al., 2020a, b).

In 2020, due to the restrictions, the migration phenomenon decreased, especially in the case of physicians, being stimulated by salary bonuses. To cope with this crisis, residents and dentists in the final years were also involved, the number of physicians increasing (Fig. 11.14), both in the state and private systems.

According to the transverse axis, most physicians practise in Bucharest-Ilfov, followed by the North-West and North-East regions (Fig. 11.15). These are also the regions where the largest medical schools are located, thus having the most graduates, and a large part of the graduates decide to remain in the city where they studied and eventually finished the residency (Apostu et al., 2020a, b).

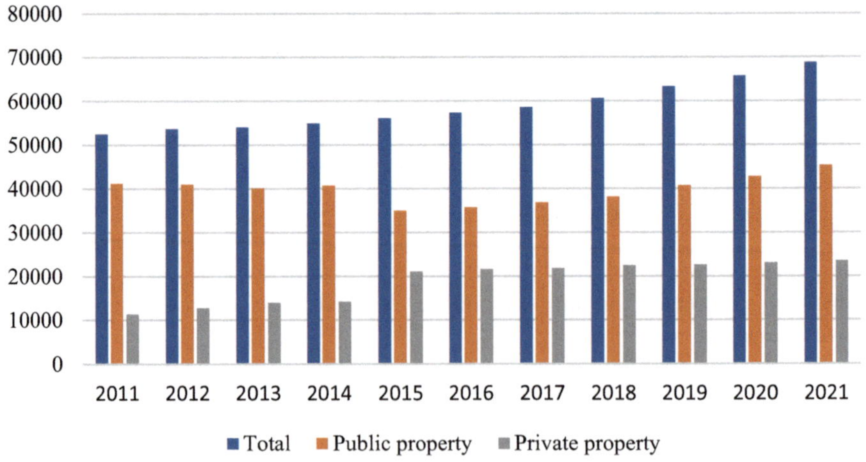


**Fig. 11.14** Physicians, Romania, 2011–2021 (Source: author's own projection)

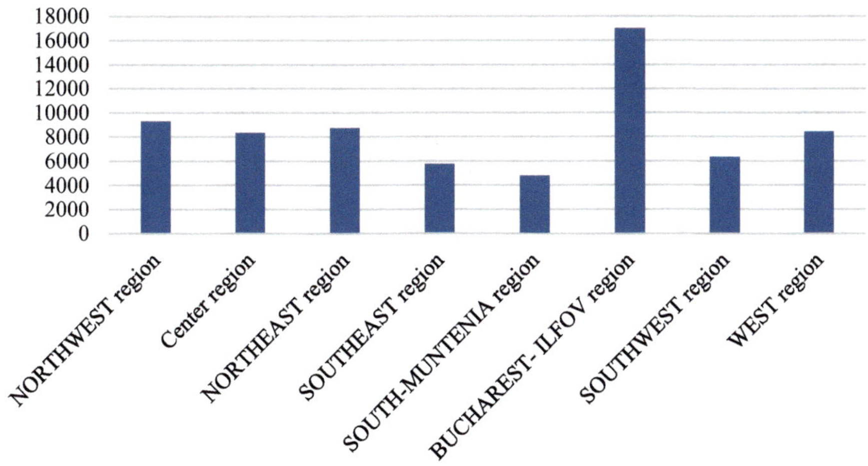


**Fig. 11.15** Physicians, Romanian regions, 2021 (Source: author's own projection)

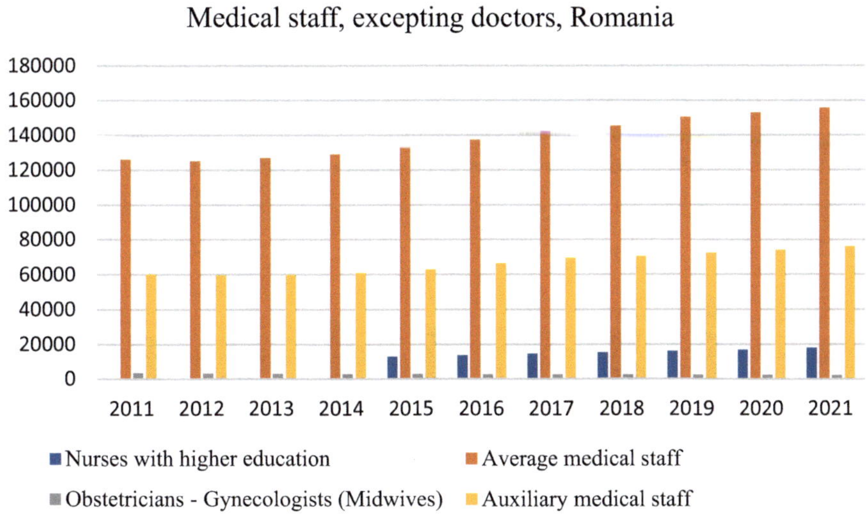


**Fig. 11.16** Medical staff, excepting physicians (Source: author's own projection)

Regarding the medical staff, other than physicians, their number did not register a significant increase in Romania (Fig. 11.16), although the number of patients increased.

From a regional point of view, as well as among physicians, the regions with the highest number of nurses are in the Bucharest-Ilfov region, the North-East and North-West regions (Fig. 11.17). With the outbreak of the pandemic, some hospitals have put out to tender a number of nurses for a period of time to make up for the shortcomings from the perspective of healthcare workers. Nurses are also affected by

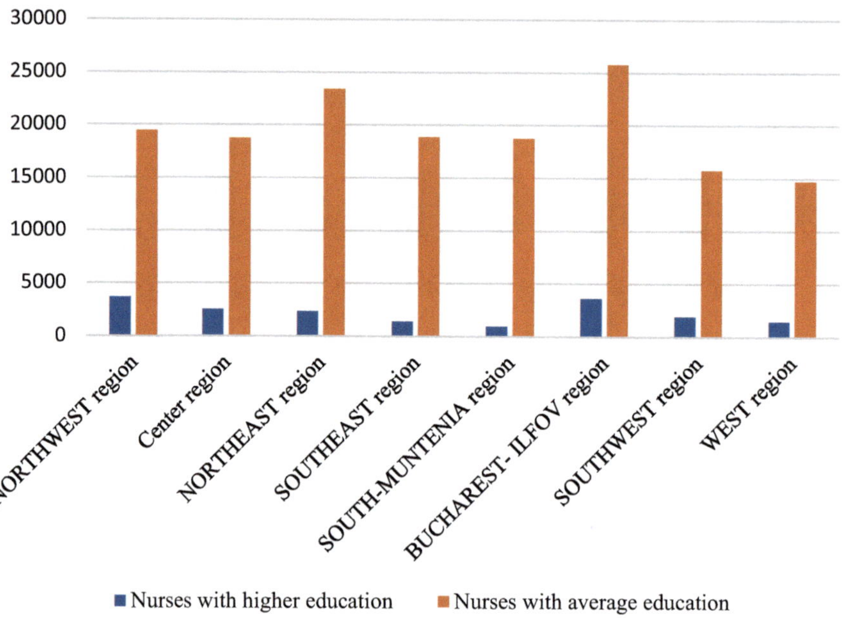


**Fig. 11.17** Nurses, Romanian regions, 2021 (Source: author own projection)

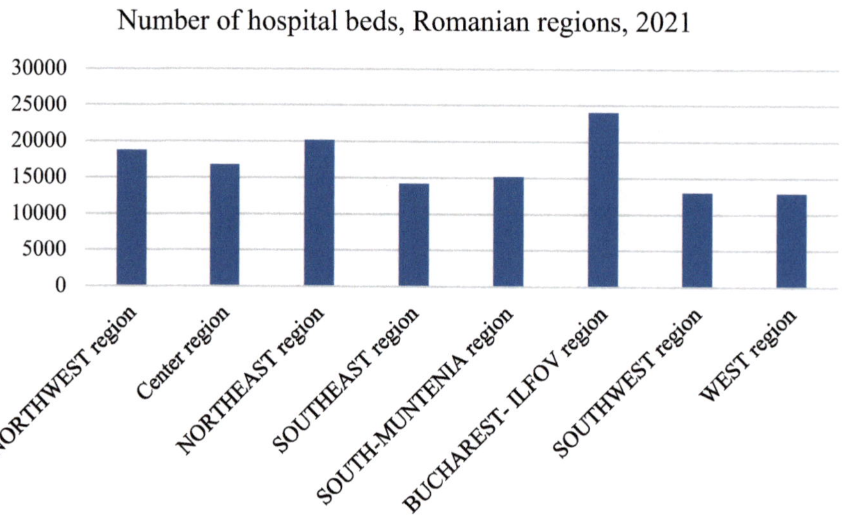


**Fig. 11.18** Number of beds, Romanian regions, 2021 (Source: author own projection)

the phenomenon of migration, many of them choosing to work in other European countries with much higher wages than in Romania.

The number of hospital beds is distributed in line with the number of physicians and nurses in large areas (Fig. 11.18). Health expenditures per capita in Romania are among the lowest, so it is expected that the efficiency of the health system will be low, with little resilience in the face of health crises.

However, the medical staff made great efforts and tried to manage the crisis to some extent, reaching the point of fatigue and exhaustion. The coronavirus pandemic has caught Romania unprepared even at the level of the minimum necessary for the protection of those who are expected to 'fight in the first line' with the coronavirus, the medical staff.

The lack of protective equipment and the disorganisation of some health units led to the infection of many medical staff and even the closure of entire hospitals, which were quarantined. The coronavirus crisis highlighted the fragility of the Romanian health system and its main problems, weak resilience and resistance to a health crisis.

## Conclusions

About 8.8% of all working hours were lost in 2020 due to pandemic cuts, the equivalent of 255 million hours of full-time work in a year. This percentage summary captures the various paths in which the pandemic has affected the global labour market.

Although a recovery occurred from the second half of 2021, it is likely to be fragile and uneven globally, with a growth projected to cover the gap created being more than likely insufficient.

The crisis is affecting employees and businesses, with the most disadvantaged being those who had problems before the crisis. In fact, the crisis has only exacerbated existing social and economic inequalities, nullifying the little progress made previously and making it considerably more difficult to implement measures for sustainable development by 2030. These intensified social and economic inequalities and the shortage of labour will lead to the creation of long-term 'scars' on economies and societies, unless precisely targeted efforts are made by policy makers to make the recovery as wide as possible and human-centred.

Two billion informal workers worldwide are left without access to social protection, which could, at least partially, have offset the loss of income. Things are not fairer on the gender either. During the pandemic, women were affected by 5% job losses, as opposed to men, among whom there was a loss of jobs in the proportion of 3.9%.

Young people have also been disproportionately affected by the crisis. The employment rate in their case fell by 2.5 times more than in the case of adults during the pandemic, thus increasing the share of young workers who became inactive.

The number of workers living in extreme or moderate poverty—that is, living on a daily income between $1.90 and $3.20 (in terms of purchasing power parity)—has increased by more than 100 million between 2019 and 2020, reaching a total of 700 million, cancelling 5 years of progress towards eradicating poverty.

The health system has been hit hardest by the coronavirus crisis. Insufficient physicians and poor working conditions highlighted the inefficiency of the system in facing the crisis. They worked to exhaustion or illness, being helped by students in their final years and stimulated by money.

The effects of the crisis could be seen in all domains, with people trying to adjust to the new normal. However, the fight against the virus continued for some time, even though we have the vaccine and a large part of the population has been vaccinated.

## References

Anon (2020). "Despescu: 250.000 De Români S-au Întors În Țară În Martie. 50.000 Au Venit Din Italia" [Despescu: 250,000 Romanians returned to the country in March, 50,000 came from Italy]. Digi24.ro, 1 April 2020.

Apostu, S. A., Roman, M., & Vasile, V. (2020a). Physicians' migration from Romania. Recent evidence from administrative data. *New Trends in Sustainable Business and Consumption*, 768.

Apostu, S. A., Vasile, V., & Chivu, R. (2020b). The analysis of push factors in case of physicians migration from Romania. *LUMEN Proceedings, 14*, 467–482.

Cleary, M., Visentin, D., West, S., Lopez, V., & Kornhaber, R. (2018). Promoting emotional intelligence and resilience in undergraduate nursing students: An integrative review. *Nurse Education Today, 68*, 112–120.

Collado-Boira, E. J., Ruiz-Palomino, E., Salas-Media, P., Folch-Ayora, A., Muriach, M., & Baliño, P. (2020). "The COVID-19 outbreak"—An empirical phenomenological study on perceptions and psychosocial considerations surrounding the immediate incorporation of final-year Spanish nursing and medical students into the health system. *Nurse Education Today, 92*, 104504.

Corley, A., Hammond, N. E., & Fraser, J. F. (2010). The experiences of health care workers employed in an Australian intensive care unit during the H1N1 influenza pandemic of 2009: A phenomenological study. *International Journal of Nursing Studies, 2010*, 577. https://doi.org/10.1016/j.ijnurstu.2009.11.015

Costa Dias, M., Joyce, R., Postel-Vinay, F., & Xu, X. (2020). The challenges for labour market policy during the COVID-19 pandemic*. *Fiscal Studies, 41*, 371–382. https://doi.org/10.1111/1475-5890.12233

Crețan, R., & Light, D. (2020). COVID-19 in Romania: Transnational labour, geopolitics, and the Roma 'outsiders'. *Eurasian Geography and Economics, 61*(4–5), 559–572. https://doi.org/10.1080/15387216.2020.1780929

Dascalu, S. (2019). Measles epidemics in Romania: Lessons for public health and future policy. *Frontiers in Public Health, 7*, 98. https://doi.org/10.3389/fpubh.2019.00098

Davidescu, A. A., Apostu, S. A., & Stoica, L. A. (2021). Socioeconomic effects of COVID-19 pandemic: Exploring uncertainty in the forecast of the Romanian unemployment rate for the period 2020–2023. *Sustainability* (2071–1050), 13(13)

Dimian, G., Vasilescu, D., Apostu, S., Aceleanu, M., & Jablonsky, J. (2022). Analysis of the Europeans' attitudes towards vaccination in the context of the Covid-19 pandemic - implications for public health policy. *Ekonomický Časopis, 10*(69), 997–1016.

Drahokoupil, J., & Müller, T. (2021). *Job retention schemes in Europe: A lifeline during the Covid-19 pandemic*. ETUI Research Paper-Working Paper.

Duval, D. T. (2003). When hosts become guests: Return visits and diasporic identities in a commonwealth eastern Caribbean community. *Current Issues in Tourism, 6*(4), 267–308.

Gherasim, O., Puiu, R. A., Bîrcă, A. C., Burdușel, A. C., & Grumezescu, A. M. (2020). An updated review on silver nanoparticles in biomedicine. *Nanomaterials, 10*(11), 2318.

Gómez-Ibáñez, R., Watson, C., Leyva-Moral, J. M., Aguayo-González, M., & Granel, N. (2020). Final-year nursing students called to work: Experiences of a rushed labour insertion during the COVID-19 pandemic. *Nurse Education in Practice, 49*(2020), 102920. ISSN: 1471-5953.

Hayter, M., & Jackson, D. (2020). Pre-registration undergraduate nurses and the COVID-19 pandemic: Students or workers?. *Journal of Clinical Nursing*. https://doi.org/10.1111/jocn.15317

Kawohl, W., & Nordt, C. (2020). COVID-19, unemployment, and suicide. *The Lancet Psychiatry, 7*(5), 389–390.

Kuhlmann, E., Dussault, G., & Wismar, M. (2020). Health labour markets and the 'human face' of the health workforce: Resilience beyond the COVID-19 pandemic. *European Journal of Public Health, 30*(Supplement_4), iv1–iv2. https://doi.org/10.1093/eurpub/ckaa122

Lam, S. K., Kwong, E. W., Hung, M. S., Pang, S. M., & Chiang, V. C. (2018). Nurses' preparedness for infectious disease outbreaks: A literature review and narrative synthesis of qualitative evidence. *Journal of Clinical Nursing, 27*(7–8), e1244–e1255.

Marcu, S. (2011). Romanian migration to the Community of Madrid (Spain): Patterns of mobility and return. *International Journal of Population Research, 2011*, 1–13. https://doi.org/10.1155/2011/258646

Marcu, S. (2014). Geography of belonging: Nostalgia attachment, transnational home and global mobility among Romanian immigrants in Spain. *Journal of Cultural Geography, 31*(3), 326–345.

Rega, P. P., & Fink, B. N. (2014). Immersive simulation education: A novel approach to pandemic preparedness and response. *Public Health Nursing, 31*(2), 167–174.

Tsamakis, K., Rizos, E., Manolis, A. J., Chaidou, S., Kympouropoulos, S., Spartalis, E., Triantafyllis, A. S. (2020). COVID-19 pandemic and its impact on mental health of healthcare professionals. *Experimental and Therapeutic Medicine, 19*(6), 3451–3453.

Vladescu, C., Scintee, S. G., Olsavszky, V., Hernandez-Quevedo, C., & Sagan, A. (2016). Romania: Health system review. *Health Systems in Transition, 18*, 1–170.

World Labor Organization Report | Covid-19 effect on the labor market: poor, increasingly poor).

Yonge, O., Rosychuk, R. J., Bailey, T. M., Lake, R., & Marrie, T. J. (2010). Willingness of university nursing students to volunteer during a pandemic. *Public Health Nursing, 27*(2), 174–180. https://doi.org/10.1111/j.1525-1446.2010.00839.x.

# Chapter 12
# Issues Regarding the Management of Hazardous Medical Waste During the COVID-19 Crisis in Romania

**Victor Platon, Simona Frone, Andreea Constantinescu, and Iuliana Pantelimon**

**Abstract** The SARS-CoV2 epidemic's course in Romania between 2020 and 2021 has exposed numerous flaws and difficulties with the country's healthcare system. These have negative effects; thus, it's critical that flaws are identified and fixed in order to build a defence against contagious diseases. This chapter provides a much-needed analysis of Romania's hazardous medical waste disposal process and makes an educated guess as to how the COVID-19 pandemic may affect the volume generated. The chapter also highlights the capacities for getting rid of dangerous medical waste.

The major goal of this chapter is to determine the amount of hazardous waste produced in Romania, the impact of the COVID-19 epidemic on the production of medical waste and the examination of safe disposal options utilising the current infrastructure. In order to achieve this, the authors developed data sets on the volumes of medical waste produced over time using the information that was available and examined the operational waste disposal facilities.

The forecasts developed in this research took into account that the data were collected in conditions of uncertainty. The severe data deficit and the availability of different data sets, strategies and reports employing computational tools that evolved over time must all be highlighted. As a result, the similarity of the data should be evaluated with caution. Future actions and initiatives to lessen and prevent the harmful effects of the COVID-19 outbreak may be supported by this research.

V. Platon · S. Frone · A. Constantinescu (✉)
Institute of National Economy - Romanian Academy, Bucharest, Romania

I. Pantelimon
Alexandru Trestioreanu Institute of Oncology, Bucharest, Romania



V. Vasile, E. Bunduchi (eds.), *The Economic and Social Impact of the COVID-19 Pandemic*, Contributions to Economics,
https://doi.org/10.1007/978-3-031-47780-5_12

## Introduction

Medical waste is a significant issue when it is not properly managed in the spirit of the EU waste acquis. If the medical waste ends up being thrown away together with household garbage and spilled into the sewerage system, the potential for transmitting contagious diseases is very high.

In Romania, several broad major categories are taken into account when managing medical waste (M.OF, 855/2012): hazardous waste (with infectious waste as subdivision) and non-hazardous medical waste. Hazardous waste comprises four sub-categories of waste (including infectious waste) defined in accordance with the second Annex of the Government Decision no. 856/2002, while non-hazardous waste refers to waste that has not come into contact with biological fluids or with patients diagnosed with contagious diseases. Infectious waste is a part of the hazardous waste category. This sub-category includes medical waste that has been in contact with microorganisms or toxins which can cause infectious diseases. This waste, which occurs during various medical procedures, comes into contact with contaminated human body fluids.

Hazardous medical waste disposal or mixing hazardous medical waste with everyday waste can cause the soil and groundwater to become polluted with harmful chemicals, viruses or bacteria, jeopardising public health and causing pathogens to spread even further. The necessary infrastructure for the secure elimination of this waste in the case of a highly dangerous epidemic like COVID-19 is crucial (Vaccari et al., 2018). If infectious waste from healthcare facilities is not dealt with appropriately, there is a risk of prolongation and recurrence of COVID-19 contaminations with all the related unfavourable effects (Bara, 2007). It should be acknowledged that prevention and proper management strategies are applicable to any dangerous medical waste and not strictly to waste from the COVID-19 patients.

Between May 2020 and December 2021, general estimates show that millions of medical items such as disposable masks and gloves, disposable gowns, shorts, overalls, goggles or visors for eye protection, extended testing, special protective suits for doctors as well as other personal protective equipment were distributed (Mihai, 2020). Accurate data on the quantity and volume of personal protective equipment are not available. All these protective devices become waste shortly after use, and as a result, extremely large amounts of medical waste are generated compared to the pre-pandemic period, requiring removal in a manner that prevents the spread of COVID-19 infection (Bojoi, 2020).

The primary goal of this research is to estimate the amount of hazardous waste issued in Romania as well as the influence of the COVID-19 epidemic and to analyse the possibility of it being disposed of safely, using the existing facilities (Platon et al., 2020). The forecasts elaborated in this paper took into account the fact that data were obtained in conditions of uncertainty. The acute data shortage as well as the existence of divergent data sets, strategies and reports using improved computational techniques must be emphasised. Consequently, it is important to analyse data consistency carefully. This study can support potential policies and initiatives to decrease and avoid the COVID-19 epidemic's negative impacts.

## Hospital Infrastructure in Romania

The hospital infrastructure in Romania has had an ascending trend in the last 12 years. The number of hospitals increased by 14.2%, from 458 in 2008 to 523 in 2021. It should be highlighted that the upward trend stopped in 2017, when many units were closed due to budget restraints.

Regarding the evolution of the number of hospital beds, Romania had a comparable evolution with the European trend: the number of beds increased slightly (on average by 1.6%/year) for the analysed period, both for total specialisations and for intensive care unit (ICU) departments. In 2021, 135,000 hospital beds were registered, of which 5762 are beds for the ICU (Table 12.1).

It can be stated that the Romanian healthcare system recorded a quantitative upward trend in the last 12 years, according to the data available. The numbers should be interpreted with caution, as patient care involves not only increasing the number of hospital beds.

## Medical Waste: Legislation and Institutions

### *Medical Waste in European Legislation*

International medical waste law has its origins in the international agreement known as the Basel Convention, signed in 1989. This was coordinated by the United Nations Environment Programme (UNEP, 2003, 2012). The Basel Convention also makes the first references to the transboundary transport of hazardous waste.

The basic international principles governing the field of environmental protection and, thus, the management of hazardous waste are:

- The 'polluter pays' principle, which implies the legal and financial responsibility of the person who produces the waste (the polluter). The producer of waste is responsible for the safe removal and final disposal of the waste generated.
- The 'precautionary' principle refers to the need to take precautions against the risks that may arise from improper management of medical waste.
- The principle of 'proximity' recommends that the final disposal of waste be carried out as close as possible to the source of production, in order to reduce the environmental and health risks associated with transport. The principle becomes applicable only when there are technical possibilities and the environment is not affected.

**Table 12.1** Number of hospital beds in Romania, 2010–2021 (no.)

| | 2010 | 2011 | 2012 | 2013 | 2014 | 2015 | 2016 | 2017 | 2018 | 2019 | 2020 | 2021 |
|---|---|---|---|---|---|---|---|---|---|---|---|---|
| Total hospital beds, of which: | 132,004 | 128,501 | 129,642 | 130,708 | 130,963 | 132,149 | 132,277 | 132,480 | 133,181 | 134,207 | 134,683 | 135,085 |
| Intensive care unit beds | 4754 | 4741 | 4872 | 4899 | 4966 | 5033 | 5025 | 5024 | 5111 | 5181 | 5722 | 5762 |
| Number of hospitals | 503 | 464 | 473 | 499 | 527 | 554 | 567 | 576 | 515 | 523 | 535 | 543 |

Source: our own processing of data from the Romanian Statistical Yearbook, INS, 2017–2022

The European legislative framework governing the transport, treatment, collection and disposal of waste is represented by four directives. The most important of these is the first, Directive 2008/98/EC on waste and repealing certain previous directives. This Directive regulates the activities of hazardous waste management, including medical waste, and covers all activities in the life cycle of waste, from generation, selective collection, storage at source, domestic and international transport, treatment, incineration and final disposal. Among the most important provisions are the following:

- Hazardous waste must be identified and collected separately from non-hazardous waste.
- Hazardous medical waste requires a special treatment route to neutralise substances potentially hazardous to human health and dangerous for the environment.
- Medical waste is stored only after it has been treated, so that it no longer poses a danger to the environment through contamination of the groundwater.

The text of the Directive states that the generation, collection, transportation, storage, and treatment of hazardous waste must all be done in a way that protects both the environment and public health. This includes taking the necessary steps to track and control hazardous waste from creation to destruction. It is the responsibility of European Union states to prevent the mixing of hazardous waste with other types of waste products, substances or materials.

## *National Legal Provisions for Medical Waste*

The European Directive has been transposed into the Romanian legal framework by the Law 211/2011 on waste, which regulates waste management activities. Each type of medical waste, whether dangerous or not, is to be disposed of in accordance with Article 2 of the law, either through sterilisation or incineration. After the sterilisation or incineration of waste, these methods' output needs to be kept in compliant landfills. Only household-type waste generated by medical units can finally be disposed of in landfills without being subjected to special treatment. If these rules are neglected in the case of hazardous medical waste and it ends up in landfills, there is a risk of biological contamination of landfills and, consequently, the danger of groundwater contamination (Curca et al., 2021). Drugs and disinfectants are harmful to the environment and cannot be disposed of together with household waste.

Hazardous medical waste must follow a clear route, in several mandatory steps: separate collection and packaging, safe transport and strict packaging, incineration or sterilisation (Fig. 12.1). Non-hazardous medical waste is collected in accordance with the regulations in force for this type of waste.

Sterilisation or incineration is recommended and used worldwide for the treatment of hazardous (including infectious) medical waste resulting from the

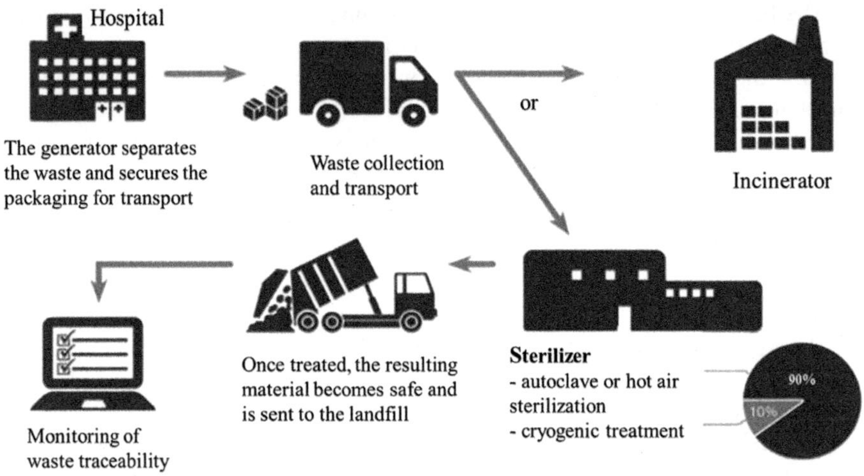


**Fig. 12.1** Disposal of hazardous medical waste (Source: Infomediu Europa, 2018)

day-to-day activities of medical facilities. Neutralisation by thermal sterilisation destroys microorganisms in vegetative form and bacterial spores by 99.9%. These neutralisation procedures are expensive, which makes the disposal of hazardous medical waste costly.

The first step Romania took for the implementation of the environmental *Community acquis*, which also includes the management of medical waste, was the legislative alignment with the norms and standards of the European Union. In this regard, the Ministry of Health has elaborated the technical regulation specific to this field, specifically MO no. 219/2002 for the approval of the Methodology for Data Collection for the National Database on Waste from Medical Activities. Applying this regulation correctly and efficiently in healthcare facilities reduces the risk of medical waste, especially hazardous waste, for the hospital staff, the general population and the environment.

It is essential to emphasise that the safe removal and ultimate disposal of the waste produced come within the purview of the waste producer. This can be accomplished either through in-house disposal facilities or through agreements with specialised operators.

Other important national legislation on the management of all types of waste is detailed in Annex 12.1.

## *The Strategy and the National Medical Waste Management Plan*

In 2016, a proposal for a draft of the National Strategy on the Management of Medical Waste was posted on the website of the Ministry of Health. The document stated that both the national plan and strategy for managing medical waste were to be developed by the Ministry of Health and endorsed by the Ministry of Environment. Additionally, the National Plan for Management of Medical Wastes would be included in the National Waste Management Plan. It must be noted that the Government Decision containing the Strategy has not been officially approved or published in the Official Monitor so far (2023). However, it should be stated that the National Waste Management Plan, developed by the Ministry of Environment (published in 2017) and adopted by Decision no. 942/2017, included a chapter on medical waste management.

The stated purpose of the National Strategy was to protect human health and the environment by implementing a proper waste management system at the level of health units in the country. The strategy presented measures aimed at applying good practices in the field of medical waste management and was supposed to be implemented through the National Plan for the management of medical waste.

The monitoring indicators proposed in the Strategy are of a generic type, without specifying clear targets to be achieved, intermediate objectives, etc. Some indicators are formulated as a simple expectation and cannot be followed in practice due to the fact that reporting of these values is not mandatory.

The national strategy for medical waste management has not been approved yet, although it has been in public discussion since 2016. The activity in this field is regulated by orders of the MoH. The National Waste Management Plan was authorised in December 2017. It includes a chapter on medical waste that lists the types of waste considered hazardous and non-hazardous. Initially, the strategy and the plan for medical waste management should have been elaborated within 12 months from the entry into force of Order no. 1226/2012 (published on January 18, 2013), based on the medical waste management plans drawn up for each county and for Bucharest.

## Quantities of Medical Waste Generated in Romania

Medical waste refers to hazardous as well as non-hazardous waste resulting from the activity of sanitary units. Out of these, hazardous wastes that present a real risk to human health and the environment are considered to be waste generated during the activities of medical diagnosis, care, therapy and recovery, involving also waste from research, testing and distribution of medicine. An important fact to note is that, until 2013, only 10–25% of the total medical waste generated was considered hazardous waste, the rest being assimilated to non-hazardous waste. After 2013, with the change of methodology, the ratio hazardous/non-hazardous was inverted.

## *Data Source*

Medical facilities are in charge of carefully collecting medical waste, keeping it in temporary[1] storage for as little time as possible and transporting it, in accordance with the legal guidelines. The sanitary units also have the obligation to transport the waste resulting from the medical activities only to economic operators authorised for the transport and disposal of the medical waste, on the basis of a service contract. In the final disposal phase, hazardous waste is incinerated or thermally treated and non-hazardous waste is eliminated at the landfill. Nearly 70% of hospital units have hired the services of specialised businesses (Min. of Health, 2016) for the low-temperature decontamination treatment or burning of hazardous waste because the great majority of them lack adequate high-performance equipment for getting rid of hazardous waste.

After more than 10 years of application of the Norms and of the Data Collection Methodology, included in the Order of the Minister of Health (MoH) no. 219/2002, a new order was initiated to comply with the European Waste Catalog, respectively the monthly monitoring of the nine waste codes from group 18 01, as well as the provision of information by the health units on waste management, materialised in the Order of the Minister of Health no. 1226/2012. The implementation of this order was achieved by using layouts in Excel format, which contributed to the accuracy of the data and to easier processing. It should be mentioned that this order specifies that the National Institute of Public Health (NIPH) has the obligation to elaborate a National Strategy and Plan for the management of waste resulting from medical activity. Thus, in the period 2013–2014, the Draft Strategy and National Plan for managing medical waste were elaborated, but neither have been finalised or approved so far.

Statistical information regarding medical waste management are gathered by the county Public Health Directorates and centralised by the NIPH, which publicly presents the centralised data through Annual Activity Reports (Health and Environment Report) or in proposals for strategies or projects. The indicated quantities symbolise the yearly averages and are calculated as the arithmetical mean of all quarterly reports (this methodology was used from 2010 to 2012). Since 2013, reporting has been done by categorising the waste in accordance with the codes on the European Waste List. It is not clear whether the reports are based on the weightiness of the waste.

Through the National Centre for Monitoring Community Environment Risks, NIPH annually prepares the national synthesis 'Monitoring the management system of waste from medical activity' and updates the national database on medical waste.

[1]Temporary storage of infectious medical waste generated by medical units may not exceed a period of 48 h, unless the waste is stored in an enclosure with a cooling system that ensures a constant temperature of less than 4 °C. In this case, the storage period can be a maximum of 7 days.

## *Evolutions in the Period 2012–2021*

At the level of the sanitary units, the waste resulting from the medical activity is collected at the source and separated by categories (nine codes) according to the MoH Order no. 1226/2012 and GD no. 856/2002.

Figure 12.2 summarises the data extracted from the annual health and environment reports of the NIPH (2013, 2014, 2015, 2016, 2017, 2018, 2019, 2020, 2021) regarding the quantities of hazardous and non-hazardous medical waste generated in the period 2012–2021, in public and private medical units with beds.

According to the NIPH Report, at the level of public and private health units that reported data in 2021, the total amount of waste resulting from medical activity which was generated and reported was 25,216 tons/year. Compared to the previous year, there is an increase of about 38.4%. Of this quantity, 21,903 tons/year represent hazardous waste. Out of this, roughly 20,152 tons/year are infectious waste resulting from the medical activity of the 1287 public and private health units. The number of reporting health units increased by more than 60% in 2021 compared to 2020. Since 2013, infectious waste has represented a very high percentage of all hazardous waste (from 84% to 96%) (Fig. 12.2).

The amount of medical waste produced by hospitals with beds decreased significantly over the 2012–2014 period, as seen in Fig. 12.2. We notice a decline in the amount of non-hazardous garbage, from 24,806 tons in 2012 to roughly 1660 tons in 2020 (more than 10 times). There is a slight increase in 2021, to 3312 tons, due to COVID-19.

It can be noted that hazardous waste replaced non-hazardous waste. From a quantity of 8900 tons of hazardous waste in 2012, 21,903 tons was reported in 2021. Infectious waste follows closely the trend of hazardous waste. An increase has been recorded, from 7500 tons in 2012 to 20,152 tons in 2021.

It should be noted that throughout a 10-year period (2012–2021), the total amount of medical waste decreased from 33,732 tons to 25,216 tons (a decrease of 25.2%). An explanation for these developments is not provided by the health and environment reports. One possible explanation would be the change in the reporting methodology in 2013, but this alone cannot be responsible for such important changes in waste quantities.

Contrary to the fact that there are more hospitals, medical waste is on the decline. As shown in the first part of this research, an increase of 18.5% brought the number of hospitals in Romania from 458 in 2008 to 543 in 2021. Given the evolution of the number of hospitals, the amount of medical waste should have increased, not decreased by 25.2%. This decrease in the amount of waste may be explained by a lower occupancy rate in hospital beds.

Another important indicator, which is often used in international comparisons, is the amount of medical waste generated by a hospital bed. By estimating a bed occupancy rate of 70%, the values in Table 12.2 could be calculated. The phenomena illustrated above, namely, the increase in the number of hospital beds, lead to relatively low levels of non-hazardous waste (0.030–0.033 kg/bed/day) in

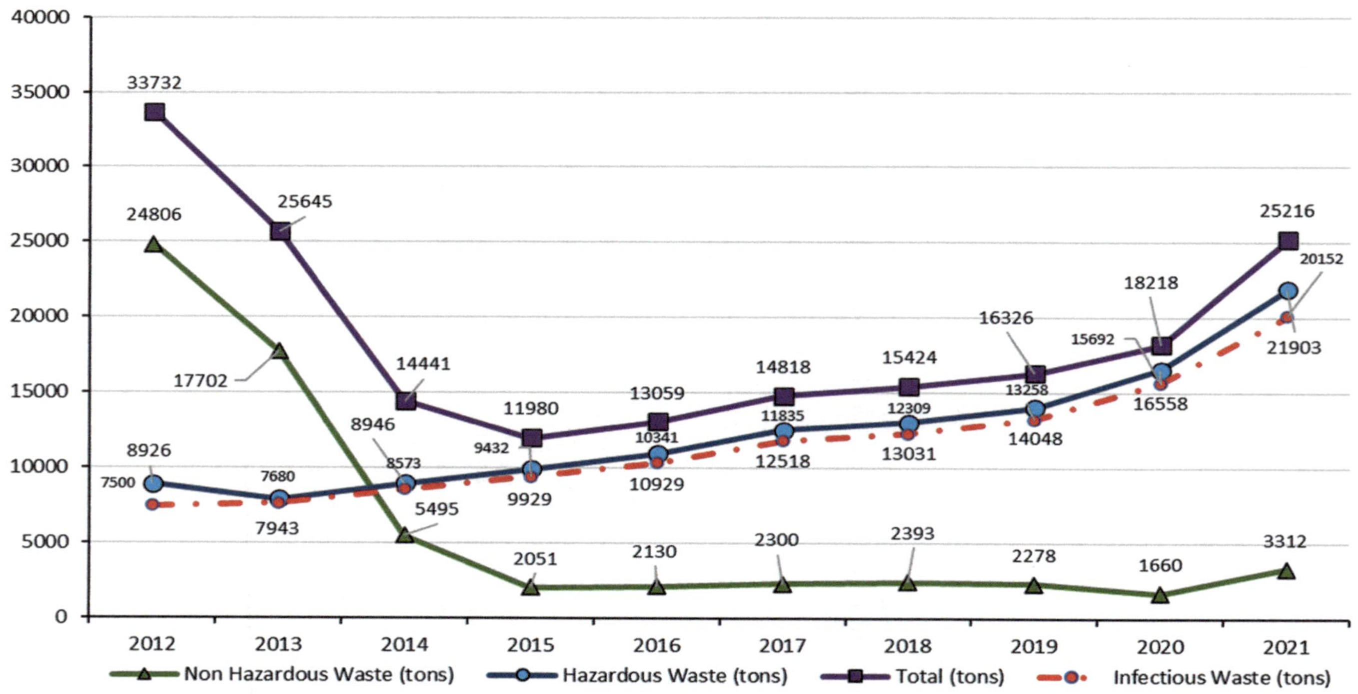


**Fig. 12.2** Progress of medical waste production in Romanian sanitary facilities with medical beds, tons (Source: NIPH own compilation, as noted below). Note: Data for this figure was extracted from the National Health Conference Summary Volumes (2012–2021) and the Annual Health and Environment Report drafted by the National Institute of Public Health, as follows: data for total medical waste and hazardous medical waste were taken from the sources presented further, and the data for non-hazardous medical waste were calculated. It is important to mention that only data on medical units with beds (hospitals) were taken into account, not those corresponding to private practices

**Table 12.2** The progress of medical waste production in relation to bed capacity (2012–2021)

| Medical waste | 2012 | 2013 | 2014 | 2015 | 2016 | 2017 | 2018 | 2019 | 2020 | 2021 |
|---|---|---|---|---|---|---|---|---|---|---|
| Non-hazardous medical waste generated (kg/bed/day) | 0.367 | 0.260 | 0.080 | 0.030 | 0.031 | 0.033 | 0.034 | 0.033 | 0.033 | 0.067 |
| Hazardous medical waste generated (kg/bed/day) | 0.132 | 0.117 | 0.131 | 0.144 | 0.158 | 0.181 | 0.188 | 0.286 | 0.330 | 0.440 |

Source: NIPH data processing, from Health and Environment Report 2021

2015–2019 and at higher levels of hazardous medical waste (0.144–0.201 kg/bed/day). These values are quite different from those reported by other countries to the WHO.

A very different situation emerged when analysing data for 2020–2021. These two pandemic years, when the epidemiological situation escalated, revealed a rise in the quantity of medical waste, especially hazardous waste. However, the volume of non-hazardous medical waste had doubled by 2021, going from 0.033 kg/bed/day in 2020 to 0.067 kg/bed/day, while the hazardous medical waste only registered a 33% increase.

## *Additional Amounts of Medical Waste Generated as a Result of the COVID-19 Epidemic*

Regarding the progression of the pandemic-related medical waste amounts, it is apparent that more medical waste was produced. As the frequency of infections rose, so did the waste produce by medical procedures. More and more single-use protective equipment (masks, gloves and suits) was being used by patients and medical professionals. These all add up as consumables, as medical waste, which must be managed safely. According to Annex 12.2, it can be found that personal protective equipment and other consumables are of several categories: infectious waste (masks, gloves, gowns, syringes and needles, etc.) and non-hazardous waste (rapid tests, vaccine vials, packaging, etc.).

For instance, in the Chinese region of Wuhan, where the novel coronavirus initially surfaced, it was essential to construct additional hospitals to accommodate the inflow of patients as well as a new fixed facility and 46 mobile facilities to process medical waste. When the outbreak was at its worst, hospitals in the Wuhan province produced six times as much medical waste as they did before the start of

**Table 12.3** Waste from the anti-COVID vaccination activity in Romania (2021)

| Vaccination wastes | Total vaccines administered in 2021 | Unit weight (kg) | Total weight (tons) |
|---|---|---|---|
| Glass vials | 15,839,807 | 0.011 | 174.2 |
| Syringes and needles | 15,839,807 | 0.006 | 95.0 |
| Boxes, packaging | 158,398.07 | 0.1 | 158 |
| Total | | | 285.1 |

Source: own processed data from ONU and https://vaccinare-covid.gov.ro/raportari/

COVID-19. A total of 240 metric tons of medical waste were produced per day (Calma, 2020).

In Romania, the additional quantities of waste generated by the COVID-19 pandemic do not have a special statistic. Some estimates may, however, be made on the basis of internationally accepted average values, as presented in Table 12.3.

As all over the world, in Romania there were many vaccination centres active in 2021. According to the Health and Environment Report 2021, there were 270 vaccination centres active at national level. The amount of medical infectious waste reported from these medical facilities was 83.31 tons/year. This number is very close to the estimations performed in the previous year, and it is based on the total number of vaccines administered in Romania in 2021 (in 2020, 10,289 vaccines were administered, whereas 617,512 vaccines were administered in 2022 (01/02) (Min. of Health Report, 2022). Glass vials, syringes, safety pins and packaging are only a few of the waste products produced by vaccination procedures. Utilising online resources, the unit weight of each of these was calculated, and the total quantity was multiplied.

The estimation stated that a quantity of waste of 285.1 tons was generated in 2021 from the vaccination activity only, out of which 95 tons of hazardous waste. These numbers were only 10% higher than the real statistical data presented in 2022 by the National Institute of Public Health.

## *Forecast of Hazardous Waste Generation in Romania*

Next, we will focus on hazardous waste because it requires specific disposal/elimination methods such as incineration, heat treatment with steam at high temperatures, cryogenic treatment, etc. The trend forecast is based on the data available for the period 2012–2021. The forecast period is that of 2022–2024, based on past trends (it has included the confidence interval of 95%).

Figure 12.3 illustrates the forecast of hazardous waste between 2022 and 2024. For 2024, the forecast indicates a quantity of 25.78 thousand tons of hazardous waste. The 95% confidence interval shows an upper threshold of 30.71 thousand tons and a lower threshold of 20.85 thousand tons. Thus, we can expect a quantity

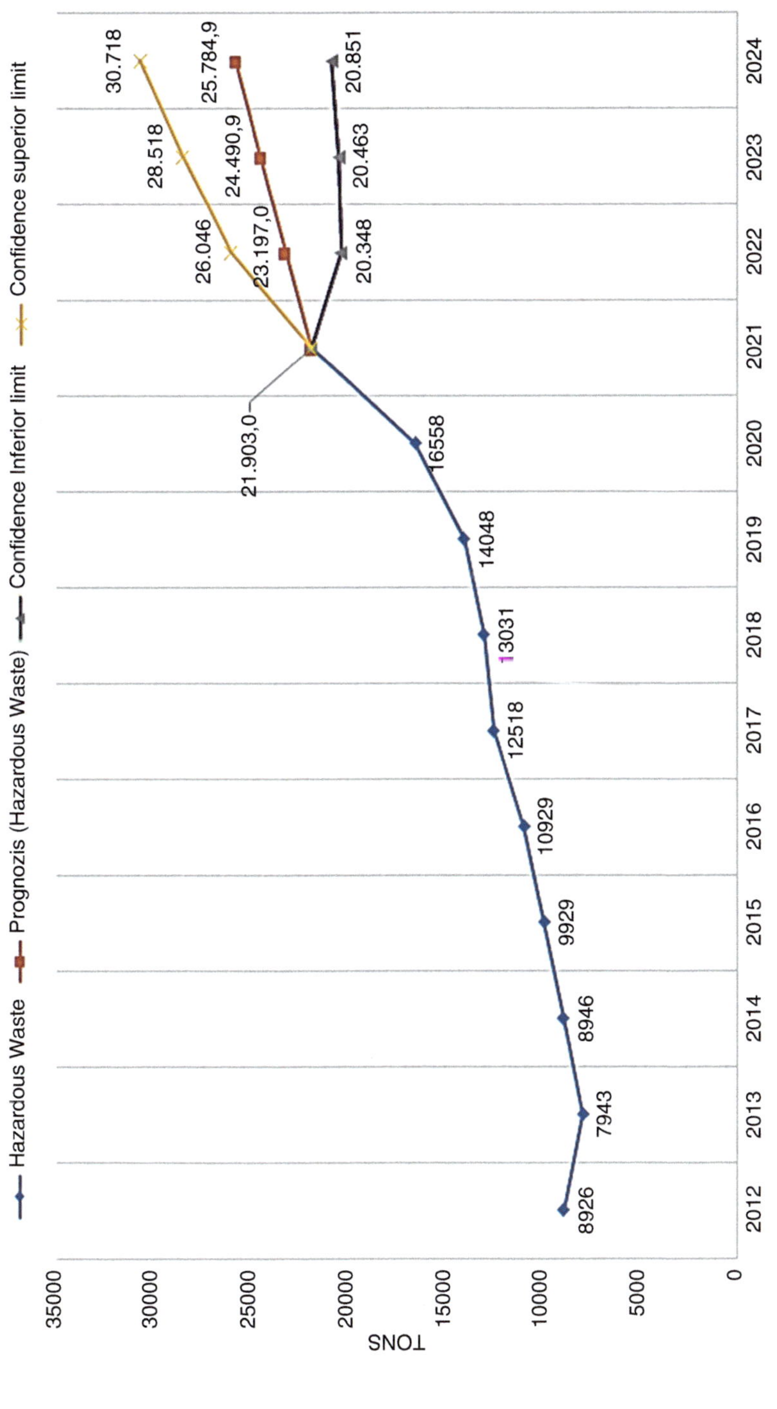


**Fig. 12.3** Forecast of hazardous medical waste generated in Romania, tons (Source: data processing from NPHI—National Public Health Institute)

of hazardous medical waste in the range of 20.85–30.71 thousand tons. This forecast was based on the 2012–2021 data.

These values should be seen as minimum values because there are still a number of medical facilities that have not sent reports on the waste produced.

Because the COVID-19 epidemic ended in 2022, the inferior confidence limit should be taken into account for the forecast period 2023–2024 (Fig. 12.3). This evolution shows a tendency to return to the values recorded before 2021.

## The System for Disposing of Hazardous Medical Waste: Analysis and Assessment

Based on the Health and Environment Reports for 2020 and 2021 of the National Institute of Public Health, following the processing of data reported by the county public health departments, a series of qualitative data on how the health units manage medical waste have been outlined. The reports on waste from medical activity were carried out in 2020, comprising a number of 796 public and private health units (about 30% are from the private system), respectively of 1287 health units in 2021.

Non-hazardous waste which does not require special measures to prevent infection is disposed of as follows:

1. 92% of the health facilities claim that waste is transported to municipal landfills by specialised companies, on a contract basis.
2. 7% of units claim that waste was cremated.
3. 1% of the units claim that the waste is treated.

Nationally, there are 35 hospitals that own 44 facilities for the thermal decontamination of hazardous medical waste at low temperatures, and there are 8 business operators that own 12 such facilities.

The substantial increase in the volume of hazardous medical waste is a major issue in the context of the COVID-19 outbreak in Romania.

In a report drafted by the Competition Council in 2019, it is specified that from the point of view of the geographical spread, both thermal decontamination and incineration plants are located in the eight regions of the country as follows (Competition Council, 2019):

1. North-East Region—Two incineration plants and four thermal decontamination plants
2. Centre Region—Six thermal decontamination installations
3. South Region—Three incineration plants and three thermal decontamination plants
4. West Region—Four thermal decontamination plants and one incineration plant
5. Bucharest-Ilfov—Three thermal decontamination plants and two incineration plants

6. South-West Region—an incineration plant and two thermal decontamination plants
7. South-East Region—an incineration plant and two thermal decontamination plants
8. North-West Region—an incineration plant and a thermal decontamination plant

From this data it can be seen that, compared to the existing 543 hospital units, there are 36 units for the disposal of hazardous medical waste, distributed unevenly at regional level. On average, a hazardous waste disposal facility serves 15 hospitals, which could cause agglomerations and queues at incineration/decontamination stations.

Another aspect that should be mentioned in this context concerns the application of the proximity principle, which requires that waste be disposed of the closest possible to the generation site. The legal provisions on the principle of proximity lack clarity, and the mechanism for selecting disposal installations is not made on the basis of compliance with the proximity principle, which would involve choice of transport routes on the basis of minimum distance.

A pressing problem in the conditions of the COVID-19 epidemic was that of the rapid elimination of contaminated medical waste, preferably through county facilities, in order to avoid long-distance transport (Doremalen et al., 2020).

At county and regional level, the distribution of the capacity to eliminate dangerous medical waste is not balanced, given that:

- There aren't enough facilities for the thermal decontamination of hazardous medical waste at low temperatures (either inside sanitary units or in a centralised system). As a result, there are now 14 counties without a facility for the thermal decontamination of hazardous medical waste at low temperatures.
- There are 20 counties where there is no close facility to burn hazardous medical waste, so the hospitals must export the harmful waste.

By type of equipment, the total capacity of the installations for the disposal of hazardous medical waste was 120,340 tons in 2018, out of which 79% are incinerators and 21% are thermal decontamination installations (Fig. 12.4). There is no information on the development of new capacities for the disposal of medical waste, and therefore we will consider the mentioned values as suitable for 2023.

As for the serviceability of the existing capacities, it can be seen from Fig. 12.5 that the average capacity in use is around 35%. In this context, it is important to state that incineration plants also process hazardous waste other than medical waste.

According to data analysis on hazardous waste disposal capacities and capacity utilisation, there is a sizable capacity reserve (of over 70,000 tons/year) that could easily handle the additional quantities of hazardous medical waste brought on by the COVID-19 pandemic.

As indicated above, the forecast of the maximum amount of hazardous medical waste is 26,000–30,000 tons/year. Even if this quantity were to double, the existing disposal infrastructure could still cope. This scenario of doubling the quantities of hazardous medical waste is highly unlikely.

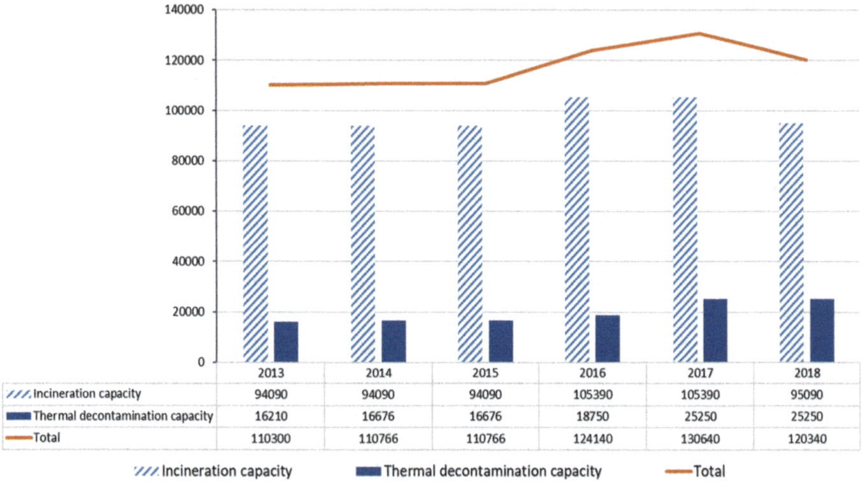


**Fig. 12.4** Existing hazardous waste disposal plant capacities in Romania, tons/year (Source: Data from Preliminary Report on Medical Waste. Sector investigation. Competition Council, 2019)

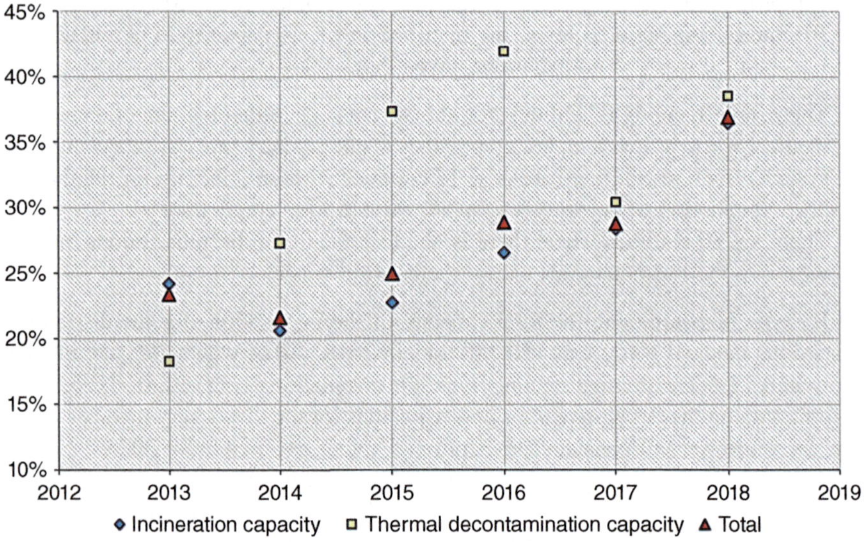


**Fig. 12.5** Use of hazardous medical waste disposal facilities, % (Source: Data from Preliminary Report on Medical Waste. Sector investigation. Competition Council, 2019)

There is, however, a problem with the validity of public data on the hazardous medical waste disposal services. Data reported by public institutions, especially those on the activity of companies involved in the disposal of waste from hospitals, contain multiple mismatches and are incomplete.

There is no indication that different institutions involved in waste disposal use the same definitions to report the same indicators. The reporting methodologies are not clear, making it difficult to correctly assess the comparability and validity of the data.

## Conclusions and Proposals

### *Conclusions*

The research undertaken on the COVID-19 epidemic's impact on Romani's medical waste management has led the research team to the following conclusions:

- Hospital infrastructure; medical waste strategy. The hospital number increased at national level from 458 in 2008 to 543 in 2021 (an increase of 18.5%). It must be noted that Romania has fully complied with all waste-related EU directives. The MoH is responsible for the supervision of the medical waste area through the National Institute of Public Health. A new public body for risk monitoring was created—the National Center for Monitoring Risks in the Community Environment—which gathers statistical data from the generators at county level. Regarding unitary national guidelines, MoH drafted in 2016 a National Strategy and Action Plan proposal for medical waste management. This document has not yet been approved and is still in draft form.
- Availability of medical waste information. It is challenging to locate and evaluate the available information on hazardous and non-hazardous medical waste. One of the factors has to do with the organisation (Ministry of Health and/or Ministry of Environment) that provides the data. The reports for the period 2012–2021 show a development extremely difficult to explain. Between 2012 and 2020, there was a steep decrease in the total volume of medical waste produced. The volume of non-hazardous garbage decreases by more than 7 times, from 24,806 tons in 2012 to 3312 tons in 2021. Basically, a reversal occurs; hazardous waste takes the place of non-hazardous ones. Hazardous medical waste increases from 8900 tons in 2012 to 21,903 tons in 2021. It should be emphasised that during the course of 10 years (2012–2021), the total amount of medical waste decreased from 33,732 tons to 25,216 tons (a reduction of 25% or 8516 tons overall). No explanation for these developments is given by the data providers. The explanation related to the change in the reporting methodology in 2012 is possible, but this alone cannot be responsible for such large changes in the quantities of medical waste generated. In addition, the fact that the number of hospitals has increased by 15% and medical waste is declining is conflictual. This should have determined an increase in the amount of medical waste generated and not a decrease of 46%.
- Evolution scenarios. During the COVID-19 epidemic in Romania, the likelihood of a rapid rise in the volume of hazardous medical waste has been a significant issue. Regarding the scenarios for the year 2023, the forecast made in this study indicates an amount of hazardous medical waste of 25.78 thousand tons. The 95%

confidence interval shows an upper threshold of 30.71 thousand tons and a lower threshold of 20.85 thousand tons. Thus, we can expect a quantity of hazardous waste in the range of [20.85; 30.71] thousand tons. These values should be seen as minimum values since there are still a number of healthcare facilities that did not send reports on waste.

- Existing hazardous medical waste disposal capacities. From the analysis of the available data, it resulted that, in Romania, there is a total capacity of 120,340 tons/year in installations for the disposal of hazardous medical waste, out of which 79% are incinerators and 21% are thermal decontamination installations. There is no data on the development of new medical waste disposal capacities.
- In terms of the use of existing capacities, it was found that it averaged around 35% which means that there were always reserves of capacity to dispose of hazardous waste of medical origin or not. This significant reserve of capacity (of over 70,000 tons/year) could take over without problems the additional quantities of hazardous medical waste coming from the COVID-19 pandemic or, otherwise, even if there would be a doubling of the amount of waste that was forecasted. This scenario of doubling the quantities of hazardous medical waste is highly unlikely.

## *Proposals (Recommendations)*

The study team makes the following recommendations as a result of their analyses:

A. The official endorsement and restoration of the National Strategy and Plan for the Management of Medical Waste. This plan should establish the quantities of hazardous medical waste produced through sampling or direct measurements. It should also produce a real inventory of the capacities currently in use for disposing of medical waste, as well as information on their quality, level of use, wear and tear, etc.

B. Optimising the infrastructure for handling waste generated by medical activity by:

   (a) Establishing the ideal conditions for the short-term storage of the medical waste within the sanitary units by setting up cool rooms
   (b) Establishing the circumstances for the internal transit of medical waste within the sanitary unit

C. Development of an online reporting program in real time (software and database) of the quantities of general health system waste and the way of disposal; the reports must be submitted on a regular basis and be based on a verified waste weighing technique.

# Annexes

## *Annex 12.1 Legislation on Medical Waste*

National waste legislation

- Law no. 426/2001 on approving Emergency Ordinance no. 78/2000 on the regime of waste
- Government Decision (GD) no. 856/2002 on the keeping of waste management records and approving a list of types of waste, including hazardous waste
- GD no. 349/2005 on the landfill of waste, with subsequent amendments
- GD no. 1862/2005 for the approval of the project 'Incineration of hazardous waste and medical activity'
- Ordinance no. 18/2005 for the amendment of Law no. 98/1994 on the establishment and sanctioning of contraventions to the legal norms of hygiene and public health
- GD no. 1175/2007 for the approval of the Norms for carrying out the activity of road transport of dangerous goods in Romania
- GD no. 788/2007 on establishing measures for the application of Regulation 1013/2006 on the shipment of waste, as amended and supplemented
- GD no. 1061/2008 on the transport of hazardous and non-hazardous waste on the territory of Romania
- GD no. 870/2013 on the approval of the National Waste Management Strategy 2014–2020
- GD no. 243/2013 on minimum occupational safety and health requirements for the prevention of injuries caused by sharp objects in activities in the hospital and healthcare sectors

Orders of the Minister of Health for the management of medical waste:

- Order of the Minister of Health no. 916/2006 on the approval of Norms for the surveillance, prevention and control of nosocomial infections in health facilities
- Order of the Minister of Health no. 613/2009 on the approval of the Methodology for the evaluation of vehicles used for the transport of hazardous waste resulting from medical activity
- Order of the Minister of Health no. 1226/2012 for the approval of the Technical Norms on the management of waste resulting from medical activities and of the Methodology for data collection for the national database on waste resulting from medical activities
- Order of the Minister of Health no. 1279/2012 on the approval of Criteria for evaluation of the operating conditions and monitoring of the equipment for the treatment of hazardous medical waste by thermal decontamination at low temperatures

## *Annex 12.2 Main Types of Medical Waste Generated by the COVID-19 Outbreak*

| Article | Type of waste | Requires safe handling and treatment |
|---|---|---|
| Medical masks | Infectious | Yes |
| Gloves | Infectious | Yes |
| Medical gowns | Infectious | Yes |
| Rapid SARS-CoV antigen tests | Non-hazardous | Most of the components are recyclable.<br>In a large number of tests, a very small volume of reagents may require safe handling and disposal |
| PCR test cartridges | Chemical | Yes (contain guanidine thiocyanate) |
| Vaccine vials | Non-hazardous | Not |
| Vaccine needles | Sharp | Yes (the packaging material is recyclable) |
| Plastic packaging and containers | Non-hazardous | Not |

Source: UN Environment Programme, 2020

## References

Bara, A. (2007). Tratarea deşeurilor medicale infecţioase, revista Green Report. https://green-report.ro/tratarea-deseurilor-medicale-infectioase/

Bojoi, A. (2020). Pachet de măsuri al CE pentru atenuarea impactului socio-economic al pandemiei de COVID 19. https://www.rri.ro/ro_ro/pachet_de_masuri_al_ce_pentru_atenuarea_impactului_socio_economic_al_pandemiei_de_covid_19-2614406

Calma, J. (2020). The COVID-19 pandemic is generating tons of medical waste, Sanitation workers need personal protective equipment too. *The Verge*, 26.03.2020. https://www.theverge.com/2020/3/26/21194647/the-covid-19-pandemic-is-generating-tons-of-medical-waste

Competition Council. (2019). Raport preliminar privind deşeurile medicale, investigaţie sectorială. https://www.concurenta.ro/ro/news/concurenta-neloiala/ancheta-sectoriala-consiliul-concurentei-suspecteaza-comportamente-anticoncurentiale-pe-piata-deseurilor-medicale.html

Curea, O., Bratu, A. M., Constantin, M., & Teodorescu, S. E. (2021). *Deşeurile rezultate din activitatea15edicală – cerinţe legale şi bune practice.* CNMRMC, Bucuresti. ISBN: 978-973-0-35381-5

Directive 2008/98/Ec of the European Parliament and of the Council of 19 November 2008 on waste and repealing certain Directives. https://eur-lex.europa.eu/legal-content/RO/TXT/PDF/?uri=CELEX:32008L0098&from=RO

Doremalen, N. et al. (2020). Aerosol and surface stability of SARS-CoV-2 as compared with SARS-CoV-1. https://www.researchgate.net/publication/339917826_Aerosol_and_surface_stability_of_HCoV-19_SARS-CoV-2_compared_to_SARS-CoV-1

Infomediu Europa. (2018). Ce se întâmplă cu deşeurile medicale periculoase generate de unităţile medicale? http://www.infomediu.eu/eco-news/9309-ce-se-%C3%AEnt%C3%A2mpl%C4%83-cu-de%C8%99eurile-medicale-periculoasegenerate-de-unit%C4%83%C8%9Bile-medicale.html

Mihai, F. C. (2020). Assessment of COVID waste flows during the emergency state in Romania and related public health and environmental concerns. *International Journal of Environmental Research* and *Public Health, 17*(15):5439. https://doi.org/10.3390/ijerph17155439. https://pubmed.ncbi.nlm.nih.gov/32731593/

Ministry of Health. (2016). Decision regarding the National Strategy and the National Plan for the management of waste deriving from medical activities, 2016, unpublished. https://lege5.ro/Gratuit/gmztmnjygq/planul-de-gestionare-a-deseurilor-rezultate-din-activitatile-medicale-propunere-de-continut-ordin-1226-2012?dp=gyztgobthe3tq

Ministry of Health Report. (2022). https://vaccinare-covid.gov.ro/raportari/

NIPH. (2013). National Institute of public health 2013, Volum de Rezumate, Conferința Națională pentru Sănătate și Mediu 2013. https://cnmrmc.insp.gov.ro/images/rapoarte/volum%20de_rezumate-2013.pdf

NIPH. (2014). *Health and environment report 2014*. National Institute of Public Health. https://cnmrmc.insp.gov.ro/images/rapoarte/Raport-SM-2014.pdf

NIPH (2015). *Health and environment report 2015*. National Institute of Public Health. https://cnmrmc.insp.gov.ro/images/rapoarte/Raport-SM-2015.pdf

NIPH. (2016). Health and environment report 2016. National Institute of Public Health. https://cnmrmc.insp.gov.ro/images/rapoarte/Raport-SM-2016.pdf

NIPH. (2017). *Health and environment report 2017*. National Institute of Public Health. https://cnmrmc.insp.gov.ro/images/rapoarte/RAPORT%202017.pdf

NIPH. (2018). Health and environment report 2018. National Institute of Public Health. https://cnmrmc.insp.gov.ro/images/rapoarte/Raport-SM-2018.pdf

NIPH. (2019). *Health and environment report 2019*. National Institute of Public Health 2019. https://insp.gov.ro/download/cnmrmc/Rapoarte/Rapoarte%20pentru%20Sanatate%20si%20Mediu/RAPORT-Sanatate-Mediu-2019.pdf

NIPH. (2020). *Health and environment report 2020*. National Institute of Public Health 2020. https://insp.gov.ro/download/cnmrmc/Rapoarte/Rapoarte%20pentru%20Sanatate%20si%20Mediu/RAPORT-Sanatate-Mediu-2020.pdf

NIPH. (2021). Health and environment report 2021, National Institute of Public Health. https://insp.gov.ro/cnmrmc/rapoarte/

Platon, V., Frone, S., Constantinescu, A., & Jurist, S. (2020). Challenges in adequate management of hazardous medical waste to reduce impact of the COVID-19 epidemic in Romania. In M. W. Staniewski, V. Vasile, & A. Grigorescu (Eds.), *Lumen Proceedings: Vol. 14. International Conference Innovative Business Management & Global Entrepreneurship (IBMAGE 2020)* (pp. 212–226). LUMEN Publishing House. https://doi.org/10.18662/lumproc/ibmage2020/16

UNEP. (2003). *Technical guidelines on the environmentally sound management of biomedical and healthcare wastes (Y1; Y3)*. https://digitallibrary.un.org/record/517098?ln=en

UNEP. (2012). *Compendium of technologies for treatment/destruction of healthcare waste*. Division of Technology, Industry and Economics International Environmental Technology Centre Osaka, Japan. https://wedocs.unep.org/bitstream/handle/20.500.11822/8628/IETC_Compendium_Technologies_Treatment_Destruction_Healthcare_Waste.pdf?sequence=3&isAllowed=y

Vaccari, M., Tudor, T., & Perteghella, A. (2018). Costs associated with the management of waste from healthcare facilities: An analysis at national and site level. *Waste Management & Research, 36*(1), 39–47.

# Chapter 13
# Conclusions: Looking Forward, Main Challenges and Limits

**Valentina Vasile and Elena Bunduchi**

**Abstract** The final chapter of the volume summarises the most significant conclusions from the thematic analyses conducted to underline the effects of the pandemic on the business environment and on the labour force. A short synthetic but not simplistic inventory of the main challenges and limits for a post-pandemic robust development is presented, underlining the importance of management of building resilience through prevention actions and flexibility in policy measures.

Practically, after each crisis, a 'new normal' is built; a new phase of human development is passed, in which the development's equilibria are reconfigured. Post-pandemic can be defined as a period of reconciliation between economy, society and nature, of reconsider inclusiveness and 'development for all'.

The COVID-19 crisis has highlighted, on the one hand, the benefits of digital transformation and the need for flexibility and innovation in employment and labour market reform, and the usefulness of lifelong learning for upskilling and reskilling. On the other hand, the need for development based on environmental protection, efficient use of resources (energy, human, food, etc.) and intelligent management of the effects of climate change was reconfirmed.

The pandemic crisis has led to significant changes in the management of the business environment and the development of national economies, caused by the restrictions imposed to manage the risks of spreading the virus, but also to adapt the health system, the supply and quality of medical services to the specific demand of the crisis—COVID-19.

---

V. Vasile (✉)
Institute of National Economy - Romanian Academy, Bucharest, Romania

E. Bunduchi
Institute of National Economy - Romanian Academy, Bucharest, Romania

Faculty of Economics and Law, George Emil Palade University of Medicine, Pharmacy, Science, and Technology of Targu Mures, Targu Mures, Romania



V. Vasile, E. Bunduchi (eds.), *The Economic and Social Impact of the COVID-19 Pandemic*, Contributions to Economics,
https://doi.org/10.1007/978-3-031-47780-5_13

The conclusions summarise the research results presented in the thematic studies, highlighting on the one hand the changes and effects and, on the other hand, the challenges for the robust post-pandemic economic and social recovery and building resilience for the future events, considering that the probabilities of future health crises cannot be ignored and it is necessary to be prepared to respond and effectively manage the associated risks and externalities. In fact, in the present society, overlapping crises have become a common feature of economic and social development, crises being both exogenous and endogenous to the economic environment—climate change, the energy crisis and the agrarian crisis, migration and demographic ageing, but also the risks generated by conjunctural and regional events—the conflict in Ukraine and the political tensions in the Europe-Asia area, as to mention just a few. A short synthetic but not simplistic inventory of the main challenges for a post-pandemic robust development is presented at the end, underlining the importance of management of building resilience through prevention and flexibility in policy measures to support robust development.

## The Most Significant Conclusions from the Thematic Analyses Conducted to Underline the Effect of the Pandemic on the Business and on the Labour Force

It is obvious that a pandemic-type health crisis affecting the population has multiple effects in the economic and social environment, from multiple perspectives:

(a) The health of the population and the need to improve as quickly as possible, both by treating the effects and causes
(b) The labour capacity of the workforce, including measures to manage real and potential human capital
(c) Flexibility of the business environment, in order to ensure the continuity of economic activities in conditions of efficiency and economic and social inclusion
(d) Governance efficiency, by adopting realistic public policies to support integrated crisis management

Starting from the analyses carried out in this volume, we consider that in order to manage the pandemic crisis, measures must be adapted to local, national, regional particularities, and their effectiveness depends on concrete actions and policy tools must be implemented, in the context of the general objectives and targets defined by the International Health Organization.

Practically, after each crisis, a 'new normal' is built from an economic, social and cultural perspective; a new phase of human development is passed, in which the balances of development are reconfigured. The COVID-19 crisis has highlighted, on the one hand, the usefulness of digital transformation and the need for flexibility and innovation in employment and labour market reform, and the usefulness of lifelong learning for upgrading or developing new skills. On the other hand, the usefulness of sustainable development with environmental protection, economical use of resources (energy, human, food, etc.) and management of climate change effects has been proven.

The main conclusions of the thematic analyses in the volume can be summarised on the following coordinates:

- The economic and social development of the last decades has been characterised by overlapping crises, with medium- and long-term effects that have changed the historical coordinates of macro- and microeconomic correlations. They have redefined international balances and conditionalities—from economic recovery we are now working for robust and resilient growth; from social inclusion we now look at equity and inclusion, reducing social inequalities and opportunity for a better life for all; from protecting the environment and reducing greenhouse gas emissions, we now focus on circular economy and green development, with the promotion of renewable energies and climate change management to mitigate the effects, etc. Moreover, the transition to a new state of normality no longer necessarily implies reaching the levels of some economic and social indicators prior to the crisis, but redefining the significance of post-crisis recovery in the context of recalibrating development on redefined strategic directions. These include the challenges posed by technological progress, changing attitudes and perceptions of quality of life, but also minimum working and living conditions, decreasing inequalities and convergent gaps. Addressing these challenges demands a comprehensive approach to adjustment measures, prioritising robust recovery over quick fixes to prevent adverse effects.
- Moreover, risk assessment and preventive measures are essential for building economic resilience. In the post-pandemic era, policymakers should strengthen social safety nets, expand unemployment benefits and support vulnerable population categories through financial aid. Retraining and upskilling workers for emerging job opportunities are also crucial. Investing in infrastructure projects, especially renewable energy and public transportation, can boost job creation and economic growth. Addressing inequalities requires equal access to healthcare, education, economic opportunities, progressive taxation and improved education accessibility. Reducing barriers to economic mobility is also essential.
- Crisis preparedness can be enhanced through research investment, bolstering healthcare systems, diversifying supply chains and improving disaster response and early warning systems. Customising actions and priorities is essential based on each country's specific crises and severity.
- A well-defined vision and inclusive community-based roadmap involving all stakeholders is vital for future development. Collaboration, partnership, inclusivity and a fair transition to the 'new normal' are essential considerations.
- Crisis management involves state and local institutions, with national measures and accountability playing a crucial role. Policymakers must support proactive measures.
- The temporary disruption of supply chains in international markets has created opportunities for indigenous firms to expand their domestic market, especially for small and micro firms. At the same time, the market was opened for social economy enterprises that provide local production and distribution chains of local agricultural products and consumer goods in households, but also the

stimulation of local tourism and agritourism that allowed compliance with the restrictions of physical interaction during the pandemic. Also, online platforms and communication and collaboration groups have been developed for current services—takeaway and home deliveries, online commerce with fixed point distribution, rigorous access planning for different personal services, etc. Keeping these connections post-pandemic represents an opportunity to develop small businesses and promote local/traditional products or to strengthen local cooperation for integrated consumer products and services, including boosting tourism through small locations in nature, capitalising on the local potential for recreation and authentic cultural consumption.

- Employment in jobs associated with digital and digital communication services (both as employees of companies and through the development of companies offering specialised services) has developed, especially in less developed countries.
- Many categories of businesses have redefined, diversified on various components of production/distribution or operational and financial management, the gains from the pandemic being able to be measured later, through flexible reorganization of the activity—online relationships with business partners, promotion and online commerce, electronic payments, hybrid work, flexibility of working time, etc.
- The recovery of exports and imports from the second half of 2020 suggests that the health crisis did not produce significant long-term changes. Moreover, companies adopted new strategies on the markets, as a preventive measure, given the risk of future crises to ensure greater resistance to possible disruptions of the supply chains.
- The COVID-19 crisis has impacted countries' budgets, leading to substantial declines in tax revenues. Measures taken by governments to support specific activities have also contributed to this situation—postponing the payment of taxes and fees, but also reducing working time and taxes and fees associated with earnings, reducing consumption and hence lower revenues from tax on value added, etc. In addition, the lack or deficient digitization of public services and also the poor financial inclusion of the population in states that in pre-pandemic were less concerned with the digitization of the sector (such as Romania) have made it difficult to pay taxes and fees.
- The pandemic has hit vulnerable groups harder, partly due to discrimination in access or lack of flexibility in public policy measures. As an example, we list some aspects resulting from the detailed analysis for Romania:

  (a) The women's situation on the labour market in Romania deteriorated, due to the feminine overrepresentation in some areas particularly affected by the pandemic (such as tourism and hospitality), but also because of their responsibility of taking care of the family health, at the expense of a balance between professional and personal life. However, in 2022, some signs of a return to normality can be seen in terms of women's employment. The relaunch of economic activity after the pandemic led to the reversal of the change in the unemployment rate among women, starting to decrease in the period 2021–2022.

(b) The pandemic crisis had some very serious economic consequences for young people (increase in unemployment more than for other categories of people, especially among low-educated young people, a trend that was also maintained in the period 2021–2022), as disruptions in the education system, jobs and income losses and difficulties in finding jobs occurred. But, on the other hand, young people showed greater adaptability to new challenges, in the post-pandemic period, through remote work, digital skills usage, reorienting towards the IT or e-commerce sectors or even through starting their own businesses.

(c) Regarding the elderly population, there were also some favourable developments on the labour market in Romania, during the pandemic and post-pandemic period. Thus, employment (in absolute and relative terms) recovered starting with the second quarter of 2021 (especially for the highly educated elderly). The unemployment rate of the elderly aged 55–64 recorded a decrease in the period 2021–2022, after an increase less pronounced than for other vulnerable groups during the pandemic (2020).

(d) Self-employed workers were disproportionately, unevenly affected by the pandemic, those who used digital technologies and services or those who managed to quickly adapt their businesses being less affected. The largest decrease in the number of self-employed workers was recorded in the first quarter of 2021, compared to the previous quarter. Although starting with the second quarter of 2021 and until the end of 2022, the indicator had an oscillating evolution, the level remained low compared to that of 2019.

- Even if the economic recovery was registered with the removal of restrictions, the labour market remains fragile and requires a deep restructuring on professions, but also from the perspective of skills required by the business environment. This raises the problem of redefining the parameters and factors supporting the quantitative and qualitative rebalancing between supply and demand (fields of education, specializations, level of qualification, type of competences, better correlation between initial and continuing education).
- Many of the economic activities closely related to the management of the pandemic crisis have been reshaped, in size, types of activities, technologies, safety and working conditions—the health sector and, associated, upstream and downstream industries (pharmaceuticals, protective and cleaning materials, medical waste management, some personal services, social services), passenger transport, activities in the hospitality industry, educational, recreation and cultural activities, etc.

## Lessons Learned: Post-Pandemic Developments

Even after only 2 years since the fierce manifestation of the COVID-19 pandemic, the new priorities of long-term development have been redefined, and many of those active in the business environment and communities have changed their life model, starting from expectations and opportunities. Post-pandemic can be defined as a period of reconciliation between economy, society and nature, with the reconsideration of the content of the phrase 'development for all', already demonetised after the failures of recovery from the financial crisis of 2008–2009. It is also obvious that debates on the issues of the decade—globalization vs. (de)globalization of markets; the role of states in the context of regionalisation; development gaps and inequities; social protection vs. opportunities for self-protection; free movement for work and integration in host countries; the role of financial stabilisers in managing macroeconomic balances; etc.—have been reactivated. Experts speak of the paradox of the pandemic (Fulford, 2023); or post-pandemic paradoxes (Krastev, 2020; Dotsey, 2023; Amankwah-Amoah et al., 2021; Yap et al., 2021; Smith et al., 2020, to mention just a few research).

Beyond individual adaptation initiatives, in managing a crisis, there is always the need for a 'safety net' to facilitate the passage through the crisis and recovery, materialised in the intervention of decision-makers through measures and policies, in sensitive areas affected by the crisis. The experience of previous crises has shown us that a major problem in crisis management, regardless of their nature and duration, is related to the public policies promoted, for prevention, intervention and post-crisis recovery, namely, their articulation with the risks, needs and characteristics of the geographical area of implementation. International or regional organisations will always make recommendations, starting from the global vision and from specialised judgements on crisis management, but the efficiency of implementation and obtaining as much as possible the expected results depend on the decision-makers' capacity to customise and monitor. The reaction to the pandemic crisis of the EU institutions was to initiate the Recovery and Resilience Facility, in order to support the efforts of economic recovery and the creation of mechanisms for the development of economic and social resilience, precisely starting from the significant gaps between member countries. The financial allocations, as amounts and destination, were negotiated by each country, but the expected efficiency depends exclusively on the capacity of national and local decision-makers and implementers to use resources intelligently and with maximum results. To this were added adjusted development strategies, adapted to post-pandemic challenges, such as the strategy for SMEs aimed at helping to become sustainable and more digitalised, improving market access and enhancing access to financing. In addition, during the pandemic crisis (but also the financial crisis of 2008–2009), companies were aware of the weaknesses in maintaining their activity due to strong dependence on certain markets, by supply chain destruction at shocks. The supply chains, affected by pandemic, are still marked by risks and scepticism. The strategies of companies, for mitigating the risks associated with their business, might take into consideration a diversification of suppliers, especially for those near their locations. Therefore, a better balanced and diversified foreign trade by geographical destinations would generate a greater resilience of companies to regional shocks (and this has already been proven to us in the post-pandemic crisis period by the new crises arising from the conflict in Ukraine—energy crisis and agricultural products crisis, to name just two of them).

Post-pandemic developments are characterised by the growth of the number of active firms by 12% (2021 vs. 2019). In 2020, the European Commission developed an SME strategy The main objectives of this strategy are capacity building and support for transition to sustainability and digitalisation, reducing the regulatory burden, and SME benefit from the (NGEU) that was adopted to help economies emerge more resilient from the pandemic. Almost 90% of NGEU resources (or 723.8 billion euros in current prices, in the form of grants and loans) form the Recovery and Resilience Facility, which has a strong SME focus, thus boosting the implementation of the SME strategy. While the RRF's 'Smart, sustainable and inclusive growth' pillar 4 supports all enterprises, around 19% of its resources are dedicated to measures directly or indirectly supporting SMEs.

Also from the perspective of national policies, coherence, credibility and social responsibility, in the context of 'development for all', a series of risks appear on specific markets—education market, labour market, financial market, etc., the combined effects of the inefficiency of implementing realistic measures being inflation, deficit and increase in external debt, instability of the business environment and lack of financial resources for recovery and robust growth. From the perspective of the case studies developed in this volume on the example of Romania, as an EU member state and with complex economic and social problems, which position it on the last places in the EU in many performance indicators, we consider that a series of comments and suggestions for policy measures, in addition to those already stated so far, are of interest:

(A) Promoting labour market policies adequate to the expected employment structure, as a result of transformations in the business environment. The analysis of the labour market policies designed and implemented during the 2020–2022 period in the context of the COVID-19 pandemic shock by the European Union member states reveals that countries deal with a combination of the best practices in recessionist situations, which were used by the most developed states like Germany, the Netherlands and Scandinavian countries and innovative solutions, issued from the preoccupations of ensuring the social protection, in the context of the block down of economic activities and activating the labour supply and maintaining the labour productivity. The respective policies were implemented in the context of the existence of variants of European Social Model. Therefore, it is possible to distinguish some differences between the labour market policies adopted by the old member states and new member states. The policy measures adopted by the most developed states were significantly more generous compared to those implemented by relatively less developed countries.

(B) A well-equilibrated and fair fiscal policy, able to stimulate voluntary compliance, that at least should include implementation of measures that can be adopted in the tax area which do not have adverse effects on economic development; enhancing tax system design to encourage workers and enterprises to transition from the shadow economy; and tax increases/new tax adoption should target those taxpayers who can bear them, sparing those for which even the current level of taxation is already a burden. Presently, the low-income population and small businesses have been significantly impacted by the pandemic, and they lack the resources to manage additional taxes; using public revenues for investments can positively influence the economy in the post-pandemic period, being essential to prioritise investments that generate the most significant positive effects in areas such as health, innovative technologies and digitalisation.

(C) Vulnerable groups of people will continue to require special attention in the post-pandemic period for their integration on the labour market. The government and other organisations will need to focus on providing support for training and upskilling programs, as well as ensuring that there are sufficient job opportunities available. This may involve promoting sectors that are expected to grow in the post-pandemic economy, such as healthcare, green jobs and digital technology. Additionally, measures such as flexible work arrangements and improved access to digital technology can help vulnerable groups participate more fully in the labour market.

(D) Promoting policies to stimulate the business environment in order to support small local initiatives—social enterprises—of the achieving of a balance between the ensuring of the social protection and the avoiding of the poverty trap and the creating of the stimulus for an active behaviour of the potential active population.

(E) The effects of the crisis can be seen in all domains, but the pandemic has identified structural problems and the need to redesign some sectors of activity. The health system has been hit hardest by the coronavirus crisis. Insufficient physicians and resources for quality services and poor working conditions highlighted the inefficiency of the system in facing the crisis. Major changes are needed to stimulate the reduction of the human capital deficit in the sector by retaining new generations of graduates, through combined measures to stimulate employment in Romania—equipment and working conditions to facilitate professional performance; efficient integration into the collaboration network for continuous training, specialisation and career advancement; reducing inequities in the system regarding labour pay and access to professional development opportunities; reducing gaps in the system regarding investments, financing, staffing and articulation with local, regional and national needs; ensuring services and financing systems adapted to health issues and client affordability; and respecting the right to medical care through quality services for all, but also reducing waste, clientelism, informal payments that condition quality or access to treatments, etc.

(F) Romania is and will remain an important supplier of labour force for Europe but also internationally as long as public policies do not support adapting the educational offer to national needs, increasing the quality of education and, especially, retaining graduates in the country.

1. The pattern of migration for work has changed irreversibly, with three components gaining ground. On the one hand, there is the mobility of essential workers, for whom host countries have developed policies to attract and thus secure the provision of minimum components for continuing activities at local level—general services for the community and households, personal care and social assistance services, local personal transport services and provision of current consumer products, current products/services of small local producers, etc. On the other hand, the policy of attracting experts in different fields of activity, especially young people, was supported during the pandemic by temporary hiring and faster and/or simplified employment procedures. Last but not least, during the pandemic, the opening of labour markets for remote work has also increased the number of migrant workers working elsewhere than the company's headquarters, communication being exclusive or mainly online. This category of migrant workers will also increase in the future, because after the pandemic there has not been a significant return to the traditional working system for activities/work tasks that can be done remotely. The advantages of this type of external mobility for work are also for the employer (minimal costs for the workplace), and for employees there are advantages from keeping the household in the country of origin, with advantages on cost of living, proximity to family, preservation of culture and customs, etc.

This book completes the analyses on the still hot or less addressed issues related to the effects of the pandemic and presents in detail some aspects related to the experience of going through the crisis and the effects for an EU member country, but with modest economic performance, with old and new social problems difficult to manage (migration for high work; in-work poverty; chronic employment deficit in areas that could support a robust recovery; poor efficiency of public policies and lack of articulation on national needs; sectors of non-performing activity through imbalances between needs and quantitative and qualitative offer to the final consumer; lack of interest in stimulating national engines of sustainable development—supporting the development of Romanian capital and the growth of market competitiveness of domestic products/services—adequate financing and allocation of human resources for the national RDI sector; real reform of the education system on segments of interest for Romania's economic and social development).

Research continues, with the team of experts absorbing other aspects of crisis management. It is certain that during the pandemic, we lived a life lesson that repositioned our individual, group and national interests, highlighted weaknesses and shortcomings in approaching development, reaffirmed the usefulness of moments of analysis and balance sheet to expectations and possibilities, as well as the need for flexibility, to adapt uncertainties and multiple risks to a month. Awareness of needs, correct assessment of potential, capitalisation of opportunities, prevention and risk management and, last but not least, acting beyond 'back to normal/back to pre-crisis performances' are defined as the minimum coordinates for a robust and resilient development, in which economic objectives correlate with social ones, crossing to a democratic society in a new vision, which goes beyond the already unsustainable model of capitalist democracy based exclusively on exacerbating the importance of immediate monetary profit from business.

## References

Amankwah-Amoah, J., Khan, Z., & Wood, G. (2021). COVID-19 and business failures: The paradoxes of experience, scale, and scope for theory and practice. *European Management Journal, 39*(2), 179–184. https://doi.org/10.1016/j.emj.2020.09.002

Dotsey, S. (2023). Foreign healthcare workers and COVID-19 in Europe: The paradox of unemployed skilled labour. *Social Sciences, 12*(4), 211. https://doi.org/10.3390/socsci12040211

Fulford, S. (2023). The pandemic paradox: How the COVID crisis made Americans more financially secure. *Princeton University Press.* https://doi.org/10.1515/9780691245348

Krastev, I. (2020). *Is it tomorrow yet?: Paradoxes of the pandemic*. Penguin UK. https://www.penguin.co.uk/books/321232/is-it-tomorrow-yet-by-krastev-ivan/9780141995182

Smith, M. L., Steinman, L. E., & Casey, E. A. (2020). Combatting social isolation among older adults in a time of physical distancing: The COVID-19 social connectivity paradox. *Frontiers in Public Health, 8*, 403. https://doi.org/10.3389/fpubh.2020.00403

Yap, S. F., Xu, Y., & Tan, L. (2021). Coping with crisis: The paradox of technology and consumer vulnerability. *International Journal of Consumer Studies, 45*(6), 1239–1257. https://doi.org/10.1111/ijcs.12724

GPSR Compliance

*The European Union's (EU) General Product Safety Regulation (GPSR) is a set of rules that requires consumer products to be safe and our obligations to ensure this.*

*If you have any concerns about our products, you can contact us on ProductSafety@springernature.com*

In case Publisher is established outside the EU, the EU authorized representative is:

Springer Nature Customer Service Center GmbH
Europaplatz 3
69115 Heidelberg, Germany

**Batch number: 10755312**

Printed by Printforce, the Netherlands